Introduction to
CRIMINOLOGY

Cliff Roberson LL.M., Ph.D.

Harvey Wallace J.D.

COPPERHOUSE PUBLISHING COMPANY
901-5 Tahoe Blvd.
Incline Village, Nevada 89451
(702) 833-3131 • Fax (702) 833-3133
e-mail info@copperhouse.com
http://www.copperhouse.com/copperhouse

Your Partner in Education
with
"QUALITY BOOKS AT FAIR PRICES"

Introduction to
CRIMINOLOGY

Library of Congress Catalog Number 97-67722
ISBN 0-942728-84-x Paper Text Edition

2 3 4 5 6 7 8 9 10

Printed in the United States of America.

PREFACE

Introduction to Criminology is designed to help the student understand the puzzles that are associated with crime and crime causation. We do not promise to solve all the puzzles; however this text does provide the readers with a framework that may be used to understand the crime problem. Professor Sutherland once remarked that the defects of criminology consist principally of the failure to integrate all the factual information regarding crime into consistent and valid general propositions regarding crime causation. This text integrates the basic concepts that are known about crime with the many theories of crime causation.

Introduction to Criminology is published as a paperback text with the goal of presenting a text that students can afford to buy and *keep* as part of their professional library. It is also written in a manner that can be understood by the student so that valuable class time is not wasted in re-explaining what the book covers.

Part I introduces students to the definition of crime, concept of law, social controls, and how crime is measured. Part II provides the theoretical approaches to crime causation. Part III discusses crimes against persons, property, and special crimes. It also covers punishments and victimology. Finally, Part IV provides the students with an introduction to all aspects of the criminal justice system. This latter discussion is designed to provide the reader with a blueprint of where we have been, where we are, and where we might be going.

All charts and graphs are sourced from B.J.S. unless otherwise noted.

ABOUT THE AUTHORS

ℭℜ   Cliff Roberson holds a Ph.D. in human behavior; LLM (advanced law degree) in criminal law, criminology and psychiatry; J.D. in law; and a B.A. in political science. He has taught criminology courses at California State University Fresno, University of Houston, St. Edwards University and Washburn University. He had the unique experience of teaching a criminology course to prisoners in a federal prison. Cliff Roberson is admitted to practice law before the U.S. Supreme Court, various federal courts and in the state courts in California and Texas.

His nonacademic experience includes Director of Programs, National College of District Attorneys; Director, Justice Center, CSU Fresno; military judge, U.S. Marine service; and staff counsel in the office of State Counsel for Offenders, Texas Department of Criminal Justice. He has authored 29 books including *Inside Criminology* and *Exploring Juvenile Justice*.

ℭℜ   Harvey Wallace is a professor and chair of the criminology department at California State University, Fresno. Professor Wallace is the academic coordinator for the U.S. Department of Justice National Victim Assistance Academy in Washington D.C. He holds a J.D. degree and is the former city attorney for Fresno, California and county counsel for Butte County. He served as a deputy district attorney in San Diego county. He has written and published numerous articles in academic and professional journals and is the author and co-author of seven textbooks in the social sciences and criminal justice field.

ACKNOWLEDGMENTS

While we are listed as the sole authors of this text, many have contributed to its development. Thanks to the faculty of the Criminology Department, California State University, Fresno and the Department of Criminal Justice, Washburn University, for their support and help; Professor Steve Russell, University of Texas, San Antonio; Glenda Hunt, Wharton Junior College, Wharton, Texas; Rob Hawkins, University of Houston, Victoria; and Kay Coen for their support and encouragement. Last, but most important, to Cathy Anderson for the many long hours devoted to transforming our manuscript into readable form. Photo credits—Mark Ide

DEDICATION

❧ *To Lynne*
— *Cliff Roberson*

❧ *To Randa, Tim,*
Laura and Billy
— *Harvey Wallace*

TABLE OF CONTENTS

PART I
The Study of Crime

Chapter 1
DEFINITION OF CRIME

Chapter 2
MEASURING CRIME

PART II
Explanation of Criminal Behavior

Chapter 3
THE CLASSICAL APPROACH

Chapter 6
PSYCHOLOGICAL AND PSYCHIATRIC APPROACHES

Chapter 7
THE CONFLICT/CRITICAL APPROACH

PART III
Crime and Punishment

Chapter 8
CRIMES AGAINST PERSONS

Chapter 11
PUNISHMENT

Chapter 12
VICTIMOLOGY

PART IV
The Criminal Justice System

Chapter 13
LAW ENFORCEMENT

Chapter 14
THE COURT SYSTEM

Chapter 15
SENTENCING AND CORRECTIONS

Chapter 16
JUVENILE JUSTICE SYSTEM

PART I

The Study of Crime

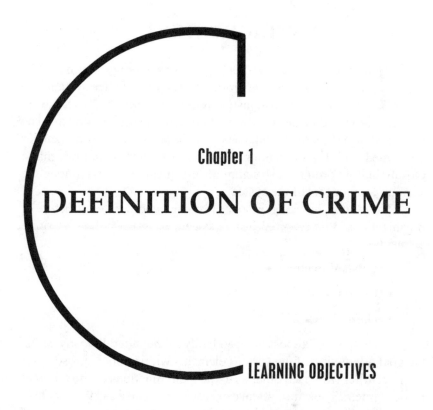

Chapter 1

DEFINITION OF CRIME

LEARNING OBJECTIVES

After studying this chapter, you should be able to:

- Explain the different types of criminal acts.

- Explain the evolution of criminology as a science.

- Distinguish between the various types of mores.

- Recognize the difference between criminal acts and deviant acts.

INTRODUCTION

In order to understand crime and criminology, we must first have a foundation regarding the criminal justice system. We refer to the criminal justice system as a "system," as if it were a system. It would be more accurate to refer to it as a non-system. The term **system** refers to the interrelationship among all those agencies concerned with the prevention of crime in society. It implies that a closely knit, coordinated structure of organizations exists among the various components of the system.

The system, however, is not a close-knit, coordinated structure of organizations. The criminal justice system is actually three separate elements:

- Law enforcement

- Courts

- Corrections

Each operates almost independently of the other. In many cases, the goal orientation of the various elements within a local jurisdiction are in conflict with each other as to the main functions of the criminal justice system. Thus, the system can best be described as "fragmented" or "divided." Accordingly, the criminal justice system is a group of agencies organized around various functions that each is assigned. While there is no single criminal justice system in this country, we have many systems that are similar but individually unique. For convenience and out of habit, however, we will use the phrase "criminal justice system" to collectively refer to all three components.

We apprehend, try, and punish criminals by means of this loose confederation of agencies at all levels of the government. Our system of justice has evolved from English common law into a complex series of procedures and decisions. Unlike many other nations, private citizens are actively involved in our justice system.

Under our form of government, each state and the federal government has its own criminal justice system. While state constitutions and state statutes define each state's criminal justice system, all the systems must respect the rights of individuals as set forth in the U.S. Constitution and interpreted by our courts.

As the *Report to the Nation on Crime and Justice* indicates, our response to crime is a complex process that involves both citizens and agencies at all levels.[1] These various levels must consider the ever-increasing costs of crime not only upon their own budgets, but upon the public as well.

Often the private sector initiates the response to crime. This first response may come from any part of the private sector: individuals, families, neighborhoods, associations, businesses, industries, the news media, or other private service organizations. Citizens response to crime involves crime prevention as well as participation in the criminal justice process once a crime has been committed. Private crime prevention is more than participating in neighborhood watch or providing private security. It also includes a commitment to stop criminal behavior by not engaging in it nor condoning it when it is committed by others.

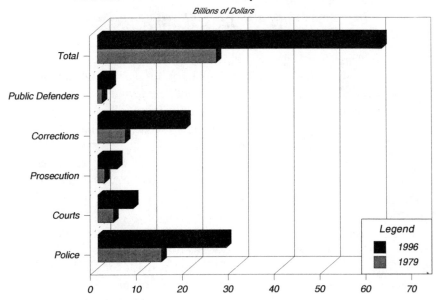

National Criminal Justice Expenditure Increases

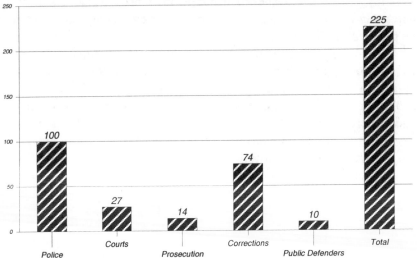

State & Local Justice System Expenditures

1997 Per Capita National Average in Dollars

WHAT IS CRIME?

Important words go beyond the assigned boundaries of their dictionary meanings. **Crime** is one such important word, a word that signifies different meanings to many different people and is always straining at the boundaries of its conventional meaning.[2]

Crime is one of the oldest problems faced by civilizations. The act of defining crime is however a difficult task. At first glance, it seems simple why we call certain acts "crimes" and certain people "criminal"; crimes are acts that pose threats to our society and criminals are people who commit those acts. This simple approach fails to consider the relativity of criminal definitions.

The relativity of criminal definitions indicates that every definition of an act as a crime must be viewed as tentative and subject to redefinition. For example, if in 1932 John and Jill Smith had walked down a street in New York City and John had a pint of whiskey in his pocket and Jill had a gold coin in her pocket, John would be committing a criminal act because of the prohibition statutes. Two years later under the same circumstances, John's conduct would be lawful since the prohibition statutes had been repealed, but Jill's would be illegal because of the new currency statutes which made the possession of gold coins for currency illegal. Thus, criminal activity may depend on one's perspective and the time frame when it occurs.

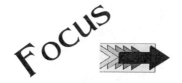

The Challenge of Crime in a Free Society

Many Americans think of crime as a very narrow range of behavior. It is not. An enormous variety of acts make up the "crime problem." Crime is not just a tough teenager snatching a lady's purse. It is a professional thief stealing cars "on order." It is a well-heeled loan shark taking over a previously legitimate business for organized crime. It is a polite young man who suddenly and inexplicably murders his family. It is a corporation executive conspiring with competitors to keep prices high. No single theory, no single generalization can explain the vast range of behavior called crime....

The most understandable mood into which many Americans have been plunged by crime is one of frustration and bewilderment. For "crime" is not a single, simple phenomenon that can be examined, analyzed and described in one piece. It occurs in every part of the country and in every stratum of society. Its practitioners and its victims are people of all ages, incomes and backgrounds. Its trends are difficult to ascertain. Its causes are legion. Its cures are speculative and controversial. An examination of any single kind of crime, let alone of "crime in America," raises a myriad of issues of the utmost complexity.

Source: President's Commission on Law Enforcement and Administration of Justice, Washington, D.C., 1967, pp. 3-5.

We generally assume that the law criminalizes particular behaviors that most people disapprove of. From this point of view, designating some acts as crimes is a simple way of sanctioning certain conduct while condemning other conduct. The law, under this perspective, is a protective reaction against behaviors and people considered by society as unacceptable.

In measuring crime, we have a tendency to accept official crime statistics at face value, i.e., crime is what is reflected in and measured by official crime statistics. A common criticism of official crime statistics, however, is that they measure only one kind of crime—the street crimes of the poor and the working-class.

Gwynn Nettler once remarked that, "Crime is a word, not a deed."[3] In this context, crime constitutes a category of events that contains numerous subcategories. And at the same time, the category of crime is itself a subcategory of a larger set of events (e.g., social harmful acts).

Terming an act a crime involves a series of judgments. First, the judgment is made that the act is harmful. Next, the decision is made that the act should be regulated by law. Finally, the decision is made that the law regulating the act should be a criminal statute rather than a civil one.

Webster's New Universal Unabridged Dictionary provides us with four definitions of **crime**:

1. An act committed in violation of a law prohibiting it, or omitted in violation of a law ordering it; crimes are variously punishable by death, imprisonment or the imposition of certain fines or restrictions.

2. An extreme violation of the law; wrongdoing of a criminal nature, as felony or treason, which affects the whole public and not just the rights of an individual; distinguishable from a misdemeanor.

3. An offense against morality; sin.

4. The acts of a criminal; habitual violation of the law.

The above definitions present two basic positions: first, crime is a defiance of a positive law; and second, crime is a breach of moral law. Henry Campbell Black in *Black's Law Dictionary* defines crime as "a positive or negative act in violation of penal law; an offense against

COMMON OFFENSES
How Many Have You Committed?

Taking office supplies or using office services for personal use
> Up to 1 year in jail and/or up to $1,000 fine.

Evading income taxes (failing to report tips, exaggerated deductions)
> Up to five years in jail and/or up to $250,000 fine.

Gambling illegally (betting on a card game or sporting event)
> Up to six months in jail and/or up to $10,000 fine

Committing computer crimes (copying software illegally, gaining illegal access)
> Up to three years in jail and/or up to $10,000 fine

Serving alcohol to minors
> Up to one year in jail and/or up to $5,000 fine

Possession of a small amount of illegal drugs (marijuana or cocaine)
> Up to four years in jail and/or up to $10,000 fine

Committing adultery in states where it is illegal
> Up to one year in jail and/or up to $1,000 fine

Shoplifting
> Up to one year in jail and/or up to $1,000 fine

Stealing TV signals (cable or satellite hookups)
> Up to one year in jail and/or up to $1,000 fine

Speeding or other moving violations
> Up to one year in jail and $1,000 fine

Parking illegally
> Up to $500 fine and your vehicle towed and impounded

Lying to a customs agent to avoid duties
> Fine not to exceed the value of the merchandise

Importing prohibited products (Cuban cigars, tortoise shell jewelry, plants, etc.)
> Up to one year in jail and/or up to $100,000 fine

Buying stolen goods (watches, books, jewelry, stereos, newspapers, etc.)
> Up to one year in jail and/or up to $1,000 fine

Unauthorized sale of tickets to events for above the listed price
> Up to six months in jail and/or up to $1,000 fine

Patronizing a prostitute
> Up to one year in jail and/or up to $5,000 fine

Lying on a government job application
> Up to one year in jail and/or up to $1,000 fine

Disregarding a jury summons
> Up to six months in jail and/or a $750 fine

Drinking in public (e.g., a park or beach where prohibited)
> Up to 30 days in jail and/or up to $100 fine

NOTE: laws and penalties vary among states

the State." Black then proceeds to discuss crimes which are *malum in se* (evil in themselves) and crimes which are *malum prohibitum* (which are crimes simply because statutes have made them crimes). It appears that both dictionaries suggest that crime has a positive definition (i.e., that which the state condemns and a moral dimension; an offense against morality).[4]

The above analysis of the definitions of crime fails to explain why a given act is a crime and another similar act is not. Johnson states that crime, as a concept, does not emerge full grown in any society. That it develops out of experience and is conditioned by social and cultural attitudes.[5] Accordingly, to understand why some acts are considered crimes and similar acts are not, not only do we need to look at the current values of our society, but also the historical background of the prohibited or sanctioned conduct.

Since religious beliefs are one of the most formative influences upon us, there is still a moral dimension to the definition of crime. At the time that our country was founded, most of our crimes were also considered moral sins. In Colonial America, those who committed crimes were also considered to be "offenders against the divine." Over the passage of time, the diversity in our society on matters of religion tended to separate crime from moral wrongs. Our movement to secularize the criminal statutes have resulted in the definition of crime as offense against the laws of state without reference to the divine. When legislatures or judges participate in the lawmaking processes, however, they are strongly influenced by their religious or lack of religious beliefs.

Crime and moral values are not the same. An adult may stand on the edge of a lake and watch a small child drown. Absent some special relationship, that adult has not committed a crime. However, society might condemn that adult for failing to attempt to save that child.

As indicated above, crime is a violation of a criminal statute. Sutherland and Cressey established four characteristics of criminal law:

1. It is assumed by political activity. The state acts as the party. It is not the victim versus the defendant, rather it is the People of the State of California/Texas/Mississippi/etc. that are prosecuting the case.

2. It must be specific. The criminal law must define both the specific offense and the punishment for that offense.

3. It must be uniformly applied. All persons must be subject to the law and its sanctions regardless of rank or station in life.

4. It must contain penal sanctions. The law must provide for punishment inflicted by the state.[6]

Establishing a definition of crime is not easy. A working definition of crime that has been adopted by most criminologists is the one proposed by Edwin Sutherland:

> The essential characteristic of crime is that it is behavior which is prohibited by the State as an injury to the State and against which the State may react, at least at the last resort, by punishment.[7]

The above definition limits crimes only to those acts which violate a criminal statute. It does not address the morality aspects of human behavior. For purposes of our discussions in this text, we will use Sutherland's definition.

The history of crime in the United States represents a pendulum-like swing between the public's fear of crime and the concept of individual rights. Criminal justice professionals generally are oriented toward one of two opposite directions—"law and order" or "individual rights." The "law and order" orientation stresses the need to solve the crime problem. The "individual rights" orientation stresses the need to protect an individual's rights and considers this need greater than the need to punish offenders. Too great an emphasis on individual rights will restrict law enforcement and allow offenders to escape punishment. Arbitrary police practices that may occur under the "law and order" orientation may infringe on human and constitutional rights. As Chief Justice Earl Warren stated in *Miranda v. Arizona*:[8]

> The quality of a nation's civilization can be largely measured by the methods it uses in the enforcement of the criminal law. . . . All of these policies point to one overriding thought: the constitutional foundation underlying the privilege is the respect a government—state or federal— must accord the dignity and integrity of its citizens. To maintain a fair state-individual balance, the government must shoulder the entire load.

Associated with the *Individual Rights v. Law and Order* issue is the concept of **due process**. This concept restricts the power of the state and more particularly the police, courts and corrections. The Bill of Rights, the first eight amendments to the U.S. Constitution, contains 23 separate individual rights, 12 of them concern procedural rights for persons accused of criminal conduct. In 1798, the U.S. Supreme Court ruled that the prohibitions against government action contained in those amendments were restrictions only on the federal government and not on state governments. The case, *Calder v. Bull*, involved a statute passed by the legislature of Connecticut which set aside a probate court judgment and directed the probate judge to refuse the recording of a will (an ex posto law).[9] The justices noted that the Bill of Rights was designed to prevent the federal abuse of power, not state abuse.

The Fourteenth Amendment, one of the antislavery amendments enacted in 1865, however, has been used by the courts to place due process requirements on the states and the state's criminal justice system in criminal matters.

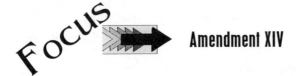

Amendment XIV

> Section 1. All persons born or naturalized in the United States, and subject to the jurisdiction thereof, are citizens of the United States and of the State wherein they reside. No State shall make or enforce any law which shall abridge the privileges or immunities of citizens of the United States; nor shall any State deprive any person of life, liberty, or property, without due process; nor deny to any person within its jurisdiction the equal protection of the laws.

The clause "without due process" of the Fourteenth Amendment has been interpreted by the U.S. Supreme Court as "incorporating" most of the provisions of the Bill of Rights. Accordingly, those rights which are incorporated under that clause apply to state as well as federal criminal proceedings. In 1897, the Court using the due process clause of the Fourteenth Amendment applied the Fifth Amendment's requirement of payment of "just compensation" for the taking of private property for public use to the states. Later in 1925, in *Gitlow v. New York*, the Court held that the First Amendment's protection on free speech restricted the state's right to control free speech. The Sixth Amendment's right to counsel was imposed on the states by *Powell v. Alabama* (1932) and the requirement of a trial by "an impartial jury" in jury cases was imposed by *Norris v. Alabama* (1935).

CRIMINOLOGY

As indicated above, society has been studying crime for centuries. Individual scientists have attempted to discover the cause of crime and how we can stop it. Whole industries have been established to protect people from the consequences of crime. Exactly what is the phenomenon call criminology?

Criminology is a relatively new science. Some would argue that it is not a true academic discipline. These detractors may claim that the study of criminology is more of a vocational pursuit than anything else. Many of the detractors are individuals that who study criminology only because they are interested in obtaining a job in the criminal justice system.

Criminology continues to grow and expand. Over thirty academic institutions offer degrees that address issues within the definition of criminology. There are professionals who now proudly engrave the word "Criminologist" on their business card. These are persons who study crime, criminals, and criminal behavior. There are several national societies that serve those studying criminology. National, regional, and state conferences are conducted where criminologists and other academic professionals present their research to peers. Finally, there are a number of referred academic journals that review, accept, and publish research in the area of criminology. By any standard, criminology can be referred to as a valid academic discipline.

Just as there are a number of different definitions of crime so are there a variety of sources to draw upon when defining criminology. One of the best known and accepted definitions comes from Edwin Sutherland, one of the best known academic researchers of criminology, who stated that criminology consists of three principle divisions:

1. The sociology of law

2. Scientific analysis of the causes of crime

3. Crime control[10]

However, for our purposes, we will use a more comprehensive definition of criminology. **Criminology** from our perspective is the scientific study of crime and criminal behavior. This definition includes all of Sutherland's elements of criminology. Additionally, this definition allows for an examination of other parties that interact with the criminal such as prosecutors, judges, correctional officials, and victims. As will be illustrated, criminology is continuously growing, evolving and maturing.

THE CONCEPT OF LAW

Types of Laws

Law can be divided into several different classifications. The most common ones include:

- Crimes and torts

- Common law and statutory law

Crime

A **crime** is a wrong involving the violation of the peace and dignity of the State. In theory, it is committed against the interest of all of the people of the State.[11] Accordingly, crimes are prosecuted by the prosecutor in the name of the *State*, *People*, or *Commonwealth*.

Tort

A **tort** is a wrong that is a violation of a private interest and thus gives rise to civil liability. The same conduct, however, may be both a crime and a tort. For example, a woman is forcibly raped by a neighbor. The criminal aspect of the conduct is a violation of the peace and dignity of the State and, therefore, a crime against all the people in the

State. It is also a violation of the private interest of the victim, and she may file a civil suit and obtain civil damages against the offender. [Note: The offender may be acquitted at the criminal trial where proof of his or her guilt is required to be established beyond a reasonable doubt and yet held accountable at the civil trial where the degree of proof required to hold the offender accountable is much less. In the recent cases against the Hall of Fame football player, O.J. Simpson, the criminal case against him resulted in a "not guilty" finding, but he was found liable in the civil case.]

Common Law

Common law is the major source of our modern day criminal law. In medieval England, courts used a traditional body of unwritten legal precedents which had been created by everyday rulings and practices. This body of law became known as the common law and it became the law of the land. At the source of its popularity and stability was this concept of precedent–the requirement of ruling the same way in similar cases.

Statutory Law

Statutory law is law that originates with specifically designated lawmaking bodies. It is enacted by legislative bodies of government. The primary statutory laws dealing with crimes and criminal procedure are the state penal codes.

The Nature of Criminal Law

Criminal law is the ultimate form of legal control by the state. The state can use criminal law to repress any conduct that threatens the state by use of the provisions for punishment and sanctions. The concept of criminal acts as injuries to the state developed when the custom of private or community redress was replaced by the principle that the state is wronged when it or one of its subjects is harmed.

A rule of conduct is a criminal law only if it is created by the state (or federal government), contains provisions for punishment to be administered upon the conviction of its violation and the punishment is administered by the state or federal government in the name of society. The basic conceptual difference between civil law and criminal law is that criminal law defines conduct that is considered against the interest of the society, whereas civil law refers to conduct that is against the interest of the individual. Crime is therefore a social wrong or a crime against society, whereas a tort is a private wrong.[12]

Substantive vs. Procedural Criminal Law

We function under two basic types of criminal laws—substantive and procedural. **Substantive criminal law** defines crimes. It lists the elements that constitute each act or omission that is classified as a crime. Substantive criminal law also attaches penalties for violations of the crimes.

Procedural law provides the rules by which we investigate, try and punish criminals. To be legally convicted of a crime, a person must be tried according to procedural criminal law and convicted of committing an act or a failure to act in violation of the substantive criminal law.

EVOLUTION OF SOCIAL CONTROL

In looking at the evolution of social control, we need first to look at our process of labeling a person a "criminal" and the relationship between sin and crime.

 Who is a Criminal?

After pleading "no contest" to charges of taking kickbacks on government contracts, a former governor of Maryland and U.S. vice-president stated, "Honesty is different things to different people."

An article in a Canadian prison newspaper stated: "There is only one difference between the men in this prison and a great number of your readers. We were caught."[13]

In defining one a **criminal**, we have the same difficulty that we discussed above in determining what a crime is. It would appear that one who commits a crime is subject to be labeled a criminal. Is it necessary to be convicted in a criminal trial before being considered a criminal? Using this approach would mean that an individual who regularly sexually abuses his daughter is not a criminal until the daughter reports it, and he is convicted. If the daughter never reports it, is he any less a criminal?

The Relationship Between Sin and Crime

Before the American Revolution, the colonies were subject to the law handed down by English judges. Accordingly, the common law of England, with its Anglo-Saxon concepts, became the basic criminal law of the colonies. After the revolution, the common law was later modified and changed by state legislatures. During the modifications, the colonies' religious beliefs became a part of our criminal code, and criminal law was used to regulate morality. To some extent, we still use criminal law to regulate morality. According to Norval Morris and Gordon Hawkins, our present criminal codes in the United States are some of the most moralistic criminal laws in history.[14]

Informal Social Controls

William G. Sumner, a noted sociologist, discussed the concept of informal social controls in his classic work *Folkways*.[15] Sumner distinguished between three types of norms. **Norms** are rules that govern our behavior in a given situation. Summer's norms included mores, customs, and folkways.

Mores are those norms that give society its moral standards of behavior. Failure to follow society's mores can lead to severe sanctions. Violation of a more causes intense feelings and extreme consequences. For example, killing and sexual assault of a child would be a violation of a basic more in our society.

Customs are the next strongest form of informal social control. Violation of a custom is not as serious as violation of a more, but it still will cause disgust and shock to those witnessing such an act. Watching someone spit out half eaten food on the floor during dinner is an example of a violation of a custom.

Folkways are the traditional methods of doing things because they are the accepted behaviors of the group or culture. When someone violates a folkway, he/she may be subjected to mild criticism or ridicule.

Crime and Deviance

Deviance refers to those acts that the majority of society views as eccentric, dangerous, bizarre, abhorrent or otherwise outside the bounds of normal behavior. Definitions of deviant behavior change according to different perspectives. For example, in Japan, it is considered acceptable behavior to go to a public bath house and bathe in the nude in front of strangers. However, such activity in the United States would cause concern, worry and possibly even the filing of criminal charges against someone who attempted to disrobe in public.

All societies have cultural values which they value and which may be viewed as strange or deviant by other cultures. Some societies in Southwest Asia accept men holding hands in public while other cultures look at this as a form of sexual deviance. However, there are certain acts that are looked upon with disfavor by almost all societies. These acts include murder and sexual assault.

Various types of drug use are also accepted in some cultures while viewed as dangerous and/or deviant in others. For example, our society accepts the use of tobacco and alcohol and, to some extent, marijuana but sees the use of drugs, such as heroin and PCP, as dangerous not only to the user but to society. Drug use among arrestees in the United States is very high.

Deviance and crime are therefore determined by a number of factors. It is a complex system of interpersonal, cultural, and societal beliefs and acts. Some acts may be deviant and not criminal in certain cultures and, in other cultures, the same acts would be deviant and criminal, while in still other cultures, those acts would not be deviant nor criminal.

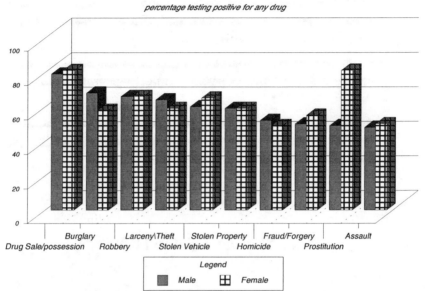

Prevalence of Drug Use Among Arrestees

percentage testing positive for any drug

SUMMARY

- While we refer to the criminal justice system as a "system," it would be more accurate to refer to it as a "non-system." It is actually three separate elements—law enforcement, courts, and corrections.

- We have a dual criminal justice system—state and federal.

- Citizens are also involved in the criminal justice system by crime prevention and by not engaging in criminal behavior.

- The word "crime" is difficult to define. For our purposes, we will accept Sutherland's definition of crime: Behavior that is prohibited by the State as an injury to the State and against which the State may react, at least as the last resort, by punishment.

- The discipline of criminology consists of three principle divisions: sociology of law, scientific analysis of the causes of crime and crime control.

- Laws can be divided into different classifications. The two most common are (1) crimes and torts and (2) common law and statutory law. A tort is a violation of a private interest and gives rise to civil liability.

- Common law is the source of our modern day criminal law. It developed from the everyday rulings and practices of the English courts.

- Substantive criminal law defines crimes and affixes permissible punishment. Procedural law provides the rules by which we investigate, try and punish criminals.

DISCUSSION QUESTIONS

1. Timmer states, "A definition of crime represents the legal conditions under which the state, as an instrument of an economically dominant class, exercises its power to punish."[16] Do you agree or disagree with this statement? Explain your opinion.

2. What are the requirements for qualifying conduct as a crime?

3. Differentiate between a tort and a crime.

4. What criteria should be used before identifying someone as a criminal?

5. Distinguish between procedural and substantive criminal law.

6. Is a state statute that defines the crime of criminal homicide a procedural or substantive law? Why?

7. Can you come up with a more comprehensive definition of criminology? Why is it preferred over the one in the text?

8. Describe some folkways that you have observed.

ENDNOTES—Chapter 1

1. U.S. Department of Justice, *Report to the Nation on Crime and Justice*, 2nd ed., (Washington D.C. 1988): pp. 56-60.

2. Richard Quinney and John Wildeman, *The Problem of Crime*, 3rd ed., (Mountain View, CA.: Mayfield, 1991), p. 1.

3. James F. Gilsinan, *Criminology and Public Policy*, (Englewood Cliffs, NJ: Prentice-Hall, 1990), p. 17.

4. Herbert A. Johnson, *History of Criminal Justice*, (Cincinnati: Anderson, 1988).

5. Ibid. p. 7.

6. Edwin H. Sutherland and Donald C. Cressey, *Criminology*, 9th ed. (Philadelphia: Lippincott, 1974) pp. 4-7.

7. Edwin Sutherland, *White Collar Crime*, (New York: Holt, Rinehart and Winston, 1949).

8. 384 U.S. 436 (1966).

9. 3 U.S. 386 (1798).

10. Edwin Sutherland, *Principles of Criminology*, 4th ed. (New York, Lippincott, 1947) p. 1.

11. *People v. Morrison*, 54 CA 469, 202 P 348 (1921).

12. Note: *Tort* is defined as a private wrong or injury, other than a breach of contract, resulting from a violation of a duty and for which the courts will provide relief in the form of damages. [John N. Ferdico, *Criminal Law and Justice Dictionary*, (St. Paul: West, 1992), p.438].

13. Gwynne Nettler, *Criminology Lessons* (Cincinnati: Anderson, 1988), p. 38.

14. Norval Morris and Gordon P. Hawkins, *The Honest Politician's Guide to Crime Control*, (Chicago: Univ. of Chicago Press, 1969).

15. William G. Sumner, *Folkways*, (New York: Dover,1906)

16. *Crime in the Streets and Crime in the Suites*, (Needham Heights, MA: Allyn & Bacon, 1989), p. 27.

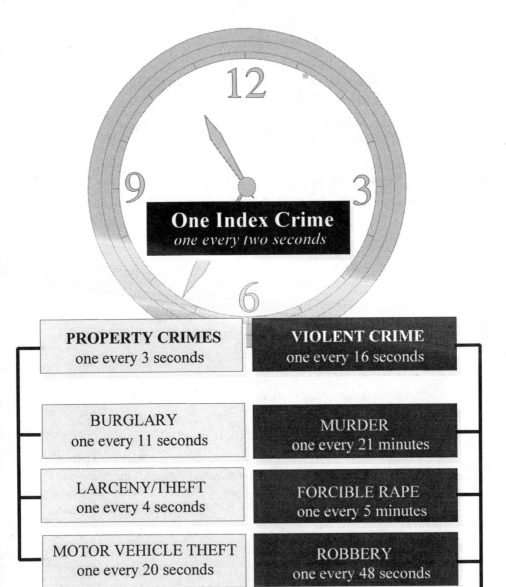

One Index Crime
one every two seconds

PROPERTY CRIMES	VIOLENT CRIME
one every 3 seconds	one every 16 seconds

BURGLARY	MURDER
one every 11 seconds	one every 21 minutes

LARCENY/THEFT	FORCIBLE RAPE
one every 4 seconds	one every 5 minutes

MOTOR VEHICLE THEFT	ROBBERY
one every 20 seconds	one every 48 seconds

	AGGRAVATED ASSAULT
	one every 28 seconds

F.B.I.'s Crime Clock

Chapter 2

MEASURING CRIME

LEARNING OBJECTIVES

After reading this chapter, you should be able to:

- Explain the differences between the various types of official reports.

- Distinguish between the types of reports that provide information regarding the commission of crimes.

- List the advantages and disadvantages of of the various mechanisms that are used to measure crime.

C rime statistics are reported in various forms and measured in many ways. We discuss these varied methods and procedures in this chapter. In examining crime statistics, we should consider the following questions: What is the extent of crime in our society? Have crime rates gone up in recent years? When and where are crimes committed? [1]

Crime occurs everyday and in every location, yet we cannot predict, with any certainty, how many crimes will occur this year or in the future. However, it is important to understand the present extent of criminal acts.

THE EXTENT OF CRIME

More than 49 million victimizations and attempted victimizations occur each year.[2] Specific categories include the following figures:

- **Fatal crimes.** These crimes, which include criminal and vehicle homicide, arson, and child abuse, claim some 31,000 lives a year.

- **Child abuse.** A conservative estimate of the number of children sexually, physically, or emotionally abused each year is 794,000.

- **Rape.** The number of rape and sexual assault victims per year is estimated at 1.1 million.

- **Assault.** The number of nonfatal assaults against children under 12 years of age comes to approximately 450,000 each year. This study estimates the number of domestic assaults at 2 million annually.

- **Drunk Driving.** Tentative estimates put the number of injuries from drunk driving at about 500,000.

- **Arson.** There were 137,000 arson victimizations, including 15,000 that resulted in injuries in 1996.

OFFICIAL REPORTS

There are many different types of official reports which are compiled by private or public agencies in the form of statistical data. This data provides a much needed resource for further research into the extent of crime and victimization. The data most commonly relied upon are reports by local law enforcement agencies, the *Uniform Crime Reports*, and the *National Crime Victimization Surveys*.

Uniform Crime Reports

During the 1920s, the International Association of Chiefs of Police (IACP) formed the Commission on Uniform Crime Reports in order to develop a uniform system of reporting criminal statistics. The committee evaluated various crimes based upon their seriousness, frequency of occurrence, commonality across the nation, and likelihood of being reported to the police. In 1929, the committee finished its study and recommended a plan for crime reporting that became the foundation of the UCR program.

The UCR prepares an annual crime index. This index is composed of seven selected offenses used to gauge changes in the overall rate of crime reported to law enforcement agencies. Therefore, the index is a combination of violent and property crimes. For example, about 14 percent of the index offenses are violent crimes and 86 percent are property crimes. These seven offenses include the following crimes:

- Murder and non-negligent manslaughter
- Forcible rape
- Robbery
- Aggravated assault
- Burglary
- Larceny-theft
- Motor vehicle theft

In 1979, Congress mandated that an eighth crime, **arson**, be added to the index. During the study phase of the project, it was recognized that differences in state criminal codes would cause the same act to be reported in various methods and categories. To avoid this problem, no distinction was made between felony and misdemeanor crimes and a standardized set of definitions was established to allow law enforcement agencies to submit data without regard for local statutes. In 1930, Congress enacted federal law that authorized the attorney general to gather crime information.[3] The attorney general designated the FBI as the national clearinghouse for all data and since that time data based upon this system has been obtained from the nation's law enforcement agencies.

The Uniform Crime Reports (UCR) program is a nationwide statistical computation involving over 1600 cities, counties and state law enforcement agencies who voluntarily report data on reported crimes. Law enforcement agencies in the UCR program represents over 245 million inhabitants or approximately 95 percent of the total population of the United States. The program is administrated by the Federal Bureau of Investigation which issues assessments on the nature and type of crimes. The program's primary objective is to generate a set of reliable criminal statistics for use in law enforcement administration, operation and management.[4]

The Federal Bureau of Investigation is tasked with administering the UCR Program and issues periodic reports addressing the nature and type of crime in the United States. While the UCR's primary objective is the issuance of reliable statistics for use by law enforcement agencies, it has also become an important social indicator of deviance in our society.

The UCR is an annual report that includes the number of crimes reported by citizens to local police departments, and the number of arrests made by law enforcement agencies in a given year. This information is of somewhat limited value since the data is based upon instances of violence that are classified as criminal and are reported to the local law enforcement agencies. Many serious acts of violence are not reported to the police and, therefore, do not become part of the UCR.

A number of factors influence the reporting or non-reporting of crimes to local law enforcement. The Bureau of Justice Statistics reports that the most common reason victims give for reporting crimes to the police is to prevent further crimes from being committed against them by the same offender.[5] For both household crimes and other theft related crimes, the most common reason given by victims in reporting the offenses is to assist in the recovery of the property.

Violent crimes are the most likely to be reported to the police. Household crimes are the next highest reported form of crime. Personnel thefts are the least likely crimes to be reported to the police.

The most common reason given for not reporting violent crimes to the police is that the crime was considered by the victim to be a private or personal matter. The most common reasons for not reporting household crimes or other theft-related crimes were that the items were recovered or the crime was committed by a non-stranger. The most common reasons for reporting household crimes or other theft-related crimes were for tax and insurance motivated reasons.

Victims give different reasons for not reporting crimes to the police when the offender was a stranger instead of an acquaintance. Victims of crimes committed by strangers gave the following reasons for not reporting the offense:

- The offender was unsuccessful.

- The victim considered the police inefficient.

- The victim felt the police did not want to be bothered.

- It was not important enough to the victim to report the crime.

Victims of crimes committed by acquaintances gave the following reasons for not reporting:

- The victim considered the crime a private or personal matter.

- The victim had reported the crime to another official.

The *Hate Crime Statistics Act* was passed by Congress in 1990 and mandates that a data base of crimes motivated by religion, ethnic, racial, or sexual orientation be collected. On January 1, 1991 the UCR program distributed guidelines for reporting hate crimes, and the first report was published in 1992. Participation in reporting hate crimes continues to grow and as of 1993, 6,840 law enforcement agencies representing 56 percent of the U.S. population were reporting hate crime data.

With the exception of the hate crime category noted above, the UCR remained virtually unchanged for 50 years. Eventually, various law enforcement agencies began to call for an evaluation and redesign of the program. Because the UCR only lists crimes that are reported to it, this presents a serious problem since not all police agencies report crimes to the FBI and the Department of Justice. Since the UCR relies on law enforcement agencies to voluntarily report crimes, there is the possibility of under reporting by some agencies based on political reasons.[6] The UCR generally provides only tabular summaries of crime and does not provide crime analysts with more meaningful information. Additionally, the method of counting crimes causes problems. For example, only the most serious crime is reported. If a person is robbed and his car stolen, police agencies are instructed to report only the robbery. Finally, some crimes, such as white-collar crime are excluded from the UCR system. After several years of study, the FBI began to institute various modifications to the UCR Program. These changes established a new, more effective crime reporting system.

National Incident-Based Reporting System

The newly redesigned UCR Program is called the **National Incident-Based Reporting System (NIBRS)**.

In 1989, the FBI began accepting data, and nine states started supplying information in the new format. NIBRS collects data on each single incident and arrest within 22 crime categories. Incident, victim, property, offender and arrestee information is gathered for each offense known to the local agency. The goal of the redesigned system is to modernize crime reporting information by collecting data presently maintained in law enforcement records. The enhanced UCR Program is a byproduct of modern law enforcement records systems that have the capability to store and collate more information regarding criminal offenses.

National Crime Victimization Surveys

The **National Crime Victimization Survey (NCVS)** attempts to correct the problems on non-reporting inherent in the UCR by contacting a nationwide sample and interviewing citizens regarding victimization.

The report was originally entitled the National Crime Survey (NCS) but was renamed to more clearly reflect its emphasis on the measurement of victimizations experienced by citizens. The NCVS began in 1972 and collects detailed information about certain criminal offenses, both attempted and completed which concern the general public and law enforcement. These offenses include the frequency and nature of:

- Rape
- Robbery
- Assault
- Household burglary
- Personal and household theft
- Motor vehicle theft[7]

The NCVS does not measure homicide or commercial crime.

A single crime may have more than one victim. For example, a bank robbery may involve several bank tellers. Thus, a single incident may have more than one victimization. A victimization, the basic measure of the occurrence of crime, is a specific criminal act because it affects a specific victim. The number of victimizations however, is determined by the number of victims of each specific criminal act.

Who They Victimized

percent of violent inmates

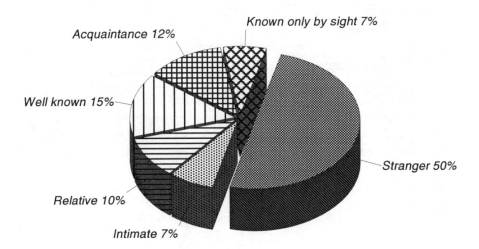

Known only by sight 7%

Acquaintance 12%

Well known 15%

Relative 10%

Intimate 7%

Stranger 50%

OMB No. 1121-0111: Approval Expires 08/31/97

NOTICE – Your report to the Census Bureau is **confidential** by law (U.S. Code 42, Sections 3789g and 3735). All identifiable information will be used only by persons engaged in and for the purposes of the survey, and may not be disclosed or released to others for any purpose.	Sample	Control number			HH
	J ___	PSU I Segment I CK I Serial			No.

FORM **NCVS-2**
(7-24-95)

U.S. DEPARTMENT OF COMMERCE
BUREAU OF THE CENSUS
ACTING AS COLLECTING AGENT FOR THE
BUREAU OF JUSTICE STATISTICS
U.S. DEPARTMENT OF JUSTICE

CRIME INCIDENT REPORT
NATIONAL CRIME VICTIMIZATION SURVEY

Notes

N C V S

2

I N C I D E N T   R E P O R T

PGM 6

1a. LINE NUMBER OF RESPONDENT ──────▶ | 801 | _____ Line number

1b. SCREEN QUESTION NUMBER ──────▶ | 802 | _____ Screen question number

1c. INCIDENT NUMBER ──────▶ | 803 | _____ Incident number

CHECK ITEM A   See item 33a on the NCVS-1. Has the respondent lived at this address for more than 6 months? *(If not sure, ASK.)*
☐ Yes (more than 6 months) – **SKIP** to 3
☐ No (6 months or less) – *Ask 2*

2. You said that during the last 6 months – *(Refer to appropriate screen question for description of crime.)* Did (this/the first) incident happen while you were living here or before you moved to this address?
| 605 | 1 ☐ While living at this address
       2 ☐ Before moving to this address

3. (You said that during the last 6 months – *(Refer to appropriate screen question for description of crime.)*) In what month did (this/the first) incident happen? *(Show calendar if necessary. Encourage respondent to give exact month.)*
| 606 | ☐☐   ☐☐
     Month   Year

4. If known, mark without asking. If not sure, ASK – Altogether, how many times did this type of incident happen during the last 6 months?
| 607 | _____ Number of incidents

CHECK ITEM B   Refer to 4. How many incidents?
| 608 | 1 ☐ 1–5 incidents (not a "series") – **SKIP** to 5b
       2 ☐ 6 or more incidents – *Fill Check Item C*

CHECK ITEM C   Are these incidents similar to each other in detail, or are they for different types of crimes? *(If not sure, ASK.)*
| 609 | 1 ☐ Similar – *Fill Check Item D*
       2 ☐ Different (not a "series") – **SKIP** to 5b

CHECK ITEM D   Can you (respondent) recall enough details of each incident to distinguish them from each other? *(If not sure, ASK.)*
| 610 | 1 ☐ Yes (not a "series") – **SKIP** to 5b
       2 ☐ No (is a "series") – *Reduce entry in screen question if necessary – Ask 5a*

5a. The following questions refer only to the most recent incident.

5b. Was it daylight or dark outside when (this/the most recent) incident happened?
| 611 | 1 ☐ Light ....
       2 ☐ Dark ....
       3 ☐ Dawn, almost light, dusk, twilight   } *Ask 6*
       4 ☐ Don't know – **SKIP** to 7

6. About what time did (this/the most recent) incident happen?

During day
| 612 | 1 ☐ After 6 a.m. – 12 noon
       2 ☐ After 12 noon – 6 p.m.
       3 ☐ Don't know what time of day

At night
       4 ☐ After 6 p.m. – 12 midnight
       5 ☐ After 12 midnight – 6 a.m.
       6 ☐ Don't know what time of night

Or

       7 ☐ Don't know whether day or night

Page 2-deleted due to irrelevancy

11. **Did the offender live (here/there) or have a right to be (here/there), for instance, as a guest or a repairperson?**

    `617` 1 ☐ Yes – *SKIP to 19*
    2 ☐ No .... } *Ask 12*
    3 ☐ Don't know

12. **Did the offender actually get INSIDE your (house/apartment /room/garage/ shed/ enclosed porch)?**

    `618` 1 ☐ Yes – *SKIP to 14*
    2 ☐ No .... } *Ask 13*
    3 ☐ Don't know

13. **Did the offender TRY to get in your (house/apartment/room/garage/shed/ enclosed porch)?**

    `619` 1 ☐ Yes – *Ask 14*
    2 ☐ No – *SKIP to 19*
    3 ☐ Don't know – *Ask 14*

14. **Was there any evidence, such as a broken lock or broken window, that the offender(s) (got in by force/TRIED to get in by force)?**

    `620` 1 ☐ Yes – *Ask 15*
    2 ☐ No – *SKIP to 16*

15. **What was the evidence? Anything else?**

    Mark (X) all that apply.

    Window

    `625` 1 ☐ Damage to window (include frame, glass broken/removed/cracked) ....
    2 ☐ Screen damaged/removed ....
    3 ☐ Lock on window damaged/tampered with in some way ....
    4 ☐ Other – *Specify*

    Door

    5 ☐ Damage to door (include frame, glass panes or door removed) ....
    6 ☐ Screen damaged/removed ....
    `626` 7 ☐ Lock or door handle damaged/tampered with in some way ....
    8 ☐ Other – *Specify*

    Other

    9 ☐ Other than window or door – *Specify*

    } *SKIP to 19*

16. **How did the offender (get in/TRY to get in)?**

    Mark (X) only one box.

    `627` 1 ☐ Let in ....
    2 ☐ Offender pushed his/her way in after door opened ....
    3 ☐ Through OPEN DOOR or other opening ..
    4 ☐ Through UNLOCKED door or window ...
    5 ☐ Through LOCKED door or window – Had key......................
    6 ☐ Through LOCKED door or window – Picked lock, used credit card, etc., other than key
    7 ☐ Through LOCKED door or window – Don't know how ....
    8 ☐ Don't know ....
    9 ☐ Other – *Specify*

    } *SKIP to 19*

17. *ASK OR VERIFY –* **Did the incident happen in an area restricted to certain people or was it open to the public at the time?**

    `628` 1 ☐ Open to the public
    2 ☐ Restricted to certain people (or nobody had a right to be there)
    3 ☐ Don't know
    4 ☐ Other – *Specify*

18. *ASK OR VERIFY –* **Did it happen outdoors, indoors, or both?**

    `629` 1 ☐ Indoors (inside a building or enclosed space)
    2 ☐ Outdoors
    3 ☐ Both

19. *ASK OR VERIFY –* **How far away from home did this happen?**

    PROBE – **Was it within a mile, 5 mile, 50 miles or more?**

    Mark (X) first box that respondent is sure of.

    `630` 1 ☐ At, in, or near the building containing the respondent's home/next door
    2 ☐ A mile or less
    3 ☐ Five miles or less
    4 ☐ Fifty miles or less
    5 ☐ More than 50 miles
    6 ☐ Don't know how far

20a. ASK OR VERIFY –
Were you or any other member of this household present when this incident occurred?

`634` 1 ☐ Yes – Ask 20b
2 ☐ No – **SKIP** to 56, page 8

20b. ASK OR VERIFY –
Which household members were present?

`635` 1 ☐ Respondent only ....
2 ☐ Respondent and other household member(s) } Ask 21
3 ☐ Only other household member(s), not respondent – **SKIP** to 59, page 8

21. ASK OR VERIFY –
Did you personally see an offender?

`636` 1 ☐ Yes
2 ☐ No

22. Did the offender have a weapon such as a gun or knife, or something to use as a weapon, such as a bottle or wrench?

`637` 1 ☐ Yes – Ask 23
2 ☐ No ...... } **SKIP** to 24
3 ☐ Don't know

23. What was the weapon? Anything else?
Mark (X) all that apply.

`638` 1 ☐ Hand gun (pistol, revolver, etc.)
* 2 ☐ Other gun (rifle, shotgun, etc.)
3 ☐ Knife
4 ☐ Other sharp object (scissors, ice pick, axe, etc.)
5 ☐ Blunt object (rock, club, blackjack, etc.)
6 ☐ Other – Specify ⤵

24. Did the offender hit you, knock you down or actually attack you in any way?

`639` 1 ☐ Yes – **SKIP** to 29, page 5
2 ☐ No – Ask 25

25. Did the offender TRY to attack you?

`640` 1 ☐ Yes – **SKIP** to 28a
2 ☐ No – Ask 26

26. Did the offender THREATEN you with harm in any way?

`641` 1 ☐ Yes – **SKIP** to 28b
2 ☐ No – Ask 27

27. What actually happened? Anything else?
Mark (X) all that apply.
FIELD REPRESENTATIVE – If box 4, ASK –
Do you mean forced or coerced sexual intercourse including attempts?
If "Yes," change entry in Item 24 to "Yes." Delete entries in 25–27.

`642` 1 ☐ Something taken without permission ....
* 2 ☐ Attempted or threatened to take something
3 ☐ Harassed, argument, abusive language ..
4 ☐ Unwanted sexual contact with force (grabbing, fondling, etc.) ....
5 ☐ Unwanted sexual contact without force (grabbing, fondling, etc.) ....
6 ☐ Forcible entry or attempted forcible entry of house/apartment ....
7 ☐ Forcible entry or attempted forcible entry of car ....
8 ☐ Damaged or destroyed property ....
9 ☐ Attempted or threatened to damage or destroy property ....
10 ☐ Other – Specify ⤵ ....

SKIP to 40, page 6

28a. How did the offender TRY to attack you? Any other way?

28b. How were you threatened? Any other way?
Mark (X) all that apply.
FIELD REPRESENTATIVE – If box 5, ASK –
Do you mean forced or coerced sexual intercourse including attempts?
If "Yes," change entry in Item 24 to "Yes." Delete entries in 25–28.

`643` 1 ☐ Verbal threat of rape ....
* 2 ☐ Verbal threat to kill ....
3 ☐ Verbal threat of attack other than to kill or rape
4 ☐ Verbal threat of sexual assault other than rape
5 ☐ Unwanted sexual contact with force (grabbing, fondling, etc.) ....
6 ☐ Unwanted sexual contact without force (grabbing, fondling, etc.) ....
`644` 7 ☐ Weapon present or threatened with weapon .
* 8 ☐ Shot at (but missed) ....
9 ☐ Attempted attack with knife/sharp weapon ..
10 ☐ Attempted attack with weapon other than gun/knife/sharp weapon ....
`645` 11 ☐ Object thrown at person ....
* 12 ☐ Followed or surrounded ....
13 ☐ Tried to hit, slap, knock down, grab, hold, trip, jump, push, etc. ....
14 ☐ Other – Specify ⤵ ....

SKIP to 40, page 6

FORM NCVS-2 (7-24-95)

NCVS is an annual survey of citizens which is collected by the U.S. Bureau of Census in cooperation with the Bureau of Justice Statistics of the U.S. Department of Justice. Census bureau personnel conduct interviews with all household members over the age of 12. These households stay in the sample for 3 years and are interviewed every 6 months. The total sample size of this survey is approximately 66,000 households with 101,000 individuals.[8]

In 1992, the NCVS underwent an extensive redesign. Based upon input from the National Academy of Sciences, the Bureau of Justice Statistics sponsored a research consortium of several institutions involving experts in criminology, research design, and statistics. The redesigned system was completed in 1985 and introduced in 1986. In 1991, BJS formed a special committee to improve questions on rape, sexual assault, and domestic violence. This committee recommended additional changes which were implemented in January, 1992 through June 1993. Since June, 1993, the redesigned methodology has been used in all sample areas.[9]

The NCVS provides data regarding the victims of crime which includes age, sex, race, ethnicity, marital status, income, and educational level, as well as information about the offender. Questions covering the victim's experience with the justice system, details regarding any self-protective measures used by the victims and possible substance abuse by offenders are included in the survey. There are periodic supplemental questionnaires that address specific issues such as school crime.

However, the NCVS suffers from problems that mitigate its validity, such as respondents under reporting or over reporting crimes. The NCVS is based upon an extensive scientific sample of American households. Therefore every crime measure presented in the NCVS report is an estimate based upon results of the sample. Since it is only an estimate, it will have a sampling variation or margin of error associated with each sample. Additionally, it is only an estimate of criminal activity and does not mean that the crime actually occurred.

Each of the methods of collecting data on violence presents a different perspective and has its own validity problems. What is certain is that violence occurs on all social and economic levels in our nation. Its toll on victims is severe and long lasting. No matter which statistic or sample one uses, all agree further research is necessary. Other researchers have gathered data regarding specific forms of violence.

Comparison of the UCRs and NCVS

UCRs	NCVS
Crimes:	
Murder-Manslaughter	
Forcible Rape	Forcible Rape
Robbery (commercial; personal)	Personal Robbery
Aggravated Assault	Aggravated and
	Simple Assault
Burglary (commercial; household)	Household
	Burglary
Larceny (commercial; household; personal)	Larceny
	(household;personal)
Motor Vehicle Theft	Motor Vehicle
	Theft
Arson	

Method of Collection:	
Crimes reported to the police	Sample survey interviews

Types of Information:	
Crime clearances, persons arrested persons charged, law enforcement officers killed and assaulted, characteristics of homicide victims	Details about victim including age, race, sex, income, education and whether victim and offender related; time and location of crime; whether reported to police; use of weapon; injury; and economic consequences

Sponsor:	
FBI	U.S. Bureau of Justice Statistics

Comparison of the Uniform Crime Reports and the Incident-Based Reporting System

UCR—Index Crimes:

Serious Violent Crimes

Murder
Non-negligent manslaughter
Forcible rape
Robbery
Aggravated Assault

Serious Property Crimes

Burglary
Motor vehicle theft
Larceny-theft
Arson

IBRS Crimes:

Arson
Counterfeiting
Extortion
Prostitution
Larceny
Robbery
Destruction of property

Assault
Drug offenses
Fraud
Criminal homicide
Motor vehicle theft
Sex offenses

Bribery
Embezzlement
Gambling
Kidnapping
Pornography
Stolen property

National Assessment Program

The National Institute of Justice conducts the National Assessment Program (NAP)survey approximately every three years to determine the needs and problems of state and local criminal justice agencies. While not technically a measurement of crime, it identifies the day-to-day issues affecting professionals in the criminal justice system. It, therefore, provides a valuable insight into concerns that are raised by the professional whose job it is to fight crime.

The 1994 NAP survey contacted over 2,500 directors of criminal justice agencies including police chiefs and sheriffs, prosecutors, judges, probation and parole agency directors, commissioners of corrections, state court administrators, prison wardens as well as other criminal justice professionals. The samples covered all 50 states and the District of Columbia. Both urban (populations greater than 250,000) and rural (populations of 50,000 to 250,000) counties were included in the survey. Respondents were asked a variety of questions dealing with workload problems, staffing, and operations and procedures.

The results of the survey indicate a great concern about the impact that violence, drugs, firearms and troubled youth are having on society and an overburdened criminal justice system. Overall, the survey indicates that cases involving violence caused problems with agencies' workloads. Police chiefs and sheriffs indicated that domestic violence was primary among crimes of violence causing them increased workload problems. Prosecutors ranked child abuse and domestic violence as significantly increasing their workload.[10] In the opinion of police chiefs and sheriffs, programs which prevent young people from obtaining guns is one of their greatest needs. In essence, it appears that law enforcement blames firearms as a large part of the juvenile crime problem.

Interest in community policing continues to grow. While the controversy around the effectiveness of community policing still exists, most law enforcement officials express a desire to implement all or portions of a community policing program in their jurisdiction. This approach recognizes the importance of involving the community in addressing the crime problem.

The program points out that we continue as a nation to become more culturally diverse. Law enforcement officials acknowledge this trend in a variety of ways. Sheriffs and police chiefs state that they are aware of the need to respond to culturally diverse populations in the wake of changing national demographics.

These findings will assist policy makers in establishing research priorities for the near future. Professionals in the field have the same concerns that researchers and citizens display—the need for an end to violence in our society. These official reports provide insight into the problem, but they do not offer any concrete solutions.

OTHER REPORTS

The National Family Violence Surveys

Within the last 10 years there have been a number of high profile cases involving family violence. The Kennedy and Tyson rape trials, the Bobbett battering and resulting attack by her on her sleeping husband, the Menendez brothers' murder of their parents, and the O.J. Simpson case all point out the high profile that family violence has attained in our society. Two of the most comprehensive studies of family violence were carried out by Murray Straus and Richard J. Gelles in 1975 and 1985.[11] Both surveys involved interviews with a nationally representative sample of 2,143 respondentsin 1975 and 6,014 respondents in 1985. The results of these landmark surveys continue to provide information and data for study in the area of family violence. They are continually cited as authorities in numerous texts, articles and research projects.

In both surveys, violence was defined as an act carried out with the intention, or perceived intention, of causing physical pain or injury to another person. Acts of violence that had a high probability of causing injury were included even if injury did not occur as a result. Violence was measured by using the Conflict Tactics Scale (CTS). This tool was developed at the University of New Hampshire in 1971 and is still used today in many studies of family violence. The CTS measures three variables: (1) use of rational discussion and agreement, (2) use of verbal and nonverbal expressions of hostility and (3) use of physical force or violence. Respondents were asked how many times within the last year they used certain responses that fell within one of the three classifications when they had a disagreement or were angry with family members.

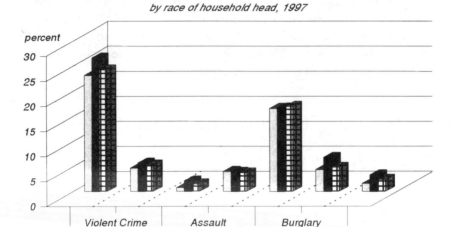

Households Experiencing Crime

by race of household head, 1997

Both studies were judged to be reliable because of the sampling procedure, the large number of respondents and the validity of the Conflict Tactics Scale as a measuring instrument. The studies surveyed families from all 50 states and assessed several different relationships: parent to child, child to parent, wife to husband, husband to wife and sibling interactions. Interviews were conducted by trained investigators and lasted approximately one hour in the 1975 study and 30 minutes in the 1985 survey.

A comparison of the results of these studies indicated that physical child abuse declined from 1975 to 1985. Straus points out that there are several explanations for such a result. First is the increased awareness of child abuse from 1975 to 1985. During that 10 year period, child abuse became a common media topic. This knowledge, on the part of the respondents, may have lessened the likelihood of their reporting such acts of violence. Second, different data collection techniques were used in the two surveys: the 1975 data was obtained via the telephone, and the 1985 results were collected by means of personal interviews. Finally, there may have actually been a decline in child abuse incidents from 1975 to 1985. Even if the last explanation is

Studies of Sexual Violence and Women

Study	Sample	Collection Method	Measured Phenomena & Prevalence Rate
Burt[20]	328	Interview	Completed rape —24% lifetime
Essock-Vitlae & McGuire[21]	300	Interview	Rape—8% since age 18
Kilpatrick and Assoc.[22]	2,004	Telephone	Forcible rape including attempts —8.8% lifetime
Riger & Gordon[23]	693	Telephone	Rape or sexual assault—2% of telephone sample
National Victim Center[24]	4,008	Telephone	Rape— 14% lifetime
Russell[25]	930	Interview	Completed rape —24%
Sorenson and Assoc.[26]	1,444	Interview	Sexual assault —13.5 %
Winfield and Assoc.[27]	1,157	Interview	Sexual assault —5.9% lifetime
Wyatt[28]	248	Interview	Completed rape —25% for blacks —20% for whites

correct, as Straus points out, this still translates into the fact that one out of every 33 children, three to seven years of age and living with their parents are victims of child abuse.

Other Sources of Data on Violence

Another social survey that has added to our knowledge of violence, *Rape in America: A Report to the Nation*, conducted by the National Victims Center, shed new light on this form of aggression. It caused an uproar across America when it was released in April of 1992.[12] The National Victim Center relied upon a comprehensive study entitled *The National Women's Study* to gather their information. This report was based upon a national sample of 4,008 women who were interviewed regarding their experience with rape. The report indicated that rape occurred at a much higher incidence than previously accepted.

Using the 1990 United States census figures, which indicate that there are approximately 96.8 million women in America, the center estimates that one in every eight women has been raped at sometime in her life. This translates into an incredible 12.1 million women in the United States who have been raped! In reviewing the figures and percentages of those women, the following statistics illustrate the number of times women have been raped:

√ 5% of the sample were unsure whether they had been raped.

√ 39% had experienced more than one rape in their lifetimes.

√ 56% of all the women surveyed indicated they had been raped one time.[13]

The information gathered from this survey indicates that 7% of all women were raped within the last year. Again using the United States census figures, this translates into approximately 683,000 women who are raped each year! These figures are higher than reported in either the *Uniform Crime Reports* or the *National Crime Victimization Survey*. The FBI's annual Uniform Crime Report has estimated that attempted or actual rapes reported to the police in 1990 was 102,560. The National Crime Victimization Survey reported attempted or actual rapes for 1990 at 130,000. While the *National Women's Survey* did not include attempted rapes, the figure is still in excess of five times that of the previously accepted figure or number of rapes occurring each year in the United States.

One of the major problems in the area of women and sexual violence is the lack of agreement among scholars, researchers and professionals regarding definitions and research methodology. Koss compiled many various studies on rape and her work illustrates different approaches that various researchers have used when attempting to determine the incidence of sexual violence against women in America.[14] Depending on which article, paper or text one reads, the estimates regarding the incident of rape will vary. This disparity has caused problems and confusion within the professional community ever since the study of women and violence began. There are a number of reasons for the disparate figures and definitions within this area. The following is a summary of some of the more common problems encountered when this phenomenon is studied:

- **Definitional Issues**: Some scholars use the term rape, while others use sexual assault, and still others define each of the forgoing terms differently. For example, one researcher may define rape as vaginal intercourse accomplished by use of force or fear while other researchers may define rape as vaginal, oral or rectal intercourse accomplished by force or fear. The simple addition of two terms changes the entire results of any study.

- **Professional Issues**: The professional community approaches rape from different perspectives. For example, attorneys view rape from a legal perspective, physicians treat it as a medical problem, and psychologists approach it from a mental health point of view.

- **Gathering Information**: Problems in the screening techniques, formation of questions, context of questioning, and issues of confidentiality all impact on the validity and type of response which the researcher will receive.[15]

The following chart indicates that a wide disparity exists in the studies that have examined violence against women.

As the above chart indicates, there is a wide discrepancy between the various studies as to the type and prevalence of sexual violence committed in the United States. The above figures indicate that rape in America is more common than previously thought, and rape is only one form of sexual violence perpetrated against women.

Clinical studies are another source of information regarding family violence. These studies are carried out by practitioners in the field;

medical professionals, psychiatrists, psychologists and counselors, all of whom use samples gathered from actual cases of family violence. These researchers collect information from hospitals, clinics and therapy sessions. Clinical studies normally have small sample sizes and therefore caution must be used when drawing any conclusions. However, these studies provide valuable data on the nature of abuse and assist in evaluating the different types of interventions utilized in family violence as well as pointing out areas for further research.

Women are not the only victims of violent crime. Researchers and professionals have attempted to study violent crime from a variety of perspectives including both the offenders' and the victims'. In 1989, Weiner conducted a review of the major research dealing with individual violent crime.[16] He reviewed over forty major studies conducted by scholars between 1978 and 1987. He concludes that the further an offender advances into the sequence of violent crime, the greater the risk that the offender will continue his violent behavior.[17]

There are also other violent acts that have only recently become criminalized. For example, stalking has become the crime of the nineties.[18] It is a newly emerging area of criminal law that is being studied by several experts in the field of human behavior. Zona and his associates are using the files of the Threat Management Unit of the Los Angles Police Department in an effort to study stalkers.[19] Meloy has published several articles and texts that examine the nature and extent of stalkers and violence.

Other Types of Crime Research

Violent crime receives most of the publicity in our society, however, it is only one of many crimes suffered by citizens. Property crimes, fraud, and white collar crimes take a tremendous toll on their victims. There is a number of reasons for this lack of attention regarding nonviolent crime: the victims' movement initially focused on serious violent crime, a lack of understanding regarding the psychological and financial consequences of property or economic crimes, and a traditional under reporting of the nature and extent of this type of crime.

Sutherland's classic definition of white collar crime is one way of viewing this offense. He defined **white collar crime** as an offense committed by a person of respectability and high social status in the course of his occupation.[29] The FBI on the other hand, defines white collar crime as those illegal acts characterized by deceit, concealment, violation of trust and not dependent upon the application or threat of physical force or violence. They are committed to obtain money, property, or services; or to avoid the payment or loss of money, property or services; or to secure personal or business advantage.[30] Both of these definitions deal with economic crimes, or crimes that have the gathering of assets from the victim as their objective.

Several prominent researchers have called for more information about economic crimes.[31] Understanding the nature and extent of economic crime is necessary if we are to attempt to respond to its consequences. One of the most common forms of economic crime is fraud. A nationwide survey of fraud revealed that a sizable portion of the adult population in the United States is affected.[32] **Fraud** was defined as a deliberate intent, targeted against individuals, to deceive for the purpose of illegal financial gain.[33] Included in this definition were various forms of telemarketing frauds, frauds involving consumer goods and services, deceptive financial advice, and insurance scams.

Fraud crosses all sociological barriers and victimization occurs in all ages, genders, races or incomes. The survey used a random sample of the adult population of the United States. The respondents were asked about 21 types of fraud plus a catch-all category and were asked if they had ever been victimized or if an attempt had been made to victimize them. More than half of those surveyed indicated that they experienced victimization, or an attempted victimization sometime in their past. Approximately one in every three respondents were potential victims of fraud within the year preceding the survey. The attempt to defraud these victims was successful fifty percent of the time.

Economic crime is a serious form of victimization that is often overlooked by those tasked with, or interested in, studying the effects of crime on individuals. The consequences of fraud will be addressed in more detail later in this text. At this stage, it is important to acknowledge that there are other forms of victimization other than violence-related crimes.

SUMMARY

- More than 49 million people experience victimization or attempted victimization each year.

- The Uniform Crime Reports (UCRs) report crime data based on the crimes reported to law enforcement agencies each year. The UCRs are concerned primarily with the eight index crimes. The FBI prepares an annual crime index based on the UCRs.

- The National Incident-Based Reporting System is designed to replace the UCRs.

- The National Crime Victimization Surveys are designed to correct the problems of non-reporting crime. It is based on interviewing a sample of citizens regarding victimization.

- The National Assessment Program Survey is conducted approximately every three years by the National Institute of Justice to determine the needs and problems of state and local criminal justice agencies.

- Other sources of data on violence include the report, *Rape in America: A Report to the Nation*, which provided new information on rape. The National Family Violence Surveys also provide information and data on family violence.

DISCUSSION QUESTIONS

1. Explain the problems with using the Uniform Crime Reports.

2. How would you improve the NCVS?

3. How does the NAP information benefit victim service professionals?

4. The National Family Violence Surveys were conducted over 10 years ago. Why is their data still important?

5. Compare and contrast the other types of crime research. Can you think of another method to collect information about crime and victims?

ENDNOTES—Chapter 2

1. Parts of this chapter are adapted from Harvey Wallace, *Victimology: Legal, Psychological, and Social Perspectives*, (Needham Heights, Maryland, Allyn & Bacon, 1998).

2. Data taken from "The Extent and Costs of Crime Victimization: A New Look," *Research Preview*, National Institute of Justice, Washington D.C. January 1996.

3. 28 USC 534 (1930)

4. "Crime in the United States, 1994," *Uniform Crime Reports*, (Washington D.C.: Superintendent of Documents, 1994).

5.

6. M.E. Milakovich and Kurt Weis, "Politics and the Measure of Success in the War on Crime," *21 Crime and Delinquency*, 1-10 (January 1975).

7. The UCR states that the NCVS started in 1973. See "Crime in the United States, 1994," *Uniform Crime Reports*, (Washington D.C.: Superintendent of Documents, 1994).

8. The UCR presents a different estimate of households than the NCVS. See "Crime in the United States, 1994" *Uniform Crime Reports*, (Washington D.C.: Superintendent of Documents, 1994).

9. "Criminal Victimization in the United States, 1993," *BJS Report*, NCJ-151657 (Washington D.C.: May 1996).

10. Tom McEwen, "National Assessment Program: 1994 Survey Results," *Research in Brief*, National Institute of Justice, (May 1995) p.2.

11. M.A. Strauss, R.J. Gelles & S.K. Steinmetz, *Behind Closed Doors: Violence in the American Family*, (New York: Anchor/Doubleday,1980).

12. Personal communication with Christine N. Edmunds, co-author and Project Director, National Victim Center, Washington D.C.

13. H. Wallace, *Family Violence: Legal, Medical, and Social Perspectives,* Allyn-Bacon, 1996.

14. M.P. Koss, "Detecting the Scope of Rape," 8/2 *Journal of Interpersonal Violence* 200-203 (June 1993).

15. *Id.*

16. Neil Alan Weiner, "Violent Criminal Careers and Violent Career Criminals," *Violent Crime, Violent Criminals*, (Newbury Park, CA: Sage) 1989.

17. *Id.* at 127.

18. H. Wallace, "Stalkers, the Constitutions and Victims' Remedies," *ABA Criminal Justice*, vol. 10/1, Spring 1995, p.16.

19. Michael A. Zona, et.al., "A Comparative Study of Erotomonic and Obsessional Subjects in a Forensic Sample," 38 *Journal of Forensic Science*, pp. 894 (July 1993).

20. M.R. Burt, "Attitudes Supportive of Rape in American Culture (Final Report, Grant #ROIMH29023). (National Institute of Mental Health, National Center for the Prevention and Control of Rape, Washington D.C. 1979).

21. S.M. Essock-Vitale and M.T. McGurie,"Women's Lives Viewed From an Evolutionary Perspective," I. Sexual Histories, Reproductive Success, and Demographic Characteristics of a Random Sample of American Women, 6 *Ethnology and Sociobiology*, pp. 137-154 (1985).

22. D.G. Kilpatrick, C.L. Best, L.J. Veronen, A.E. Amick, L.A. Villeponteaux and G.A. Ruff, "Mental Health Correlates of Criminal Victimization: A Random Community Survey," 53 *Journal of Consulting and Clinical Psychology*, pp. 866-873, (1985).

23. S. Riger & M.T. Gordon, "The Fear of Rape; A Study in Social Control," 37 *Journal of Social Issues*, pp. 71-92 (1981).

24. D.G. Kilpatrick, C.N. Edmunds & A.K. Seymour, *Rape in America: A Report to the Nation*, (Arlington, VA: National Victim Center, 1992).

25. D.E.H. Russell, *Sexual Exploitation*, (Beverly Hills: Sage, 1984).

26. S.B. Sorenson, J.A. Stein, J.M. Siegel, J.M. Golding & M.A. Burnam, "Prevalence of Adult Sexual Assault: The Los Angeles Epidemiologic Catchment Area Study," 126 *American Journal of Epidemiology*, pp. 1154-1164 (1987).

27. I. Winfield, L.K. George, M. Swartz & D.G. Blazer, "Sexual Assault and Psychiatric Disorders Among a Community Sample of Women," 147 *American Journal of Psychiatry*, pp. 335-341 (1990).

28. G.E. Wyatt, "The Sociocultural Context of African American and White American Women's Rape," 48 *Journal of Social Issues*, pp. 77-92 (1992).

29. E.H. Sutherland, *White Collar Crime, The Uncut Version,* (New Haven, CT:Yale University Press, 1983).

30. Report of the Attorney General, *National Practices for the Investigation and Prosecution of White Collar Crime,* U.S. Department of Justice, (Washington D.C.: Office of the Attorney General, 1990).

31. Geis, Gilbert, and Stotland, *White Collar Crime: Theory and Research,* (Newbury Park, CA: Sage, 1980).

32. Much of the material presented in this section dealing with fraud comes from Richard Titus, Fred Heinzelmann, & John M. Boyle, "The Anatomy of Fraud: Report of a Nationwide Survey," Research in Action, *National Institute of Justice Journal* (August 1995) p. 28.

33. *Id.*

PART II

Explanation of Criminal Behavior

Cesare Beccaria

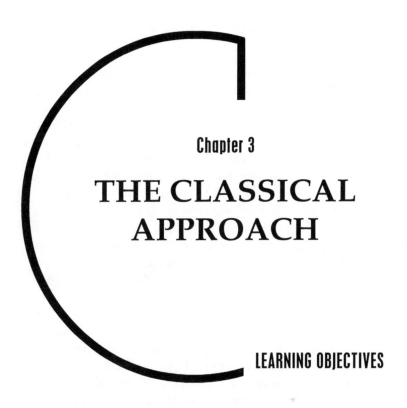

Chapter 3

THE CLASSICAL APPROACH

LEARNING OBJECTIVES

After reading this chapter, you should be able to:

- Analyze the basic concepts of the classical school of thought on crime causation.

- Explain the concept of free will.

- Describe the influence of the social contract theorists on the classical school.

- Differentiate between the classical and neoclassical concepts.

- Explain the importance of the classical school concepts on our present legal system.

INTRODUCTION

From the earliest times, crime has been recognized as a violation of social imperatives. Even the primitive societies recognized the necessity of utilizing social norms as means of social control. Law regulates not only what is, but also what should be. Crime has a long history, criminal law is younger, and criminology is even younger. Criminology was originally considered the study of laws and their effects on society. The first researchers in criminology were lawyers, physicians, philosophers, and physical scientists.

In this chapter, the classical and neoclassical schools of criminological thought are explored. We have adopted the term *school* to include not only a system of thought and collection of similar concepts, but also those spokespersons who advocated those thoughts and concepts. The term *classical* refers to the fact that the school was one of the first to develop an organized perspective of the criminal's nature. **Classical** is merely a descriptive term that has traditionally been associated with the fact that it was the first, similar to Latin's reference as a "classical language." The classical school was the dominant theory for almost a century until it was replaced by the positivist school. In the 1970s, there was a revival of the classical concepts, and the theory is alive and well today in the American administration of justice.

In the literature of criminology, the labels, classical and neoclassical, are used to designate some important concepts involved in the study of crime causation. Both of these schools are very similar in that both are based on the concepts of free will and rationalistic hedonism.

DECLINE OF NATURAL LAW

To even the casual observer, much of our criminal law, past as well as present, are clearly formalized statements of religious doctrines. Some interesting questions in this regard include: How much of criminal law was derived from religious beliefs? Should moral factors influence the lawmakers in formulating criminal laws? What is a "just" law? What should our relationship be between legal and moral obligations?

The term **natural law** is based on the belief that law has a supernatural origin. Under this concept, crime and sin are merged into a single phenomenon. For example, the Ten Commandments is not only a body of criminal law, but also an ethical code and a divine declaration. In ancient Greece and Egypt law, morals, and religion were integrated into a single idea. Generally crime and sin were indistinguishable in early European societies. Even today, however, religion plays a major role in lawmaking since the definition of wrongdoing is in part determined by our theological concepts. One of the problems with the concept of natural law is that even "eternal" and "true" justice changes, as do theological truths from which so many of the ethical truths are derived.[1]

During the development of the classical school, many utopians such as Dante, Hobbes, Hume and Bentham attacked the concept of natural law that resulted in the subordination of law to morality. According to those writers, law had no necessary relationship with morality, which is not rational and cannot be proved. Laws are only the commands of human beings.

FORERUNNERS OF
THE CLASSICAL SCHOOL

To the ancient Hebrews, laws were expressions of God's commands. Any violation of the law was a transgression against God. Deviant behavior, at that time, was believed to destroy the bonds of society. Any criminal behavior on the part of any member of God's chosen people could incur God's wrath on everyone.

Greek philosophers considered crime an offense against the society or the state. Persons who committed crimes were infected with corruption and evil. Later, the Greeks developed a naturalistic explanation of criminal behavior. Plato (428-348 B.C.) contended that man had a dual character. The individual was rational and sought perfection, but was limited by his or her own weaknesses and imperfections. He concluded that crime would also be present because of man's greedy nature. Plato saw punishment as man's right to cleanse himself of evil. Aristotle (384-322 B.C.) contended that our ability to reason separates us from animals and that crime is caused by our irrational acts. He, however, was not clear on what causes the irrational acts (crimes).

The early European churches equated crime with sin. Criminals were possessed by the devil. St. Augustine (354-430 A.D.) contended that crime and criminals resulted from influences of the devil. If the devil was driven out, then the criminals would no longer be bad (criminal). St. Thomas Aquinas (1225-1274) contended that the "soul" which is implanted in the unborn child by God was the source of our reasoning power. The conscience part of the soul drives us toward rational and just behavior. Our human appetites, however, are influenced by the devil. When our appetites overrule our conscience, evil or crime occurs.

It was during the fifteenth and sixteenth centuries that astral influences (moon and stars) as a cause of criminal behavior became popular. Hohenheim [1490-1541], a Swiss physician, was a proponent of the concept that criminal behavior was caused by influences of the stars and moon. According to him, people acted strangely and irrationally because of astral influences. The word "lunatic" comes from the Latin word "luna" meaning moon. Even today, we comment that it must be a "full moon" when a lot of crazy things happen.

By the late sixteenth century, the European churches' authority declined, and governments took greater control of the criminal justice system. At that time, however, the legal codes were confusing and inconsistent. Their procedures which were incomplete were left primarily to the whim of judges. It was under these conditions that the classical theory of criminology developed.

Preclassical

The classical school of criminology is regarded as the beginning of the study of crime causation as a separate field of study. The search for the causes of crime, however, started long before the classical school. Topinard, a French anthropologist, is credited with coining the term "criminology."[2] J. Baptiste della Porta (1535-1615) attempted to develop a relationship between physical characteristics and the type of crime the criminal committed.

While the background of the classical school involves the entire scope of preceding intellectual history.[3] Beccaria's essay was based on the theories of the social contract writers including Hobbes, Locke, Voltaire, and Rousseau. During the period when Beccaria was writing, the theology of the Church and the doctrine of the divine right of kings were challenged by the intellectualism and rationalism of the social contract thinkers.

The conflict was apparent in explaining why the government had a right to rule over the people. According to the theology of the Church Fathers, all people live in suffering and pain because the first human pair chose to disobey divine injunction. The **divine right of kings** contended that kings governed under a "divine right." The social contract theory discounted the concept of "divine right." Under social contract theory, it was theorized that individuals come together and contract to form a government rather than live in the wild. Each person gives up some freedom to gain protection from society. Rousseau had contended that the desire for companionship was the basis for the formation of society. Hobbes, however, considered fear as the essential reason that humans formed societies and accepted the necessary restraints for protection from wild beasts and other unrestrained humans.

A second major conflict between the fathers of the Church and the social contract writers involves the degree of control that an individual has over him or herself. According to the Church Fathers, God and the Devil could influence will. Generally, the social contract thinkers accept human will as a psychological reality, a faculty or trait of the individual that regulates and controls behavior. They also contended that the will was free and that there were no or few limitations to the choices that an individual could make. Voltaire, while recognizing that will may be strong or weak, and thus influence human behavior, accepted the basic doctrine of will as the motive or mainspring of human behavior.

To understand the development of the classical school, we need to also look at the **Age of Enlightenment**. The Enlightenment movement dominated Europe for most of the eighteenth century. The enlightenment movement promoted optimism, certainty, reason, toleration, humanitarianism, the belief that human problems could be solved and a belief in human progress. The enlightenment leaders were philosophers who, with logic and rationality, attempted to solve the world's problems. This movement followed the Age of Science, during which scientists and mathematicians such as Copernicus, Descartes, Newton, Galileo, Locke, Rousseau, and others discovered new ideas that revolutionized thinking. The movement influenced all aspects of European and early American life, including social thinking, the arts, literature, and politics. Enlightenment concepts are present in the U.S. Constitution and especially in the Bill of Rights.

THE CLASSICAL SCHOOL

Cesare Beccaria

The classical school is associated with the name of the Italian scholar Cesare Bonesana, Marchese de Beccaria (1738-94) and his essay *On Crimes and Punishment,* which was written in 1764. The classical school was an outgrowth of the Age of Enlightenment.

The fact that Beccaria had the ability to write the renowned essay on penal reform, which resulted in him being showered with acclaim and plaudits, was not demonstrated in his early life. He was born in Milan on March 15, 1738 and died on November 28, 1794. His father and mother were members of the aristocracy, and his ancestors had achieved distinction in many areas of endeavor. Beccaria attended the Jesuit College in Parma and then studied law at the University of Pavia. During his early years at Jesuit College, he rebelled against the authoritarian methods of instruction and the inflexible and dogmatic demeanor of his teachers. For a brief period of time, he found mathematics interesting, but he soon tired of it. He was considered by many to be lazy. It is said that rather than work he would prefer to explore the world's problems over a beer at a local pub. It is stated by several researchers that his mother was concerned about her son's ability to function in the business world. Accordingly, she sought a safe, prestigious, but not too demanding position for him. She used her influence to get him appointed as a professor at the university.

After his formal education was completed, he returned to Milan, where he developed an interest in philosophical works. His interest was apparently kindled by Montesquieu. Montesquieu contended that society results from four impulses or desires: peace, hunger, sex, and social desires.

Beccaria's interest in philosophical works led him to read the philosophical writings of others including the French Encyclopedists. This interest caused him to develop a close association with two stimulating and keen brothers, Pietro and Alessandro Verri. Pietro was a distinguished Italian economist and Alessandro was a creative writer. The three (the two brothers and Beccaria) and several others formed a group of young men dedicated to the study and discussion of literature and philosophical subjects. During one of these stimulating discussions, which were followed by serious study of the current social problems of the day, Beccaria was challenged by the Verri brothers to lead the discussion on the penal system of that day. The Verri brothers proved to be the spark needed to bring out Beccaria's creative powers. He was given the assignment on the penal system which culminated in the essay. At the time, Beccaria knew nothing about the penal system. According to his friend, Pietro Verri, Beccaria was easily discouraged. He needed prodding and even had to be given assignments upon which to work. Beccaria began to work on the essay in March 1763 and completed it in January 1764. At first, it was published anonymously. The essay was an immediate success, acclaimed by almost all who read it.[4]

In the essay, Beccaria objected to the existing practices in the penal system. He especially disliked the capricious and purely personal justice that judges were dispensing. He also objected to the severe and barbaric punishments of that day. The judges exercised their power to add to any punishments prescribed by law and thus to promote their personal views as to the special circumstances involved.

In his writings about the concept of the contractual society and the need for punishment, Beccaria stated that laws are the conditions under which independent and isolated men unite to form a society and that men weary of living in a continual state of war, and enjoying a liberty rendered useless by the uncertainty of preserving it, sacrificed some of their liberty so that they may enjoy the rest of it in peace and safety.[5] Tangible motives in the form of punishments are needed to protect society and to prevent it from plunging into its original chaos. Infractors of the law must be punished in order to protect society.

He contended that only laws can decree punishments for crimes and authority for making those laws resides only with the legislator who represents the entire society united by a social contract. A magistrate should not be allowed, under any pretext of zeal or concern for the public good, to augment the prescribed punishments.

Judges should not have the authority to interpret laws and the reason, again, is that they are not legislators. The laws should be sufficiently clear and precise so that what constitutes criminal behavior does not need to be interpreted by a judge.

The true measure of crimes is the harm that they do to society. It is an error to believe that the true measure of crimes is to be found in the intention of the person who commits them. Sometimes men with the best intentions do the greatest injury to society and at other times, intending to worst for it, they do the greatest good. To determine the severity of the criminal conduct, one should consider the extent of the harm that is done to society.

Because it is in the common interest that crimes not be committed, and also that they be less frequent in proportion to the harm they cause society, there must be a proper proportion between crimes and punishments. Obstacles that deter man from committing crime should be stronger in proportion as the crimes are contrary to the public good. Thus the greater the harm to society, the more harsh the punishment should be for that conduct.

If punishments are too severe, men are driven to commit additional crimes to avoid punishment for a single one. For punishment to attain its goal, the evil which it inflicts need only to exceed the advantage derived from the crime.

The more prompt and the more closely the punishment follows the crime, the more just and useful the punishment will be. There should be a close association in the human mind of the two ideas-- crime and punishment.

One of the greatest curbs on crime is not the cruelty of the punishments, but their certainty. Do you want to prevent crime? To prevent crime, the laws should be clear and simple with the entire force of the nation united in their defense. The laws should favor not the classes of men but men themselves. Men should fear the laws and fear nothing else. Fear of the law is salutary, but one's fear for another man is fertile for crime.

It is better to prevent crime that to punish them. The ultimate goal of every good legislation should have that as its ultimate end. Laws should be published so that the public may know what they are and support their intent and purpose. Torture and secret accusations should be abolished. Capital punishment should be abolished. Jails should be made more humane institutions. The law should not distinguish between wealthy and poor or between nobles and commoners. A person should be tried by a jury of his peers, when there is a class difference between the offender and the victim, one-half the jury should be from the class of the offender and the other half from the class of the victim.

Beccaria concluded that for punishment not to be an act of violence of one or many against a citizen, it must be public, prompt, necessary, the least possible under the circumstances, proportionate to the crimes, and dictated by the laws.

Becarria's ideas were quite radical for his time. In 1766, the book was condemned by the Catholic church. The essay was, however, extremely well received. It was first translated into French in 1766 and into English in 1767. A one translator noted, perhaps no book, on any subject, has ever more generally read and more universally applauded.

Beccaria on the Death Penalty

Was there ever a man who could have wished to leave to others the choice of killing him? It is conceivable that the least sacrifice of each person's liberty should include sacrifice of the greatest of all goods, life? . . .The punishment of death, therefore, is not a right, for I have demonstrated that it cannot be such; but it is the war of a nation against a citizen whose destruction it judges to be necessary or useful. If, then, I can show that death is neither useful nor necessary I shall have gained the cause of humanity.

There are only two possible motives for believing that the death of a citizen is necessary. The first: when it is evident that even if deprived of liberty he still has connections and power such as to endanger the security of the nation-when, that is, his existence can produce a dangerous revolution in the established form of government. . . I see no necessity for destroying a citizen, except if his death were the only real way of restraining others from committing crimes; this is the second motive for believing that the death penalty may be just and necessary.

The French Code of 1791 which was adopted after the French Revolution was based on Beccaria's principles. The code was arranged in a scale, that to each crime the law fixed a penalty, and that the legislatures should make the laws and the judges should only apply it to the cases that came before them. The code was an attempt to legislate on every crime and to fix by statute the penalty for each degree of crime. The only question left to the judges was the question of guilt. After a finding of guilty, the prescribed penalty was to be imposed regardless of extenuating circumstances. The punishments were absolutely fixed.

Jeremy Bentham

Jeremy Bentham (1748-1832) followed Beccaria as the spokes-person for the classical school. Bentham was a prolific writer and was often described as an "armchair philosopher." His writings covered a variety of topics including those of prison building and the purpose of law. He has been considered by many as the greatest legal philosopher and reformer the world has ever seen. Bentham's great grandfather was a prosperous pawnbroker in London. His father and grandfather were attorneys. Bentham studied law and was admitted to the "bar." Bentham, however, had great scorn for the legal profession. He once commented humorously that "only lawyers escape punishments for their ignorance of the law."[6]

Unlike Beccaria, who enjoyed being with people, Bentham was ill at ease in public and preferred books to social outings. His mother died when he was young, and he did not like his stepmother. Apparently, he had his first and only relationship with a woman at the age of 57. When she refused his proposal of marriage, he had nothing further to do with her. Jeremy Bentham died in 1832. Following the terms of his will, his body was dissected. His skeleton was dressed in his usual attire and is on display at the University College in London. For over 160 years, the fully dressed skeleton has attended the college faculty assemblies. Speakers at the assembly traditionally first voiced recognition to Mr. Bentham and then to the other members of the assembly and guests.

Bentham was intensely influenced by the times in which he worked. He undertook the task of expounding a comprehensive code of ethics, but later believing that such an undertaking alone was sterile and too non-utilitarian, he then put great emphasis on the practical problem of eliminating or, at least, decreasing crime.[7] He was aiming at a system of social control that would be a method of controlling human behavior according to a general ethical principle of utilitarianism. This **principle of utilitarianism** is that an act is not to be judged by an irrational system of absolutes but by a supposedly verifiable principle of the greatest happiness for the greatest number. Bentham said that an act possesses "**utility**" if it tends to produce benefit, advantage, pleasure, good or happiness or prevents pain, evil, or unhappiness. According to him, the "goodness" or "badness" of an act should be judged by its utility. To Bentham, all human action is reducible to one simple formula of motivation—the pursuit of pleasure and the avoidance of pain. He contended that motive necessarily refers to action. Pleasure, pain, or other events prompt the action. There is no such thing as any sort of motive that is bad.; it is only the consequence of the motive that can be bad because of its effect on others. Bentham contended that is was obvious that all persons might derive considerable pleasures from uncontrolled orgies of criminal behavior if there were no pains attached to this criminal behavior. Bentham recognized that any legal sanction must be acceptable to the majority of people before it would be effective. He advocated social engineering to establish effective punishments for criminal behavior. He dismissed any recourse to natural law. He caustically labelled "natural law" as "nonsense on stilts."

Bentham saw punishment as an evil, but a necessary evil to prevent greater evils from being inflicted on society and thus diminishing happiness. According to him, punishment should not be an act of anger, resentment or vengeance. Punishments should not produce any more pain that necessary to accomplish its purpose. He advocated two principles regarding punishment:

1. The general concept that the less certain the punishment, the more severe that it must be to have any possibility of deterrence.

2. Overtly equivalent punishments are not really equivalent because of the variations among the offenders. Regarding the second principle, a fine to a rich man is a mild punishment compared to a similar fine against a poor man.

Bentham contended that extensive capital punishment statutes produce contempt for the laws and make perjury appear meritorious by founding it on humanity.

Administrative and Legal Criminology

The classical school is often referred to as the administrative and legal school of criminology. Following the classical concepts, the laws should clearly establish what constitutes criminal behavior, and each crime should have a fixed penalty attached to it. The uncertainties of motive and intent, and the unequal consequences of an arbitrary rule are ignored for the sake of administrative uniformity. As a practical matter, however, motive and intent do matter. Accordingly, modifications were needed to make a code of laws that can be enforced in everyday situations. These modifications are the essence of the neoclassical school that will be discussed later in this chapter.

Human Nature

The classical school's concept of **human nature** was that human beings are rational and their behavior is governed by the doctrine of "free will." The classical school's concept of human nature marked a shift in the theoretical concepts from that of the divine right of kings to the intellectualism and rationalism of the social contract followers. According to the classical school, humans will freely choose either criminal paths or noncriminal paths, depending on which path they believe will benefit them the most. People, including criminals, will avoid behaviors that will bring them pain and will engage in behaviors that will bring them pleasure. Prior to making the decision as to which course of action to take, individuals will weigh the expected benefits against the expected pains.

Prior to deciding on criminal misconduct, criminals go through a thinking process whereby they take a variety of factors into account before they make a final decision on whether or not to commit a criminal act. Accordingly, criminals are totally responsible for their criminal behavior. According to the classical theorists, environmental forces do not push, pull, or propel individuals to act in a criminal fashion, the individual acts willfully and freely. Offenders are not helpless, passive or propelled by forces beyond their control. In summary, criminals should be held accountable for their behavior because they act willfully and freely.

Individuals, including criminals, are responsible for their behaviors. They are able to interpret, analyze, and dissect the situations in which they find themselves. Criminals are not victims of their environments since they act over and against their environments.

Crime Causation

Crime is the result of a rational decision by an individual to commit criminal behavior. The individual makes a logical and rational decision after weighing the pros and cons of the course of action. The inconsistencies in the justice system help promote crime causation in that there is a general awareness that punishments are not administered rationally and fairly. The lack of uniformity and consistency in sentencing is also related to the cause of crime.

Purpose of Punishment

As noted earlier, there is no room for individual offender's reformation or cure in the original classical thinking. The classical concept of punishment is that it should be prompt, certain, useful, and fit the crime. The punishment, to serve its purpose, must be proportional to the crime. If punishments are too severe, they would cause individuals to commit other offenses solely to avoid detection or punishment. The only purpose that punishment should have is to protect society. The concept that punishments should be used to deter others from committing crimes was nonexistent during that time.

NEOCLASSICAL SCHOOL

The neoclassical school also holds that people are guided by reason and have free will. The neoclassical school differs from the classical school in that it incorporates the practical modifications necessary for the administration of criminal law and justice. The neoclassical school, while supporting the concept of free will, believes that some people, such as juveniles and persons with unstable mental conditions, lack the ability to reason or have limited ability to reason. The application of criminal codes based on classical thinking without regard to any disabilities of the offender creates an inflexible system of justice. Accordingly, the neoclassical school advocates giving judges limited discretion in the handling of criminals.

The insanity defense is based on the neoclassical concept that man has **"free will"** to choose between good and bad behavior. If, however, for some reason a person lacks the ability to choose (i.e., no free will) that person should not be punished for his or her criminal behavior because he or she was unable to make a rational choice. The M'Naughten test for insanity, which developed from a famous English case in 1843, holds that a defendant is not culpable for his or her conduct if he or she was "laboring under such a defect of reason, from disease of the mind, as not to know the nature and quality of the act he

Classical and Neoclassical Perspectives

Perspective	Spokesperson(s) and Period	Concepts
Ancient Hebrews		Laws were expressions of God's commands.
Greek Philosophers	Plato Aristotle 400-300 B.C.	Crimes caused by man's greedy nature. Crime caused by irrational acts.
Early European Churches	St. Augustine St. Aquinas 400-1300 A.D.	Equated crime with sin. Crime results from influences of the devil.
Classical	Beccaria Bentham 1750-1850	Free will; individuals choose to commit crimes. Social contract; due process- natural rights.
Neoclassical	Many spokespersons 1970s- present	Free will, except for people incapable of making a choice.

or she was doing; of if he or she did know it, that he or she did not know that the conduct was wrong. Under the American Law Institute's insanity test, a defendant is not guilty if the defendant lacks "substantial capacity" either to know right from wrong or to conform to the law. Both tests are based on the inability of the defendant to make a rational choice. Accordingly, a person must have free will under those tests in order to be considered guilty of a crime.

Today's neoclassical supporters point to the irrationality in the administration of justice as one of the major causes of the high crime rates. They contend that if the criminal justice system imposed punishments quicker, with greater certainty, and appropriate to the crime, many would-be-criminals would not commit crimes. Many criminals know that when they commit certain types of crimes, there is little likelihood they will go to prison because of the overcrowding problem.

The classical theory was attractive to legal authorities because it was based on the social contract theory. The social contract theory holds that all people have a stake in the continued existence of an authority structure, since without it society would degenerate into a "war of all against all." Its inflexibility, made it generally unworkable. The neoclassical theory, while still based on the social contract theory, provides the needed flexibility. The neoclassical view is, with some modifications, the major model of human behavior held by agencies of social control in all advanced industrial societies. Its widespread acceptance in contemporary legal systems is probably the result of the fact that this view supports the fundamental assumptions on which legal systems are based.[8]

SUMMARY

- The classical school was the first organized system of thought and concepts on crime causation. It was the dominant theory until it was replaced by the positivist school.

- Natural law is based on the belief that law has a supernatural origin . With the development of the social contract theory, the belief in natural law declined.

- The forerunners of the classical school included the ancient Hebrews who believed that laws were an expression of God's commands and the Greek philosophers who considered crime an offense against society. The early European churches equated crime with sin.

- J. Baptiste della Porta, a French anthropologist coined the term "criminology." He attempted to develop a relationship between physical characteristics and the type of crime the criminal committed.

- The classical school is associated with Beccaria and his essay. The school developed during the Age of Enlightenment which dominated Europe for most of the eighteenth century.

- Beccaria advocated the concept of "free will" and the prompt and certain punishment of criminal behavior. He stated that it was better to prevent crime than to punish criminals.

- Bentham followed Beccaria as the spokesperson for the classical school. He developed the principle of utilitarianism that holds that an act is not to be judged by an irrational system of absolutes but by a principle of the greatest good for the greatest number.

- The classical school is also referred to as administrative and legal criminology, based on the concept that laws should clearly establish what constitutes criminal behavior and should affix definite punishments for their violation.

- The neoclassical school accepts the classical concept of "free will," but holds that not all persons have the ability to reason.

DISCUSSION QUESTIONS

1. Explain the basic concepts of the classical school.

2. Discuss the differences between the classical and neoclassical schools.

3. What parts of Beccaria's essay do you agree with?

4. Explain the importance of the classical and neoclassical schools to our present legal system.

ENDNOTES—Chapter 3

1. Stephen Schafer, *Theories in Criminology*, (New York: Random House, 1969).

2. J. Baptiste della Porta, *The Human Physiognomy,* 1586.

3. George B. Vold and Thomas J. Bernard, *Theoretical Criminology*, 3d ed. (New York: Oxford University Press, 1986).

4. Elio Monachesi, "Cesare Beccaria," *Pioneers in Criminology*, edited by Hermann Mannheim (Monclair, NJ, Patterson Smith, 1973).

5. Cesare Beccaria, *On Crimes and Punishment,* translated by Henry Paolucci (New York: Bobbs-Merrill Company, 1963).

6. Charles Milner Atkinson, *Jeremey Bentham:His Life and Work,*(London: Charles Smith 1905).

7. Gilbert Geis, "Jeremy Bentham", *Pioneers in Criminology*, (Montclair, N.J.: Patterson Smith ,1973).

8. George B. Vold and Thomas J. Bernard, *Theoretical Criminology*, 3rd ed. (New York: Oxford University, 1986).

Cesare Lombroso

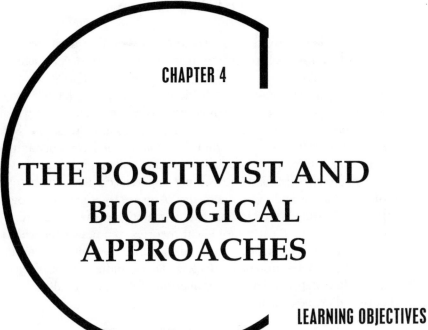

CHAPTER 4

THE POSITIVIST AND BIOLOGICAL APPROACHES

LEARNING OBJECTIVES

After reading this chapter, you should be able to:

- List the biological explanations of violence.
- Describe the importance of the Age of Realism.
- Explain the concept of *determinism* and the role it plays in the positivists' theories.
- Define *phrenology*.
- Identify the approaches used by the positivists in explaining crime.
- List the contributions of Cesare Lombroso.
- List the various classifications of criminals and their importance.
- Illustrate the problems with accepting biological reasons as the cause of crime.

INTRODUCTION

These days, biological explanations of violence are much in vogue. According to an article in *Discovery* magazine: "Part of the reason for this surge in popularity is that scientists studying the brain and its genetic underpinnings have learned a lot in recent years."[1] The tendencies toward violence, according to the article, may reside in our genes or be hard-wired into our brains. Some neuroscientists have mapped brain abnormalities in laboratory animals and human murderers that seem to correlate with aggressive behavior. Other neuroscientists have teased out apparent connections between violent behavior and brain chemistry. Apparently, today's biological theories of violence are far more sophisticated than their forbearers. In addition, unlike the early biological theories, the newer theories are concerned with behavior in individuals rather than groups, and they tend to allow for environmental factors. These studies will be discussed later in this chapter after an examination of the traditional biological theories of crime causation.

AGE OF REALISM

To understand the different viewpoints between the positivist school and the classical school, we need to examine the marked shift in thinking by the intellectual leaders that was of such magnitude that it could well be considered as an "intellectual revolution." The end of the Age of Enlightenment was followed by the **Age of Realism**. Realism was the prevailing intellectual temper during the third quarter of the nineteenth century. Realism discounted sentiment, idealism, mysticism, and the belief in the supernatural. During the century between Beccaria and Cesare Lombroso (1835-1909), the logic and basic methodology of objective science became well entrenched. The interpretations of scientific investigations provided a new intellectual approach that looked for the answers of all phenomena in the terms of objective science rather than religion or philosophy.

Charles Darwin's book *On the Origin of Species*, written in 1859, was considered by most researchers as the final break with the Age of Enlightenment.[2] In his famous book, Darwin presented evidence in an attempt to prove that humans were the same general kind of creatures as other animals, but were more highly evolved or developed; humans were merely one type of creature with no divinity links. According to his view, our ancestors were less highly evolved and were part of a continuous chain linking humans to the earliest and simplest forms of animal life. As creatures, they could be understood by biological and cultural antecedents rather than as individuals with "free will." Accordingly, free will was replaced by the concept of **determinism**. Determinism was based on the notion that behavior is governed by physical, mental, environmental, and social factors beyond the control of the offender.

THE POSITIVIST APPROACH

Auguste Comte

Auguste Comte was born in January 1798 in southern France near the city of Montpelier. His father was a devoted Catholic and a low-level governmental employee. His father despised the French Revolution and its attack on the Catholic church.

Comte was frail and in poor heath as a young boy. He was, however, a good student. Early, he became disillusioned with his father's attacks on the evils of a republican form of government and the supremacy of the church. After developing a strong belief in the republican form of government, he advocated a return to those principles. He spent two years at the prestigious Ecole Polytechnique University in Paris. He left after being upset with the handling of six students who objected to the antiquated methods of administrating examinations.

In 1827 while presenting a series of lectures on his philosophy, Comte had a mental collapse. During that time, he tried to commit suicide. During this period, his marriage also ended. He later blamed his problems on his preoccupation with the elaboration of his positivist philosophy. He resumed lecturing in 1829 and died in 1857.

Comte originally labelled his methods of research "social physics." He quickly abandoned this term when the Belgian social statistician, Adolphe Quetelet also referred to his work as "social physics."[3] Comte contended that there were three stages in the evolution of human thinking:

1. Theological stage—characterized by mythological thinking

2. Metaphysical or abstract stage—characterized by classical thinking

3. Scientific or positive stage—which he considered as the highest stage in human thinking

Comte repudiated the metaphysical and speculative concepts. He envisioned a society in which all social problems are solved by scientific methods and research. He contended that by studying large groups of people, we could learn the specific laws that govern human behavior. This concept became known as empiricism. Under empiricism, it was thought that all social sciences could be dealt with by empirical research and scientific methods, not by the abstract intuitive philosophy that was relied on by the classical thinkers.[4]

Cesare Lombroso

More has been written by and about Cesare Lombroso (1835-1909) than any other criminologist. Lombroso is generally referred to as "the father of modern criminology." His influence is still alive in European contemporary research. In America, he is often used as a straw man for an attack on biological analyses of crime causation.

Lombroso was born in Venice of Jewish family. He was educated in medicine and became a specialist in psychiatry. At the age of 15, he had two noteworthy historical papers published. At the age of 16, he published a review of Paolo Marzolo's *Introduction to Historical Monuments.* Marzolo, a leading philosopher and physician, was impressed by the review and requested an interview with Lombroso. Marzolo was shocked to learn that a 16-year-old schoolboy had written a comprehensive review of his works.

After graduating from medical school in 1859, Lombroso volunteered for medical service in the Army. While serving in the army, he began a systematic measurement and observation of over 3,000 Italian soldiers. His purpose was to ascertain and analyze the physical differences that he had noted among Italian soldiers from various regions of Italy. During this time, he concluded that the practice of tattooing was a characteristic of criminals.

His personal life was rather typical. At the age of 34, he married a young Jewish girl. They had two daughters. Both daughters married professional men who were involved in Lombroso's work. With his daughter Gina's husband, G. Ferrero, he spent many hours examining human skulls. Together, Ferrero and Lombroso published *The Female Offender.*

While a professor of legal medicine at the University of Turin, Lombroso's name became prominent with the publication of his book, *L'uomo Delinquente (The Criminal Man)* in 1876. In the book, Lombroso proposed that criminals were biological throwbacks to an earlier evolutionary stage when people were more primitive and less highly evolved than their noncriminal counterparts. He described those people as "atavistic." The word is apparently taken from the Latin word "atavus" which means ancestor. Darwin had previously written that "With mankind some of the worst dispositions which occasionally and without any assignable cause make their appearance in families, may perhaps be reversions to a savage state, from which we are not removed by many generations."[5]

As noted earlier, Lombroso is given credit for founding the positivist school of criminology. Some researchers (e.g., George Vold) contend that it is something of an anomaly that it was Lombroso's fate to be known principally for the earliest formulation of his theory of criminality of the atavistic criminal because the real basis for the positivist school is the search for the causes of criminal behavior. The search is based on the multiple factor causation approach, and some of the factors may be biological, others psychological, and still others social.[6] Lombroso's thinking changed over the years, and in later years, he looked more and more to environmental rather than biological factors.

Lombroso was the first clinical criminologist who "got his hands dirty" by spending numerous hours measuring criminally insane persons and epileptics' skulls. He was referred to as a "scientific Columbus." He attempted to categorize and classify types of offenders. Although his system of classification is considered crude by today's standards, he developed the first criminal topology. His general theory suggests that criminals are different from noncriminals because of the manifestation of multiple physical anomalies which are of atavistic or degenerative origin. Lombroso classified criminals as follows:

- Epileptic criminal
- Insane criminal
- Born criminal
- Occasional criminal

Lombroso designated the epileptic criminal, the insane criminal, and the born criminal as separate types, all stemming from an epileptoid base. Lombroso believed that the moral imbecile and the criminal were fundamentally alike in physical constitution and mental characteristics. In addition to the physical stigmata, Lombroso also noted that the born criminal had sensory and functional peculiarities, including a greater insensitivity to pain and touch, more acute sight, less than average acuteness of hearing, smell and taste. The born criminal also had a lack of moral sense, including an absence of repentance and remorse. The occasional criminal, which he added later, referred to a large number of individuals who do not seek the occasion for the crime but who are almost drawn into it or fall into the meshes of the criminal codes for very insignificant reasons. He subdivided the occasional criminal types into categories: pseudocriminals, criminaloids, habitual criminals, passionate criminals, and political criminals.

Lombroso, like Beccaria, advocated that the first objective of punishment should be the protection of society. The second objective should be toward the improvement of the criminal. He maintained, however, that we should not treat crime in the abstract and that we should make the punishment fit the offender. Like a physician applying remedies according to the illness, we should adapt the punishments to each individual. We must, according to him, make a difference according to whether we have under our eyes a born criminal, an occasional criminal, or a criminal by passion. He recommended the concept of indeterminate sentencing and restraining the criminal until he or she has been corrected.

Gabriel Tarde

While Lombroso concentrated on the biological and physical causes of criminal behavior, Gabriel Tarde (1843-1904) examined the sociopsychological factors. Even though he was not a positivist advocate, a discussion of Gabriel Tarde is included in this section. He did advocate the scientific investigation of crime causation and many of the other attributes of the positivist school of thinking. He attempted to arrive at a happy marriage between psychology and sociology. Tarde did not lead the usual scholar's life. For 15 years, he was a provincial magistrate in the small village of Sarlat, his birthplace and home. Later he directed the Bureau of Statistics in France's Department of Justice.

Unlike Lombroso, Tarde indicated that individual choice played a limited role in the crime causation process. Tarde's major contribution was his concept of the criminal as a professional type. He was of the opinion that most criminals went through an apprenticeship before becoming a criminal, and it was an accident of birth or chance that put them in an atmosphere of crime. He also attempted to classify criminals and was very critical of Lombroso's classifications.

Raffaele Garofalo

Raffaele Garofalo (1852-1934) is one of the three leading exponents of the positivist school of criminology. Often referred to as one of the "unholy three of criminology," because of his Darwinistic beliefs (the other two being Lombroso and Ferri). He was born a member of Italian nobility in Naples. He worked as a lawyer, prosecutor, and magistrate. Later in life, he was a professor of criminal law and procedure. Garofalo also enjoyed a long and productive scholarly career. He is known principally for his major work, *Criminology*, first published in 1885.

Criminology contained the influence of social Darwinism and the speculations of Herbert Spencer. Garofalo rejected the definition of crime as conduct for which the law has provided penalties and denominated as criminal. His concept of "natural crime" was substituted for the general definition of crime. To him, "natural" is defined as that which is not conventional, which exists in human society independently of the circumstances and exigencies of a law maker's concepts of crime. Natural crime, thus, consists of that conduct which offends the basic moral sentiments of pity and probity. Pity, in this case, refers to a revulsion against the voluntary infliction of suffering on others. Probity is the respect for property rights of others. To be a criminal act, he stated that the act must be harmful to society. The concept of natural crime, however, does not consist of a catalogue of acts which are universally conceived to be criminal. True crime is conduct which, upon evaluation by the average person's moral sense, is deemed as offensive to society.

According to Garofalo, the criminal has a "moral" deficiency that is of an "organic" basis and hereditarily transmissible. He believed in the biological transmission of criminality but not necessarily in the physical manifestation of criminality, as did Lombroso. Garofalo classified criminals as: murders, violent criminals, thieves, and lascivious criminals. He accepted Darwin's theory of survival of the fittest and if the criminal did not adapt or conform to society, he should be eliminated. He supported capital punishment for those who would not adapt. Garofalo viewed criminality as something organic and innate.

Enrico Ferri

Enrico Ferri (1856-1929) was one of the most colorful and influential figures in the history of criminology. He was born in the province of Mantua and his active life spanned more than fifty years. During a substantial portion of that time, he was the acknowledged leader of the positivist school of criminology. He was also a highly successful trial lawyer and a member of Parliament. He was even the editor of the socialist newspaper *Avnati*. His book, *Principles of Criminal Law,* which was published in 1928, was his most important contribution to the legal principles of the positivist school. According to him, the concept of free will had no place in criminal law, and the social defense was the prime purpose of criminal justice, criminals should be classified into five categorized, and penal substitutes should be used as a means of indirect social defense. He also saw three principle types of factors in crime causation. He is actually credited with coining the term "born criminal," which Lombroso used in his theory.

Ferri's three principle types of crime causation factors are anthropological, physical, and social. Anthropological factors are the offender's age, sex, civil status, occupation, residence, social class, degree of training and education. The physical factors include race, climate, fertility and the distribution of soil, the daily cycle, the seasons, the meteorological factors, and annual temperature. The social factors include an increase or decrease in population, customs and religion, the nature of the family, political, financial, and commercial life.

Ferri's five types of criminals are:

1. The born or instinctive criminal—who carries from birth an evident and precocious propensity to crime

2. The insane criminal—who is affected by a mental disease

3. The passional criminal—who commits the crime through a prolonged and chronic mental state of passion or emotion (explosive and unexpected mental state)

4. The occasional criminal—who constitutes the majority of lawbreakers and is the product of family and social conditions and, therefore, has less deviating psychological traits from those of the social class to which he belongs

5. The habitual criminal—who is a criminal by habit and is mostly a product of the social environment in which he belongs. Ferri clearly recognized that not every criminal fits neatly into his classification system.

Later, Ferri added a sixth type of criminal, the involuntary pseudo-criminal, who causes damage by his or her lack of foresight, imprudence, negligence, or disobedience of regulations rather than through malice.

In support of the positivist school, Ferri contended that the principal reason for the rise of a positivistic view of criminal justice was the necessity to put a stop to the exaggerated individualism in favor of the criminal in order to obtain a greater respect for the rights of honest people who constitute the greatest majority. The positivist school first studies the natural origin of crime and then its social and legal consequences in order to provide, by social and legal means, the various remedies which will have the greatest effect on the various causes of crime.[7]

Determinism

As noted earlier, the classical school emphasized the concept of free will and the position that punishment should be based on the crime that was committed. The positivists rejected the free will concept and substituted the doctrine of **determinism** and the position that punishment be tailored to fit the needs of the criminal. Determinism is based on the concept that the individual has no choice in his or her behavior, and because of biological or other factors, the concept of choice has been removed. The criminal is propelled by social, biological, emotional, and/or spiritual forces beyond his or her control. Accordingly, the criminal did not voluntarily commit the crime. "Hard determin-

Differences Between the Classical and Positivist Schools

Classical School	Positivist School
Legal definition of crime	Rejects legal definition of crime
Free Will	Determinism
Definite sentences	Indeterminate sentences
Punishment should fit the crime	Punishment should fit the criminal
Anecdotal reasoning— no empirical research	Inductive reasoning—empirical research

ism" is based on the concept that the individual has no freedom of choice. **Soft determinism** is based on the concept that the individual has limited choice in the matter.

Importance of Positivism

The positivist approach was a reaction to the inflexible and harshness of the classical school. The positivists emphasized not the crime as had the classical thinkers, but the criminal as an individual and the concept that the punishment should be tailored to fit the criminal. They contended the criminal had no choice in the crime because of determinism. Only by treating the criminal, not punishing him, could crime be eliminated. The positivists advocated scientific methodologies for studying the cause of crime. Accordingly, by careful study and scientific observation, the causes of crime could be determined and thus eliminated. One of their important contributions is evidenced by the juvenile justice system, where treatment and punishment is directed toward what is best for the juvenile.

BIOLOGICAL APPROACHES TO CRIME CAUSATION

Until recently, the biological theories enjoyed more popularity in Europe than in the United States. The common assumption of the biological theories is that crime is caused by a biological process. The process could be the product of our genetic makeup or by the things we eat. The biological approaches to crime causation that will be discussed in this section include heredity and crime, inferiority and body-type theories, difference and defectiveness theories, and nutrition.

Heredity and Crime

Do criminals inherit bad genes which cause their antisocial behavior? The concept of the "bad seed" was popularized by *The Bad Seed*, a 1950s play and later movie about a prepubescent pigtailed blond girl who was a multiple murderer. According to the tale, she appeared to be an angelic girl whose parents were homicidal, antisocial people. She was raised by a foster family and had no contact with her biological parents. While she appeared to have model behavior, her bad seed or aberrant gene eventually took control, and she committed deceptive, shocking, atrocious criminal acts. The public tended to forget that the tale was fictional.

Two studies of "bad seeds" were compiled in the early part of the twentieth century. One was about the famous Juke family and the other involved the Kallikak family. Henry Goddard, a leading U.S. advocate on heredity and crime conducted the research on the Kallikak family. Researchers concluded in both studies that there was evidence of hereditary transmission of criminology. Today, most researchers who have reviewed the two studies conclude that there is little evidence to support the findings of hereditary transmission of criminology. Henry Goddard also taught that the feebleminded were a form of undeveloped humanity, "a vigorous animal organism of low intelligence, but strong physique.

A 1992 publication by the National Research Council discussed the findings of a team of Dutch and American scientists who had discovered a Dutch family in which, for the past five generations, the men had been unusually prone to aggressive outbursts, rape and arson. According to the report, the men in that family had a genetic defect which made them deficient in an enzyme that regulates levels of neurotransmitter serotonin. The report, however, cautioned that the results concerned only one family and should not be generalized to the population at large.

Edward O. Wilson's book, *Sociobiology: The New Synthesis* received a great deal of attention when it was published in 1975. Sociobiology is the study of genetic explanations for such behaviors as altruism, homosexuality, male dominance, and conformity. Wilson's book examined crime causation based on sociobiology concepts. As the result of his book, the subdivision of criminology known as "biosocial criminology" developed.[8] Biosocial criminology deals with the study of crime from a biological perspective. Biosocial theories assume that criminal behaviors cannot be understood unless the interaction between the offender's biology and his or her environment is understood.

Biological explanations of crime causation are based on the assumption that structure determines behavior. People behave differently because their body structures are different. The structural differences may be the result of chromosomes, genes, chemistry, hormones, or even body type. The biological theories assume that the causes of criminal misconduct are often beyond his or her control because the person is "different."

According to many researchers, brain scans seem to give a dramatic view into the biological dynamics of violence. In the 1980s, brain scan studies indicated that the brains of many convicted criminals had areas of inactivity relative to the brain scans of control subjects. In 1997, one psychologist at the University of Texas, Medical Branch, conjured up red-and-blue reconstructions of the brains of violent offenders and used them to support his thesis that hair-trigger tempers are the result of an impairment of the frontal and parietal lobes of brains. Neuroscientists are attempting to isolate and study the roles of several neurotransmitters in suicidal patients, depressives, and people prone to impulsive violence.[9]

Inferiority Theories

According to the inferiority theories, the criminal is different from the noncriminal. The criminal is inferior because of constitutional, intellectual or mental reasons. The first inferiority theories focused on the criminal's physical characteristics (constitutional). At the time that the inferiority theories developed (16th century), unusual physical characteristics were considered as inherently evil. J. Baptiste della Porte (1535-1615) is considered as one of the first researchers to study the relationship between a person's physical characteristics and crime causation. He concluded that thieves had small ears, small noses, slender fingers, and bushy eyebrows.

Physiognomy became popular in the latter part of the eighteenth century. Physiognomy is the study of judging a person's character by studying facial features. According to the thoughts of that day, a person's facial features were related to their conduct. Later, physiognomy gave way to phrenology. As noted earlier, phrenology is the study of bumps on the skull.

Franz Joseph Gall (1758-1828) investigated the bumps and other irregularities of the skulls of criminals in the late 1700s. It was then that phrenology emerged as a discipline. **Phrenology** is based on the concept that the exterior of the skull corresponds to the interior and the brain's conformation. That the brain can be divided into functions and those functions are related to the shape of the skull. By examining the shape of a person's skull, one can measure behavior. While these concepts developed about 70 years before the contributions of Lombroso, most look to Lombroso as beginning the positivist school of criminology. The positivist or positive school was probably founded by Auguste Comte (1798-1857), but Lombroso made it popular.

Cesare Lombroso examined and measured many Italian prisoners' craniums before and after their deaths in order to determine character traits and development. He concluded that criminals were physically inferior to noncriminals and that criminals possessed certain physical stigmata that distinguished them from noncriminals. He also concluded that many criminals were born inferior and, for the most part, they were helpless to do anything about their differences. According to Lombroso, criminals have excessive dimensions of the jaw and cheek bones, eye defects, ears of unusual size, asymmetry of the face, and fleshy lips.

Phrenology was short-lived as a science. It disappeared as a scientific discipline because no one was able to substantiate its conceptions of physiological organs of the mind and their relationship to human conduct.

Charles Goring (1870-1919), based on a study of 3,000 convicts, refuted Lombroso's concept of criminal atavism but never rejected the idea that serious criminality was the result of a constitutional, physical, mental or moral proclivity. He believed that this proclivity was biological and inherited. He concluded that criminals were physically smaller in stature and weight than the general population. Goring, in his study, attempted to control for some environmental influences, but ignored others. His work is only considered as evidence of an association between crime and heredity.

Many of the later inferiority theories assume that the criminal is inferior to the noncriminal in intelligence. There is some evidence that intelligence is inherited, and there appears to be a number of studies that find "a clear and consistent link" between criminal behavior and low intelligence. One of the problems in this area is that of measuring intelligence. There are numerous studies that attack the credibility of the most frequently used IQ measurement instrument (Benet and Simon test). In addition, it appears that IQ scores are affected by socioeconomic and cultural factors.

Some of the arguments that are used to reject the link between criminal behavior and low intelligence include:

- Low mentality is not a significant cause of criminal behavior because there are smart criminals and dumb criminals.

- Intelligence appears to be more of a factor in the type of crime the individual will commit rather than whether he or she will become a criminal.

Body-type Theories

The body-type theories have been popular with the general public. We seem to believe that fat people are always jolly and redheads are hot tempered. The criminal, therefore, should be hard in appearance with a malformation in general facial structure or have a scar. Who were the criminals in the Dick Tracy comic strips? They were all deformed.

Ernst Kretschmer (1888-1964) studied the relationship between physique and mental illness. After researching 4,417 cases, he concluded that bodies could be divided into three distinct body types.

1. Asthenic type—The asthenic person has a thin and narrow build, with long arms and delicate bone structure and appearance. He concluded that this type of person tended to be idealistic, introverted, and withdrawn. This body type, he also associated with schizophrenia. He concluded that this type of person is generally associated with violent crimes.

2. Pyknic type—The pyknic type person has a round body and is fat and fleshy. This body type is associated with manic-depressiveness. He concluded that the pyknic type person tended to exhibit moodiness, extroversion, joviality, and realism. He concluded that pyknic types are generally associated with the crimes of larceny and fraud.

3. Dyplastic type—The dyplastic type person has a body type that is part pyknic and part asthenic. He did not indicate an identifiable mental illness for this type of person.[10]

Earnest A. Hooton, a Harvard physical anthropologist, studied 17,000 people, including 13,873 prisoners. He was attempting to corroborate Lombroso's biological theories. Hooton concluded that there were differences between criminals and noncriminals. Criminals were more likely to have long thin necks, thinner beards and body hair, more red-brown hair, and thinner lips than noncriminals. Criminals also had low foreheads, compressed faces, and narrow jaws. Criminals were physically inferior to noncriminals and differences were due to hereditary factors. His theories were often criticized because his famous book was published in 1939 and supported the Nazi belief of a "superior race."[11]

In 1949, William H. Sheldon studied delinquent male youths between the ages of 15 and 21. He concluded that delinquents had greater mesomorphy (tendency to be big-boned and muscular) than did nondelinquents. He developed his own method of body typing. He attempted to isolate three poles of physique, which he called somatotypes, and devised three classes of them:

1. Endomorph—a person who is fat, round, and fleshy with short tapering limbs and small bones.

2. Ectomorph—a person who is thin, small, and bony with a small face, sharp nose, fine hair, and relatively little body mass and relatively great surface area.

3. Mesomorph—a person who is big-boned and muscular and tends to have a large trunk, heavy chest and large wrists and hands.[12]

Later, William Sheldon, in his text on delinquent youths, listed both physique and temperament types. He then concluded that each person possesses the characteristics of the three types of physique and temperament. Sheldon used three numbers, each between one and seven, to indicate the extent to which the characteristics of the various types were present in a given individual. For example, an individual whose physique is 7-1-4 would have many characteristics of an endomorph, almost none of the ectomorph, and some of the mesomorph. He also concluded that most delinquent youths were significantly more mesomorphic than those least involved in delinquent behavior.

Sheldon and Eleanor Gluecks, a husband and wife research team, studied the association between physical body types and delinquency. They concluded that strength, physical ability and activity level of mesomorphy can, under certain circumstances, be a factor in whether a juvenile becomes antisocial and criminal.[13]

The body-type theories have been criticized for the following reasons:

- The theories have not actually demonstrated the relationship between physique and behavior.

- In most studies on body-types, cultural factors were not considered.

- Most body-type tests were conducted exclusively on males.

- Most body-type theories were conducted on confined individuals and probably do not represent a normal sample. The test may really indicate which body-types are more likely to be detected when involved in criminal behavior.

Difference and Defectiveness Theories

The difference and defectiveness theories are based on the concept that criminals are biochemically different from noncriminals. Linus Pauling, who twice won the Nobel Prize in chemistry, suggested that behavior disorders are mostly caused by "abnormal reaction rates" in the body which result from constitutional defects, faulty diets, and abnormal concentrations of essential body elements.[14] The concept of **biochemical imbalances** may be traced to Fredrick Wohler, a German chemist. In 1828, Wohler demonstrated that the organic compound "urea" could be synthesized. This lead to the concept that people were chemical beings. Earlier, researchers had been able to identify some physiological and psychosocial effects caused by secretions of the endocrine glands (hormones). Max Schlapp and Edward Smith, in 1928, presented the theory that crime was the result of emotional disturbances caused by biochemical imbalances. The imbalances were in the secretions of endocrine glands. According to them, if the secretions were the product of chemical imbalances, the physiological and psychosocial effects of these secretions on individuals could cause irrational behaviors. They also contended that over 30 percent of all prison inmates suffered from irregular glandular functioning.[15]

Research has also been conducted on the relationship between high levels of testosterone and criminal conduct. Since females tend not to be as aggressive as males, maybe males with high levels of testosterone, a hormone secreted by the testes that simulates the development of masculine characteristics, would be more aggressive than males with low levels.

Premenstrual Syndrome/ Premenstrual Tension

Premenstrual syndrome (PMS) and premenstrual tension (PMT) have been considered as factors in violent personal crime by women. However, the rate of violent personal crime by women is much lower than the rate of males. Researchers estimate that approximately 40 percent of woman between the ages of 20 and 40 years are affected by PMS/PMT. Generally the symptoms begin 10 to 14 days prior to the onset of the menstrual period. In some cases, it continues until the onset of menstruation. Some researchers contend that severely afflicted women are most vulnerable to extreme behavior during this period. One study of 249 female prison inmates indicated that 62 percent of the violent crimes committed by the females were during the PMT period and only two percent were committed in the postmenstrual week.

The popularity of the PMS theory exceeds the empirical evidence supporting the theory. The PMS/PMT defense has been successful in reducing murder to manslaughter in several English cases. One famous case involving this defense was that of Sandie Smith, an English barmaid. She had previously been convicted of carrying a knife and threatening a police officer. She was also on probation for having stabbed another barmaid to death. Her background included nearly thirty convictions for assault and battery and eighteen attempted suicides. Her attorney was successful in getting the British court to accept PMT as a mitigating factor.[16]

Chromosomal Abnormality

In a normal person, there are 23 pairs of chromosomes in each cell, including a pair of sex chromosomes, X and Y for men and XX for women. A relatively small number of males have the extra Y chromosome (XYY individuals). Over 200 research studies have failed to support the thesis that the XYY men are more aggressive and violent than XY men. In addition, the XYY condition is so rare in the population that it cannot be a major factor in criminality.

In the 1960s, a team of British researchers reported that a disproportionate number of male inmates in a Scottish hospital for the criminally insane had an extra Y chromosome accompanying the normal male complement of one X and one Y chromosome. Next, attorneys for Richard Speck, the notorious Chicago multiple murderer, announced that they planned to appeal his case based on the fact that he was XYY, and therefore not responsible for his actions. It was later determined that Speck was not an XYY. Several popular novels, including *The XYY Man* and *The Mosley Receipt*, came out in the late 1960s which featured XYY characters who struggled against their compulsion for violence.

Central Nervous System

The central nervous system (CNS), which includes the brain and the spinal column, is involved in conscious thought and voluntary motor activities. Some researchers have concluded that criminals have an excessive amount of slow-brain wave activity when compared to non-criminals. Accordingly, criminal behavior, in some cases is the result of brain damage. As with many other theories, there is a definite lack of clear evidence that criminal behavior is the direct result of brain damage.

Nutrition and Criminal Behavior

Nutrition as a causative factor in criminal behavior is generally traced to the biochemical imbalance, with the imbalance being caused by nutrition. Generally, nutrition is considered the primary cause of an individual's chemical imbalance. A number of studies have maintained that delinquents and criminals suffer from vitamin deficiencies, cerebral allergies and low blood sugar. Like the studies on hormone imbalances, much of this research is based on case histories, with reports of spectacular changes in behavior attributed to changes in a person's diet.[17]

Problems with Biological Explanations

The use of biological factors to predict an individual's tendency to commit violent crimes causes difficult problems for our society. Suppose it was determined that males with certain biological factors were twice as likely to commit a violent crime as males without this factor. Would this give us the right to take precautionary measures

Positivist and Biological Perspectives

Perspective	Spokesperson(s) and Period	Concepts
Positivist	Comte; Lombroso Garofalo- & Ferri 1880-1930	biological approach to crime causation determinism lack of free will punishment designed for the criminal
Heredity	Goddard & many others 1930-1940s & 1960-present	Criminals inherit bad genes which cause their antisocial behavior.
Inferiority	Gall, Lombroso, della Porte & Goring 1600-1860	Criminal is inferior because of constitutional, intellectual, or mental reasons.
Body-type [also known as constitutional]	Kretschmer, Sheldon, Dugdale, Hooton, Gluecks, & Goddard 1930-1940s	Direct association between body or constitutional type and criminal behavior.
Chromosomal Abnormality	Peter Jacobs 1960s	Aggression caused by extra Y chromosome.
Difference & Defectiveness	Wohler; Schlapp; and Edward Smith 1920-1930s	Crime caused by chemical imbalances.

against someone discovered with this factor? Should this fact be made public and violate the individual's right of privacy? What about the concept of "self-fulfilling prophecy?" Telling individuals, especially children, that they are prone to violence might just encourage them to commit violence.

SUMMARY

- Biological explanations of violence are popular today because of recent discoveries regarding the brain and its genetic underpinnings.

- The positivist school of criminology grew out of the Age of Realism and Darwinism.

- The concept of "free will" was replaced by the concept of "determinism." Determinism was based on the notion that behavior is governed by physical, mental, environmental, and social factors beyond the control of the individual.

- Cesare Lombroso is referred to by many as the "father of modern criminology." He is credited with the founding of the positivist school of criminology. He was also the first criminologist who "got his hands dirty" by spending many hours in labs studying criminals' bodies. He concluded that criminals are biologically different from noncriminals.

- Positivism was a reaction to the inflexibility and harshness of the classical school. The school is based on the scientific study of the causes of crime.

- Biological approaches to criminal behavior were more popular in Europe than in the United States. The biological approaches to crime causation include: heredity, inferiority, body-type, difference and defectiveness, and nutrition theories.

- The positivist's approach is based on the concepts of determinism, indeterminate sentences, punishment designed to fit the criminal, rejection of the legal definitions of crime, and inductive reasoning with empirical research.

- According to the inferiority theories, the criminal is biologically inferior to the noncriminal. Franz Joseph Gall studied the bumps and irregularities of the skulls of criminals and concluded that by examining the shape of a person's skull, one can measure behavior.

- The body-type theories are based on the belief that there is an association between criminal behavior and body type. The difference and defectiveness theories are based on the concept that criminals are biochemically different from noncriminals. PMS/PMT have been considered as factors in violent personal crime by women. Chromosomal abnormality has also been considered as a factor in crime causation.

DISCUSSION QUESTIONS

1. If the causes of criminal misconduct are in fact biologically related, then the concept of responsibility and choice becomes moot. Wouldn't it be cruel to punish a person for a crime he or she was not responsible for?

2. Explain the differences between the concepts of "free will" and "determinism."

3. What are some of the biological reasons given for crime causation? Do you agree with them?

4. Compare and contrast Ferri and Lombroso.

ENDNOTES—Chapter 4

1. *Discovery*, October 1997, p.59.

2. George B. Vold and Thomas J. Bernard, *Theoretical Criminology* 3rd ed. (New York: Oxford University, 1986).

3. Lewis Coser, "The Sociology of Poverty," *Social Problems*, vol. 13, Fall, 1971.

4. Julis Gould, "Auguste Comte," in T. Raison ed., *The Founding Fathers of Social Science,* (Harmondsworth, England: Penguin, 1969).

5. Charles Darwin, *Descent of Man,* (London: John Murry, 1871), p. 137.

6. Vold and Bernard, 1986, p. 37.

7. Thorsten Sellin, "Enrico Ferri," in *Pioneers in Criminology*, 2d ed. Edited by Hermann Mannheim (Montclair, NJ: Patterson Smith, 1972).

8. Frank H. Marsh and Janet Katz, eds. *Biology, Crime and Ethics* (Cincinnati: Anderson, 1985).

9. Bettyann H. Kevles and Daniel J. Kevles, "Scapegoat Biology," *Discovery*, (October, 1997) pp. 58-64.

10. Ernst Kretschmer, "Physique and Character" (translated by W.J.H. Sprott) (London: Trubner, 1925).

11. Earnest A.. Hooten, *The American Criminal: An Anthropological Study*, (Cambridge, Mass: Harvard Univ. Press, 1939).

12. W.H. Sheldon, *Varieties of Delinquent Youths*, (New York: Harper, 1949).

13. S.Glueck and E. Glueck, *Unraveling Juvenile Delinquency,* (New York: Commonwealth Fund, 1950).

14. A. Hoffer, "Some Theoretical Principles Basic to Orthomolecular Psychiatric Treatment," in L.J. Hippen, ed. *Ecologic-Biochemical Approaches to Treatment of Delinquents and Criminals,* (New York: Van Nostrand Reinhold, 1978).

15. Max G. Schlapp and Edward H. Smith, *The New Criminology,* (New York: Boni, 1928).

16. Ruth Masters and Cliff Roberson, *Inside Criminology* (Englewood Cliffs, NJ: 1990) p. 251-253.

17. George B. Vold and Thomas J. Bernard, *Theoretical Criminology,* 3rd ed. (New York: Oxford, 1986) pp. 98-90.

Emile Durkheim

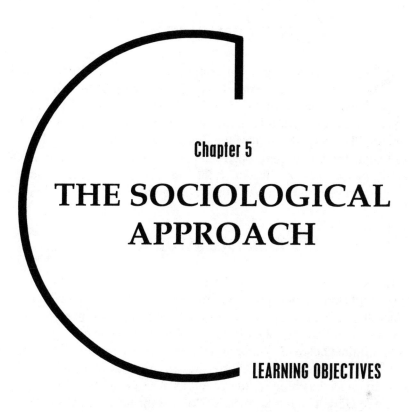

Chapter 5

THE SOCIOLOGICAL APPROACH

LEARNING OBJECTIVES

After reading this chapter, you should be able to:

- Compare and contrast the different types of control theories of crime causation.

- Explain the strain theories of crime causation.

- Outline the differential association theory and explain why it is so popular.

- Explain the subculture of violence theory.

- Explain the concept of neutralization of criminal behavior.

- List the contributions of Emile Durkheim and Robert Merton to the sociological theories of crime causation.

INTRODUCTION

S ociological theories of crime causation are popular in the United States. **Sociology** was developed by Auguste Comte in the first half of the nineteenth century.[1] The discipline resulted from turmoil caused by the French Revolution of 1789 and the rapid industrialization of the French society. It was part of the effort to construct a rational society out of the ruins of the traditional French society. The clear leader in the development of sociological theories of crime causation was Emile Durkheim.

EMILE DURKHEIM

Emile Durkheim (1858-1917), like Lombroso, rejected the classical concepts that humans were free and rational in a contractual society. Durkheim, writing approximately 20 years after Lombroso, focused on society and its organization and development for explanations of criminal behavior. Durkheim's theories are complex and overlapping with different social approaches to criminal behavior. Like Lombroso, much has been written about Durkheim and his concepts.

Emile Durkheim has been called "one of the best known and one of the least understood major social thinkers." He was born of Jewish parents in a small French town on the German border. He was schooled in Paris and taught philosophy at various secondary schools in France. Later, he spent a year in Germany studying under the famed experimental psychologist Wilhelm Wundt. After the publication of two articles, he obtained a professorship at the University of Bordeaux. At the university, he taught the first course in a French university on sociology. Later, he received the first doctor's degree awarded by the University of Paris in sociology and an appointment to the faculty at the University of Paris, and he taught there until his death in 1917.

Durkheim's first major publication was *De la Division du Travail Social (The Division of Labor in Society),* which was his doctoral dissertation and was published in 1893. In this publication, he describes the processes of social change involved in industrialization of societies. According to him, the processes are part of the development from a primitive society which he labeled as "**mechanical**" to the more advanced form called "**organic**." In the mechanical society, each social group is relatively isolated from all other social groups, and each group is basically self-sufficient. In the mechanical society, individuals live largely under identical circumstances, do identical work and have identical values. There is little division of labor since only a few persons in the clan or village have specialized functions. Accordingly, there is little need for individual talents, and because of the uniformity of its members, there is social solidarity among the clan or village members.

In the organic society, however, different segments of the society depend on each other in a highly-organized division of labor. Since individuals are no longer working and living under identical circumstances, social solidarity is no longer based on these circumstances. Durkheim indicated that all societies are in some stage between the mechanical and the organic structures, with no society being totally one or the other.

According to Durkheim, law plays different roles in maintaining the social solidarity of each of the two types of societies. In the mechanical society, law functions to enforce uniformity of the members of the group and is oriented toward repressing deviations from the norm. In the organic society, however, law functions to regulate the interactions of the various groups in society and provides restitution in cases of wrongful transactions. Crime is also different in the two forms of society. In the mechanical society, crime is "normal." And a mechanical society without crime would be pathologically over controlled. As society develops toward the organic form, it is possible for the pathological state of "anomie" to occur, and such a state would produce a variety of social maladies. In his later works, *The Rules of the Sociological Method* and his most famous publication *Suicide,* Durkheim develops the concept that crime is normal in both types of societies.

Anomie (a Greek term defined as "lawlessness") is a state or a condition that exists within people when a society evolves from a mechanical to an organic entity. Anomie occurs as a result of wide-sweeping scientific, technological, and social changes. Anomie is a condition of normlessness, not a lack of norms, but the condition whereby norms have lost their meaning and become inoperative for large numbers of people. Anomie may also be described as the fragmentation or disassociation of one's center; the feeling of being a number, not a person; social isolation; or social loneliness. Durkheim believed that anomie was the product of societal transition. When society is in transition and anomie is high, institutions and laws become meaningless to people, and crime results.

Durkheim used his concept of anomie to explain the phenomenon of suicide. According to him, the degree of integration of a society was inversely related to its rate of suicide. He noted that there were low suicide rates in predominantly Catholic countries where religion provided a unifying theme. He also noted that there is increased social solidarity during wartime and in prolonged economic depressions. Whenever there is unification and high social solidarity within a society, anomie is low and suicide rates (and crime rates) are lower.

Durkheim took a broad approach to crime. He looked to the very nature of society to explain crime. He concluded that crime was imminent in society and that it was a normal and necessary phenomenon in any society. According to Durkheim, all the uniformity that exists in a society is the "totality of social likenesses" or the "collective conscience." The collective conscience may be found in every culture. In addition, every society has a degree of diversity in that there are many individual differences among its members. He contended that there can not be a society in which the individuals do not differ more or less from the collective type. Pressure is exerted in varying degrees for uniformity within the society. Its strongest, however, will consist of criminal sanctions. The pressures result in certain conduct being designated as criminal behaviors or beliefs as morally reprehensible. The demands or dictates of social solidarity, such as the rules regarding social conduct, are constructed in a manner that certain individuals cannot fulfill them. The number who cannot fulfill the demands must be large enough to constitute an identifiable group, but not so large as to include a substantial portion of the society. This allows those in society who fulfill the demands of the collective conscience to feel a sense of moral superiority by identifying themselves as good and righteous, and those who fail as criminals. Thus, criminals play an important role in the maintenance of the social solidarity. They are identified as inferior and allow the rest of society to feel superior.

Durkheim contended that even punishment plays a role in the maintenance of social solidary. When the rules of the collective conscience are violated, society responds with repressive sanctions, not for retribution or deterrence, but because those of us who conform will be demoralized. When a criminal is punished, those of us who are not punished receive the award of "not being punished" because of our "good" behavior.

It would be a pathological state of society if there were no crime. A society that had no crime would be one in which the constraints of the collective conscience are so rigid that no one could oppose them. In this type of situation, crime would be eliminated, but so would the possibility of any progressive social change because no one would dare deviate from the norm. On a personal level, individual growth could not occur in a child if it was impossible for the child to misbehave. And a child who never did anything wrong would be pathologically over controlled. Elimination of misbehavior would also eliminate the possibility of independent growth.[2]

ECOLOGICAL THEORIES

The University of Chicago established the first department of sociology in 1892 and was the leader in American sociological thought from then until the mid-twentieth century. The diverse group of scholars who were collected at the University of Chicago became known as the Chicago School. The one recurring theme of the Chicago School is that human behavior is developed and changed by the social and physical environment of the person rather than simply by genetic structure.

The school made two major methodological contributions to criminology. The first was by the use of official data (crime figures, census reports, housing and welfare reports). The second contribution was the use of the case study or life history approach to analyze the criminal behavior of an individual (ethnography). Borrowing the idea of studying plants and animals in their natural habitat, researchers attempted to present the human ecology to explain criminal behavior in certain individuals. For this reason, the Chicago school became known as the "ecological school."

Social Disorganization Theory

Using the organic approach to the study of a community, Robert Park and Ernest Burgess concluded that a relationship existed between increasing crime rates and the increasing complexity of our society and that social disorganization was a causative factor in criminal behavior. **Social disorganization** is defined as a breakdown in the bonds of relationship, coordination, teamwork, and morale among different groups in society so as to impair the functions of society. According to social disorganization theorists, society is a complex whole whose parts are interdependent, and society needs to maintain basic equilibrium. **Social organization** exists when there is a high degree of harmony and internal cohesion in the society. The harmony unites a society and creates common goals and values that are reflected in a high degree of behavioral predictability. Internal cohesion consists of general acceptance by people in society of goals worth striving for (values) and rules on how to behave (norms). When the consensus of values and norms is disrupted, traditional rules do not apply, and social disorganization occurs. When social disorganization occurs, social controls will be lax or nonexistent and deviant behavior will occur.

Park and Burgess divided the cities into a series of distinctive concentric circles radiating from the central business district. They found that the farther one moves from the center of these concentric zones, the fewer social problems one encounters. They concluded that the growth of cities, and the location of various areas and social problems is not random, but is instead part of a pattern. The concept of the concentric zone pattern of city growth provided the foundation for other later Chicago School explanations of crime and delinquency.

The critics of the social disorganization theory contend that the concept of social disorganization is, in itself, disorganized, vague, ambiguous and subjective. The critics also contend that the concept of disorganization is equated with its consequences of social problems and not all social disorganization results from social problems. Others contend that the social disorganization theory is bias in favor of homogeneity and against heterogeneity.

Park and Burgess, and later, Clifford Shaw and Henry McKay, studied the crime rate in Chicago by using concentric zones. Based on the ecological concepts of dominance, invasion, and succession from plant and animal ecology, they maintained that there are dominant uses of land within the zones.

The first zone was the **central business district**, which had businesses and factories but few residences. The zone next to it is the **zone of transition** because, as businesses and factories encroached into this area, the residences were squeezed out. What was once a residential area when the city was smaller is being transformed into a business and factory area. This zone is not a desirable location for residences, but owing to its state of deterioration was the cheapest place to live. Immigrants usually settled there because of the low cost of housing, and it was close to the factories. Other zones radiating out from the central business district were increasingly more expensive to live.

Social ills, according to the researchers, followed a pattern in which the most problems were found in the first zone and progressively fewer problems were found in each succeeding zone. They noted that the neighborhoods in the zone of transition were more socially disorganized than the outer areas, and many of the neighborhood support organizations were either weak or nonexistent. Later, researchers Byron Groves and Robert Simpson noted four elements that constitute social disorganization:

1.   Low economic status

2.   A mixture of different ethnic groups

3.   Highly mobile residents moving in and out of the area

4.   Disrupted families and broken homes[3]

Symbolic Interactionism

One lasting perspective from the Chicago School was the social-psychological theory of **symbolic interactionism.** From symbolic interactionism two theories of crime causation developed—**differential association** and **labeling**. The labeling theory is discussed in Chapter 7 and the differential association theory later in this chapter. George Herbert Mead originated the concept, but the phrase "symbolic interaction" was coined by Herbert Blummer in 1937. It developed from a belief that human behavior is the product of purely social symbols communicated between individuals. Accordingly, the mind and the self are not innate but are products of the social environment.

Symbolic interaction is based on the concept that people act toward "things" on the basis of meanings that those "things" have for them. The meaning that a thing has is derived from, or arises out of, the social interaction that one has with others. The meaning that a thing has is handled in, and modified through, an interpretative process used by a person in dealing with the things that he or she encounters. Herbert Blummer summarizes symbolic interactionism as follows:

> The meaning of a thing for a person grows out of the ways in which other persons act toward the person with regard to the thing.... Symbolic interactionism sees meanings

as social products, as creations that are formed in and through the defining activities of people as they interact.[4]

The general principles of symbolic interactionism crime causation theories are: (1) the symbols we learn and use become our social reality; (2) we become socialized by the people with whom we associate; and (3) individual's definitions of their situations are the sources of their behaviors(i.e., the causes of our behavior are in our interpretation of reality).[5]

STRAIN THEORIES

The strain theories are based on the following assumptions:

1. If an individual fails to conform to social norms and laws, it is because there is excessive pressure or strain that propels the individual to commit criminal behavior.

2. Lawbreaking and deviance is not normal.

3. Misconduct or deviance is caused by immense pressures on the individual.

4. People are basically moral and innately desire to conform to society's laws. The critical question for strain theorists is, What is the nature of the strains (pressures) that cause an individual to commit criminal behavior?

Robert Merton

Robert Merton revised Durkheim's conception of anomie and applied it directly to American society. Merton's paper on the subject, "Social Structure and Anomie," is probably the most frequently quoted paper in modern sociology and criminology. Merton examined the question of how malintegration in society related to deviance. Using the value of economic success as an example, and relating this example to institutional ways of achieving economic success, he applied his concepts to the United States using the premise that anomie is the greatest in societies where certain ends or goals are elevated but there are no means or limited means (access) to attain those goals.

Merton pointed out that the culture of any society defines certain goals it deems worth striving for and that there are many such goals in every society. He saw the desire to acquire wealth as one of the most prominent cultural goals in American society. Accumulated wealth is generally equated with personal value which is associated with a high degree of prestige and social status. Accordingly, our culture encourages all individuals to seek the greatest amount of wealth. Cultures also have approved norms or institutionalized means that individuals are expected to follow in pursuing the culture's goals. The American culture is also based on the egalitarian ideology in which it is maintained that all people have an equal chance to achieve wealth. The ideology is often illustrated by Horatio Alger stories in which the poor kid makes it big.[6] Merton contended, in American culture, that the approved goal to acquire wealth and the institutionalized means of obtaining that goal by the Protestant work ethic can be identified as "middle-class" values and that the use of force or fraud to obtain this wealth is not acceptable. According to him, only the most talented and the most hard-working individuals in the lower socioeconomic class will be able to obtain the goal in the accepted means. Attaining the goals are much easier for those from the upper social economic class. For the majority of individuals in the lower socioeconomic class attaining the goal through accepted means is not realistic. This places severe cultural strains (pressures) on them.

Merton referred to the person's acceptance of society's goals and the blocked access to achieving those goals as the **goals-means dysfunction**. This dysfunction is the essence of his theory. When there is a dysfunction between the culture's goals and the means to achieve those goals, Merton contended that specific and predictable adaptations would develop. Merton theorized that there were five adaptations or ways that a person could deal with anomie. The five adaptations are listed below.

- **Conformity:** The individual accepts both the culture's goals and the institutionalized means for attaining those goals. Conformity generally does not lead to deviance and is considered as the typical middle-class response. For example, with the cultural goal of getting a good job, one attends school and obtains an education (an acceptable institutionalized means for attaining the goal).

- **Innovation:** The individual accepts the culture's goals, but rejects the institutionalized means to achieve them. Innovation is like taking a shortcut. Merton believes that this adaptation was greater among the lower-socioeconomic status groups and that most crime that exists in society will be in the form of innovation by individuals who accept the goal of acquiring wealth but find they can not succeed through the institutionalized means. Therefore they look for new methods to acquire wealth.

- **Ritualism:** Ritualists reject the culture's goals and accept the institutionalized means to achieve goals, however, they believe the goals to be of little importance. The maintenance of a strict set of customs and manners which serve no purpose characterizes ritualism. College fraternities, clubs, and some religious practices are examples of ritualism. Merton believed that this was a lower-middle socioeconomic status group response.

- **Retreatism:** This individual rejects both the culture's goals and the institutionalized means to achieve them. Retreatism is an escape response. Addicts, alcoholics, psychotics and vagrants could be viewed as retreating. These individuals are dropouts from society.

- **Rebellion:** This individual rejects the culture's goals and institutionalized means of obtaining those goals and replaces them with his or her own goals and means. He or she is angry and revolutionary. This individual differs from retreatism in that goals are not secretly desired by the rebel. Rebels, however, generally do care and have strong feelings about their own goals.

Merton notes that the modes of adaptation are designed to account for some, but not all forms of criminal behavior.[7]

Durkheim contended that the driving forces of criminal behavior can be traced to appetites and impulses toward cultural goals that are inherent in human nature. Since human nature does not change, differences in the amount of crime cannot be explained by differences in the forces driving people to commit criminal behavior. Accordingly, the differences in the amount of criminal behavior can only be explained by differences in the restraining forces. He argued that societies restrain human nature either through culture (consensus of values) or through structure (the interrelationships among the different functions

Merton's Modes of Adaptation

Modes	Cultural Goals	Institutionalized Means
Conformity	+	+
Innovation	+	-
Ritualism	-	+
Rebellion	+/-	+/-

+ = signifies acceptance   - = signifies rejection

+/- = signifies rejection of prevailing values and substitution of new values

in societies), and that these restraints break down during periods of rapid social change, resulting in higher levels of crime. Merton, in contrast to Durkheim, contended that the drive to commit crime was cultural in nature and not human nature, and that the forces restraining individuals from committing crime were also cultural. Merton maintained that the high level of crime in American society was caused by a cultural imbalance—the imbalance between the cultural forces that drive the individual toward criminal behavior and the cultural forces restraining the individual from criminal behavior. He believed that the distribution of criminal behavior is inversely related to the distribution of legitimate opportunities.

Albert Cohen

Albert Cohen saw American society as primarily consisting of middle and working classes, and that our society places a high premium on ambition, getting ahead and achievement. Both the middle and lower classes tend to teach certain values to their young. The values that each class taught their children are not necessarily the same, although both classes believe in ambition, getting ahead, and achievement. Since lower-class boys are taught a different value system, they are not "properly" socialized to meet the requirements of middle-class society. The lower-class boys, however, are measured or evaluated by the standards and aspirations of the middle class in which they are not properly trained and lack the resources to fulfill. This is called the **middle-class measuring rod**. The following chart compares the differences between the two systems of values according to Cohen. Cohen contended that our school system emphasized the middle-class value system and that the lower-class boys were at a definite disadvantage in the school environment. Cohen stated that "all children were subjected to the middle-class measuring rod," and that the lower-class boys learn early in school that they are at a disadvantage. This produces strains (pressures) on them. Another way of describing what happens to the working-class children is that they become anomique and frequently react with violence. This **reaction formation** is a result of stimuli which cause the child to "overreact" to any perceived threat or slight.

Cohen contended that gang activity by lower-class youths was merely a flouting of middle-class values. To use Merton's modes of adaptation, the youths would be considered in rebellion. According to Cohen, the characteristics of a delinquent gang are: (1) a strong sense of gang solidarity with hostility to the outside world; (2) an in-group solidarity free of adult inference; (3) acts committed not for financial gain, instead "purposeless"; (4) short-run hedonism; (5) the possession of malice and negativism toward the middle class. While Cohen only studied males, he believed that the patterns he studied were more likely to develop among boys than among girls. He also contended that delinquent subcultures emerged among boys whose status, power, and income were relatively low but whose aspirations were high.

Cohen has been criticized over his claim that many working-class boys accept and are taught middle-class values and do not accept working class values and goals as he theorized. Other criticisms include the fact that empirical studies have failed to establish that delinquent gangs

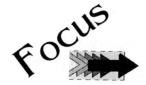

Values Comparison

Middle Class Values	Lower Class Values
• Self control	• Nonchalantness
• Postponement of immediate gratifications and self-indulgence in favor of long-term goals	• Easy going
• Planning for the future	• Lack of order
• Orderliness	• Lack of punctuality
• Individual responsibility	
• Ambition	• Ethic of reciprocity
• Cultivation of skills and manners	
• Respect for property	• Toughness
• Control of aggression and anger	

reject middle-class values and goals, and that he makes no attempt to explain middle-class delinquency which appears to be quite extensive. In addition, much of what delinquent gangs do, according to Cohen's critics, have been labeled "for kicks" and is not done against middle-class or mainstream American society as Cohen contends.[8]

Opportunity Structure

Richard Cloward and Lloyd Ohlin, also strain theorists, attempted to explain subcultural delinquency by using an "opportunity theory."[9] They explored the linkage between the socially structured patterns of youth opportunity in the communities and the dominant patterns of subcultural formation among youth which would occur in response to that system. They concluded that communities have sets of legitimate and illegitimate opportunities which conditioned the shape of the deviant subcultures that developed.

Cloward and Ohlin contended that lower-class boys also share the American dream for success and that success is a value to them that they measure materially. Since lower-class boys, however, do not have access to legitimate means to attain their success goals as do the middle-class youth, lower-class boys perceive their chances of success as limited. There is a severe gap between their aspiration levels and expectations which creates pressures or strains. The pressures or strains result in deviancy and crime. Many of the youth then attempt to use illegitimate means to achieve their goals. Cloward and Ohlin indicated that there were three basic types of subcultures:

- **Criminal subculture:** These subcultures primarily conduct illegal activities such as drug sales. Out of the illegal activities, new opportunity structure emerges that provides an alternative way for its members to achieve success.

- **Conflict subculture:** These subcultures are characterized by violent and aggressive gangs in unstable transient neighborhoods attempting to gain status. The members of the subculture are under great pressure and perceive that legitimate opportunities are blocked for them.

- **Retreatism subculture:** This subculture is made up of individuals who have failed to find a place for themselves in the criminal and conflict subcultures and have, thus, withdrawn.

As noted earlier, the strain theorists assume that people commit crimes as the result of extreme pressures or strains placed on them by society. Some of the theorists believe that humans are innately moral and want to be law abiding. Others assume that humans are subject to external social forces that may alter their risk of engaging in crime. It is the structural forces in society that produce the pressures and enhance the likelihood of criminal misconduct. According to strain theorists, we should attempt to isolate the types of strain that cause individuals to commit crime and reduce or eliminate them.

CONTROL THEORIES

The control theorists contend that delinquency or criminal conduct occurs when an individual's bonds to society are weak or severed. During the socialization process, we learn how to fit in harmoniously into society. This process is also key to whether we become criminal. It controls us. If the socialization process is effective, the control mechanisms will prevent us from committing criminal behavior. If the process is defective, our control mechanisms will not connect us to society, and we may become criminal.

The control theory is concerned with order and conformity to rules. The control theorists contend that human beings are amoral by nature and have the proclivity to commit crimes. Society, however, requires social order and demands people to conform. Most people conform because they are restrained by their relationships to conventional institutions and individuals such as family, school, friends and peer groups. While the stain theorists are concerned with why individuals commit criminal behavior, the control theorists ask the question, "Why does anyone conform; that is, why are we not all deviant?"

The social control theories, like the strain theories, are not really theories in the sense of rigorous scientific procedures for developing and testing hypotheses. They are an approach or an explanation for criminal behavior. There are three types of control theories: containment, social-control, and the social-learning theory which is a psychological approach and is discussed in Chapter 6. All three approaches have these common assumptions:

√ Humans require nurturing.

√ Differences in nurturing account for variations in attachment to others and commitment to an ordered way of living.

√ Attachment and commitment are internal controls commonly called "conscience" and recognized in "guilt."

√ External controls are usually tested by the presence of "shame."

Emile Durkheim believed that mechanical societies controlled people better than did organic ones. In the mechanical society, which was small and tradition-directed, people knew each other by sight. Everyone knew what the other person was doing. Accordingly, every person in society served as a police officer and provided surveillance. It was difficult for anyone under such close scrutiny to commit transgressions. Similar conditions exist today in small communities. In contrast to mechanical societies, organic societies do not control people as well. Organic societies are large, heterogeneous, and people can easily disappear in groups. Often, individuals do not know their neighbors, and thus, the neighbors do not serve as police officers. In addition, most people in organic societies do not want to get involved. Accordingly, people in those societies lack significant bonds to society.

Albert Reiss

Albert Reiss conducted a study of Chicago working-class boys between the ages of 11 and 17 who were on probation. He found that revocation of probation was more likely when boys had weak egos and superego controls which prevented them from internalizing society's norms. (Note: he borrowed the ego and superego concepts from psychiatry which is discussed in Chapter 6). He contended that the youths had weak personal control mechanisms. The primary control mechanism, according to Reiss, is the attachment people had for others and that people are controlled by the norms held by those to whom they are attached and hopefully such persons are law abiding. He saw delinquency as emerging from the failure of personal and social controls to produce behavior in conformity with the norms of the social system.[10]

Containment Theory

The containment theorists stress that we live in a society that provides a variety of opportunities for conformity or nonconformity. Both illegal and legal opportunities are available and not everyone will choose to commit criminal behavior. Accordingly, the existence of subcultures, the location of goods and services within a city, the population density, and other variables do not adequately explain criminal behavior. What we need to know is why these phenomena affect some people and not others. That is, why are some individuals immune to such influences? Walter Reckless attempted to answer this question by use of his containment theory.

Reckless defined his containment theory as follows:

> The assumption is that there is a containing external social structure which holds individuals in line and that there is also an internal buffer which protects people against deviation of the social and legal norms. The two containments acts as a defense against deviation from the legal and social norms, as an insulation against pressures and pulls, as a protection against demoralization and seduction. If there are "causes" which lead to deviant behavior, they are negated, neutralized, rendered impotent, or are paired by the containing buffers.[11]

Reckless saw two types of containment—outer containment and inner containment. The **outer containment** is also considered as social pressures and represents the structural buffer in the person's immediate social world. It consists of such items as a presentation of a consistent moral front to the person, and institutional reinforcement of his or her norms, goals, and expectations.

The **inner containment** consists mainly of self components, such as self-control, good self-concept, ego strength, well-developed superego, high tolerance for frustration, high sense of responsibility, strong goal orientation. Reckless considered that the inner containments provided the most effective controls on a person. Together, the inner and outer containments work to prevent people from becoming criminals. There are many social pressures that pull and push a person toward criminal behavior and interact with their containments. The pulls to-

Travis Hirschi's Elements of the Social Bond

1. **Attachment:** Attachment refers to our affective ties to people who are important to us and to our sensitivity to their options.

2. **Commitment:** Commitment is the rational component of the bond. Commitment refers to the time and energy that we invest in our way of living. Individuals without a commitment to conventional values are more likely to become delinquent.

3. **Involvement:** The more a person is involved in conventional things, the less the opportunity the person has to commit criminal behavior.

4. **Belief:** When a person's belief in the values of the society or group are weakened, criminal behavior is more likely to occur.

ward criminal behavior include such factors as poverty, poor family life, and deprived education. The pushes are individual factors such as hostility, personality, and aggressiveness. Hopefully, according to Reckless, inner and outer containment interacts with the pushes and pulls on a person to prevent criminal behavior.

Social Control

Travis Hirschi stated, in his 1969 book *Causes of Delinquency*, that the real question is why, with so many opportunities and pressures to commit crimes, are most of us law-abiding citizens? The basic concept of the social control theory is that the social bond of an individual to society determines whether or not the individual commits criminal behavior. According to Hirschi, there are four components of the social bond: attachment, commitment, involvement, and belief. We are more likely to commit deviant behavior if the social bond is weakened.[12]

The social control theorists do not view human nature as inherently evil, a blank state, or inherently good. They see the human being as a "free spirit." Free to do whatever is most convenient and advantageous at a given time. We all have nonconformist impulses. According to these theorists, we all would deviate if given the chance. They do not see deviant behavior as problematic and therefore do not feel the need to explain it. If socialization is effective, a social bond will result, giving the person a stake in conformity and preventing him or her from committing crime. If the socialization is ineffective, a social bond will not result, thus the person will not have a stake in conformity and will probably commit criminal acts.

Delinquency and Drift

David Matza and Gresham Sykes contend that delinquents have no commitment either to societal norms or to criminal norms. Instead, delinquents drift in and out of crime. While delinquents tend to spend most of their time in law-abiding behaviors, they are flexible in their commitment to the values of the dominant society and that the majority of them are drifters into criminal activity. Matza and Sykes contend that people do not commit crimes when they are controlled by morals; however, when the morals can be neutralized, the controls lessen and then individuals are more likely to commit criminal behavior. Accordingly, people need to neutralize their morals before violating laws they believe in. To explain this concept, Matza and Sykes formulated the **techniques of neutralization**. The techniques act to lessen the effects of social controls. Those techniques are listed below:

- **Denial of Responsibility**: The delinquent defines himself or herself as lacking responsibility for the behavior in question. The acts are the product of forces beyond the control of the delinquent. The delinquent feels that he or she is being pulled/pushed into situations beyond his or her control. Typical response: "I didn't mean to do it, but..."

- **Denial of Injury**: There is no harm to victims. For example, auto theft is viewed as borrowing. Gang fighting is seen as a private quarrel and no one else's business. The victim (e.g., insurance company, large company, or government) can easily afford the loss or damage. The delinquent may also feel that his or her behavior does not cause any great harm despite the fact that it runs counter to the law.

- **Denial of the Victim**: The injury is not wrong in light of the circumstances. The offender is retaliating for a previous act of the victim. The victim deserves the injury or there is no real victim. For example, the victim had it coming to him because the victim was a drug user.

- **Condemnation of the Condemners**: This technique involves a shift in focus. It is a rejection of the rejecters. For example, to the offender, the police are corrupt, stupid, and brutal. The offender thinks that many condemners are hypocrites and deviants in disguise.

- **Appeal to Higher Loyalties**: The norms of the group or gang are more important than those of society in general. For example, you always help a buddy and never squeal on a friend. Bombing an abortion clinic for God.

Roberson, one of the authors of this text, once taught a criminology course to prisoners in a federal prison. Often during discussion on the causes of crime, offenders were asked if they agreed with certain theories on crime causation and asked how the theories related to any crimes they may have committed. The traditional answer was that they agreed with certain theories, but these theories did not apply in their particular case because. . . . They would then attempt to neutralize their conduct.

CULTURAL CONFLICT

Most of the cultural conflict concepts may be traced back to the Chicago School. Thorsten Sellin published the first systematic discussion of the relationship between culture conflict and crime called *Cul-*

ture, Conflict and Crime.[13] Sellin considered crime as a violation of group conduct norms.[14] Sellin opined that different cultures have different conduct norms. He defined **conduct norms** as rules that reflect the attitudes of a group about the manner in which a person should act in a given situation. He stated that the dominant class in a society decides what the conduct norms are and which conduct is criminal and which is not. The values which receive the protection of criminal law are those which the dominant class treasures. His theory may be summarized as follows:

√ For every person there is a right or wrong way to act in each given situation, according to the conduct norms of the group to which he or she is a member.

√ The conduct norms of one group may allow a person to act in one way, whereas the conduct norms of another group would prohibit such conduct.

√ Problems occur when a person acts in a manner permitted by the conduct norms of his or her group but not permitted by the conduct norms of the groups in control of political organizations.

Sellin indicated that there were two types of culture conflicts—**primary** and **secondary**. A primary conflict occurs when one's native cultural conduct norms conflict with those of the new culture. A primary culture conflict occurs when one's native culture conduct norms conflict with those of the new culture. A secondary culture conflict occurs in complex societies comprised of a variety of subcultures when the behavior required by one group's conduct norms violates the conduct norms of another group.

SUBCULTURAL THEORIES

The subculture theories are based on the assumption that there are subcultures with different value systems from the conventional value systems in a society. Subcultures differ from the larger culture, in part, because they have similarities (i.e., age, ethnic background, etc.) and have like interests, goals and values. Edwin Lemert suggested that American values are not always clear and that Americans tend to be values "plural." He also suggested that criminality is the result of a positive response to one set of subcultural values that happen to be out of tune with society's values. In the delinquent subcultures, criminal values are normal and criminal behavior is a legitimate means of attaining desirable goals. In both the culture conflict theories and the subcultural theories, the general theme is that differences in norms and values are significant factors in the causation of criminal behavior.

Albert Cohen contended that lower-class delinquent youths belong to a subculture that has different value systems from those of society in general. According to Cohen, the delinquent subculture is a mode of reaction and adjustment to the dominant middle-class society that discriminates against certain youths because of their lower-class status.

Marvin Wolfgang contends that there is a "subculture of violence." His theory is summarized as follows:

1. Members of the subculture hold values different from those of the dominant parent culture.

2. Those who belong to the subculture of violence have values that are not, however, totally different from those of the dominant culture.

3. Individuals who belong to the subculture of violence have a favorable attitude toward the use of violence and learn a willingness to resort to violence to solve conflicts.

4. Members of the subculture of violence have different psychological traits from those who are not members of that culture.

5. Persons who commit violent acts are distinctly more pathological and display more guilt and anxiety than those persons who do not commit violent acts.

Wolfgang and Franco Ferracuti later listed the below seven corollary propositions to the subculture of violence:[15]

1. No subculture can be totally different from, or totally in conflict with, the society of which it is a part.

2. The existence of a subculture of violence does not require that the actors sharing these basic value elements express violence in all situations.

3. The potential resort or willingness to resort to violence in a variety of situations emphasizes the penetrating and diffusive character of this culture theme.

4. The subcultural ethos of violence may be shared by all ages in a subsociety, but this ethos is most prominent in a limited age group, ranging from late adolescence to middle age.

5. The counter norm for the subculture of violence is nonviolence.

6. The development of favorable attitudes toward, and the use of, violence in a subculture usually involves learned behavior and a process of differential learning, association, or identification.

7. The use of violence in a subculture is not necessarily viewed as illicit conduct, and the users, therefore, do not have to deal with feelings of guilt about their aggression.

DIFFERENTIAL ASSOCIATION

Edwin H. Sutherland published his first version of this theory on differential association in 1939 and the final version in 1947. According to Sutherland, all behavior is learned in a social environment. He contended that the major difference between conforming behavior and criminal behavior is in what is learned rather than how it is learned, because we learn both criminal and noncriminal behavior is much the same way. He considered that criminal behavior is not necessarily different from noncriminal behavior, that values are important in determining behavior, and that certain locations and people are more crime-prone than others. A statement out of his 1934 text, *Principles of Criminology,* became the basis for his theory. He stated:

First, any person can be trained to adopt and follow any pattern of behavior which he is able to execute. Second, failure to follow a prescribed pattern of behavior is due to the inconsistencies and lack of harmony in the influences which direct the individual, Third, the conflict of culture is therefore the fundamental principle in the explanation of crime.[16]

By the term **differential association**, Sutherland meant that the content of the patterns presented in association would differ from individual to individual. Sutherland does not, as some claim, mean that mere association with criminals would cause one to commit criminal behavior. Instead, he apparently meant that the content of the communications from others was given different degrees of significance depending on the relationship with the person making the verbal or non-verbal communication. For example, a communication from a close personal friend would have more significance in affecting our behavior than communications heard on a radio from a stranger.

In Sutherland's final version, he expressed the belief that all behavior is learned and, unlike others at that time, moved away from the concept of social disorganization and to the concept of differential social organizations. By doing this, he was able to apply the learning process to a broader range of society. The final version is summarized in his nine points, with number six being the heart of the theory.

1. Criminal behavior is learned.

2. Criminal behavior is learned in interaction with other persons in a process of communications.

3. The principal part of the learning of criminal behavior occurs within intimate personal groups.

4. When criminal behavior is learned, the learning includes: (a) techniques of committing the crime, which are sometimes very complicated, sometimes very simple; (b) the specific direction of motives, drives, rationalizations, and attitudes.

5. The specific direction of motives and drives is learned from definitions of the legal codes as favorable or unfavorable.

6. A person becomes delinquent because of an excess of definitions favorable to violation of the law over definitions unfavorable to violation of law.

7. Differential associations may vary in frequency, duration, priority, and intensity.

8. The process of learning criminal behavior by association with criminal and noncriminal patterns involves all of the mechanisms that are involved in any other learning.

9. While criminal behavior is an expression of general needs and values, it is not explained by those general needs and values, since noncriminal behavior is an expression of the same needs and values.[17]

Sociological Perspectives

Perspective	Spokesperson(s) and Period	Concepts
Ecological [Chicago School]	Mead, Blummer, Park, Burgess, Shaw, & McKay 1920s-1930S	Social disorganization Symbolic Interactionism Demographics Concentric Zones
Strain	Merton, Cloward Cohen & Ohlin 1930s-present	Deviance is not normal. Excessive society pressures causes crime. Differential opportunity Goals-means dysfunction Opportunity Structure
Goals-means Dysfunction	Merton & Cohen 1930-present	A strain theory Middle-class measuring rod
Opportunity Structure	Cloward & Ohlin 1930s-present	A strain theory Use of illegitimate means to attain goals Differential opportunity
Control	Reckless, Hirschi, Reiss, Matza, Sykes, 1950s- present	Ask why people do not commit crime. Humans require nurturing Containment Social control Drift
Containment	Reckless 1950s-present	A control theory Inner and outer containments
Social Control	Hirschi 1960s-present	A control theory Social bonds
Drift	Matza & Sykes 1960s-present	A control theory Techniques of neutralization
Subcultural	Wolfgang & others 1920s-present	Subculture of violence Different value system
Differential Association	Sutherland & others 1930s-1960s	Behavior is learned

The theory holds that criminal behavior is learned in association with intimate others by interacting and communicating with those others. Two things are learned—the techniques for committing the criminal behavior and the definitions of values, motives, drives, rationalizations, and attitudes to support such behavior. The techniques may be considered as the "how" and the definitions as the "whys."[18]

Criminal behavior occurs, according to the theory, when there is an excess of definitions favoring criminal behavior. The excess of definitions does not mean a simple number of excesses, but the weight of the definitions as determined by the quality and intimacy of interaction with others. The theory holds that one learns to commit criminal behavior the same way one learns to play baseball. Note, the resulting behavior is often determined by not only the persons to whom one was been exposed but also by the absence of alternative patterns to fall back on.

For Sutherland, the real question concerns criminal behavior, not how certain conduct came to be criminal. Differential association theory is a process theory. Today, it is one of the most popular theories to explain criminal behavior. The theory has been criticized as being too general in nature and does not account for the fact that for most people, involvement in crime decreases as they grow older. It does not explain crimes of violence, and it fails to consider the role of "free will" in criminal behavior.

In an attempt to provide a more adequate specification of the learning process, Robert Burgess and Ronald Akers formulated the *differential association reinforcement theory*. Their purpose was to merge Sutherland's theory with the more general theory of behaviorism and the works of B.F. Skinner. The key points of their theory are as follows:

1. The primary learning mechanism in social behavior is operant conditioning, in which behavior is shaped by the stimuli and that follows, or are consequences of, the behavior.

2. Direct conditioning and imitation of others are important in determining behavior.

3. Rewards, or positive reinforcement, as well as avoidance of punishment, strengthen this behavior.

4. The determination of whether the behavior is deviant or conforming depends on differential reinforcement.

5. People learn norms, attitudes, and so on, from those who are important to them; that is, our associations with the people who are important to us provide the stimuli for shaping our behavior.[19]

SUMMARY

- Emile Durkheim is considered the leader in the development of sociological theories of crime causation. He rejected the concept of "free will" and looked for sociological causes for human behavior. Under his concept of "anomie," there is a condition of normlessness whereby norms have lost their meaning and become inoperative as a society moves from a mechanical to an organic one.

- The ecological theories look at the relationship between ecological factors and criminal behavior. They were the first to use official data and the case study approach in studying crime causation.

- The social disorganization theory is based on the breakdown in the bonds of society and criminal behavior. The elements of social disorganization include low economic status, a mixture of different ethnic groups, highly mobile residents, and disrupted families.

- Two theories of crime causation developed from the social-psychological theory of symbolic interactionism—differential association and labeling. Symbolic interactionism sees meanings as social products, as formations that are formed in and through the defining of activities of people as they interact.

- The strain theories are based on the assumption that excessive strains or pressures cause people to commit crimes and that people are by nature moral and lawabiding. Merton's modes of adaptation illustrate the various reactions that individuals have as the result of their goal-means dysfunction. Cohen contended that lower-class boys are measured by the "middle-class measuring rod" but do not have the resources to meet those measurements.

- The opportunity structure approach is based on the concept that communities have sets of legitimate and illegitimate opportunities which condition the shape of deviant subcultures. Lower-class boys, lacking access to legitimate means to attain their goals, experience pressures or strains and thus turn to illegitimate means.

- Control theories are based on the concept that individuals are by nature immoral and need society's bonds to control their behavior. The internal controls of attachment and commitment and external controls keep most individuals from committing criminal conduct.

- According to the containment theory, there are inner and outer containments which keep individuals from committing crimes. The inner containments include self-control, good self-concept, ego strength, well-developed super-ego, high tolerance for frustration, high sense of responsibility, and strong goal orientation. The outer containments include the presentation of a consistent moral front and institutional reinforcement of his or her norms, goals, and expectations.

- Hirschi's social control theory consists of four social bonds—attachment, commitment, involvement, and belief. Individuals are more likely to commit deviant behavior if the social bonds are weak or non-existent.

- Matza and Sykes concluded that delinquents have no committment either to societal norms or to criminal norms. The delinquents use techniques of neutralization to neutralize their immoral behavior. The techniques include denial of injury, denial of responsibility, denial of victim, and condemnation of the condemners.

- Cultural conflict theories see delinquent behavior as the result of value conflicts between the conduct norms of the dominant class and those of the delinquents. There are two types of culture conflicts—primary and secondary.

- Similar to the cultural conflict theories, the subcultural theories are based on the assumption that there are subcultures with different value systems from the conventional value systems in our soiety. The subculture of violence tends to value conduct that is violent as opposed to nonviolent conduct.

- Differential association is based upon the preemise that criminal behavior is learned through interactions with other people. We also learn the techniques for committing crime. The learning process for criminal behavior is by association with criminal and noncriminal patterns. A person becomes delinquent because of an excess of definitions favorable to violation of the law over definitions unfavorable to criminal behavior.

DISCUSSION QUESTIONS

1. Why are sociological theories popular in the United States?
2. What are the contributions of Emile Durkheim and Robert Merton to sociological theories of crime causation?
3. Explain the concept of "anomie."
4. What are the differences between the differential association theories and the subcultural theories?
5. Analyze the concept of social bonding.
6. Which of the social theories do you agree most with? Why?

ENDNOTES—Chapter 5

1. George B. Vold and Thomas J. Bernard, *Theoretical Criminology*, 3rd ed. (New York:Oxford University, 1986) pp. 141-42.

2. Kai T. Erikson, *Wayward Puritans*, (New York: John Wiley, 1966).

3. Frank P.Williams III and Marilyn D. McShane, *Criminological Theory*, 2d ed. (Englewood Cliffs, NJ: Prentice Hall, 1994).

4. Herbert Blumber, *Symbolic Interaction: Perspective and Method*, (Englewood Cliffs, NJ:1969) pp. 4-5.

5. Ruth Masters and Cliff Roberson, *Inside Criminology*, (Englewood Cliffs, NJ, 1990).

6. Vold and Bernard, 1986:187.

7. Robert K. Merton, *Social Structure and Anomie*, (New York: Free Press, 1938).

8. Albert K. Cohen, *Delinquent Boys: The Culture of the Gang*, (New York: Free Press, 1960).

9. Robert A. Cloward and Lloyd E. Ohlin, *Delinquency and Opportunity*, (New York: Free Press, 1960).

10. Albert J. Reiss, "Delinquency and the Failure of Personal and Social Controls," *American Sociological Review*, vol. 16, 1951, pp. 196-207.

11. Walter C. Reckless, "Containment Theory," in Marvin Wolfgang, et al., eds. *The Sociology of Crime and Delinquency*, 2d ed. (New York: John Wiley, 1970). pp.402-3.

12. Travis Hirschi, *Causes of Delinquency*, (Berkeley, Univ. of Calif. Press, 1969).

13. Vold and Bernard, 1986.

14. Thorsten Sellin, *Culture Conflict and Crime*, (New York: Social Science Research Council, 1938).

15. Marvin E. Wolfgang and Franco Ferracuti, "The Subculture of Violence," in L.D. Savitz and N. Johnson, eds. *Crime in Society* (New York:Wiley, 1978).

16. Edwin H. Sutherland, *Principles of Criminology,* 2d ed. (Philadelphia:Lippincott, 1934) p. 54-55.

17. Edwin H. Sutherland and Donald R. Cressy, *Criminology,* 10ed, (Philadelphia: Lippincott, 1978) pp. 80-82.

18. Williams and McShane, 1994: 76-77.

19. Ruth Masters and Cliff Roberson, *Inside Criminology,* (Englewood Cliffs, NJ: Prentice Hall, 1990). pp. 209-10.

Sigmund Freud

Chapter 6

PSYCHOLOGICAL AND PSYCHIATRIC APPROACHES

LEARNING OBJECTIVES

After studying this chapter, you should be able to:

- Examine the psychological and psychiatric approaches to crime causation.

- Describe how those approaches differ from the sociological approaches.

- Explain emotional problems theories.

- Describe the social learning theories.

- Outline the thinking pattern theories.

- Explain the tests for insanity.

INTRODUCTION

This chapter examines the psychological and psychiatric approaches to crime causation. Most of these approaches discussed in this chapter argue that criminal behavior originates primarily in the personalities of the offender rather than from the environmental situations they encounter. In addition, some of the approaches argue that criminal behavior is the result of normal learning patterns, such as one approach considered under the discussion of differential association in the previous chapter.

Psychiatry grew out of the experiences of medical doctors in dealing with basic problems of mental disease. **Psychiatry** may be defined as a field of medicine that specializes in the understanding, diagnosis, treatment, and prevention of mental problems. Psychiatry has divided the mental disorders into organic disorders and functional disorders. **Organic disorders** are those disorders that can be traced to a physical problem (e.g., head injuries, distorted vision, or those due to disease or degeneration). **Functional disorders** are those disorders where there is strange behavior but no known organic problems. An example of a functional disorder would be a person with no apparent brain pathology who hears voices or who sees things that others do not see.

Psychoanalysis is a branch of psychiatry which is based on the theories of Freud and a particular method of treatment involving individual case study. While psychiatry is as old as medicine, psychoanalysis is a relatively recent development with the work of Sigmund Freud (1856-1939) and Alfred Adler (1870-1937) and Carl Jung (1875-1961).[1] The psychological approaches tend to focus not only on the mental but also the behavioral characteristics of a person. Despite the differences in the approaches studied in this chapter, the basic connecting theme is the concept that the person is a unique personality and that the only way that a person can be understood is through a thorough case study.

Before the development of the scientific theories of criminal behavior involving mental illness, **demonology** was used to explain criminal behavior. Individuals were thought to be "possessed" by evil spirits and their behavior could not be changed until the evil spirits were exorcized. Methods of exorcism included the drinking of horrible concoctions, praying, and making strange noises to scare away the evil. Many considered that the only way to drive out the evil spirits was to insult them or to make the body an unpleasant place to inhabit. Flogging and other types of corporal punishment were also used in an attempt to drive out the evil spirits. By the eighteenth century, the discovery of an organic basis for many physical illnesses lead to the discovery of an organic basis for some mental illnesses as well. As the organic view replaced demonological theory of crime causation, the concept that psychological problems could also cause mental illness became popular.

William Healy is credited with taking the positivists' emphasis in studying anatomical characteristics and shifting it to the psychological and social elements. He believed that the only way to find the causes of criminal behavior was to deeply study the individual's background, including emotional development. He measured personality disorders and environmental pathologies with the thesis that criminal behavior was purposive behavior resulting when individuals were frustrated in their attempts to fulfill their basic needs. Healy also noted that delinquents have a higher frequency of personality defects and disorders than nondelinquents.[2]

The psychological/psychiatric theories of crime causation include emotional problem theories, mental disorder theories, sociopathic personality theories, and thinking pattern theories.

PSYCHOANALYTIC THEORIES

Sigmund Freud

Sigmund Freud was born in Freiberg, Moravia in 1856 of Jewish parents, and he died in 1939. He was a distinguished student at the University of Vienna, where he graduated in 1881 with a medical degree. From 1881 to 1885 he did research in physiology while on the staff of the Vienna General Hospital. He then was in private practice until 1902, when he was appointed professor of neuropathology at the University of Vienna School of Medicine. Freud remained there until 1923 when he was forced to retire because of cancer in his jaw. Freud was one of the most controversial and influential persons of the twentieth century.

While Freud did not discuss criminal behavior to any great extent, he did suggest that the criminal wants to be caught and punished for his or her guilt. According to him, criminals are their own worst punishers. Freud focused on the pathological, not the healthy part of human beings. He was concerned with the unconscious mental life of the individual.

Freud believed that aggression and violence have their roots in instinct. According to him, violence is a response to thwarting the pleasure principle. He developed the idea that each of us has a "death wish." This **death wish** is a constant source of aggressive impulses and tries to reduce the organism to an inanimate state. Freud contended that this death wish may be expressed directly, manifested indirectly as in hunting, or sublimated into sadomasochism.

Freud contended that behavior based on "guilt" arising from the Oedipus conflict was the basis of criminal activity. The conflict was named from a character in Greek mythology who kills his father and marries his mother. He contended that we have a hidden desire to act out similar behavior. The equivalent complex for girls is known as the Electra complex and is taken from a classic tragedy in Greek mythology. Both the Oedipus and Electra complexes are based on the Freudian premise that incest is a basic human desire.

Freud's concepts of the id, ego, and superego are well known. According to him, these form the basis of personality. The **id** is the primary, rash, impulsive part of the personality. It is governed by the pleasure principle. The id is hedonistic and has no regard for responsibility and sensible things. The **ego** is considered the sensible and responsible part of the personality. It is governed by the reality principle. The ego appraises the external situation and then enables the person to make rational decisions. The ego should repress unacceptable social impulses and/or drives into the unconscious. The **superego** is the "conscience." It is unconscious. This part of the personality allows a person to feel pride, shame, and/or guilt. It is the person's moral faculty and sets moral and ethical standards.

Freud's contribution of the concept of human development phases are also important. According to him, there are certain developmental stages that humans go through—oral, phallic, latency, and neophallic or genital stages. The **oral stage** is the first stage and occurs during infancy and the first year of life. During this stage, the child is totally antisocial and laden with primitive urges. The infant is beset by a variety of oral urges. The urges can be sadistic, cannibalistic, and antisocial.

Freud's Structure of Personality

Superego	Based on ethical principles; the force of self-criticism; may contain the conscious elements in the form of moral and ethical codes; primarily unconscious in operation
Ego	The conscious personality; the reality principle; mediates between the demands of the id and the prohibitions of the superego
Id	Permanently unconscious; reservoir of biological and psychological drives; source of the pleasure principle

The second stage is the **anal stage** which lasts until the child is about three years old. During this stage, the child is stubborn, spiteful, and cruel. The **phallic stage** is next, and during this stage, the genitals are a major focus. This stage lasts until approximately the age of six. During the **latency period**, which lasts from age six to puberty (approximately twelve years of age), it appears that no urges are present. The last stage is the **genital** or **neophallic stage** where the pre-teenager is again obsessed with his or her genitals, sex, oral urges, and anal urges.

Freud invented the technique of **psychoanalysis** to treat problems caused by traumatic experiences in early childhood that the individual was not consciously aware of. He used the concept of free association where the patient relaxed completely and talked about whatever came to mind. By exploring these associations, the individual was able to reconstruct earlier events and bring them to consciousness.

Psychoanalytic Theory of Juvenile Delinquency

According to C.G. Schoenfeld, the adolescent who is likely to commit delinquent or criminal behavior is a person whose superego has criminal tendencies and does not oppose the antisocial instincts of early childhood. Delinquent behavior may also occur in a youngster whose superego is rigid, prim, and proper. This child's superego is so offended by the reactivated urges that his or her superego becomes guilty. To deal with the overwhelming guilt, the youth commits crimes, with the unconscious aim of being caught and punished.[3]

Most psychoanalytic theories take the position that criminality and delinquency are caused from insecurity, inadequacy, inferiority, unconscious motivation and conflict within the person.

Crime Causation

The psychoanalytic theories of crime causation are summarized by Yablonski and Haskell as follows:

- An inability to control criminal drives (id) because of a deficiency in ego or superego development. Because of the faulty development, the criminal is believed to possess little capacity for repressing instinctual (criminal) impulses. The individual who is dominated by the id is consequently criminal.

- Antisocial character formation resulting from a disturbed ego development. This occurs during the first three years of life.

- An overdeveloped superego, which makes no provision for the satisfaction of the demands of the id. Offenders of this type are considered neurotic.[4]

The psychoanalytic theorists assume that criminality is a part of human nature. Most assume that the difference between a criminal and a noncriminal is that the normal person can control his or her criminal drives and find other socially acceptable outlets for them, whereas the criminal cannot.

EMOTIONAL PROBLEM THEORIES

The emotional problem theories assume that the criminal commits crimes because of the inability to cope with everyday emotional problems. Instead of possessing gross pathological problems, the criminal is responding to very subtle psychological factors that prevent him or her from functioning normally. Generally, these theorists assume that the criminal is normal in psychological makeup and that he or she is not psychotic, neurotic, or sociopathic. The deterioration of coping skills caused by emotional problems is the root of the criminal behavior. The emotional problems could spring from any number of events such as problem relationships, crises, finances, employment, sickness, lack of adequate self-concept, and so on. Once the criminal's coping ability is restored, it is unlikely that he or she will commit additional crimes.

There is considerable overlap between the emotional problem theories and the mental disorder theories discussed in the next section. Both groups contend that there is something mentally wrong with the criminal (i.e., the criminal is not a normal person).

MENTAL DISORDER THEORIES

Mental disorders have been studied for years, but there is still much disagreement regarding the definitions, classifications, causes, and methods of identification, diagnoses, and treatment. There is also difficulty in determining the extent of any disorders diagnosed. Accordingly, any conclusions should be viewed with caution.

The mental disorder theories attempt to classify criminal behavior by the use of certain mental disorders such as psychosis, neurosis, and impulse disorders. **Psychosis** is a common category of mental disorder used to explain criminal behavior. Psychoses can be functional and/or organic. Psychotic people lose contact with reality and have difficulty distinguishing reality from fantasy. **Neurosis** is a common type of mental disorder that was first used to cover a class of diseases that referred to "affections of the nervous system." Neuroses have no demonstrable organic cause and **neurotic behaviors** are behaviors that do not grossly violate social norms or represent severely disordered personalities. **Impulse disorders** are sudden, explosive, and driven to action. A person with an impulse disorder does not necessarily lose touch with reality or lose communication. Impulse disorders include kleptomania (compulsive thievery), pyromania (an irresistible impulse to burn), and explosive disorder (sudden assaultive or other destructive behavior that occurs in a person who otherwise demonstrates good control).

As noted earlier, there are two general types of mental disorders—organic disorders which have an identifiable physiological cause and functional disorders which are characterized by no apparent brain pathology that can be identified by existing techniques.

There is a popular tendency to view deviant irrational behavior as psychologically abnormal behavior. Often the public confuses socially unacceptable behavior with "mental illness" and therefore, the psychotics and schizophrenics are guilty by association. As noted by Bartol, unpredictable, irrational, bizarre, disoriented people are frightening and thus, dangerous. It is important to note, however, that murderers and violent offenders, although socially deviant, are not necessarily psychotic or crazy. In fact, the research literature, according to Bartol, is highly consistent in pointing out that psychotic or severely disturbed individuals are no more likely to commit serious crimes against others than the general population.[5]

Sociopathic Personality Theories

Psychiatrists use the term **psychopath** to describe individuals who exhibit a certain group of behaviors and attitudes.[6] The term psychopath is also considered synonymous with the more modern terms of **sociopath** and **antisocial personality**. The three terms are often used interchangeably. A working definition of them is listed below:

The term is reserved for individuals who are basically unsocialized and whose behavior patterns brings them repeatedly into conflicts with society. They are incapable of significant loyalty to individuals, groups, or social values. They are grossly selfish, callous, irresponsible, impulsive, and unable to feel guilt or to learn from experience and punishment. Frustration tolerance is low. They tend to blame others or offer plausible rationalization for their behavior.[7]

The above definition implies that the behaviors originate in the personality of the individual. Others contend, however, that it is possible that the behaviors may be explained by factors other than personality. Yablonsky contended that core members of violent gangs tended to be sociopaths and led their gangs in mob-like violence while acting out their own hostility and aggression.[8] Samuel Guze argued that sociopathy, alcoholism, and drug addiction are the only psychiatric conditions consistently associated with criminal behavior.[9] He also contended that psychiatry has no consistently effective methods of treating individuals who are sociopaths and recommended that they be confined until they reach middle age.

The Diagnostic and Statistical Manual of Mental Disorders (DSM) refers to a sociopathic disorder. DSM-III replaces the terms psychopath and sociopath with the term antisocial personality disorder. The fourth and revised edition of the DSM, commonly referred to as DSM-IV, again refers to such behavior as antisocial personality disorder.

Hervey Cleckley points out that the terms psychopath or antisocial personality are so broad that they might be applied to almost any criminal.[10] He contends that psychopathy is distinctly different from criminality, that the majority of psychopaths are not criminals, and the majority of criminals are not psycopaths. He also states that psychopaths may be found in any profession including business, science, and medicine. He believes that the typical psychopath differs from the typical criminal in that his actions are less purposeful and his goals more incomprehensible and that while he causes himself needless sorrow and shame, he usually does not commit criminal behavior. Vold and Bernard state that the terms, psychopath, sociopath, and antisocial personality, may have some use for psychiatrists who want a shorthand way to describe a certain type of person with whom they come in contact in the practice of their profession, and that the terms seem to be simply labels that psychiatrists attach to more serious offenders and which do not seem to add anything to our ability to identify these offenders in the first place or to understand why they behave this way.[11]

Future Dangerousness

Should we, as recommended by Guze, lock up sociopaths until they reach middle age? Recently, several states have enacted **"violent sexual predator" laws** that allow for the confinement of individuals based on the concept of future dangerousness. In general, these laws rely on a psychiatric evaluation of the individual and a prediction of the future dangerousness of that individual. In 1966, a U.S. Supreme Court decision required that 967 patients, being held in a New York State Hospital for the criminally insane because they were "dangerous," be transferred to a regular mental hospital. During the next five years, only 26 of them were returned to hospitals for the criminally insane. One-half of the original group were later discharged from the hospital altogether. Of those discharged, only 17 percent had any additional arrests. Accordingly, the prediction of dangerousness was incorrect for 83 percent of those released. Prior to release, they had been held an average of 13 years.[12]

Charles Whitman, the University of Texas Tower Killer, while on active duty with the U.S. Marines, was tried by a special court-martial several years before his killings in Austin. He was charged with assault and battery. A psychologist testified on Whitman's behalf that he was a non-dangerous person and not the type of person who would commit an assault and battery. He was, nevertheless, convicted.

Post Traumatic Stress Disorder

Post traumatic stress disorder (PTSD) was first recognized in the 1980s. It is considered as a brain dysfunction. The PTSD defense has been raised by war veterans who contend that they suffer nightmares, flashbacks, depression, and survivor guilt. They contend that they lose their orientation and believe they are back in Vietnam and that their actions are taken to protect their buddies by shooting or attacking or maiming the people around them. Their attorneys argue that the flashbacks appear so real to the veterans that they have destroyed their ability to distinguish right from wrong. The defense has been used in murder cases, cases involving battered women, and in cases involving armed robbery and drug law violations.

BEHAVIOR AND SOCIAL LEARNING THEORIES

The **social learning theory** was developed by Albert Bandura. Using the works of B.F. Skinner and Skinner's operant learning theory, Bandura focuses on violent and aggressive behavior. He asserts that not only is learning reinforced through actual rewards and punishments but also that we learn by watching others receive rewards and punishments for certain forms of behavior. We then imitate or model those behaviors that are rewarded.[13]

Earlier learning theories see criminal behavior as normal learned behavior and were focused on how learning takes place. The later versions of the learning theories also considered the social environment. **Learning** refers to habits and knowledge that develop as the result of the experiences of the individual in entering and adjusting to the environment. Learning is distinguished from unlearned or instinctive behavior, which seems to be present in the individual at birth and determined by biology. Bandura recognized that all persons have self-regulatory mechanisms, and thus can reward and punish themselves according to internal standards for judging their own behavior. Aggression may be inhibited in some people (e.g., high moral standards, religious beliefs, etc.); however, these people may still engage themselves in aggressive behavior through the process of **disengagement**. Disengagement may result from (1) "attributing blame to one's victims"; (2) "dehumanization through bureaucratization, automation, urbanization, and high social mobility"; (3) "vindication of aggressive practices by legitimate authorities"; and (4) "desensitization resulting from repeated exposure to aggression in any of a variety of forms."

Social learning theory considers the concept of imitation or modeling central to the learning process. Accordingly, as per the learning theorists, we learn criminal behavior by observing the behavior of others in the context of the social environment.

The learning theories rely on behavioral psychology and are based on Skinner's operant learning theory. **Operant learning theory** is con-

cerned with the effect that an individual's behavior has on the environment and the consequences of that effect on the individual. Behavior,
therefore, is shaped and maintained by its consequences. An individual
is the product of present and past events in his or her life. The determination as to whether the frequency of any particular behavior is increased or diminished is based on the contingencies of reinforcement
and punishment (aversive stimuli). There are six basic principles: positive reinforcement, negative reinforcement, positive punishment, negative punishment, discriminative stimuli, and schedules. **Reinforcement**
is any event that follows the occurrence of behavior and that alters and
increases the frequency of the behavior. Those that directly increase
the behavior are positive reinforcers and those that remove something
undesirable are negative reinforcers. **Punishment** is the opposite of
reinforcement. **Discriminate stimuli** do not occur after the behavior,
but are present either before or as the behavior occurs. The **schedules**
refer to the frequency with which, and the probability that, a particular
consequence will occur. Learning takes place because of the consequences associated with behavior.

Burgess' and Akers' differential reinforcement theory accepts the
six basic principles and adds satiation and deprivation to them. They
contend that a stimulus will be more or less reinforcing depending on
the individual's current situation. For example, a person who already
has money (satiated) will be less reinforced by robbing someone than a
person who is impoverished (deprived). Since individuals do not have
the same past experiences, their conditioning histories are different.
Accordingly, some stimuli that people experience daily will produce
different responses in different individuals.

THINKING PATTERN THEORIES

The thinking pattern theories are psychological theories that are
focused on the offender's cognitive processes. In most part, the theories focus on the criminal's intellect, logic, mental processes, rationality, and language usage. They explore the concept that a link between
crime and intelligence exists. It has been argued many times that low
intelligence causes crime. Research in this area has not demonstrated
that low intelligence causes crime, only that low intelligence and crime
often appear together in the same groups.

Cognitive Development Theories

The cognitive development theorists contend that the way in which people organize their thoughts about rules and laws results in either criminal or noncriminal behavior. This organization of thoughts is referred to as **moral reasoning** by psychologists. When that reasoning is applied to law issues, it is termed **legal reasoning**, although this term has a different meaning to lawyers.

Later some cognitive development theorists developed the thesis that both criminal and noncriminal behaviors are related to cognitive development and that people choose the behaviors in which they wish to engage, just as the classical theorists did several centuries earlier. They argued that criminal behavior exists because of the way people think and either the criminal must be confined forever, or he must be taught how to change his ways of thinking. According to these theorists: "The root causes of crime are thought and choice."[14]

The cognitive development theories are based on the early works of **Jean Piaget**, who believed that there are two stages in moral reasoning. First, the belief that rules are sacred and immutable. Second, the belief that rules are the products of humans. Piaget contended that we leave the first stage at about the age of thirteen. The second stage leads to more moral behavior than the first.

Lawrence Kohlberg called the first stage "preconventional" and the second "conventional." He also added a third and higher stage called "post-conventional reasoning." According to him, those who do not make this transition from preconventional to conventional may be considered as arrested in their development of moral reasoning, and they may become delinquents. He noted that the progression to higher stages should preclude criminal behavior and that most criminals do not progress beyond the preconventional stage.[15]

The Criminal Personality

The most detailed study on the way that offenders think and the criminal's mind was conducted by Samuel Yochelson and Stanton Samenow and discussed in their book, *The Criminal Personality.* They conducted their study over a 15-year-period and involved intensive interviews, therapy and follow-up studies of 255 male patients committed to the Saint Elizabeth's Hospital in Washington, D.C. The researchers concluded that traditional psychiatric ideas and treatment modes did not work with criminals. They concluded that criminals use language differently from noncriminals and that the criminal has a different frame of reference when compared to the noncriminal. They concluded that to change the criminal, we need to change the criminal's way of thinking, They identified 52 criminal thinking errors. They also concluded that the criminals told self-serving stories and tended to tell what they thought the authorities wanted to hear. Yochelson and Samenow recognized that most offenders are aware of society's ways of thinking, but many used life's adversities to justify their behavior.

Some of the common thinking errors listed by Yochelson and Samenow are listed below:

1. The criminal's mental life includes fantasies of triumph, power, and control over others.

2. The criminal has a different concept of normal energy. If his energy level is not full of vitality and energy, he thinks something is wrong with him.

3. Criminals are preoccupied with and fear death.

4. The criminal is fearful of being put down or being a "zero." He believes that everyone can see how worthless he or she is.

5. Criminals have an unyielding criminal pride and think that they are better than and above others.

6. Criminals are concrete thinkers. They tend to think in terms of isolated events. In addition, their thinking is fragmented.

7. Criminals view themselves as one of a kind and as unique.[16]

Yochelson and Samenow have been criticized since they do not answer the question of why criminals think in certain ways and others do not and what causes criminal thinking patterns. They appear to be more concerned with a description of criminal thinking. In addition, they researched only criminals confined to institutions and never looked as criminals who were never confined.

Psychological and Psychiatric Perspectives

Perspective	Spokesperson(s) and Period	Concepts
Psychoanalytic	Freud, Schoenfield, Yablonski, & Haskell 1920s-present	Id, ego, superego Sublimation Criminality part of human nature
Emotional Problems [Psychiatric]	many 1930s- present	Criminal not a normal person Inability to cope with everyday problems Psychological problems
Mental Disorder [also a psychiatric theory]	Cleckley & others 1930s-present	Psychosis Impulse disorders Sociopathic personality
Sociopathic Personality	Cleckley & others	A mental disorder theory Psychopaths-sociopaths
Post Traumatic Stress	many 1970s-present	A mental disorder theory Brain dysfunction based on flashbacks
Behavior	Skinner and others 1940s-present	Operant behavior Conditioning Stimulus-response
Social Learning	Bandura and others 1950s-1970s	Modeling Disengagement Learning Discriminate stimuli
Thinking Patterns	Piaget, Kohlberg, Yochelson, Samenow, & others 1960s-present	Cognitive process are different Moral development Cognitive development Criminal personality
Criminal Personality	Samenow & Yochelson 1970s	Thinking patterns theory Thinking errors Self-serving Preoccupied with death Fearful of being put down

INSANITY

The insanity defense is a controversial defense and is generally based on psychological factors. Insanity is a legal, not a medical term. There is no general agreement as to its meaning. It is only a legal conclusion that the defendant was not responsible for his or her actions. As noted in Chapter 3, the most often used test for insanity is the **M'Naghten test**. This test was developed from the case of Daniel M'Naghten, who intending to kill the British Prime Minister Robert Peel, shot and killed Edward Drummond instead. At his trial, M'Naghten claimed that he was insane and therefore should not be held responsible for his actions because of his insane delusions. Under the M'Naghten test which developed from the case, to be considered insane the defendant must have suffered from a defect of reason or from a disease of the mind so that at the time of the act the accused did not know the nature and quality of the act or that the act was wrong.

A second test used by some states is the **irresistible impulse test** which includes the M'Naghten test and, in addition, allows the defendant to use the insanity defense if a mental disease has rendered the defendant incapable of choosing between right and wrong. Under this test, the defendant is also considered insane if he or she cannot control his or her behavior. A few jurisdictions use the Durham Rule which is also known as the Product Rule. The **Durham Rule** is based on an assessment of whether the offender's behavior was the product of mental disease or defect. Another test for insanity is the **ALI Rule**, named after the American Law Institute, also called the substantial capacity test. Under the ALI Rule, the question is whether the defendant had the substantial capacity to appreciate the criminality of his or her conduct or, if so, to control that conduct.

After the defense was successful in the case of John W. Hinckley, who on March 30, 1980, attempted to assassinate President Reagan, the federal test was modified to the effect that the test is whether the defendant lacks the capacity to appreciate the wrongfulness of his or her conduct. The insanity defense has also been expanded in cases involving posttraumatic stress disorder and premenstrual tension syndrome which were discussed in Chapter 4.

Despite the fact that the insanity defense is frequently unsuccessful, it is very unpopular with the general public. States are looking for suggestions for dealing with the problem of the mentally ill defendant.

COMPARISONS OF TESTS

Test	Standard
M'Naghten	Did not know what he was doing or did not know it was wrong
Irresistible Impulse	Could not help himself
Durham	The act was caused by mental illness
ALI	Lacks substantial capacity to appreciate the wrongfulness of his conduct or to control it
Federal Rule	Lacks capacity to appreciate the wrongfulness of his conduct

One method for dealing with the mental illness problem is by using the Michigan procedure of "guilty, but mentally ill." Under this rule, insanity and mental illness are two distinct concepts. To find a defendant guilty, but mentally ill, the jury must determine that the defendant is guilty of the offense, that the defendant was mentally ill at the time of the act, and was not, however, insane at the time of the act. A defendant found guilty, but mentally ill, may have any sentence imposed upon him or her that could be imposed with a finding of guilt. In addition, psychiatric treatment will be provided the defendant and any time spent in any treatment facility will be applied toward the sentence to be served.

 **Criminally Responsible?**

In 1997, Theodore Kaczynski, more commonly known as the unabomber, reopened the divisive debate about when people should be held criminally responsible. His lawyers claimed that he was a paranoid schizophrenic who was incapable of forming the intent necessary to be found guilty of the 18-year string of bombings around the country.

According to his defense attorneys, there is extensive evidence that Kaczynski suffered delusions and believed he was controlled by others. The classic insanity defense states that the defendant did not know right from wrong. Because of the restrictions imposed after the Hinckley acquittal, a defendant who tries to use this defense has the burden of proving it by "clear and convincing evidence."

John Hinckley was acquitted by reason of insanity in the 1982 attempted assassination of President Ronald Reagan. Because of the public's reaction to his acquittal, Congress and many state legislatures made it more difficult to assert what many call the "insanity excuse."

On the other hand, Kaczynski did not want his attorneys to use the insanity defense. After much debate, he was allowed to enter a guilty plea and avoid a trial and the death penalty.

The assertion of a mental defect is different from that of the insanity defense. The assertion of a mental defect is used by the defense to argue that the government has failed to establish beyond a reasonable doubt a necessary element of a crime (i.e., that he sent the bombs intending to cause harm). According to the defense, he lacked the mental state required to form a specific intent to harm anyone.

SUMMARY

- Generally, the psychological and psychiatric approaches to crime causation contend that criminal behavior originates primarily in the personality of the offender rather than from the environmental situations he or she encounters.

- Sigmund Freud suggested that the criminal wants to be caught and punished for his or her own guilt. He believed that aggression and violence have their roots in instinct. The id, ego, and superego form the basis of personality. When one of those aspects dominates the personality, criminal behavior may result.

- The emotional problem theories assume that the criminal commits crimes because of his or her inability to cope with emotional problems.

- The mental disorder theories attempt to classify criminal behavior by the use of mental disorders.

- Predictions of dangerousness are used to hold individuals in mental institutions. There are serious questions regarding the ability to successfully predict future dangerousness.

- The behavior and social learning theories are based on the concept that learning is reinforced through actual rewards and punishments and that we learn by watching others receive rewards and punishments.

- The thinking pattern theories are based on the premises that criminals have different thinking patterns from noncriminals and that certain thinking errors of criminals can be identified.

- Insanity is a legal, not a medical term. The M'Naghten test is the most popular test used in the United States. It is based on the question of whether the accused suffers from a defect of reason or from a disease of the mind so that he or she does not know the nature and quality of the act or that the act was wrong.

DISCUSSION QUESTIONS

1. What are the basic concepts of the psychological theories of crime causation?

2. How does Freud explain criminal behavior?

3. How do mental disorder theorists explain crime causation?

4. Explain the various tests for insanity.

5. Explain the difference between the social learning theories and the emotional problem theories.

ENDNOTES—Chapter 6

1. George B. Vold and Thomas J. Bernard, *Theoretical Criminology*, 3rd ed. (New York: Oxford, 1986) pp. 110-111.

2. Sue Titus Reid, *Crime and Criminology*, (Fort Worth: Harcourt Brace Jovanovich, 1991).

3. C.G. Schoenfeld, "A Psychoanalytic Theory of Juvenile Justice," in E. Peoples, ed., *Correctional Casework and Counseling*, (Pacific Palisades, CA: Goodyear, 1975).

4. L. Yablonski and M.R. Haskell, *Juvenile Delinquency* (New York: Harper & Row, 1988) p. 355.

5. C.R. Bartol, *Criminal Behavior: A Psychosocial Approach*, (Englewood Cliffs, NJ: Prentice-Hall, 1980).

6. Vold and Bernard, 1986:122-123.

7. *Diagnostic and Statistical Manual of Mental Disorders*, 4th ed. (Washington, D.C.: American Psychiatric Association, 1994).

8. Louis Yablonsky, *The Violent Gang* (New York: Penguin, 1970).

9. Samuel Guze, *Criminology and Psychiatric Disorders* (New York: Oxford University Press, 1976).

10. Hervey Cleckley, *The Mask of Insanity* (St.Louis: Mosby, 1976) p. 263.

11. Vold and Bernard, 1986:124.

12. H.J. Steadman, "The Psychiatrist as a Conservative Agent of Social Control," *Social Problem*, vol. 20 (2), 263-71 (1972).

13. Albert Bandura, *Aggression: A Social Learning Approach* (Englewood Cliffs, NJ: Prentice Hall, 1973).

14. Glenn D. Walters and Thomas W. White, "The Thinking Criminal: A Cognitive Model of Lifestyle Criminality," *Criminal Justice Research Bulletin 4* (No. 4, 1989).

15. Lawrence Kohlberg, "The Development of Modes of Moral Thinking and Choice in Years 10 to 16," PhD. Diss., Harvard University, 1958.

16. S. Yochelson and S. Samenow, "The Criminal Personality," Vol. 1. *A Profile for Change,* (Northvale, NJ: Jason Aronson, 1976).

Karl Marx

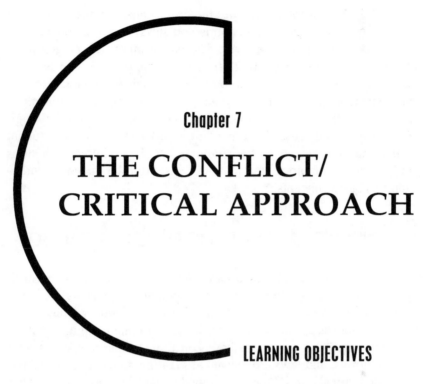

Chapter 7

THE CONFLICT/ CRITICAL APPROACH

LEARNING OBJECTIVES

After studying this chapter, you should be able to :

- Understand the crime causation theories based on the conflict approach.

- List the key concepts of the critical theories.

- Explain how Marxist theories differ from other sociological theories.

- Identify Quinney's social reality of crime and its propositions.

- Describe the concept of "new criminology."

- Differentiate conflict criminology from realist criminology.

- Explain the labeling concepts.

This chapter examines the crime causation theories which view our values, norms and laws from the conflict and critical perspectives. The two primary theory groups in this classification are conflict/critical criminology and the labeling theory. Conflict/critical criminology theories include the radical theory, Marxist theory, new criminology, and realist criminology. While many would place the labeling theory in Chapter 5, because it is a sociological theory, it is discussed at this point in order to provide the student with a chance to review it after studying both the sociological theories and critical criminology, thus making it easier for the student to understand its basic concepts.

CONFLICT AND CRITICAL CRIMINOLOGY

Most sociological theories are based on the consensus approach that views emerging norms and laws of society as representative of the common feeling of society about what is right and proper. They represent a consensus of views and a mechanism for maintaining social order. The conflict theories are based on the conflict perspective that values, norms, and laws are viewed as creating dissension, clash, and conflict. Critical criminology developed in the 1970s, as some conflict theorists rejected the earlier conflict approach and shifted toward the Marxist perspective.

Central to the conflict and critical theorists' conceptions of crime is the concept that crime is simply behavior that threatens the ruling class. They stress that a relationship exists between deviant behavior and the process of making and enforcing laws and that many acts of rule breaking are committed in the name of a group or cause.

Conflict Theories

According to the conflict theorists, conflict is a fact of life. Resources are scarce and the attempt to control the resources generates the major portion of conflict in a society. The control of resources creates power which is used to maintain and expand the resource base of the controlling group at the expense of others in society. Law is a societal mechanism used by the group in power to maintain control of less powerful groups. Laws are formulated so that they express the values and interests of the power group and restrict the behavior common to the less powerful groups. The application and enforcement of laws leads to a focus on the behaviors of the less powerful groups, thus disproportionately criminalizing them.

Marxist Theory

Karl Marx originated the idea that crime was a product of capitalism. To him and **Friedrich Engels,** the criminal was a person who had been brutalized and demoralized by capitalism. As noted by Vold and Bernard, Marxist criminology theories are difficult to summarize for several reasons. First, they are based on complex theories of society and social change. The complexity has lead to profound disagreements among different Marxist theorists. Second, the theories have changed significantly since they were first developed.[1] Karl Marx (1818-1883) linked economic development to social, political, and historical change. He based his theory on the conflict between the material forces of production and the social relations of production. He used the term "material forces of production" to refer to a society's capacity to produce material goods, including technological equipment and the knowledge, skill, and organization to use that equipment. The term "social relations of production" refers to relationships between people and includes property relationships. The term also includes the distribution of goods and who get what.

Marx argued that capitalist societies would inevitably tend to polarize into two groups, one growing smaller and smaller while getting richer and richer, and the other growing larger and larger while getting poorer and poorer. The tendency toward polarization is what Marx call the "contradiction" in capitalism. While Marx himself did not discuss crime causation or its relation to the economic system at length, he did address it. He believed that it was essential to human nature that people be productive in life and in work. Marx saw crime as the struggle of the isolated individual against the prevailing conditions that are dictated by those in power who represent only their own interests. He also believed that in industrialized capitalist societies there are large numbers of people unemployed and underemployed and that these individuals become demoralized and are subject to all forms of crime and vice.[2]

Willem Bonger, an early Marxist criminologist, argued that the capitalist economic system encouraged all people to be greedy and selfish and to pursue their own benefits without regard to the welfare of others in society. Since the justice system criminalizes the greed of the poor while it allows legal opportunities for the rich to pursue their selfish desires, crime is concentrated in the lower classes. Bonger argued that a socialist society would ultimately eliminate crime since it would promote a concern for all in society, not just the rich. In addition, a socialist society would remove the present legal bias that favors the rich.[3]

Marxist criminology is based on four propositions:

1. Crime is best understood under the perspective of the scarcity of resources and the historical inequality in the distribution of those resources.

2. Crime constitutes more than the state definition of crime;

3. The state version of crime and other social harms are a product of the class struggle.

4. Crime represents the alienation of individuals by capitalist social structures and institutions.

After Willem Bonger advocated Marxist criminology in the 1920s, it virtually disappeared from the scene. In the 1970s, many of the concepts reappeared in the form of critical criminology advocated by Richard Quinney[4] and in Great Britain as "new criminology" with the works of Taylor, Walton, and Young.[5]

Critical Theories

Critical criminology may be considered as a mixture of the labeling and radical theories. It evolved from the social turbulence of the 1960s caused by the reaction to the American involvement in the Vietnam war and the development of the drug counterculture. This social turbulence caused many individuals to question the traditional assumptions of the criminal justice system. Generally, there are three major themes to critical criminology.

- Criminologists should focus on why some people and not others are labeled as criminals rather than focusing on the characteristics that distinguish criminals from noncriminals. Under this theme, the critical criminologists take issue with theories that view crime as a result of biological and psychological maladjustments and with sociological theories that rely on such factors as inadequate socialization and peer group pressures.

- The criminal justice system is a tool used for the purpose of maintaining the status quo and serves the interests only of those powerful members of society.

- Criminal laws reflect not our morality, but the desires and interests of only a small segment of our society. Law is, in reality, the rules imposed on society by the ruling class.

The leading spokesman for the critical criminologists is William Chambliss. His theory looks at the questions of why some acts are defined by law as criminal, and others are not, and why crime is distributed as it is by social class, race, and gender. Chambliss also wonders why given the definition of certain acts as criminal, some people are arrested, prosecuted, convicted and sentenced, whereas others are not. He contends that criminal behavior is generated because of the contradictions and conflicts that inevitably arise in the course of life. These contradictions lead to conflicts between groups, classes and strata and the contradictions tend to intensify with time and cannot be resolved within the existing social framework. He maintains that the amount and type of crime depends on the nature of existing contradictions, the conflicts that develop as people respond to the contradictions, and the mechanisms institutionalized for handling the conflicts and dilemmas produced by the contradictions.

Radical Criminology

The radical theory of crime causation is explained in the works of William Chambliss in the 1960s and 1970s. Chambliss examined the making of law and the process by which it is applied. He also focused on the importance of labor, resources and control for the existing social order. Chambliss argued that the ruling class exercises control in two ways: first by creating laws that emphasize the behaviors of the lower classes whereby their conduct is criminalized and second, by encouraging the myth that law serves the interests of everyone. According to him, the criminal justice system favors the more-powerful at the expense of the powerless.[6]

Social Reality of Crime

In the early 1970s, **Richard Quinney** began to question the definitions of crime and the legal process. At the time that he formulated his **"social reality of crime,"** his approach to crime causation and criminal justice was the more conservative variety of conflict criminology. Later he became a Marxist criminologist. In his early works, Quinney viewed crime, like the labeling advocates, as the product of society's reactions to certain behaviors. The reactions that were the most important, according to him, were the reactions of those persons with legitimate authority. The powerful in society use their power to create and place into criminal law those behaviors that they consider as unacceptable and those behaviors that favor their position in society. As a result, those in the lower-class positions are more likely to engage in objectionable behavior. According to Quinney, crime is the product of legal definitions constructed through the exercise of political power. Just as crime is constructed, so is non-crime constructed. Accordingly, behavior which is favorable to the ruling class is defined as noncriminal, and the behavior that is not favorable to the ruling class is defined as criminal.

Quinney advocated that criminal law is used by the state and the ruling class to secure the survival of the capitalist system, and, as capitalist society is further threatened by its own contradictions, criminal law will be increasingly used in an attempt to maintain domestic order. He stated that the traditional ideas about the causes of crime should be abandoned, and we should attempt to understand what could be, not what is. By focusing on what causes crime, we focus our study on the criminal rather than understanding that crime is a product of the authority that defines behavior as criminal.

Quinney's social reality of crime consists of the following seven propositions:

1. **Definition of Crime:** Crime is a definition of human conduct that is created by authorized agents in a politically organized society.

2. **Formulation of Criminal Definitions:** Criminal definitions describe the behaviors that conflict with the interests of the groups in society that have the power to shape political policy.

3. **Application of Criminal Definitions.** Criminal definitions are applied by the segments of society that have the power to shape the enforcement and administration of criminal law.

4. **Development of Behavior Patterns in Relation to Criminal Definitions:** Behavior patterns are structured in segmentally organized society in relation to criminal definitions, and within this context persons engage in actions that have relative probabilities of being defined as criminal.

5. **Construction of Criminal Conceptions:** Conceptions of crime are constructed and diffused in the segments of society by various means of communications.

6. **Social Reality of Crime:** The social reality of crime is constructed by the formulation and application of criminal definitions, the development of behavior patterns related to criminal definitions, and the construction of criminal conceptions.[7]

New Criminology

New criminology was the first major theory to challenge traditional criminology and advocated a new critical look at the American criminal justice system. It first appeared around the 1970s in Great Britain and was developed, like the labeling theory, from the social reaction perspective.

Taylor, Walton, and Young explain their concepts in the below excerpt from their book:

> This "new" criminology will in fact be an old criminology, in that it will face the same problems that were faced by the classical social theorists. Marx saw the problem with his usual clarity when he began to develop his critique of the origins of German idealism... We have argued for a political economy of criminal action, and of the reaction it excites, and for a politically-informed social psychology of these ongoing social dynamics. . . .

It should be clear that a criminology which is not normatively committed to the abolition of inequalities of wealth and power, and in particular of the inequalities in property and life-chances, is inevitably bound to fall into correctionalism (even with social reform of the kind advocated by the Chicagoans, the Mertonians and romantic wing of Scandinavian criminology) precisely because, as this book has attempted to show, the causes of crime must be intimately bound up with the form assumed by the social arrangements of the time. Crime is ever and always that behaviour seen to be problematic within the framework of those social arrangements; for crime to be abolished, then, those social arrangements themselves must also be subject to fundamental social change.[7]

Taylor, Walton and Young contend that deviance is normal, not in the Durkheim sense, but in the sense that men are now consciously involved in asserting their human diversity. They assert that the task is not merely to penetrate these problems, question the stereotypes, or act as carriers of alternative phenomenological realities, but to create a society in which the facts of human diversity, whether personal, organic or social, are not subject to the power to criminalize.

Realist Criminology

Realist criminology emerged after the Marxist theories were criticized for being too simplistic. It surfaced in the 1980s, based on the writings of Jock Young and Walter Dekeseredy. The British version (Jock Young) may have been the product of the radical's disenchantment with their ability to change and reform society and the conservative direction that the British Labour Party was taking.[9] Their concepts are discussed earlier under new criminology. Probably the realists' greatest contribution to criminology is the concern for specific analyses of crime and crime policies, resulting in the need to consider crime as a social policy. Considering crime as a social problem is a deviation from the Marxist view that all crime is the product of the capitalist system. The realists also recognized that crime is a problem for society and is also in socialist countries. They departed from the radical argument that the causes of crime are unemployment and poverty and presented a very complex explanation of crime that was based on four variables—the victim, the offender, the state, and the community.

LABELING THEORY

The **labeling theory** developed in the early 1960s. It was first known as the **societal reaction school**. The theorists, supporting the development of the labeling concepts, argued that earlier theories of crime causation placed too much emphasis on individual deviance and neglected the reactions of people to this deviance. Labeling theorists contend that criminologists overemphasize the original deviant act as well as the character of the deviant. They attack the concept that because crime is bad, those who commit crime are also bad. They take some of their concepts from the **culture conflict theories** that hold that the definition of crime changes from time to time and from place to place.

While the labeling perspective reached its height of popularity in the 1960s, most researchers attribute the development of the labeling perspective to the early works of Frank Tannenbaum and his 1938 book *Crime and the Community*.[10] He formalized the "dramatization of evil" which suggested that deviant behavior was not so much a product of the deviant's lack of adjustment to society as it was the fact that he or she had adjusted to a special group and that criminal behavior was a product of the conflict between a group and the community. The conflict results in two opposing views of appropriate behavior. The community then places a **"tag"** on the child which identifies the child as a delinquent. This causes the child to change his or her self-image and causes people to react to the tag, not the child. Accordingly, the process of tagging criminals or delinquents creates crime.

In the 1960s, as our society was becoming more conscious of racial inequality and civil rights, the issues of the underprivileged members of society became one of the topics of concern. The social atmosphere promoted by the "Great Society" of presidents Kennedy and Johnson increased the popularity of the labeling theory. Labeling was accepted as the answer to the question of why certain people were more frequently involved in the criminal justice system.

One concept that the labeling theorists use is the **"looking-glass self."** This concept defines the social self as made up of what a person sees others seeing in him or her. Others are a mirror (looking glass) to one's self. If a person thinks that others see him as lazy, the person will tend to be lazy. If others see him or her as criminal, then he or she will act out the part. This concept is similar to the "self-fulfilling prophecy."

The effects of labeling theory on criminology has been substantial, according to Williams and McShane. It has caused criminologists to question the middle-class values, which they were using in their descriptions of deviance and criminality. In addition, researchers take a more critical examination of criminal justice agencies and the way in which those agencies process individuals.[11]

Focus — The Process of Labeling Behavior

The process of making the criminal is a process of tagging, defining, identifying, segregating, describing, emphasizing, making conscious and self-conscious; it becomes a way of stimulating, suggesting, emphasizing, and evoking the very traits that are complained of.

The person becomes the thing he is described as being. Nor does it seem to matter whether the valuation is made by those who would punish or by those who would reform. In either case the emphasis is upon conduct that is disapproved of. The parents or the policeman, the older brother or the court, the probation officer or the juvenile institution, insofar as they rest on the thing complained of, rest upon a false ground. Their very enthusiasm defeats their aim. The harder they work to reform the evil, the greater the evil grows under their hands. The persistent suggestion, with whatever good intentions, works mischief because it leads to bring out the bad behavior it would suppress. The way out is through a refusal to dramatize the evil. The less said about it the better.

[SOURCE: Frank Tannenbaum, Crime and the Community, (1938) pp.18-20. Reprinted with permission of Columbia University Press.]

The basic points of the labeling theory are:

1. Society has multiple values with differing degrees of overlap.

2. The quality of behavior is determined by the application of values to that individual's behavior. The identification of that behavior as deviant occurs through a reaction to that behavior.

3. Deviance exists only when there is a reaction to the behavior.

4. Once behavior is perceived and labeled deviant by a social audience, the individual who is responsible for the behavior is also labeled as deviant.

5. The reaction to behavior and the labeling process is more likely to occur when the actor is a member of the less socially powerful class.

6. Society tends to observe more closely those whom have been identified as deviant and therefore find even more deviance in those persons. Subsequent acts are reacted to more quickly and the label more firmly affixed.

7. Depending on the strength of an individual's original self-concept, once a person is labeled as deviant, the person may accept that label as self-identity.

8. A person labeled as criminal is perceived to be first and foremost a criminal; other attributes are generally ignored.

9. Further deviant behavior (secondary deviance) is a product of living and acting within the deviant label.

The labeling theory has had a great influence on the study of crime causation. It has caused us to re-examine our basic concepts regarding crime and criminals. It has also had its critics. One of the most serious criticisms is that it is not a theory, but a perspective, and that it has no systemic theoretical basis. In addition, empirical testing of the labeling theory is impossible.

Conflict & Critical Perspectives

Perspective	Spokesperson(s) and Period	Concepts
Conflict & Critical	many 1930s to present	Conflict of values, norms and laws Laws and enforcement tools of powerful
Marxist	Marx, Engel & Bonger 1870s-1930s	Crime should be viewed with scarcity of resources Crime more that state definition Product of class struggle
Conflict	many 1920s-1960s	Conflict fact of life Laws an attempt to control resources Laws express values of the powerful
Critical	Chambliss 1960s- present	Should focus on why some are considered criminal Justice system a tool for maintaining status quo
Social Reality	Quinney 1970s	Crime defined by those in power Laws used by ruling class to secure capitalist system
New Criminology	Taylor, Walton, & Young 1970s	Social reaction Crime is behavior that harms ruling class
Realist	Young & Dekeseredy 1980S	Marxist theories too simplistic Crime is also a problem in socialist countries Concern for specific analyses of crime and crime policies
Labeling	Tannenbaum 1930s-present	Labeling process Deviance exist only in relation to the reaction Should look at how behavior is perceived and labeled Secondary deviance Dramatization of evil

SUMMARY

- Most sociological approaches to crime causation view the social norms and laws of society as representative of the common feelings of society about what is right and proper. Both the conflict/critical and labeling theories, however, view our values, norms, and laws from the conflict perspectives.

- The conflict and critical theories contend that crime is simply behavior that threatens the ruling class. These theories hold that a relationship exists between deviant behavior and the law-making and law enforcing processes.

- To Marx and Engels, crime was a product of capitalism and the criminal is a victim of capitalism. Bonger contended that the economic system encouraged all people to be greedy and pursue their own interests. He also contended that we could eliminate crime by establishing a socialist society.

- According to the conflict theorists, law is a societal mechanism used by the group in power to maintain control of less powerful groups.

- Critical criminology is a mixture of the labeling and the radical theories. We should focus on why some people and not others are labeled as criminal rather than on the characteristics that distinguish criminals from noncriminals. The leading spokesperson for the critical criminologists is William Chambliss. Chambliss formulated the "social reality of crime" in order to question common assumptions that we hold regarding the nature of crime.

- New criminology advocated a critical look at the American criminal justice system. Its followers contended that our task should be to create a society in which the facts of human diversity are not subject to the power to criminalize.

- Realist criminology recognized that crime was also a problem in socialist countries and presented a very complex explanation of crime that was based on the victim, offender, state, and community.

- The labeling theory is concerned with the labels we place on people and the effects of those labels. By tagging a person as criminal, the individual becomes a criminal. The labeling theorists contend that the process of making a criminal is a process of tagging, defining, identifying, segregating, describing, and making conscious. In addition, they hold that deviance exists only when there is a reaction to the behavior, accordingly, we should also examine our reactions to the behavior.

DISCUSSION QUESTIONS

1. Explain the concepts involved in the critical approach to crime causation.
2. How would a Marxist explain crime?
3. Compare and contrast conflict criminology with the labeling theory.
4. Explain the labeling theory.

ENDNOTES—Chapter 7

1. George B. Vold and Thomas J. Bernard, *Theoretical Criminology*, 3rd ed. (New York:Oxford, 1986).

2. Karl Marx and Friedrich Engles, *The German Ideology,* (London: Lawrence and Wishart, 1965).

3. Willem Bonger, *Criminality and Economic Conditions*, (Boston: Little Brown, 1916).

4. Richard Quinney, *Critique of Legal Order,* (Boston: Little Brown, 1973 and Richard Quinney and John Wildeman, *The Problem of Crime,* 2d ed. (New York: Harper & Row, 1977).

5. I. Taylor, P. Walton, and J. Young, *The New Criminology: For A Social Theory of Deviance* (New York: Harper and Row, 1973).

6. William Chambliss, "Toward a Political Economy of Crime," *Theory and Society,* (1975) vol. 2 pp. 151-157.

7. Richard Quinney, *The Social Reality of Crime,* (Boston: Little Brown, 1970) pp 14-23.

8. Taylor, Walton, and Young, 1973: 281-282.

9. Williams and McShane, 1994:166.

10. Frank Tannenbaum, *Crime and the Community,* (Boston:Ginn, 1938).

11. Frank P. Williams III and Marilyn D. McShane, *Criminological Theory,* 2d ed. (Englewood Cliffs, NJ: Prentice-Hall, 1994), p. 141.

PART III

Crime and Punishment

Chapter 8

CRIMES AGAINST PERSONS

LEARNING OBJECTIVES

After studying this chapter, you should be able to:

- Understand the different types of murder.

- Differentiate between murder and manslaughter.

- List the different kinds of robbers.

- Recognize the various types of sex offenses.

- Differentiate between assault and battery.

MURDER

While the killing of another human being has been recognized for centuries as prohibited conduct, the exact nature of the crime was not clearly defined during early historical times. The English Common Law established three forms of homicide: justifiable homicide, excusable homicide and criminal homicide. All three of these homicides involved the killing of another human being. The distinction between them involved the circumstances surrounding the killing.

Justifiable homicide involved killing under circumstances sanctioned by the sovereign. Killing during war or acting as an executor for the state are examples of justifiable homicide. In this form of homicide, the person doing the killing does not harbor any evil intent and acts under "color of law."

Excusable homicide occurs when one kills another by mistake or in self-defense. When one kills another as a result of an unprovoked attack, the law would deem this to be an act of self-defense and thus the killing is "excused." If a person were driving his car in a neighborhood at 10 miles per hour and struck and killed a child who darted out from behind a bush, the law may hold the person was not at fault and therefore the killing would be labeled excusable homicide.

Criminal homicide is the most serious type of homicide. This type of killing involved unlawful conduct and evil intent on the part of the killer. Criminal homicide is not sanctioned by the state and is considered one of the most serious types of crimes in our society.

Criminal homicide is a common law crime created by English judges rather than the English legislature.[2] The early common law decisions have, in some instances, been translated into statutes in many of our states. These statutes have broken down the crime of criminal homicide into graded levels—murder, voluntary and involuntary manslaughter and negligent manslaughter. The most serious type of criminal homicide is *murder*. Anyone who has watched a television show believes he understands what is involved in murder. However, the laws surrounding murder can be confusing and complex. It requires a specific set of circumstances to establish the elements of murder.

Murder is the most serious of the criminal homicide classifications. According to the Federal Bureau of Investigation, there is one murder committed in the United States every 26 minutes.[3] While there have been, and will continue to be, sensational murderers such as the Manson Family Cult that killed pregnant actress Sharon Tate and several others, most homicides are not the stuff of movies or television. They range from killings stemming from arguments with family or acquaintances to deaths that occur as a result of simply not following the rules of the road when driving a car. Since early times, there has been controversy over the definition, classification, and types of murder. The following discussion of the elements of murder attempts to clarify this controversy.

Murder Defined

Murder is the purposeful, knowing, or reckless unlawful killing of another human being. The crime of murder can be divided into two basic elements:

1. **The defendant must have acted with the necessary specific intent to kill or engage in conduct so outrageous that the specific intent to kill will be inferred**.

   Courts and scholars have debated over the years on the proper name to use when describing the intent or *mens rea* necessary for murder. [4] The term **"malice aforethought"** was, at one time, the favored term when describing the defendant's intent in a murder case. Many states have moved away from using "malice aforethought" and have substituted other terms to define the necessary specific intent. For example, Pennsylvania uses the terms poison, lying in wait, willful, deliberate, or premeditated to establish the necessary specific intent. [5] New York uses terms such as "with the intent to cause the death of another" and "a depraved indifference to human life, or he "recklessly engages" in conduct causing a great risk of death.

   Contrary to popular television shows, murderers very seldom announce their state of mind before or during the commission of the crime. Courts are, therefore, required to review the facts of the case to determine if the defendant exhibited, via his actions, the necessary intent for murder. By whatever term or name it is called, the *mens rea* necessary for murder is a specific intent to kill or conduct so outrageous that the specific intent to kill will be inferred.

LOS ANGELES
Police Bulletin

2

(For Circulation Among Police Officers Exclusively)

OFFICIAL PUBLICATION OF POLICE DEPARTMENT, CITY OF LOS ANGELES, CALIFORNIA
Willie L. Williams, Chief of Police

APRIL 8, 1994   94-16

ARREST FOR MURDER

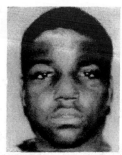

Suspect: **Tyree Jamal Dabney**

(Right Thumb)
Fingerprint Classification

4	1	At	4	
	1	tAat	-	
4	1	At	4	
	1	tAa	3	Possible reference

Felony Juvenile warrant #JUVYJ 0733101, charging Welfare and Institution Code Section 602/Penal Code Section 187(a), (murder), has been issued for the arrest of **Tyree Jamal Dabney**; alias: Tyree Dabnay, "Menace 3"; male Black, 17 years, DOB: 1-18-77, 5'4", 160 lbs., black hair, brown eyes, dark complexion; LA #2386335D, Main #04388973, NCIC file #W798225001, California Driver License #B3974125; no bail; will extradite.

On January 26, 1994, at approximately 1800 hours, the suspect and a co-suspect, attempted to rob a furniture store at 2220 South Vermont Avenue. During the robbery both suspects shot and killed the store owner. The co-suspect was also shot to death by the store owner. The suspects' vehicle and weapons are in custody.

Suspect Dabney's parents live in the 1900 Block South Harvard Blvd. in Los Angeles.

Caution: This suspect should be considered armed and dangerous.

REFER TO: DR #94-03 07060

INFORMATION FOR:

Detectives Moran and Masuyama, South Bureau Homicide, phone: (213) 237-1310. Between 1600 and 0800 hours, and on weekends and holidays, phone Detective Headquarters Division at (213) 485-2504.

KINDLY NOTIFY CHIEF OF POLICE, LOS ANGELES, CALIFORNIA

2. The defendant's conduct must have caused the death of another human being.

This element requires a death as a result of the defendant's acts or failure to act. Any behavior by the defendant will suffice. This element also includes the term "another human being." This term presumes a living person. Similarly, the definition of murder precludes suicide since that is the taking of one's own life.

The Model Penal Code (MPC 210.2) attempts to solve problems inherent in the various statutory definitions of murder. The code separates criminal homicide into three basic categories:

- Murder

- Manslaughter

- Negligent manslaughter

The Model Penal Code traces the history of murder from its common law background up to the adoption of the code. It points out that the common law definition of murder included the term "malice aforethought."[6] The drafters of the code then reviewed the legislative background involving the use of "malice aforethought" in the United States and concluded that use of the term should be abolished as it was too imprecise.[7]

The Model Penal Code states that the crime of murder occurs when:

- The defendant causes the death of another human being

  √ It is committed purposely or knowingly, or

  √ It is committed recklessly under the circumstances manifesting extreme indifference to the value of human life. Such recklessness is presumed if the defendant is an actor or an accomplice in the attempt or commission or flight after commission of the crimes of robbery, rape, deviate sexual intercourse by force or fear, arson, burglary, kidnapping, or felonious escape.

The majority of states have failed to adopt the Model Penal Code's definition of murder and continue to use terms such as *willful, deliberate,* and *premeditated killing of another*. Other states continue to use the term *malice aforethought* to encompass the terms *intentionally*, *knowingly*, or *recklessly*. Simply knowing the definition of murder is only the first step in understanding this crime. When someone kills another in a premeditated or reckless way, the courts and society must examine the killing to determine how serious or heinous the act was. This determination assists in defining the degree of murder.

Degrees of Murder

In early English common law there were no degrees of murder. However, America developed the "first degree" and "second degree" concept of murder in Pennsylvania as early as 1794. This law contained a preamble which explained the rationale behind establishing different degrees of murder. The statute stated: "And whereas the several offenses, which are included under the general denomination of murder, differ so greatly from each other in the degree of their atrociousness, that it is unjust to involve them in the same punishment." [8]

The two forms or degrees of murder are based upon the seriousness of the type of criminal homicide. **First degree murder** is normally classified as a killing which is premeditated. This type of killing occurs when it is determined the defendant had time to reflect on the act and form the intent to kill.[9] Examples of premeditated murders include those where the defendant carries out the killing by the use of explosives, lying in wait to ambush the victim, using poison to accomplish the homicide, or killing by torture. Most states have very simple second degree murder statutes that hold all other murders are **murders of the second degree**.

The establishment of degrees of murder is an effort on the part of the society to divide this type of homicide into two classifications. The classification of murder into degrees assists us in determining the seriousness of this crime.

VOLUNTARY MANSLAUGHTER

Voluntary manslaughter is considered the second most serious form of criminal homicide. While it requires the same type of intent that is necessary for murder, the crime is "downgraded" to voluntary manslaughter if there was a factual pattern that provoked the defendant into killing a person. This provocation does not excuse the defendant's acts, rather society has made a determination that some facts inflame the passions of a reasonable person to the point that he will react by killing the instigator. This killing, while intended, is not in the same class as murder and, therefore, should be treated differently.

Voluntary Manslaughter Defined

Voluntary manslaughter can be defined as the intentional and unlawful killing of another person in response to adequate provocation. It is composed of three elements:

1. The defendant must have acted with the same intent required for the crime of murder (express or implied intent to kill).

Voluntary manslaughter is an intentional killing of another. However, a majority of states downgrade this killing from murder to manslaughter based upon the fact that the defendant was provoked into killing the victim.

In order to reduce the crime from murder to voluntary manslaughter, the provocation must be of such a nature as to cause a reasonable person to kill. Yet, reasonable people, no matter what the provocation, do not kill. The law recognizes this fact by holding that one who kills upon adequate provocation is guilty of manslaughter, and one who acts in a reasonable manner in killing another, such as in self-defense, is not guilty of any crime.

2. There must be adequate provocation for the defendant's actions.

For the defendant to claim adequate provocation, two requirements must be satisfied: (1)The provocation must be adequate. While the Model Penal Code dispenses with this requirement, a majority of the states still use it.[10] (2)The killing must be in the heat of passion. The provocation must be so extreme that the defendant acted in a murderous rage. The defendant's passion must be sudden and with no cooling-off period. The Model Penal Code also eliminates this requirement. The drafters of the code reasoned that if the defendant was not under the influence of extreme mental or emotional distress at the time of the killing, no cooling-off period had occurred. The majority of the states still retain this requirement and use the **reasonable person standard** to determine if sufficient time has elapsed to enable a reasonable person to gain control of his or her passion.

3. **The defendant's conduct must have caused the death of another human being.**

The traditional view requires a causal relationship between the defendant's act and another's death.

The Model Penal Code does away with use of the term "voluntary" or "involuntary" manslaughter. It defines **manslaughter** as:

- The unlawful killing of another human being

  √ Committed in a reckless manner, or

  √ Committed under the influence of extreme mental or emotional disturbance for which there is a reasonable explanation or excuse.

The drafters of the code did not believe the law of manslaughter was well developed by the states. The basis upon which this section of the code was founded was that the pattern of statutory treatment of manslaughter by the states was substantially deficient for failing to confront the major policy questions raised by this offense.[11] New York has accepted the Model Penal Code view in it's definition of manslaughter of the first degree.[12]

A majority of states, as well as the federal government, still use the concept of voluntary manslaughter. We as a society seem to be reluctant to punish a person by charging him or her with murder when there were objective facts to support the position that he or she was provoked into killing another human being.

Voluntary manslaughter is based upon the concept that a killing that would ordinarily be classified as murder may be downgraded to voluntary manslaughter if adequate provocation exists. While the Model Penal Code has eliminated the term voluntary manslaughter, a majority of states still retain this classification of homicide which is based upon the concept of provocation. **Adequate provocation** requires the defendant be provoked, that the provocation be so grievous that he/she acted in the heat of passion and without his/her rage cooling off. While voluntary manslaughter requires intentional acts as part of the killing, the next form of homicide only requires an act which results in a death.

INVOLUNTARY MANSLAUGHTER

Involuntary manslaughter is one of the most confusing forms of criminal homicide in that this crime involves the death of another person under factual situations that do not establish a wicked and depraved mind. Rather in some cases, the death resulted from activity that many persons in society engage in on a daily basis—drinking and driving, speeding in a school zone, cleaning a handgun or playing with a weapon without checking to insure that it is unloaded.

Involuntary Manslaughter Defined

Involuntary manslaughter is the unintentional killing of another human being caused during the commission of an unlawful act not amounting to a felony or as the result of criminal negligence. The crime of involuntary manslaughter can be divided into three elements:

1. **The killing of another human being was unintentional**.

   The defendant need not intend to kill the victim to be found guilty of involuntary manslaughter. He need only have the general intent to commit the act, or acts that caused the death.

2. **Death occurred as a result of an unlawful act or the defendant's criminal negligence.**

   If the defendant commits a misdemeanor and death results, she may be charged with involuntary manslaughter. This type of unlawful act is sometimes referred to as the **Misdemeanor-Manslaughter Doctrine**.[13] The most common form of misdemeanor is a traffic offense; however, other misdemeanors will meet this requirement. For example, a simple battery may suffice. An unintentional killing caused by any criminally negligent act of the defendant is involuntary manslaughter. The courts require more

The Au Pair Murder Trial

A teen-age British girl, working as an au pair (i.e., a nanny who cares for children in exchange for living expenses), Louise Woodward, became the center of an international media feeding frenzy when she was accused of killing eight-month old Matthew Eappen.

On February 4, 1997 Louise Woodward called the police and stated that Matthew Eappen was having difficulty breathing. When the paramedics arrived, they diagnosed Matthew as suffering from a two-and-a-half-inch skull fracture. The baby spent four days in the intensive care unit of the hospital before he died. In addition to the skull fracture, Matthew also had a month-old wrist fracture.

Woodward was charged with first degree murder for allegedly shaking Matthew to death. The prosecutors stated that she admitted to shaking the baby and to dropping him on the floor and tossing him on a bed. The prosecutors also asserted that Matthew hit the floor with the force equivalent to being thrown from a second-story window. They concluded by stating that the injuries from the fall and the shaking caused Matthew's death, and in Massachusetts, that conduct constitutes murder.

The defense team argued several theories: (1) a pre-existing medical condition caused the death, and (2) that Matthew's two-year old brother inflicted the injuries.

On October 7, 1997, the first day of the trial, the prosecution began to present the evidence against Woodward. This evidence included testimony by the officers who responded to her 9-1-1 call and a series of medical experts who testified on direct examination that Matthew died as a result of severe head trauma normally associated with shaken baby syndrome. However, the defense was able to cross-examine the experts in such a manner as to weaken the effect of their testimony. The defense presented a number of character witnesses regarding Woodward's honesty and affection for children. Expert testimony by the defense raised the specter that William died from an earlier injury. Finally, Louise Woodward testified and denied ever shaking Matthew.

Outside the presence of the jury, the prosecution asked for jury instructions that would allow the jury to consider the verdicts of murder, voluntary manslaughter or involuntary manslaughter. The defense objected to these instructions and asked the judge to instruct the jury to limit their options to first or second degree murder or acquittal. The defense's motion was based upon the assumption that Woodward would stand a greater chance of conviction if the jury had several options to choose from. Judge Hiller Zobel agreed with the defense's request.

The jury deliberated approximately 30 hours before returning with a second degree murder verdict against Louise Woodward. During sentencing, Woodward maintained her innocence, claiming not to know what happened to Matthew. The 19-year-old au pair was sentenced to mandatory life imprisonment with the possibility of parole after 15 years.

The trial and verdict caused an uproar on both sides of the Atlantic with Britishers forming committees to raise funds to help Woodward.

The defense filed a motion to set aside the verdict or reduce the charges to manslaughter. On November 10, 1997, the judge issued his ruling and reduced Woodward's charge to manslaughter. He then released her with credit for time served.

Drug-Related Murders, 1988-95

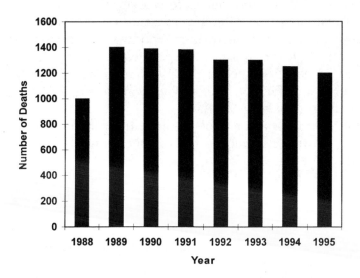

than simple "civil negligence." The criminal negligence standard involves a high and unreasonable risk of death to another.

The handling of firearms calls for a higher degree of care than normal, and criminal negligence will be found in the unintended killing by the defendant when he was handling or using a weapon.[14] The Model Penal Code deals with these situations under negligent manslaughter which is discussed below.

In addition to the causal link between the defendant's act and the death, some courts require a close connection between the time and place of the act and the death. [15] Additionally, for the defendant's conduct to be unlawful, it is not necessary that he know that some law forbids his conduct. [16] There is no requirement that the defendant have any specific intent to violate the law which makes his conduct unlawful.

3. The defendant's unlawful act or negligence caused the death.

The defendant may violate a statute or act in a criminally negligent manner but unless her conduct causes the victim's death, the courts will not hold her criminally liable. For example, a person who is required to have a license to perform services might perform those services and the victim might die. Unless the failure to obtain a license was the activity which caused the death, the courts will not hold the defendant liable. [17]

The Model Penal Code does not classify unintentional killing as involuntary manslaughter. Rather it classified homicides that are committed recklessly as manslaughter. The code defines **recklessly** as follows:

A person acts recklessly with respect to a material element of an offense when he consciously disregards a substantial and unjustifiable risk that the material element exists or will result from his conduct. The risk must be of such a nature and degree that the actor's failure to perceive it, considering the nature and purpose of his conduct and the circumstances known to him, involves a gross deviation from the standard of care that a reasonable person would observe in the actor's situation.

The federal system defines **involuntary manslaughter** as the killing during the commission of an unlawful act not amounting to a felony or killing that results from the commission of a lawful act without due caution.[18] A majority of the states still retain the involuntary manslaughter classification. These states define this crime in much the same terms as the federal government.

Involuntary manslaughter is the unintended killing of another person. The law will hold the defendant accountable in any one of two situations: (1) a death resulted when the defendant was committing an unlawful act, not amounting to a felony, or (2) the defendant acted with criminal negligence which caused the death of another.

NEGLIGENT MANSLAUGHTER

Negligent manslaughter is a "new" form of criminal homicide. It is based upon the Model Penal Code position that voluntary and involuntary manslaughter are difficult concepts to apply in some instances. As a result, the drafters of the Model Penal Code established the concept of the crime of negligent manslaughter.

Negligent Manslaughter Defined

Negligent manslaughter is the unintentional killing of another human being caused by the negligence of the defendant. The crime of negligent manslaughter is composed of three elements:

1. The killing of another human being was unintentional.

Similar to involuntary manslaughter, the defendant does not have to intend to kill another person. The death of the person may be unintentional.

2. The death resulted from a negligent act by the defendant.

The Model Penal Code and those states that have adopted it's position require more than "civil" negligence to hold a defendant liable for negligent homicide. The courts usually require "gross negligence." This is a higher standard than mere "civil negligence" but does not reach the level of recklessness necessary for voluntary manslaughter.

In those states, such as California, that have adopted a separate vehicular manslaughter statute, mere negligence may be sufficient to charge a defendant with vehicular manslaughter. Criminal negligence involves the failure of the defendant to perceive the risk in a situation where the offender has a legal duty of awareness.

3. The defendant's negligence caused the death.

This is the traditional causation requirement. The negligent act or actions of the defendant must cause the death of the victim.

As stated earlier, the Model Penal Code has abolished the distinction between voluntary and involuntary manslaughter. It classifies manslaughter into two crimes: manslaughter and negligent manslaughter. The manslaughter classification was discussed under voluntary manslaughter earlier. Under the Model Penal Code, negligent manslaughter is defined as follows:

- Criminal homicide constitutes negligent homicide when it is committed negligently.

The code's definition of negligence requires proof of substantial fault and limits criminal sanctions to cases where "the significance of the circumstances of fact would be apparent to one who shares the community's general sense of right and wrong."[19] The code imposes criminal liability for inadvertent risk situations only on those cases where the defendant is grossly insensitive to the interests and claims of another person in society.

A majority of the states and the federal government have not adopted the Model Penal Code view. These states still retain the voluntary/involuntary classification. However, many of these states use criminal negligence as a grounds for conviction under their involuntary manslaughter statutes.[20]

Negligent manslaughter is a relatively new crime. The line between gross negligence and recklessness is thin, yet courts and legislatures use the distinction as a method of classifying homicides by degree of seriousness.

The negligent manslaughter statutes are attempts by the states to hold persons accountable when they violate society's norms beyond mere negligence, but below the standard of recklessness.

ROBBERY

Robbery is considered as a violent personal crime. It is also one of the most serious forms of theft-related crimes in America. It is included as one of four major violent crimes grouped together by the FBI for purposes of comparison. The other three crimes are rape, assault, and murder.

Some texts include robbery and extortion in chapters that deal with property crimes.[21] Even when these crimes are included in chapters dealing with property crimes, they are discussed together.[22] We have decided to place robbery in this chapter on Crimes Against Persons for several reasons. First and foremost, the scholars that drafted the Model Penal Code believed that robbery was of such a distinctive nature that it deserved a separate article. The drafters explained that this crime was being defined as a distinct offense because of the special danger associated with the commission of the crime against the victim.

The second reason that robbery deserves special attention is that it is a crime that combines both theft and assault into one menacing act. The specter of an armed robber lurking nearby in the darkness rests in the mind of every person as they walk to their car late at night. From 1980 to 1989, the number of arrests for robbery increased 7.9% from 102,821 to 110,952.[23] Citizens are afraid to leave their homes to go shopping for fear of being robbed even in broad daylight. We are becoming a nation of individual armed fortresses which in fact are our homes. Any student of criminology, criminal Justice, or sociology needs to understand the dynamics of this violent theft-related crime on our law enforcement agencies, our cities and our society.

On a recurring basis, we read of persons being robbed as they leave work. Stores, both large and small, have been the target of armed robberies. Daily news reports cover the drama of bank and armored car robberies. It is no wonder that the average citizen is frightened by the prospect of facing a street mugger. Statistics validate this fear. Fifty-five percent of all robberies take place between 6:00 p.m. and 6:00 a.m. One in every three involves injury to the victim. Seventeen percent occur at or near the victim's home, and ten percent occur in a parking lot or garage.[24] Less than one percent of the victims suffered no monetary loss. Over 28 percent lost less than fifty dollars, and at the other extreme, 18 percent were robbed of five hundred dollars or more.[25]

Typology of Robbers

There have been numerous studies and reports concerning the crime of robbery. These range from statistical analysis of the crime to attempts to classify robbery by patterns. One classic typology was conducted by McClintock and Gibson who categorized robberies into five distinct areas:

- *Robbery of persons who control money or goods*. This category includes robberies of commercial establishments such as jewelry stores, banks, and offices.

- *Robbery in an open area*. These robberies include street mugging, purse snatching and other attacks on streets, parking lots and open garages.

- *Robbery in private residences.* These robberies normally occur after the offender has broken into the victim's home.

- *Robbery by a short term acquaintance.* This classification includes robbery that occurs after a chance encounter. A meeting at a party, a bar, or after a brief sexual encounter are examples of this type of robbery.

- *Robbery by a long term acquaintance.* This type of robbery is relatively rare, but does occur on a regular basis. This robbery may include the robbery from persons who have been romantically involved with the offender for a short period of time.[26]

Another well known typology was conducted by John Conklin.[27] He classified robberies by identifying the type of offender rather than the location of the robbery. Conklin classified robberies into four major categories:

- *Professional Robber.* The professional robber is a career criminal. This is a way of life with these offenders. They plan and execute these robberies very carefully. They operate in groups with specific tasks assigned to each member. They may plan and carry out three to four major robberies in any given year.

- *Opportunist Robber.* This is the most common type of robber. They do not specialize in robbery. These offenders will commit all types of larceny offenses with robbery being just one of the many crimes they commit. They normally do not plan their crime, but act when the opportunity presents itself.

- *Addict Robber.* These offenders are addicted to a controlled substance and rob to support their habit. However, most drug abusers are interested in quick and safe crimes and will commit burglary or other theft-related crimes before turning to robbery. The addict robbery does not plan the robbery in the same detail as the professional robber, but is more cautious than the opportunist robber.

- *Alcoholic Robber.* These offenders have little interest in planning their offenses. They engage in robberies to support their addiction. Many of them commit the crime while intoxicated, and as a result, they are caught more often than the other classes.

These and other scholars have attempted to classify various aspects of the crime of robbery in an effort to explain why or how it occurs. This information assists society in understanding this dangerous and personal crime. Robbery is a personal crime in that the victim comes into contact with the offender for a period of time necessary to cause fear or fright. The length of time of contact and the level of fear necessary to constitute robbery is explained under the discussion of the elements of robbery.

Robbery Defined

Robbery is the theft of property from the person or immediate presence of another by use of force or fear. The crime of robbery has three distinct elements:

(1) Theft of Property.

This element of robbery is very similar to the element contained in the discussion of larceny. One of the distinctions between larceny and robbery is that many larceny statutes establish a value that determines whether the theft will be treated as a misdemeanor or felony. This is not the case when dealing with robbery. The amount of the item taken is immaterial to establishing the seriousness of the crime. It will be considered robbery if the mugger on the street demands and receives one dollar or five thousand dollars.

The offender must intend to keep the property. Thus robbery is a specific intent crime. Similar to larceny, there must be specific intent to deprive the owner of the property. In robbery this is fairly easy to prove by looking at the defendant's words or actions or both. The defendant does not have to retain the property for any length of time to establish this intent. For example, if an offender pulls a gun on a citizen, demands the money and then flees the scene with the money, the fact that a police officer arrests the offender one block from the scene does not allow the defendant to claim he did not intend to keep the money. The courts will infer the specific intent to keep the property.

The property may be anything or of any value. An empty wallet is property for purposes of robbery. If a victim were required to part with the wallet, this element is complete. It does not matter that the fair market value of the wallet may be two dollars. The reason the legislatures and courts have taken this position is based upon a combination of the second and third element of the crime—robbery is a personal crime involving danger to the victim.

(2) Taking.

The taking of the property must be from the "person or immediate presence" of another. The term **immediate presence** is broadly interpreted to include any place within sight or hearing, or even smell. In one famous case, a cow was stolen from a large heard of cattle that was scattered for a mile or more on a plain. The heard was being watched by a cowboy. The court held that the taking of the cow was from the immediate presence of the cowboy.[28]

(3) From the person or presence of another.

Someone may commit a burglary, and the victim will not find out until they discover the property is missing from their home or business. Robbery requires the property to be taken from the person or from that person's immediate presence. The term "presence of another" means simply that the offender must take property that he does not own.

This element of robbery does not require that the victim physically have possession of the item which is taken. The property does not have to be attached to the victim by a string, belt or other item. It is sufficient if the victim has control over the item. For example, if the victim were sitting on a park bench with his package laying next to him and the offender approached him, pulled a gun and stated, "I'm taking your package, don't try to stop me," a robbery has been committed, even though the victim was not holding onto the package at the time the offense occurred. If a person has physical control over property, and is prevented from stopping the crime because of force or fear exerted by the actions of the offender, this element has been satisfied. A different problem arises if the victim has control over the property but is unaware that the offender has taken it. This issue is addressed in the final element of the crime.

(4) By use of force or fear.

The traditional robbery occurs when the offender confronts the victim, brandishes a weapon of some sort and demands money. This is clearly an act of placing the victim in fear for his or her safety. The second situation arises when the robber physically assaults the victim, and as a result, the victim surrenders his or her property or is prevented from resisting as a result of the assault.

There are other situations that are not so clear as it relates to this element of the crime. Is a pickpocket guilty of robbery? The offender has removed property from the person of another. However, the victim is unaware of the act, therefore the final element of robbery, force or fear, is missing, Accordingly, a pickpocket is guilty of larceny, not robbery. What if force is added to the situation? Is the mugger who approaches from behind and snatches an old lady's purse from her hand quickly without giving her a chance to resist guilty of robbery? There is the removal of property from the presence of another and force is used to accomplish the crime. The courts are divided on this issue with some holding that because the victim was unaware of the act until after it was completed, the final element of robbery is missing and the crime is larceny.[29] The rationale for this position is that the victim was not touched, nor placed in fear of bodily harm. Other states specifically include this type of act as robbery.[30] The better position is that because the victim may be harmed as the purse is jerked from her possession, the rationale for robbery, that of specific harm to the victim during a taking of property, has been satisfied, and this type of act should fall under the definition of robbery.

The force or fear necessary for the commission of robbery is a complex factual determination. Questions such as where the property is located, when the victim became aware of the crime and whether there was physical force or intimidation used must be answered when addressing this element. As the above discussion indicates, robbery is both a dangerous and personal crime. It is a combination of larceny and assault that is considered to be of such a distinctive nature that the drafters of the Model Penal Code set it apart from other theft crimes by including the offense as a separate article in the code.

The drafters of the Model Penal Code examined the history of the crime of robbery and pointed out that the average citizen is especially frightened of the violent petty theft that operates in the streets and alleys of almost every city. The ordinary citizen may become angry at surreptitious larceny, embezzlement or fraud, but the specter of a street mugger committing a robbery late at night on a deserted street raises terror in the minds of almost everyone.

The Model Penal Code defines robbery as:

- A person is guilty of robbery if, in the course of committing a theft, he:

√ Inflicts serious bodily injury upon another; or

√ Threatens another with or purposely puts him in fear of immediate serious bodily injury; or

√ Commits or threatens immediately to commit any felony of the first or second degree.

An act shall be deemed "in the course of committing a theft" if it occurs in an attempt to commit theft or in flight after the attempt or commission.

The drafters of the Model Penal Code examined the question of whether the crime of robbery should continue to be treated as a separate offense since the core of the crime is the combination of theft and the fact or threat of immediate harm. One argument is that the offense could be treated as two separate crimes and punished accordingly. However, this course was not adopted by the drafters of the code for two reasons: First, the combination of some types of assault with theft is properly regarded as a more serious offense than the gradation yielded by the cumulation of penalties for the two offenses viewed separately. The second justification was that long tradition reinforced the judgment that robbery be considered as a separate crime.[31]

The Model Penal Code modernizes the common law rules regarding robbery by punishing the act as a crime even if the robber does not obtain anything of value. In addition, the code makes it a crime to lawfully obtain property, then use force or fear to prevent the owner from reclaiming it. At the same time, the code retains the essence of the common law crime—that of a theft committed by force or fear.

SEX OFFENSES

The discussion of sex offenses is a necessity in any examination of crimes against persons. This section is not intended to cause anyone displeasure or discomfort. For some students, this will be their first exposure to physical acts that are not considered normal or even talked about in polite company. Some of the acts discussed in this section will show a twisted and sick mind. Sex crimes or offenses are repulsive to modern society, and they range from violent and gross to simply a seamy side of modern day life.

Many of these crimes, while they involve acts that could be classified as having sexual connotations, are from many experts' points of view nothing more than violent acts of aggression against women. Some authorities have placed rape under the heading of violent crimes, and reserved discussion of other sex offenses to general public disorder chapters. [32] We have elected to place all serious sex-related offenses in one section for purposes of discussion and comparison. One of the most well-known and publicized sex offenses is that of rape.

Rape

Rape is one of the most feared, misunderstood and repulsive crimes in the United States. Until the trial of Senator Ted Kennedy's nephew, William Kennedy Smith, many Americans had unrealistic images of rapists. They believed a rapist was some sort of low-life animal who prowled the night and looked like a Neanderthal with a sloping brow and beady eyes. While William Kennedy Smith was acquitted of all charges, the publicity surrounding the trial in Florida, exposed millions of people to the courtroom drama of a rape case. The "experts" that were hired by the various media discussed all aspects surrounding the crime of rape. A rapist looks just like the neighborhood boy or man who delivers the morning paper. He can be anywhere and strike at anytime. While many scholars have researched the issue, no one has yet to come forward with a single acceptable reason on why men engage in the crime of rape. There is no known cause or genetic factor that predisposes some men to engage in this type of assaultive sexual behavior. However, there have been several theories that have been advanced which attempt to explain the reasons why certain persons carry out these acts against women.

Donald Symons suggests that man's biological sex drive is behind his aggressive assault. Rape is viewed as an instinctive drive associated with the need of perpetuating the species. Symons' theory holds that men still have this primitive sex drive that mandates they have sex with as many women as possible. His position holds that rape is intertwined with sexuality as well as violence.[33]

Paul Gebhard sets forth the position that rapists are suffering from psychotic tendencies or have sadistic feelings toward women.[34] In addition, A. Nicholas Groth suggests every rapist exhibits anger, power and sadism.[35] These two scholars accept the psychological explanation for the cause of rape.

Diana Russell, in her book *The Politics of Rape*, sets forth the theory that rape is part of the masculine qualities accepted in U.S. society. Russell's position is that in our society, young boys are taught to be aggressive and dominate. Men learn to separate their sexual desire from other intimate feelings such as love and respect. Rape is viewed as a form of domination over women.[36]

There are numerous other theories on why men engage is this assaultive behavior towards women. At the present time, there does not appear to be one generally accepted cause for this crime. What most authorities will agree upon is that rape is a violent crime; it is a crime involving the sexual organs of both the offender and the victim, and it is a crime that subjects the women to psychological duress and pain.[37] The crime of rape may appear at first glance to be a relatively simple crime with two basic elements, however, these elements contain numerous complex issues that raise both legal and emotional issues.

Rape is an unlawful act of sexual intercourse with another person against that person's will by force, fear or trick. The crime of rape has two elements:

(1) Unlawful sexual intercourse.

This element is specifically gender neutral in its approach. Traditional common law and early statutes authorized prosecution of rape against a man. As will be discussed, this is the view of the Model Penal Code. Early courts and legislators took the position that a man cannot be raped either by another man or by a female. In fact, many of the existing statutes hold to this position. Michigan is an example of a state with a more progressive statute that defines rape in gender-neutral language.[38] To assume that men can rape women and not to accept the possibility that a women can rape a man is to perpetrate a position that women are the weaker sex and naturally submissive to the demands of men.

For purposes of rape, **sexual intercourse** requires penetration of the penis into the vagina. Penetration does not have to result in a completed act of sexual intercourse. There is no requirement for ejaculation or emission by the male for the crime to have been complete. This position allows for a virgin to be raped and still retain her hymen.

In early court cases, the prior sexual history of the victim was admitted. There were a variety of theories upon which the victim could be cross-examined regarding her previous sexual activity. For example, to show that, because she had intercourse with another person, she is more likely to have consented to intercourse with the defendant, thus illustrating that she is a person of loose morals and therefore would have intercourse with anyone including the defendant. Modern day statutes prevent introduction of this kind of evidence. These statues are normally called **rape shield laws** and prohibit the defendant or his attorney from questioning the victim regarding her previous sexual activity or introducing other evidence surrounding her past sexual practices.[39]

Closely related to the victim's past sexual history, but separate from it, is the issue of consent. This is one of the most complex and emotional issues in the crime of rape. The classic defense in most rape cases is that the victim consented to sexual intercourse. Of course defendants do not raise this issue if there has been physical force involved or the victim was underage and therefore incapable of granting consent. However, many rapes involve the use of threats or slight force which result in overcoming the victim's initial resistance. In these cases, the defendant will argue that the victim consented, and therefore it was not rape but consensual sexual activity between adults. Tied to the issue of consent is society's position that minors cannot knowingly give consent to certain acts. One of these acts is sexual intercourse. Issues regarding intercourse with minors, unconscious persons and incompetents will be discussed in more detail in the following section.

(2) Committed by use of force, fear or trick.

There are three distinct situations that are covered by this element of the crime of rape. It may occur as the result of **force** which overcomes the victim's resistance, the victim may be placed in a situation where she **fears** for her safety and therefore submits to the act, or the victim may be **tricked** and become incapable of giving consent.

In the first situation, the defendant utilizes brute force to require the victim to submit to the sexual acts. This force may take the form of a physical beating with fists, clubs, or other objects. The victim is left battered as a result of the defendant's acts. There are physical marks on her body as a result of the violent assault by the perpetrator. She may receive bruises, her clothing may be ripped from her body and she may in a state of physical and emotional shock as a result of her encounter.

The second situation is very similar to the first, but occurs when the victim no longer resists the attackers advances as a result of fear for her safety. This fear may be caused by the defendant's banishing of a weapon whether it be a knife, gun or club. In these situations, the victim may comply with the attackers demands and not have any marks on her as a result of the incident.

The third situation involves the defendant "tricking" the victim. This is a very broad category that includes sex with minors and incompetents as well as use of alcohol or drugs to render the victim incapable of giving informed consent. As briefly discussed above, our society has determined that persons under a certain age cannot legally give consent for purposes of engaging in sexual intercourse. The common law held consensual intercourse with a minor under the age of 10 was rape.[40] In modern society, the general rule is that when a female reaches the age of 18, she is considered an adult and capable of entering into binding contracts and giving consent for purposes of engaging in lawful sexual intercourse. This issue does not normally arise, however, at this age. Consent becomes important when the defendant engages in sexual intercourse with a minor between the ages of 3 to 16. There are numerous incidents of child sexual abuse where the defendant has engaged in a course of sexual intercourse with a minor over a period of years. Because the victim cannot *legally* agree to intercourse, the defendant may be charged with rape. There are wide variations among the states regarding the age at which a minor can give consent. Many jurisdictions have special statutes that prohibit sexual relations with young children. Some of these statutes entitle this type of sexual intercourse statutory rape, and some impose penalties as severe as forcible rape for this type of conduct.

A person who is classified as mentally incompetent cannot legally give consent to sexual relations. When a person takes advantage of these types of victims and has intercourse, the law allows him to be charged with rape. The issue with this type of situation is defining what constitutes **mental incompetence**. States have approached this issue in a variety of ways: Some states hold a person to be incompetent if she is incapable of expressing any judgment on the matter.[41] Other states impose a requirement that the woman did not have the ability to comprehend the moral nature of the act.[42] A third group of states addressed the issue of incompetence by asking if the women had the capacity to understand the character and probable consequences of sexual intercourse.[43] The first approach is too restrictive and would only protect those women suffering from an extreme form of mental retardation. The second alternative is vague in that the courts would have to examine the victim's moral values. The last approach seems to allow the most latitude and protect both the defendant and victim. The drafters of the Model Penal Code have adopted this approach with a slight variation which requires the defendant to know that the victim is suffering from a mental condition which renders her incapable of appraising the nature of her conduct.[49]

This third category also involves "tricking" the victim by causing her to use alcohol or drugs to the point that she cannot legally consent to the act or she is rendered unconscious as a result of her ingestion of liquor or drugs. In these cases, the victim may be unconscious or so impaired that she cannot consent to the act of sexual intercourse. The test in this area is similar to the approach used when dealing with incompetent victims.

ACQUAINTANCE RAPE

Acquaintance rape is the crime of the 1980s and 1990s. Acquaintance rape involves cohesive sexual advances that conclude in intercourse. It normally occurs between persons that are dating or have a social relationship. It may involve threats or actual force which cause the victim to submit to the act. Many of the victims do not report such incidents because it does not involve a stranger "jumping out of the bushes."[44]

From 1973 to 1992, 47% of all rapes reported to the police by female victims involved nonstrangers. Of these rapes, 47% of the offenders were able to complete the act simply by threatening the victim. What is more startling is the fact that 22% of all females raped by nonstrangers did not report the crime because they were afraid of reprisals by the offender or his family or friends.[45]

Authorities in the field are split regarding the actual percentage of rapes involving nonstrangers. Some believe the actual number of "acquaintance rapes" is very low in comparison to violent rapes by strangers.[46] Others accept the Department of Justice statistics regarding the percentage of rapes by nonstrangers and attribute the low numbers to a reluctance on the part of the victim to report these types of sexual advances.[47] One survey reported that on Midwestern college campus 100 Percent of all the rapists knew their victim.[48]

The states and courts have adopted various laws regarding the crime of rape. At present, there is no single definition that is accepted by all the jurisdictions. Because of this confusion, the drafters of the Model Penal Code studied this crime in detail and adopted a proposal that attempts to address the many diverse issues surrounding the crime of rape.

The Model Penal Code was concerned with the divergent listing of acts involved with the crime of rape and attempted to establish a single definition with different grading schemes by dividing the crime into three felony levels. The code reserves the most serious category for those acts of aggression resulting in serious bodily injury or where there is no voluntary social or sexual relationship between the parties.

The Model Penal Code defines **rape** as:

- A male who has sexual intercourse with a female, not his wife, is guilty of rape if:

  √ He compels her to submit by force or by threat of imminent death, serious bodily injury, extreme pain or kidnaping to be inflicted on anyone, or

  √ He has substantially impaired her power to appraise or control her conduct by administrating or employing without her knowledge drugs, intoxicants or other means for the purpose of preventing resistance; or

√ The female is unconscious; or

√ The female is less than 10 years old.

Rape is a felony of the second degree unless (i) in the course thereof the actor inflicts serious bodily injury upon anyone, or (ii) the victim was not a voluntary social companion of the actor upon the occasion of the crime and had not previously permitted him sexual liberties, in which case the offense is a felony of the first degree. [50]

The Model Penal Code does not classify unlawful sexual intercourse between a husband and his wife as rape. This is the case event if the husband physically assaults his wife and forces her to submit to the act. Today, many states have statutes which authorize the prosecution of a husband for the rape of his wife.[51]

In addition, the code is specific that only a man can rape a woman and not vise versa. Both of these positions are out of date with modern society. Today, we understand the dynamics of spousal abuse and can accept the fact that a husband may rape his wife. As discussed above, modern thinking legislators have made the crime gender neutral thereby allowing a female to be charged with raping a male.

The drafters of the code seemed to be concerned with the burden of proof in the crime of rape and required the victim to suffer bodily injury or be raped by a stranger to constitute the most serious form of this crime. This flies in the face of modern society and imposes a stigma on a person who is raped by an acquaintance and does not resist to the point that she is physically injured. In addition, the drafters ignore the realities of modern-day life and the fear that a woman may endure when dragged from a street and raped. The drafters of the Model Penal Code would require her to either resist to the point that she is physically injured or require the assailant to beat her before the crime is considered one of the more serious felonies. The more acceptable view is set forth in the discussion above which does not require bodily injury for the crime of rape. The federal statutes are in accord with this position. The Model Penal Code attempted to define, very narrowly, the crime of rape, and in the process, imposed an additional burden of proof on the victim of this crime. As the above discussion indicates, rape is not a simple crime.

Rape is more than a simple violent assault that ends when the perpetrator finishes his or her physical act. It can have long term psychological effects on its victims. These consequences include Rape Trauma Syndrome, Acute Stress Disorder, and Post Traumatic Stress Disorder.

Rape trauma syndrome is a type of posttraumatic stress disorder. The essential feature of this disorder is the development of characteristic symptoms after the sexual assault that are usually beyond the range of ordinary human experience. Often the victim will have recurrent painful memories of the incident, or recurring dreams or nightmares in which the incident is reexperienced. Diminished responsiveness to the external world, called **psychic numbing** usually starts after the rape. A victim may feel detached from others and complain that she has lost the ability to become interested in activities that were previously meaningful to her—particularly those associated with intimacy, tenderness, and sexuality.

Acute stress disorder (ASD) is acute stress that is experienced in the immediate aftermath of a traumatic event. This is a newly categorized disorder that was first listed in the *Diagnostic and Statistical Manual of Disorders*, 4th edition (DSM-IV) in 1994.[52] The characteristic feature of Acute Stress Disorder is the development of anxiety, dissociative symptoms, and other manifestations that occur within one month after exposure to the traumatic event. In order to receive a diagnosis of ASD, the victim must have experienced, witnessed, or have been confronted with an event that involved actual or threatened death, serious injury, or a threat to the physical safety of the victim or others. Additionally, the victim's response to such a condition must involve intense fear, helplessness or horror. This diagnosis requires that the victim experience several of the symptoms of Posttraumatic Stress Disorder (PTSD), and that he or she must experience three of five PTSD dissociative symptoms during or immediately after the traumatic incident.

These symptoms must persist for at least two days, but last no more than 30 days. The dissociative symptoms are derealization, depersonalization, dissociative amnesia, subjective sense of numbing, and reduction in awareness of surroundings. In the event these symptoms last longer than 30 days, the victim may be suffering from Posttraumatic Stress Disorder.

Posttraumatic Stress Disorder was first identified when some Viet Nam Veterans began experiencing flashbacks of events that occurred during combat. Posttraumatic Stress Disorder is defined as the development of characteristic symptoms following a psychologically distressing event that is outside the range of usual human experience.[53] Traumatic events include, but are not limited to, military combat, violent personal assault, kidnapping, being taken hostage, terrorist attack, torture, incarceration as a poisoner of war, natural or man-made disasters, severe automobile accidents, or being diagnosed with a life-threatening illness. The characteristic symptoms require that the person experience, witness or be confronted with an event or events that involved actual or threatened death or serious injury, or a threat to the physical integrity of self or others and the person's response involved intense fear, helplessness or horror.

The symptoms the victim may experience include re-experiencing the traumatic event, avoidance of stimuli associated with the event, numbing of general responsiveness, and increased agitation.[54] Victims of any type of crime can experience Posttraumatic Stress Disorder. However, several scholars have carried out research regarding the effect of rape on victims.[55] Victims of rape have reported, or been diagnosed as suffering from, Posttraumatic Stress Disorder. Rothbaum's study found that 94% of rape victims displayed classic symptoms of PTSD one week after the assault. This figure dropped to 47% 12 weeks after the incident.[56] Kilpatrick's study, *Rape in America,* reported that

11% of all women raped still suffer from PTSD, and the authors estimate that 1.3 million women in the United States are currently suffering from Post-Traumatic Stress Disorder as a result of a rape or multiple rapes.[57]

Sodomy

The ancient city of Sodom was allegedly destroyed by God because of its residents unspeakable sexual acts. The term **sodomy** was derived from this biblical description of a city and its citizens who engaged in certain erotic sexual acts.[58] In early England, this act was considered so vile, that the famous legal commentator, Blackstone, refused to name it. He referred to the act as "the infamous crime against nature."[59] This early revulsion continued in America and some statutes still refer to the crime by the term coined by Blackstone. One state charges sodomy as "the abominable and detestable crime against nature."[60]

Similar to rape, the definition and elements of sodomy include the requirement that force or fear be used to overcome resistance. While numerous states have modified their earlier position regarding acts between consenting adults, some states still punish the act whether it is homosexual or heterosexual in nature. These states do not require any physical coercion be used by the perpetrator for the statute to apply. In other words, some states punish sodomy even if it is a consensual act among consenting adults in the privacy of their own bedroom.

Sodomy is the unlawful sexual penetration of the penis of one person and the anus of another committed by use of force or fear. The crime of sodomy can be divided into three basic elements:

(1) Unlawful sexual penetration of the penis of one person

At one time in England, it was required that there not only be penetration, but an emission or ejaculation for the crime to be complete.[61] However, the modern view is that any penetration by the penis of a person is sufficient to establish this element of the crime. The crime is complete upon any penetration.

(2) With the anus of another

Early English law punished the crime if the act was with an animal or another human. However, American statutes have divided these acts into two separate crimes, and to be convicted of the crime of sodomy, the offender must penetrate another human's anal cavity. The crime, as written, applies to both female and male partners.

(3) By use of force or fear

Similar to the crime of rape, knowing voluntary consent is a defense to the crime of sodomy. Thus, sodomy between consenting adults would not be a crime. This is the case whether the act is homosexual or heterosexual in nature. There same type or amount of force or imposition of fear that is required in rape is necessary in sodomy.

Oral Copulation

Oral copulation is the unlawful act of copulating the mouth of one person with the sexual organs or anus of another by use of force or fear. The crime of oral copulation has three elements:

(1) The unlawful act of copulating the mouth of one person

This element of oral copulation requires either the offender or the victim to use his or her mouth during the commission of the crime. Penetration is not required. Any form of contact, such as kissing or other action, is sufficient.

(2) With the sexual organs or anus of another

The crime traditionally punished the copulation of another's sexual organs or anus. It is immaterial if the act is committed by the offender on the victim or the victim is forced to commit the act on the assailant. In either situation, the crime is complete with the touching of the mouth to another's sexual organs or anus.

(3) By use of force or fear

The act to be punished as a crime must not be consensual. Force or fear must be used to overcome resistance. The amount of force or fear necessary is the same for rape, sodomy or oral copulation.

A distinction must be made between consensual sexual acts between consenting adults and oral copulation which is criminal in nature. Consensual acts of this nature are called fellatio and cunnilingus. **Fellatio** is the consensual oral stimulation of male sex organs and **cunnilingus** is the consensual oral stimulation of the female sex organs.

The crime of oral copulation may be committed by a woman on another woman, by a man on another man, by a woman on a man or by a man on a woman.

At the time of the adoption of the Model Penal Code, most states did not limit "crimes against nature" to only sodomy. The states punished fellatio and cunnilingus as well as anal intercourse and **bestiality**. States enacted specific criminal statutes prohibiting these acts. These state statutes punished consensual as well as forced acts of deviate sexual acts. The drafters of the code made a determination that private sexual acts between consenting adults should not be viewed as criminal in nature and therefore excluded them from coverage of deviate sexual intercourse.

The Model Penal Code defines **sexual deviate intercourse** as sexual intercourse, with some penetration however slight; emission is not required.[62] The code defines sexual deviate intercourse by force or imposition as:

- **By force or its equivalent**

  √ A person who engages in deviate sexual intercourse with another person, or who causes another to engage in deviate sexual intercourse, commits a felony of the second degree, if:

  √ He compels the other person to participate by force or threat of imminent death, serious bodily injury, extreme pain or kidnaping, to be inflicted upon anyone; or

  √ He has substantially impaired the other person's power to appraise or control his conduct, by administrating or employing without the knowledge of the other person drugs, intoxicants or other means for the purpose of preventing resistance; or

  √ The other person is unconscious; or

  √ The other person is less than 10 years old.

- **By other imposition**

  A person who engages in deviate sexual intercourse with another person, or who causes another person to engage in deviate sexual intercourse, commits a felony of the third degree if:

√ He compels the other person to participate by any threat that would prevent resistance by a person of ordinary resolution; or

√ He knows that the other person suffers from a mental disease or defect which renders him incapable of appraising the nature of his conduct; or

√ He knows that the other person submits because he is unaware that a sexual act is being committed upon him.

The drafters of the code were attempting to establish a uniform set of rules that would apply to offenses that society, as a rule, did not care to discuss or, in some instances, even acknowledge. They were able to bring a uniformity to this area of the law and yet accept that certain consensual acts performed by adults in the privacy of their own home should not be considered criminal.

ASSAULT

Assault and battery are frequently considered as the same offense although they are separate and distinct offenses. A **battery** consists of the unjustified offensive touching of another. An **assault** is either an attempted or threatened battery. The critical difference between assault and battery is that battery requires an actual or constructive touching of the person. In some aggravated assault crimes, the "assaults" actually refer to batteries. For example, the crime of assault causing serious bodily injury is actually a battery rather than an assault.

Battery

Battery is the unlawful, willful, and offensive touching of the person of another. Battery has three distinct elements:

√ The willful and unlawful

√ Use of force or violence

√ Against the person of another

The unjustified offensive touching is the *actus reus* of the crime of battery. In most states no actual bodily injury is necessary to constitute battery. The Model Penal Code, however, requires at least a slight bodily injury to constitute the crime of battery. It is not necessary that the victim actually fear physical harm as the result of the touching. For example, the offensive touching of the breasts or kissing of a women may be a battery.

In many cases, it is unclear as to whether the touching should be considered offensive. For example, a hug or kiss from an elderly aunt may be offensive to the young child, but certainly not of the criminal type. The test generally used is whether a **reasonable person** would consider the touching as offensive.

It is immaterial how the offender caused the offensive touching. For example, it can be the firing of a weapon or the hitting with the fist. There is no requirement that the touching actually touch the person; a constructive touching is sufficient. In one famous case, the accused was convicted of battery when he hit the horse that the victim was riding. In another case, a defendant was convicted of battery when he convinced a six-year-old girl to touch his sexual organs.[63]

Consent may be a defense to battery as long as the contact is not "unlawful." For example, a person may consent to being kissed, fondled and the consent would be a defense to a battery charge. Participation in sporting events are a common example of consent to battery, e.g., the quarterback of a football team cannot claim he was unlawfully struck by the charging linebacker. If, however, the contact is unlawful, consent is no defense, e.g., a person cannot legally consent to being shot with a pistol nor can a minor legally consent to sexual contact.

Assault

An **assault** is an attempt to injure the person of another or an intent to frighten without actual injury. Assault ("attempted" battery type) has three distinct elements:

√ An unlawful attempt

√ With apparent present ability

√ To commit an injury to the person of another.

Assault ("threatened" battery type) has three distinct elements:

√ A threat

√ With apparent present ability

√ To commit an injury to the person of another

There are two standard types of assault: (1) the attempted battery and (2) placing a person in fear of a battery by menacing behavior. In several states, like California, the second type of behavior is not an assault. In those states, assault is only an attempted battery. Since an assault is, in many cases, an attempted battery, a defendant may be convicted of an assault even though a battery was actually committed.

In most states, the courts have extended battery liability not only for intentional conduct, but also those situations where the defendant has acted in a criminally negligent fashion. Normally criminal negligence is conduct that the accused knew, or should have known, would result in harm to others. Several states have limited battery liability to situations where the accused acted in a willful, wanton, or reckless manner.

The doctrine of transferred intent is applied to those cases where the offender intended to injure one person and by mistake or accident injures another. Thus, if one intends to strike someone but instead accidentally harms another, the intent to injure is transferred to the actual victim. The intent may still be used to justify an assault on the intended victim. For example, D shoots at X intending to kill her. He misses and hits V. D is guilty of assault on X and battery on V. The battery of V is based on the doctrine of transferred attempt.

SUMMARY

- The exact nature of crime was not clearly defined in early historical times. The English had three forms of homicide— justifiable, excusable, and criminal. Presently in the United States, most jurisdictions retain that classification. Murder is the most serious of the criminal homicides. It is the purposeful, knowing, or reckless killing of another human being. First degree murder is generally murder that was premeditated. In most states, all other murders are murders of the second degree.

- Voluntary manslaughter is the voluntary and unlawful killing of anothr but with adequate provocation. Involuntary manslaughter is the unintentional killing of another human being caused during the commission of an unlawful act not amounting to a felony or as the result of criminal negligence. Negligent manslaughter is the unintentional killing of another human being caused by the negligence of the defendant.

- Robbery is considered as a violent personal crime. It involves the theft of property from the person of another by use of force or fear.

- Rape is a feared, misunderstood, and repulsive crime. There are many theories on why individuals commit rape; none appear acceptable. Some view rape as a sex crime and others view it as a crime of dominance over women. It is unlawful sexual intercourse with another person against that person's will by force, fear, or trick. Many jurisdictions are broadening their rape statutes to include all types of forcible sex crimes and consider the crime as sexual assault.

- Assault and battery, often considered as the same offense, are separate and distinct crimes. A battery is an unjustified offensive touching of another and an assault is an attempted or threatened battery.

DISCUSSION QUESTIONS

1. How do we prove intent in murder cases. Can we rely simply on statements made by the perpetrator?

2. Should heat of passion be accepted as a mitigating circumstance?

3. In the typology of robbers, who is the most dangerous robber?

4. Which type of sex offense is the most serious? Why?

5. Should we be able to impose the death penalty for rape of a 25-year-old woman? What about rape of a child under the age of five? What about rape of an elderly women over the age of 85?

ENDNOTES—Chapter 8

1. Portions of this chapter have been adapted from Wallace and Roberson, *Fundamentals of Criminal Law*, (White Plains, New York, Longman, 1996).

2. Wayne R. LaFave and Austin W. Scott,Jr., *Criminal Law*, 2d Ed. (West Publishing Co.: St. Paul, Minn. 1986)

3. U.S. Dept. of Justice, BJS, *Report to the Nation on Crime and Justice*, 2nd ed. (Washington D.C.: GPO,1988).

4. LaFave & Scott, *Criminal Law*, p. 528-545.

5. Title 18, Pennsylvania Statutes, Sections 2501-2502.

6. American Law Institute, *Model Penal Code and Commentaries,* Part 2, Section 2.10.2, p. 14-15.

7. *Id,* p.15-20.

8. Pennsylvania Laws of 1794 Chapter 257, Section 1 and 2 (1794)

9. See *State v. Snowden,* 313 P 2d 706 (Idaho 1957)

10. For a discussion of provocation and adultery, see Note, 86 *Just. P.* 617 (1922) [English Cases] and for a discussion of provocation and mutual combat, see Comment, "Manslaughter and the Adequacy of Provocation: The Reasonable Man," 106 *Univ. of Penn. Law Review* 1021 (1958)

11. See *People v. Velez,* 144 CA 3d 588 (1983)

12. See *New York Statutes*, Penal Law Section 125.20 subsection 2 and Section 125.25 (a)

13. See LaFave & Scott, *Criminal Law,* p. 594 (1972).

14. See *People v. Velez*, supra.

15. See *People v. Mulcahy,* 318 Ill 332, 149 N.E. 266 (1925)

16. *People v. Nelson*, 309 NY 231, 128 NE 2d 391 (1955)

17. *People v. Penny,* 44 Cal 2d 861, 285 P2d 926 (1965)

18. Manslaughter as: "(a) Manslaughter is the unlawful killing of a human being without malice. It is of two kinds: Involuntary—In the commission of an unlawful act not amounting to a felony, or in the commission in an unlawful manner, or without due caution and circumspection, of a lawful act which might produce death."

19. See Wechsler & Michael, "A Rationale of the Law of Homicide," 37 *Columbia Law Review* 701, 747-751(1937)

20. See for example Pennsylvania Title 18, Section 2504.

21. Sue Titus Reed, *Criminal Law,* (New York, MacMillan Publishing 1989) Chapter 6 which includes both robbery and extortion along with other traditional theft crimes such as larceny, false pretenses, burglary and others. p. 210-247.

22. See Joel Samaha, *Criminal Law*, Third Edition, (St. Paul, Minn.: West 1990) Chapter 11 which has a separate subheading entitled Robbery and Extortion,

23. *Sourcebook of Criminal Justice Statistics--1990.* U.S. Department of Justice, (Government Printing Office, Washington D.C. 1990) Table 4.5, p. 419.

24. See *Sourcebook of Criminal Justice Statistics--1990,* Tables 3.47 and 3.48, p. 283-4.

25. *Supra*, at Table 3.8,p. 258

26. See, F.H. McClintock and Evelyn Gibson, *Robbery in London*, (London: Macmillan 1961) p. 15.

27. John Conklin, *Robbery and the Criminal Justice System*, (New York: Lippincott, 1972) p. 1-80.

28. As reported in B.E. Witkin and Norman L. Epstein, *California Criminal Law*, 2d. ed. Vol. 2, p.720.

29. *People v Patton*, 76 Ill 2d 45, 389 NE 2d 1174 (1979)

30. The statutory definition of robbery has been extended in some states to include robbery by snatching. See Georgia Statutes Section 26-1901(1978)

31. See Model Penal Code and Commentaries, Part II, Section 222.1, p. 98.

32. See for example, Joel Samaha, *Criminal Law*, 3rd Ed. (St. Paul: West Publishing Co., 1900) where the author has a chapter entitled "Crimes Against Persons," which includes rape, battery, assault, and kidnapping.

33. Donald Symons, *The Evolution of Human Sexuality,* (London: Oxford University Press, 1979).

34. Paul Gebhard, et al., *Sex Offenders: An Analysis of Types*, (New York: Harper & Row, 1965), p 198-205.

35. A. Nicholas Groth and Jean Birnbaum, *Men Who Rape,* (New York: Plenum, 1979) p. 101.

36. Diana Russell, *The Politics of Rape,* (New York: Stein and Day, 1975), For a more modern article that supports Russell's position, see Donald Mosher and Ronald Anderson, "Macho Personality, Sexual Aggression and Reactions to Guided Imagery of Realistic Rape," *Journal of Research in Personality* , 20 (1987) 77.

37. For a survey of literature in the field, see, "New Research Examines Psychology of Sexual Violence," *Law Enforcement News*, (John Jay College of Criminal Justice, New York: January 15, 1992) p. 1.

38. Michigan does not use the term rape and substitutes instead the term criminal sexual conduct. In addition, the statute is gender neutral and refers to the "actor" as the person who is accused of criminal conduct. See Michigan Statutes 750.520a to 750.520i.

39. Vermont Statute , Title 13, Chapter 72, Section 3255 (3)(A)(B) is an example of such a Rape Shield Law.

40 W. Blackstone, *Commentaries*, 212.

41 For an early case taking this position, see *Whitaker v. State,* 199 Ga 344, 34 SE 2d 499 (1945)

42 *State v Dombroski*, 145 Minn 278, 176 NW 985 (1920)

43. *State v. Meyers*, 37 Wash 2d 759, 226 P 2d 204 (1951)

44. Ruth Masters and Cliff Roberson, *Inside Criminology*, (Prentice-Hall, Englewood, N.J. 1990) p. 380.

45. *Sourcebook of Criminal Justice Statistics--1992* Table 3.31, p. 271.

46. For a survey supporting this position, see Joan M. McDermott, *Rape Victimization in 26 American Cities,* (Washington D.C.: Government Printing Office, 1979)

47. Clifford Kirkpatrick and Eugene J. Kanin,"Male Sex Aggression on a University Campus," 22 *American Sociological Review,* (February 1957) p. 52-58.

48. Thomas Meyer, "Date Rape: A Serious Campus Problem that Few Talk About," *Chronicle of Higher Education, (5 December 1984) p. A 15.*

49. MPC Section 213.1 (2)(b)

50. MPC Section 213.1

51. Virginia Statute Section 18.2-61 is an example of such a statute. For an excellent discussion of martial rape, see Robert T. Sigler and Donna Haywood,"The Criminalization of Forced Martial Intercourse," in *Deviance and the Family*, edited by Frank E. Hagen and Marvin B. Sussman, (NY: Haworth Press 1988) p. 71-85.

52. *Diagnostic and Statistical Manual of Mental Disorders* (4th ed.) American Psychiatric Association, Washington D.C. 1994.

53. *Id.*, p. 427-429.

54. DSM-IV, p. 427-429.

55. For an excellent discussion of the effects of rape on victims, see Bruce Taylor, "The Role of Significant Others in A Rape Victim's Recovery: People Who Are More Likely to Be Harmful Than Helpful," paper presented at the 1996 ACJS Annual Meeting, Las Vegas, NV, March 1996.

56. B.O. Rothbaum, E.B. Foa, T. Murdock, D.S. Riggs & W. Walsh,"A Prospective Examination of Post-Traumatic Stress Disorder in Rape Victims," *Journal of Traumatic Stress* 455-475 (1992)

57. D.G. Kilpatrick, C.N. Edmunds & A.K. Seymour, *Rape in America: A Report to the Nation*, (National Victim Center, Arlington, VA. 1992)

58. See *Commonwealth v. Poindexter,* 133 Ky 720, 118 SW 943 (1909)

59. W. Blackstone, Commentaries, 215.

60. See *Phillips v State*, 248 Ind 150, 222 NE 2d 821 (1967) for a case upholding the filing of an indictment using this language for the crime of sodomy.

61. East P.C. 480 (1803)

62. MPC Section 213.0 (3)

63. *Beausoliel v. United States* 107 F.2d 292

Chapter 9

CRIMES AGAINST PROPERTY

After reading this chapter, you should be able to:

- Explain the various types of burglars.

- Distinguish between the different types of larcencies.

- Illustrate the different types of arson.

BURGLARY

One of the most well-known property crimes at common law was burglary. This crime was classified as an offense against habitation. The rationale behind classifying this crime as a felony was to protect the innocent landowner in his home. A home was more than a mere dwelling where someone resides, it was a person's kingdom. Since only rabble roamed the countryside at night, the common law crime of burglary was to protect the property owner from intrusion during the night.

Modern statutes have enlarged the scope of burglary. This crime is still considered serious, especially when the offense is committed upon an inhabited dwelling. While it is true that burglary is a theft related crime, it is such a unique offense that it deserves special and separate treatment.

Burglary Defined

Burglary is defined as the entry into the dwelling of another with the intent to commit a crime. The crime of burglary has four distinct elements:

1. The Entry

Early common law required "breaking and entering" for the crime of burglary to be complete.[2] However, today there is no requirement of damage to or destruction of the property during the entry into it. Opening a door or a window is sufficient. In fact, pulling open a screen door closed by a spring will constitute entry.[3]

The offender does not have to enter the structure with his entire body for this element to be satisfied. If the defendant puts his hands inside while raising a window, courts will hold entry has occurred.[4] There is a distinction between any part of the offender's body and any tools he may use to effect entry. The fact that a tool may have intruded into the structure does not establish entry within the meaning of this element unless the tool was used to complete the crime. One court held where the defendant used a drill to bore a hole in the floor which allowed the grain to run out of the hole was sufficient for burglary where the tip of the drill "entered" the dwelling.[5] However, if the defendant used a drill to bore a hole in a door near the lock for the purpose of unlocking the door, courts have held this did not satisfy the entry requirement even though the tip of the drill intruded inside the dwelling during the boring.[6]

The entry must not be authorized or consented to for this element of burglary to be satisfied. If the defendant enters a department store that is open, he has not satisfied this element since anyone can enter the store. If he commits a theft while inside, he may be guilty of larceny, but may not be convicted of the crime of burglary. However, if once in the building, the defendant enters a room or section not open to the general public and commits a theft, he has satisfied this element and may be convicted of burglary.

2. Into a Dwelling

Under common law, burglary was limited to a person's home or those buildings within the curtilage. A **curtilage** was that area surrounding the home which included separate buildings and structures necessary for the landowner to carry on his business. Thus, a barn, stable, or dairy house were included within the definition of dwelling under common law.[7] Modern statutes have broadened this definition to include any structure. Many states impose an additional penalty if the structure that was burglarized was a dwelling. States vary in the definition of what constitutes a dwelling, however, the majority require that it be occupied by persons in order to fall within this classification.

Many businesses are occupied only during the day, however, they are now included within the scope of this element. Thus, commercial stores may be burglarized. Industrial plants or warehouses may be entered with the intent to commit a crime and this requirement will be satisfied. So long as there are four walls and a roof, this requirement is satisfied. In addition, the legislatures and courts have modified this requirement to adapt to changing technology. They have held that a motor home is a dwelling for purposes of burglary.[8]

3. Of Another

The law of burglary was designed to protect the occupant of a building, not necessarily the owner. Thus, the crime can be committed on a rental property by the owner if he enters without permission with the intent to commit a crime inside the building. However, one cannot be guilty of burglarizing his own home.[9]

4. With the Intent to Commit a Crime

The defendant must have the intent to commit a crime before he enters the building. Normally burglary is committed with the intent to commit a theft; however, any felony will suffice. Therefore, entry with the intent to commit robbery, rape or murder will be burglary. The defendant does not have to complete the intended crime, only enter with the necessary intent. If a defendant were to enter with the intent of killing another, but was unable to find the prospective victim, he would be guilty of burglary.[10]

The issue of proving the defendant had the requisite intent prior to entry has caused some courts problems. How do you prove what was in the offenders mind prior to her entry into the structure? One approach holds that an unexplained intrusion into the dwelling of another will support a finding of intent to commit theft.[11] Some statutes establish a *prima facie* presumption of the necessary intent based upon such unexplained entry.[12] One court held, " Under Michigan law, intent to commit larceny may be inferred from the totality of circumstances disclosed by the testimony. Such intent may be inferred from the nature, time, or place of the defendant's acts before and during the breaking and entering."[13]

As the above discussion indicates, burglary is a complex crime that can be very difficult to analyze depending on the circumstances. The drafters of the Model Penal Code attempted to simply this process when they set forth the modern position on the crime of burglary. The Model Penal Code defines burglary as:

(1) Burglary Defined. A person is guilty of burglary if he enters a building or occupied structure, or separately secured or occupied portion thereof, with the purpose to commit a crime therein, unless the premises are at the time open

to the public or the actor is licensed or privileged to enter. It is an affirmative defense to prosecution for burglary that the building or structure was abandoned.

(3) Multiple Convictions. A person may not be convicted both for burglary and for the offense which it was his purpose to commit after the burglarious entry or for an attempt to commit that offense, unless the additional offense constitutes a felony of the first or second degree.

The drafters of the Model Penal Code reviewed the history of the crime of burglary and pointed out that the initial development of the offense of burglary probably resulted from an effort to protect property owners from existing defects in the common law crime of attempt. Early common law did not punish a person for the crime of attempt unless the actor had embarked on a course of criminal conduct and was very near completion of the crime. This position would allow a perpetrator who was breaking into a dwelling to commit a crime to escape punishment if he was captured during the entry or was unable to complete the intended crime since he had not progressed far enough down the path towards the ultimate criminal act to be charged with the crime of attempt. The development of the crime of burglary provided a solution to this dilemma and imposed criminal sanctions for the breaking and entry of a dwelling with the intent to commit a crime whether or not the defendant was successful in completing the ultimate objective of the entry.

The Model Penal Code retained the crime of burglary but narrowed it coverage. The code reviewed the purpose behind maintaining the offense and restructuring the scope of the crime. The code accomplishes this by redefining the nature of the entry, the structure or building covered by the offense and the criminal purpose accompanying the entry. The language in the Model Penal Code establishes that entry into a premise open to the public cannot be considered burglary even if it can be proved that the defendant had the intent to commit a crime prior to entry. The code narrows the definition of dwelling or structure that is covered by the statute and establishes an affirmative defense for entry into an abandoned building or structure. The rationale behind this narrow definition of dwelling was to restrict the application of the crime of burglary to those situations that are considered the most dangerous to citizens. However, the code does not require actual presence in the dwelling because it is a matter of chance that the perpetrator has no control over. The final major change in the code deals with the objective of the perpetrator. The defendant must intend to commit any crime that would result in imprisonment. Thus, infractions or minor violations that are punished by fines only are excluded, and if the defendant entered to commit these offenses, the crime of burglary has not occurred.

The Model Penal Code retains and redefines the crime of burglary. It narrows the scope of the crime and does away with many of the precedents established by early common law and statutes. By limiting burglary to non-privilege entry, it highlights the importance of the offense of criminal trespass.

Many states have specific statutes dealing with criminal trespass. The Model Penal Code sets forth a comprehensive statute concerning this crime. The code defines **criminal trespass** as:

- Buildings and Occupied Structure. A person commits an offense if, knowing he is not licensed or privileged to do so, he enters or surreptitiously remains in any building or occupied structure, or separately secured or occupied portion thereof. An offense under this Subsection is a misdemeanor if it is committed in a dwelling at night. Otherwise is a petty misdemeanor.

- Defiant Trespasser. A person commits an offense if, knowing that he is not licensed or privileged to do so, he enters or remains in any place as to which notice against trespass is given by:

  √ Actual communication to the actor; or

  √ Posting in a manner prescribed by law or reasonably likely to come to the attention of intruders; or

  √ Fencing or other enclosure manifestly designed to exclude intruders.

An offense under this subsection constitutes a petty misdemeanor if the offender defies an order to leave personally communicated to him by the owner of the premises or other authorized person. Otherwise it is a violation.

- Defenses. It is an affirmative defense to prosecution under this section that:

√ A building or occupied structure involved in an offense under this Subsection (1) was abandoned; or

√ The premises were at the time open to members of the public and the actor complied with all lawful conditions imposed on access to or remaining in the premises; or

√ The actor reasonably believed that the owner of the premises, or other person empowered to license access thereto, would have licensed him to enter or remain.

The Model Penal Code defines criminal trespass in such a manner as to penalize those persons who do not fall within the definition of burglary and yet commit crimes in buildings or structures open to the public. The purpose of all these prohibitions is to afford the property owner or person in possession of property a secure working and living environment.

Typology of Burglars

While modern day burglars do not steal from tombs, they are just as imaginative in that they will steal from any location that offers a profit. Just as there are different types of burglaries—residential, commercial and industrial—so is there a wide spectrum of burglars. Walsh in her classic work, *The Fence*, set forth a continuum of these offenders ranging from the most adept to the least organized.[14] The following is a listing of Walsh's typology of burglars:

- **The Professionals**. These are skilled burglars who exhibit the characteristics of career criminals. These offenders plan their crimes and concentrate on lucrative targets because they earn their living by engaging in burglaries.

- **Known Burglars**. This group is not as skilled as the professionals, nor are they as successful. They may plan their crimes, but are not as adept as the professional. Their title is appropriate since this class of criminal is known to the police because of prior arrests.

- **Young Burglars**. These are usually offenders in their late teens or early twenties. They do not plan as well as the known or professional burglar.

- **Juvenile Burglars**. These criminals are under the age of sixteen. They confine themselves to local neighborhoods which are chosen by chance. Many times these juvenile burglars will operate at the direction of an older fence or burglar.

- **Junkies**. These burglars are the least organized offenders. They wait for the opportunity and quickly dispose of the stolen property to feed their drug habit.

Other scholars have conducted research which supports Walsh's basic classification.[15] While they may differ in description or groupings, it is clear there are classes of burglars that range from the very good to the inept.

Once a burglar steals property, he must dispose of it. The fence, a dealer in stolen property, is a critical link in the crime of burglary as well as other property crimes. The professional fence is a full-time career criminal who buys and sells stolen property. Other fences occasionally buy or sell stolen goods to supplement their full-time law abiding occupation.

People commit burglaries for a variety or reasons, and they dispose of the property in a number of ways. We are all "victims" of the crime of burglary. If we are the victim, we feel a sense of outrage and loss. If we are the neighbors of the victim, we wonder if we will be next. All citizens end up paying higher insurance premiums because of this property crime. Just as there is no simple answer to the crime of burglary, there is no simple outline on the elements of the crime. While, at first glance, it may seem to be a rather straightforward property crime, the long history of burglary and its evolution has made any discussion of its elements interesting and complex.

LARCENY/THEFT

The term **theft** is often used to refer to three different and distinct crimes—larceny, embezzlement, and obtaining property by false pretenses. In examining theft crimes, the terms personal property, ownership, custody, control, and possession are frequently used.

Larceny was a common law felony. The origins of the other theft crimes can be traced to English misdemeanor statutes. At early English common law, protection of personal property was limited to the crime of robbery.[16] Later, larceny was developed as a crime to handle the situations where the personal property was taken from the possession of another without consent and nonviolently by stealth. In recent years, there has been a trend by states to consolidate the offenses of larceny, embezzlement, and false pretenses into the crime of theft.

Personal property is generally defined as all property except land and buildings attached to land. **Ownership** is the highest form of interest that you may own in a piece of property. It confers complete and unlimited discretion over the property. While an owner may temporarily give up possessory rights in the property, legal title, the essence of ownership, is still retained by the owner. **Custody** is the physical control of an item. It is less than possession. Custody of property confers no right to exercise discretion as to its use or handling. **Possession of property** occurs when a person has control of the property and discretion in the use and handling of that property. For example, if A owns a truck and leases it to B, A has ownership rights of the truck and B has possessory rights of the truck. If B hires C to drive the truck, C has custody of the truck when C is driving it, but not possession of it.

Larceny is a crime directed against the possession, not ownership, of property. It is directed at those who take personal property and carry it away from the person who has the right of possession.

Larceny Defined

Common law larceny is defined as the trespassory taking and carrying away of the personal property of another with the intent to deprive the other of the property permanently.[17] The crime of larceny has five elements:

1. The Wrongful Taking

To constitute the offense, the taking must be wrongful, i.e., "a trespassory taking." If the taking is with permission of the person with the right of possession, then the crime committed, if any, is not larceny. The element of "carrying away" is also referred to as **asportation**.

The most complicated issue is usually whether there has been a "taking" of the property. The **wrongful taking** must be the taking of possession rather than mere custody. As noted earlier, a person has possession when he or she has sufficient control over the property in a generally unrestricted manner. The line between "custody" and "possession" is often fuzzy and more technical than practical.

Actual possession of property is when the person is in physical control of the property. **Constructive possession** is when a person with the right of possession is not in actual physical control of the property and no one else has actual physical possession of it (i.e., the property has been mislaid). Unless the property has been abandoned, it is in the actual or constructive possession of someone.

2. Carrying Away

As noted earlier, one key element of larceny is the "carrying away" or "asportation" of the property. As stated in an old law review article, virtually any movement of the property—even a "hair's breath" away from the place where the defendant took possession of the property—is sufficient to constitute the offense.[18] The "carrying away" must be directed toward carrying the property away from the possession of another.

3. Personal Property

Larceny was designed to protect the possession of personal property. As noted earlier, the crime is completed when there is asportation (i.e., the taking and carrying away). Since land cannot be taken and carried away, the crime of larceny does not protect land from wrongful taking. Items attached to the land, tend to take on the characteristics of the land (i.e., real property) and also are not subject to larceny as long as they are attached to the land. Once they are severed from the land, however, the property such as trees, crops, lumber, etc., becomes personal property and therefore protected by the larceny crimes.

4. Of Another

Property that the victim has no right to possess may still be stolen from him or her. For example, marijuana, which is contraband, is subject to the crime of larceny. In addition, a person who steals personal property from a thief is guilty of larceny. Accordingly, a person may be guilty of larceny when he steals personal property from a person who has stolen the property from another. This concept is based on the legal fiction that when two people's rights to possession of certain property are equal, the first in time prevails (i.e., since neither thief had a right to possess the property the first has greater right of possession than the second thief). This concept also demonstrates that the larceny statutes are based more on history than logic.

To be guilty of larceny, the person must know that he or she has no right to take the property. If a person believes that he or she has the right to take certain property, the person is not guilty of larceny for taking the property even if the belief is unreasonable.

5. With the Intent to Permanently Deprive

If D takes property that is for sale with the intent to pay for it later, D lacks the intent to deprive the possessor of the property permanently of its value. In most states, this would *not* be larceny. The taking of property that is for sale without paying, however, raises the presumption that the taking was with the intent to steal. Accordingly, it would be up to D to prove that he or she intended to pay for the property. In addition, if D lacked the current ability to pay for it, this would also be evidence that he intended to permanently deprive the possessor of the property. If one takes property that is not for sale with the intent to pay fair market value for it, this is larceny.

Lost or mislaid property is subject to special rules regarding whether or not the finder is guilty of larceny for keeping the property. **Mislaid property** is property that was intentionally placed where it was found. **Lost property** is property that was unintentionally placed where it was found. Mislaid property remains under the constructive possession of its owner. Accordingly, when someone picks up mislaid property with the intent to keep the property, he or she has committed the crime of larceny. Lost property is under the constructive possession of the owner if the property has reasonable clues as to the ownership of the property.

At early common law, there were no degrees of larceny. All larcenies were felonies. By statute in most states, larceny has been divided into grand larceny and petty larceny depending on the fair market value of the property taken: grand larceny being a felony and petty larceny being a misdemeanor. The dividing line in many states is property value. If property is valued at over $100.00, it is subject to grand larceny. In addition, in many states the nature of the property rather than the fair market value may also be used. For example, in California it is a felony to steal a horse regardless of value.

Embezzlement

The first general embezzlement statute was passed in 1799.[19] As noted earlier, larceny requires a wrongful taking of personal property. To cover those situations where there was a legal taking of property that was later wrongfully converted to another's use, the crime of embezzlement was enacted in the eighteenth century. Under common law, embezzlement was only a misdemeanor. Presently, embezzlement is either a felony or misdemeanor, depending on the value of the property embezzled.

Embezzlement is a crime against ownership. It is defined as the conversion of property by someone to whom it has been entrusted. Another definition of embezzlement is the fraudulent conversion of the property of another and whose fraudulent conversion has been made punishable by statute. Most of the rules applicable to larceny also apply to embezzlement. The chief difference between the two crimes is that in the case of embezzlement the embezzler is entitled to possess the property at the time of the taking whereas the thief has no right to possess the property in question. Unlike larceny, the essence of the crime of embezzlement is the violation of a trust. Like larceny, embezzlement requires that the defendant know that his or her conduct is wrong when the property is appropriated. Accordingly, a "claim of right" defense, in which the defendant honestly claims a right to the property, applies to both crimes.

False Pretenses

Obtaining property by false pretenses is similar to larceny and different from embezzlement in that the taking was wrongful. However, it is like embezzlement and unlike larceny in that possession was given to the thief by the person in lawful control of it. When property is obtained by false pretenses, the title to the property is also transferred to the thief. The essence of this crime is that the owner of the property was induced to transfer title to personal property as the result of false pretenses. **False pretenses** is defined as the obtaining title to property by making a material false representation with the intent to permanently deprive owner of possession. The elements of the crime of false pretenses include:

- The obtaining title to property
- By making a material false representation
- With the intent to permanently deprive owner of possession

The false pretense must be of a material fact, not an opinion. The pretense also must be relied on by the victim. The false representation must be of an existing fact, not an opinion. A promise of future conduct is not a fraud unless at the time the individual made the promise, the individual had no intentions of carrying out the promised conduct.

Larceny by trick is similar to obtaining property by false pretenses, except only possession, not title, to the property is passed to another. For example, D intending to steal a car, rents one for one day and then sells the car. In this case, because D got only possession of the property not its title, it is larceny by trick.

To eliminate some of the subtle distinctions between the various theft offenses, the trend is to consolidate them into a single theft offense. In many states, the prosecutor need only to allege that the defendant "stole" the property. In other states, he or she must allege how the defendant "stole" the property. In the latter states, the prosecutor still faces the problem of alleging the correct type of theft involved.

ARSON

Arson is an ancient crime that continues to take a human and economic toll on today's society. In 1989, there were 688,000 incendiary or suspicious structural fires attributed to arson. These fires caused 4,655 civilian fire-related deaths and resulted in over $7.5 million in property loss.[20]

Arson Defined

Arson is the malicious burning of the dwelling or structure of another. The crime of arson consists of four elements:

1. Malicious

The requirement of malicious action does not require a specific intent to commit arson. Rather the law will infer the necessary intent if the act was done voluntarily and without excuse or justification and without any claim of right.[21] In an early case, a prisoner set fire to the building in which he was confined, with the intent of burning a hole in the wall for the purpose of escaping. The court found him guilty of arson, stating his action was malicious even though he did not intend that the entire building should be damaged by the fire.[22]

Simple negligence, which results in the burning of a structure, will not satisfy this element. The defendant must have intended to burn the building of another or commit an act done under such circumstances that there is a strong likelihood of such a burning.[23]

2. Burning

There is no requirement that the burning consume or totally destroy the building. The traditional test is whether "the fiber of the wood or other combustible material is charred."[24] It is immaterial how the defendant starts the fire—matches, gasoline, focusing the sun's rays through a magnifying glass—if the structure is charred as a result of the defendant's actions, this element of the offense is satisfied.

The element of burning also includes explosions. Many statutes specifically include explosions within the definition of burning for purposes of defining the crime of arson. These statutes apply even if the explosion did not cause a fire.

3. Dwelling or Structure

Similar to the definition of dwelling in the crime of burglary, the offense of common law arson applied only to a "dwelling." This early restriction was based upon the same rationale of limiting burglary to dwellings—the protection of a person's home. The structures protected under arson have been greatly expanded from early common law and now includes any dwelling, shop, or structure used by persons for living or the conduct of business.

4. Of Another

Since arson is intended to protect the security of another's property, the burning of one's own property does not fall within the definition of the offense. However, similar to the crime of burglary, it is possession or occupancy, not title to property, that determines whether the structure falls within the definition of this element. For example, it would not be arson for the owner of a house to burn the house. However, if the owner had rented the property to another person and then set it afire, it would be arson since the owner had title, but not legal possession to the property at the time of the fire.

With the invention of insurance, the burning of one's own home or business to collect the insurance raised issues of whether such acts were prohibited by the traditional arson statutes. State legislatures responded to this phenomena by amending arson statutes to include this type of conduct. These sections require a specific intent to defraud the insurer be proved for this crime to apply.

The Model Penal Code defines **arson** as:

- **Arson.** A person is guilty of arson, a felony of the second degree, if he starts a fire or causes an explosion with the purpose of:

  √ Destroying a building or occupied structure of another; or

  √ Destroying or damaging any property, whether his own or another's, to collect insurance for such loss. It shall be an affirmative defense to prosecution under this paragraph that the actor's conduct did not recklessly endanger any building or occupied structure of another or place any other person in danger of death or bodily injury.

- **Reckless Burning or Exploding.** A person commits a felony of the third degree if he purposely starts a fire or causes an explosion, whether on his own property or another's, and thereby recklessly:

  √ Places another person in danger of death or bodily injury; or

  √ Places a building or occupied structure of another in danger of damage or destruction.

- **Failure to Control or Report Dangerous Fire.** A person who knows that a fire is endangering life or a substantial amount of property of another and fails to take reasonable measures to put out or control the fire, when he can do so without substantial risk to himself, or to give a prompt fire alarm, commits a misdemeanor if:

  √ He knows that he is under an official, contractual, or other legal duty to prevent or combat the fire; or

  √ The fire was started, albeit lawfully, by him or with his assent, or on property in his custody or control.

The code established a grading or degree of seriousness of the offense by considering both the kind of property destroyed or imperiled and the danger to persons as a result of the act. Under the code, arson, as a second degree felony, carries a maximum sentence of 10 years. However, if the arson results in serious bodily injury to another person, the crime of aggravated assault may be added if the circumstances of the offense manifest "extreme indifference to the value of human life."[25]

The Model Penal Code includes explosions as well as burning within the definition of arson. Under the code, as well as a majority of the state statutes, the crime is complete if the explosion occurs even if there is no fire or flame after the explosion.

The Model Penal Code has established a uniform and rational approach to the crime of arson. It classifies the crime as serious offense by making it a second degree felony. In addition, it allows for the charging of other crimes if, as a result of the act, persons suffer great bodily injury. Similar to many states, it includes explosions within the definition of arson even if no fire results from the bombing.

Arson Typology

Arson may be committed with a single match or a complex electrical or mechanical device. There are numerous reasons or motives behind this crime. McCaghy classified arson into six major categories:

- **Vandalism Arson**: Vandalism arson occurs when the offender is using arson to express hatred towards a particular group or culture.

Abandoned properties are the normal target for vandalism arsonists.

- **Profit-motivated Arson**: The classic profit-motivated arson is when a person burns a structure to collect on insurance from a company. This is a form of insurance fraud that is all too common in the United States.

- **Crime-concealment Arson**: This form of arson is used by a person in the hopes of concealing another crime that was committed on the premise that was burned.

- **Sabotage Arson**: Acts of sabotage arson are most common during labor strikes, prison riots or other civil rebellion.

- **Revenge Arson:** This arson is motivated by the desire to get even, whether the object is an employer who fired the arsonist or a jilted spouse.

- **Excitement Arson**: The **pyromaniac** is a person who sets fires because they excite him. There is no other motive other than experiencing the feelings that result from setting and watching a structure burn.[26]

Because the crime of arson may involve emotions, psychological compulsive actions or simple greed, explaining why people commit this offense is complex and presents overlapping classifications. There is no single series of classifications for why persons start fires. Other authorities have classified arson into three basic categories: vandalism, pyromania, and arson for profit or other crime concealment.[27]

Arson vandalism, like other acts of vandalism, is the result of juveniles. Fires set by juvenile arsonists do not represent isolated criminal behavior. These adolescent offenders are usually involved in other criminal activity. There are numerous explanations of why juveniles start fires. One source lists the following factors: below normal intelligence; motor-neural complications, such as brain damage; unstable family relationships; insufficient parental guidance and adverse peer influence.[28] Fires started by juveniles are crudely set, indicating a lack of sophistication and knowledge of the chemistry of fire on the part of the arsonist. Most fires started by juveniles occur during the day.

Pyromaniac arsonists are classified in the same manner as McCaghy's. The term pyromaniac is controversial in the behavioral

sciences and the law. The pyromaniac receives some form of gratification from the act of setting fires and seems to act from some form of
compulsion. However, it is difficult, both medically and legally, to establish a specific pyromania personality.

Arson for profit or for other crime concealment purposes are
simply persons who have committed a crime and are attempting to
hide it behind a wall of flame or are using the fire to attempt to collect
money from insurance companies. They are the most common form of
arsonist and the easiest to understand, since their motive is simply money
or the hiding of another criminal act.

Arson may appear to be a relatively simple crime to define, but
the reasons for the offense are complex and varied. The crime of arson
has evolved from its common law origins to its present statutory form.
While there are many similarities between the various statutes which
define this crime, each state enacted arson laws which contain minor
differences. The drafters of the Model Penal Code attempted to establish a uniform definition for this dangerous property crime.

SUMMARY

- Burglary is the most popular of the common law crimes against
  property. Most state statutes have expanded the common law
  crime of burglary to include almost all structures and locked
  vehicles and to include entries made anytime during the day.

- Burglary is the entry into the structure with the intent to commit
  a crime. In some jurisdictions, criminal trespass is a lesser
  included offense to burglary. Walsh classifies burglars as
  professionals, known burglars, young burglars, juvenile
  burglars, and junkies.

- Theft is often used to include the common law crimes of
  larceny, embezzlement, and obtaining property by false
  pretense. Larceny is the oldest common law crime.
  Embezzlement and obtaining property by false pretense may
  be traced to the early English misdemeanor statutes. Larceny
  is the wrongful taking and carrying away of personal property
  of another with the intent to deprive the other of the property
  permanently. Embezzlement is a crime against ownership,
  whereas larceny is a crime against possession. Embezzlement

is the conversion of property that has been entrusted to the defendant. False pretenses is like larceny in that the taking of the property was wrongful and like embezzlement in that it is a crime against ownership.

• Arson is the malicious burning of a dwelling or structure of another. The reckless or unlawful burning of the property of another is a lesser included offense to arson in many jurisdictions. McCaghy classifies arson into six classes— vandalism arson, profit-motivated arson, crime-concealment arson, sabotage arson, revenge arson, and excitement arson.

DISCUSSION QUESTIONS

1. Why is burglary considered a property crime and not a crime against persons since it occurs in the home?

2. What is the difference between larceny and robbery?

3. Differentiate between embezzlement and false pretenses.

4. What is the most dangerous form of arsonist? Why?

5. Which is the most serious form of property crime with regard to the danger to its victims/financial costs/impact on society?

ENDNOTES—Chapter 9

1. Portions of this chapter have been adapted from Wallace and Roberson, *Fundamentals of Criminal Law*, (White Plains, NY: Longman, 1996).

2. *State v. Boon,* 35 NC 244, 246 (1852)

3. *U.S. v. Evans*, 415 F 2d 340, 342 (5th Cir 1969)

4. *State v. Allen,* 125 Ariz 158, 608 P2d 95, 96 (App 1980)

5. *Walker v. State*, 63 Ala 49 (1879)

6. *The King v. Hughes*, 1 LEACH 406, 168 English Reports 305 (1785)

7. *Devoe v. Commonwealth,* 44 Mass 316, 325 (1841)

8. See *U.S. v. Lavender*, 602 F2d 639 (4th Cir 1979) which held a Winnebago mobile home where a family lived while touring the United States was a dwelling within the meaning of a burglary statute

9. *People v. Gouze,* 15 Cal 3d 709, 524 P 2d 1365 (1975)

10. *Ziegler v. State*, 610 2d 251, 252 (Okl Cr 1980)

11. *State v. Hopkins,* 11 Utah 2d 363, 359 P 2d 486 (1961)

12. *State v. Bishop,* 90 N 2d 185, 580 P 2d 259 (En Banc, 1978)

13. *Goldman v. Anderson*, 625 F 2d 135, 137 (36th Cir 1980)

14. Marilyn Walsh, *The Fence*, (Westport, CT: Greenwood Press, 1977)

15. See Harry A. Scarr, *Patterns of Burglary*, (Washington D.C.: GPO 1973) and Carl Pope,"Patterns in Burglary: An Empirical Examination of Offense and Offender Characteristics," 8 *Journal of Criminal Justice*, 39-51 (1980)

16. J. Hall, *Theft, Law and Society* (1952) and N. Kidd, "The Jurisprudence of Larceny," 33 Vand. L. Rev. 1101 (1980).

17. *United States v. Waronek*, 582 F.2d 1158

18. Jerome Hall, *Theft, Law and Society*, 2nd ed.(American Law Institute, 1952).

19. *Id.*

20. *Sourcebook of Criminal Justice Statistics*, (1990) Table 3.158, p 406.

21. *State v. Scott*, 118 Ariz 383, 576 P 2d 1383, 1385 (App 1978)

22. *Lockett v. State*, 63 Ala 5 (1879)

23. Perkins and Boyle, *Criminal Law*, (NY: Foundation Press 1982) p. 277.

24. *People v. Losinger,* 331 Mich 490, 502, 50 NW 2d 137, 143 (1951)

25. MPC Section 220.1, p. 10

26. Charles McCaghy, *Crime in American Society*, (NY, NY: Macmillan, 1980)

27. International Association of Chiefs of Police, Training Key # 300, "The Arsonist"p 67-71.

28. *Id.*, p. 68.

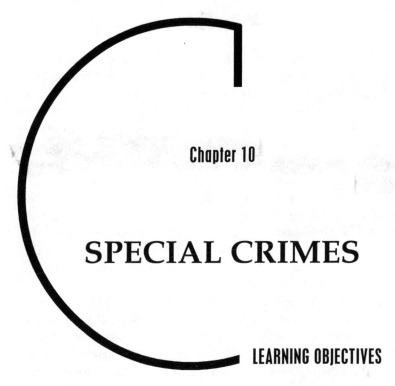

Chapter 10

SPECIAL CRIMES

LEARNING OBJECTIVES

After reading this chapter, you should be able to:

- Describe the controversy surrounding the definition of gangs.

- Explain the use of graffiti in gang culture.

- Identify the impact of hate crimes on its victims.

- List the various types of groups that may commit hate crimes.

- Describe the various theories regarding child abuse.

- Explain the various theories regarding spousal abuse.

- Analyze the dynamics involved in stalking.

229

GANGS

Gangs are becoming more widespread and gang-related violence is increasing. Federal, state, and local criminal justice professionals face a number of distinct challenges when dealing with gangs. One of the first challenges is to agree upon what constitutes a gang. There is continuing controversy regarding the definition of the term **gang**. One authority defines gang as any group of people who band together for criminal activity or who commit crime as a group.[1] Various local or municipal jurisdictions have developed their own definition of what constitutes a gang. Many states have statutory definitions of gangs that vary from state to state. One scholar has suggested that we identify gangs based upon certain common traits. These features include: 1) formal organizational structure, 2) identifiable leadership, 3) a territory, 4) recurrent interaction, and 5) engaging in serious or violent behavior.[2]

A second controversy concerns the number of gangs and the number of serious crimes committed by them. At present, there is no national reporting system regarding the number of gangs. One estimate places the number of gangs at 4,881, with 250,000 members.[3] Since there is no reliable reporting system regarding gangs, it is hard to estimate the number of serious crimes committed by members. However, most law enforcement agencies agree that gang violence continues to grow.

Some gangs form along ethnic or racial lines.[4] Many gangs identify themselves by a name derived from a street or neighborhood where they live, a rock band they like, a cult they follow or their ethnicity. Examples of gangs formed along ethnic lines include:

- **Asian**—Vietnamese, Hmong, Thai, Japanese, or Chinese (e.g., Cheap Boys, Natoma Boys, Wah Ching, Lady Rascals [female] and Southside Scissors [female])

- **African American**— (e.g., Crips, Bloods)

- **Hispanic**—(e.g., White Fence, Los Vatos Locos, Midnight Pearls [female])

- **White**—White Supremacist, Satanic, Punk (e.g., Skinheads, Stoners)

Another type of gang is known as a **tagging crew**. Tagging crews are individuals known as "taggers" who join together for the sole purpose of placing their names or slogans in visible places. While taggers can be individuals with no gang affiliation, recent trends in Southern California indicate that more and more taggers belong to street gangs.

Gangs use **graffiti** (i.e., drawings or writings scratched on a wall or other surface) to identify themselves and their territory and, in some instances, to communicate messages. The graffiti may include a gang member's name, the member's nickname, a declaration of loyalty, a memorial to a slain gang member, threats, challenges and warnings to rival gang members. Gang graffiti is most commonly found on neighborhood walls, fences, and mailboxes. Some gangs purposefully destroy property in order to leave their trademark graffiti behind. Abandoned houses are also a favored target for graffiti, however, any building can be a target.

The graffiti of various gangs can be generally identified by their "signatures." Hispanic gang graffiti is often written in blocked letters and is very stylized. Some Asian gangs are now mimicking the blocked Hispanic style of graffiti. African American and white gang graffiti tend to be similar to each other and use a simple crude style. However, the white gang graffiti may include Nazi symbols and other graphically violent drawings.

Characteristics of Gangs

Gangs, drugs and violence are continuing problems in our society. However, not all gangs engage in drug dealing, nor do all gangs consist of juveniles or former prison inmates. Gangs are as varied as any other facet of our modern society. Although gangs appear to be more highly structured than other delinquent groups, they vary from region to region. It is impossible to examine all the various gangs that exist today, however, we can list some of the more common characteristics that are common to most gangs:[5] diversity, change, concentration, gang structure, social contexts, family, schools, organized crime, and prisons.

- **Diversity.** There is a great deal of variability in gangs, gang activity, and gang problems. Gangs vary by ethnic makeup, involvement in violent crimes, drug-related activities, age of members, and organizational stability.

- **Change.** Gangs evolve due to a number of factors including demographic shifts, economic conditions and other influences.

- **Gang problems are concentrated.** A small percentage of gang members account for most of the harm done by their gangs. More than 60 percent of crimes are committed at a few particularly dangerous locations, with crime rates being much higher in neighborhoods in which most potential offenders live or visit.

- **Gang structure.** Although gangs appear to be more highly organized than simple delinquent groups, there are wide differences between different gangs. Some gangs base their membership on geographic areas such as neighborhoods while other only admit members of a certain age span. Some gangs are part of a larger alliance known as nations. Estimates of gang size range from four members to thousands in a gang or a nation.

  Gangs have different types of members. There are as many different types of memberships as there are gangs; however two classes appear to be common to most gangs—**core members** who include gang leaders and regular members and **wannabees** who are those that desire to join the gang or who are new members in the gang.

Most authorities agree that male gang members are almost exclusively responsible for gang-related crime including violent offenses. About five percent of gang crimes appear to be committed by females. Male gang members outnumber female members by 20 to 1, however many gangs have female auxiliaries or affiliates.

Gang socialization differs by age, context and situation. Reasons for joining gangs include a need for recognition, status, safety, power, excitement, and new experiences. Youths raised under extreme social deprivation are drawn to gangs. Gang affiliation may be viewed as an expected socialization process in certain communities when they are viewed as embodying such values as honor, loyalty, and fellowship. The gang may be seen as part of the family and contributing to the development of the clan.

- **Social contexts.** Rapid urban development, lack of community identity, increasing poverty, and social isolation contribute to institutional failures and the development of gangs. The interplay of social disorganization and the lack of access to legitimate resources contribute to deviant behavior. Families, schools, politics, organized crime, and prisons impact gang development.

- **Family.** Family disorganization, such as single parent families, does not by itself lead children into gangs. A variety of other factors must accompany a weak or disorganized family structure to produce a youth who becomes involved in gangs. These factors include the availability of a peer group that does not support the family and school.

- **Schools.** A gang member is likely to be a youth who has done poorly in school and has little identification with school staff. He does not like school and uses it for gang-related activities instead of academic-related learning. Few schools directly address gang related problems. Gang-related violence usually does not erupt in schools, although gang recruiting may occur on the school grounds. Schools that have strong leadership and more concerned learning environments usually have lower rates of gang problems.

- **Organized crime.** Greater competition among various criminal organizations, the relative increase in older youths and adults in gangs, and the expanded street-level drug market have contributed to the integration of violence and organized gang activity. Many youth gangs have become subunits of organized crime for purposes of drug distribution, car theft, extortion, and burglary.

- **Prisons.** Prison gangs and street gangs are interdependent. The prison or training school may be regarded as facilitating and responding to gang problems. In most states, prison gangs are outgrowths of street gangs, but there is some evidence that prison gangs may emigrate to the streets. Prison incarceration has led to increased gang cohesion and membership recruitment in many institutions.

Several factors seem to motivate youths to leave gangs: (1) growing up and getting smarter, (2) fear of injury, (3) serving time in prison, (4) a girlfriend or marriage, (5) a job, (6) drug dealing, (7) concern for youth, (8) interest in politics, (9) religion, and (10) the assistance of an adult.[6] In some cases, the departure from a gang was accompanied by a complete break with gang peers and a leaving of the neighborhood. In most cases, it simply involved a lack of involvement in criminal activity.

Communities are responding to gang problems by mobilizing neighborhoods, increasing social interaction, especially with youth, increasing economic opportunities such as special schools and job programs and more active law enforcement responses include gang suppression units. Gang violence is a serious problem that will not simply disappear as the gang members grow older. Society must be willing to pay the price to deal with the conditions that draw youths to gangs. Only by identifying those conditions and responding to them can we hope to address this serious form of violence.

HATE CRIMES [7]

Identifying Bias Crimes

In order to identify hate or bias crimes, we must first define these offenses. In this text, **hate crime** or **bias crime** is used interchangeably. Finn and McNeil define hate crimes as "words or actions designed to intimidate an individual because of his or her race, religion, national origin or sexual [preference]."[8] In the Hate Crimes Statistics

Act of 1990, **bias crimes** are those offenses that are motivated by hatred against a victim based on his or her race, religion, sexual orientation, ethnicity, or national origin.[9] Many states have also adopted hate crime statutes that prohibit the same or similar type of conduct. As indicated above, hate or bias crimes are not new, what is new is that we are beginning to recognize these crimes and respond to them.

Recognizing bias crimes involves an evaluation of a number of factors. There is no generally accepted foolproof list of indicators that indicate the offense is motivated by bias or hate of a particular group. However, the Office for Victims of Crime has identified seven general factors that should be examined when evaluating criminal acts.[10] These factors include: cultural differences, written or oral comments, use of symbols, representation of organized hate groups, prior hate crimes, victim/witness perceptions, and lack of other motive. Depending on the situation, one of these factors standing by itself may strongly indicate that the offense may be classified as a bias or hate crime. On the other hand, several of these indicators may not present conclusive evidence that the crime was motivated by hate or bias. Each case should be evaluated on its own merits.

- **Racial, Ethic, Gender and Cultural Differences.** Is the victim of a different culture than the offender? Investigators may not be able to establish this fact from the victim. They may have to look for other indicators that point to any cultural differences between the victim and the offender. These other factors include the cultural diversity of a number of locations including the place of attack, the victim's home or work place. Inquiry should be made as to whether or not the victim was engaged in activities that represent or promote his or her group, such as a gay rights march and if the incident occurred on a date that has a special significance to certain cultures such as Martin Luther King's birthday. Even if the victim is not a member of any recognized cultural or ethnic minority, he or she may have supported such a group and the attack may be in reprisal for that activity. Finally, questions must be asked as to whether there is a history of violence between the victim's culture and any other group.

- **Written or Oral Comments or Gestures.** Inquiry should be made as to whether the attackers made any comments or gestures before, during or immediately after the attack. These comments might refer to the victims race, sex or gender. Likewise, the attackers may make certain gestures indicating affiliation with another group.

- **Drawings, Markings, Symbols, and Graffiti.** Care should be taken to look for any drawings or symbols that might indicate membership in a group. These may be on the victim's house, place of work, house of worship, or where the attack occurred.

- **Representations of Organized Hate Groups.** Sometimes, hate groups will call members of the media and take credit for a bombing, burning or other act of violence. They may also leave their trademark at the scene of the crime. For example, a burning cross may be found outside the victim's home.

- **Previous Existence of Bias or Hate Crime Incidents.** Did the incident occur in a location where previous hate crimes have occurred? If there have been a series of crimes involving victims of the same culture, or the incidents occurred in the same location that is frequented by members of a specific culture, those facts may indicate that the crimes are motivated by hate or bias. Interview the victim to determine if he or she has received previous harassing mail or phone calls based upon his affiliation or membership in a group.

- **Victim/Witness Perception.** The victim should be questioned to determine if he or she perceives the crime as motivated by bias. This may not always be accurate, but the victim's input in this area is critical.

- **Lack of Other Motives.** If there is no other motive for the incident and the victim is a member of a minority culture, the fact that it may be motivated by bias or hatred of that group should be considered.

As indicated above, the presence or absence of these factors does not establish the existence of a hate-related crime. In fact, there are several caveats that must be exercised when evaluating these crimes. These caveats might appropriately be called **false-positive factors**. These factors include the following:

- **Requirement for a Case-by-Case Assessment.** Each crime must be evaluated on its own merits. The existence or nonexistence of bias or hate as the motivation for the offense must be evaluated in light of all the facts and circumstances surrounding the crime.

- **Misleading Facts.** Care must be taken not to rush to judgment in what appears to be a hate crime. There may be other facts that negate this first impression. For example, the victim may tell the officers that the perpetrator used a racial epitaph during the assault. Further investigation may reveal that the victim and the offender were both of the same race or culture.

- **Feigned Facts and Hoaxes.** Some offenders may leave hate symbols in an effort to give the false impression that the offense was motivated by bias or hatred when in fact is was simply an ordinary crime. Other perpetrators may leave symbols or signs of certain groups as a hoax or to mislead investigators.

There are occasions when determining whether the offense was really a hate crime may be difficult. Even if police officers cannot prove that the offense was a hate crime, the victim may believe that hate or bias was, in fact, the motivation. The effect of such crime on victims is unique, and, in many cases, more devastating that other crimes because of the psychological impact on the victim.[11]

The victim must live with the realization that the crime was not a random act of violence, rather the victim was targeted or selected for victimization based upon his/her beliefs, race, culture, religion or sexual preference. Bias crimes are "message crimes" that send a message of terror to the victim because the victim is different than the majority of other Americans. Some victims of bias crimes may not have any community support systems within their community. They may have recently arrived within the United States and have not developed a support base within the general community or their specific culture. Other victims may fear discovery of their status and, therefore, decline to report suspected hate crimes. This aspect of this type of victimization is especially true for closeted gays and lesbians, undocumented aliens, and those who suffer from other disabilities such as HIV/AIDS infection.

Bias crimes also impact the victim's immediate community and culture. Such crimes increase tension with the minority community and raise the specter of retaliation by members of that community. As a result of these factors, bias or hate crimes pose special problems for victim service professionals.

Targets of Hate Crimes

Hate violence has a long history in the United States. However, some sources are suggesting that it has increased in the recent past.[12] Accurately measuring the number of hate crimes that are committed is extremely difficult because the Hate Crime Statistics Act of 1990, while requiring reporting, is still a relatively new procedure. Additionally, two other factors contribute to the lack of meaningful statistics in this area: the lack of training of law enforcement officers which causes many officers to fail to recognize incidents of racial violence and the natural reluctance on the part of many victims of hate crimes to report such incidents to law enforcement agencies.[13]

Acts of racial violence reflect a racial prejudice or interpersonal hostility which is based upon the view that different cultures do not merit treatment as equals or that they deserve blame for various problems within society. Many minority cultures are viewed in a certain manner.[14] These stereotypes are race-based generalizations about a person's behavior or character that are typically not substantiated with scientific data. This stereotyping may act as a trigger to violence with different cultures. Stereotyping does not cause violence, however physical violence is easier to perform on a dehumanized victim. Attackers may believe that the minority is "invading their turf." This may occur when a minority family moves into a traditional neighborhood that has not had any previous experience with that particular culture. Attackers may also claim that minority cultures are taking jobs that rightfully belong to "real Americans." These and other rationalizations deny minority cultures status as accepted citizens.

Persons of color and certain religious groups have traditionally been the target of hate crimes. These groups have been victimized both on a national and international scale. They continue to be victimized today. For example, in New York in 1988, 30 percent of all bias incidents were committed against African Americans and another 30 percent were perpetrated against Jews. In Los Angeles in that same year, the majority of racial incidents were against African-Ameri-

Bias Crimes by Motivation and Type as Reported to the FBI for 1992

Bias Motivation	Crimes Against Person	Crimes Against Property	Total Bias Offenses	% Against Persons	% Against Property
Race	4015	1053	5068	79%	21%
Ethnicity/Nat'l Origin	680	166	846	80%	20%
Religion	492	751	1243	40%	60%
Sexual Orientation	774	175	949	82%	18%
Total	5961	2145	8106	74%	26%

cans and more than 90 percent of religiously motivated incidents were against Jews.[15] The arson of African-American churches is but another example of the continuing victimization of persons of color.[16]

Disabled persons are also victims of hate/bias crimes. As the number of disabled persons in our nation has increased, so too has the number of hate crimes and abuse against them. A **disabled person** is one who has a physical or mental impairment that substantially limits one or more of the major life activities of that individual or that person has a record of such impairment or that person is regarded as having such an impairment. Major life activities include such activities as walking, seeing, hearing, speaking, breathing, learning and working. Some perpetrators seek out disabled victims because their disability makes them "easy prey" for these type of offenders.[17] An example is a developed disabled woman who has an intellectual ability of a 7-year-old child who may be sexually assaulted by a caretaker.

Anti-gay and lesbian violence became a national issue with the murders of San Francisco Mayor George Moscone and City Supervisor Harvey Milk. Their deaths became symbols of both the strength of the homosexual community as well as the hostility that is directed at them. Attacks against gays infected with HIV/AIDS have increased in the last several years.[18]

Women also have been the subject of hate/bias crimes. They continue to be targets of violence because of their gender. Many states include gender as a classification within their hate crime statutes. Crimes against women, including sexual assault and spousal abuse, will be discussed in a separate chapter. The next section examines the conflict between the First Amendment of the U.S. Constitution which protects freedom of expression and prosecuting hate or bias crimes.

Legal Aspects of Hate Crimes

Prosecuting a perpetrator for violation of a hate crime raises several emotional and constitutional issues. The First Amendment prohibits the federal government and the states from enacting any law that unduly regulates a person's freedom of expression. However, from the founding of our nation, the Supreme Court has held that such freedom of expression is not unlimited. There are situations where conduct or other activities while expressing beliefs or thoughts are outside the scope of First Amendment protection.

Hate crimes deal with both the expression of beliefs and action. The expression of beliefs reflect hatred or loathing toward a certain group while the action is criminal in nature. Thus, drafting a criminal statute that regulates hate crimes is no easy task.

In 1992, the Supreme Court struck down a local hate crime ordinance in St. Paul, Minnesota which criminalized the use of hate symbols, such as the burning of a cross, on the grounds that it violated an individual's right to freedom of expression.[19]

On June 11, 1993 in *Wisconsin v. Mitchell*, the United States Supreme Court unanimously upheld the constitutionality of Wisconsin's hate crime statute which increased penalties for crimes motivated by hate or bias.[20] Todd Mitchell was a 19-year-old black male who was outraged over a scene in the film, *Mississippi Burning*, which depicted a young black child being attacked by a white racist. Upon seeing a 14-year-old white male, Mitchell asked his companions if they wanted to get that white boy. They attacked him, leaving the victim comatose for four days with possible brain damage. Mitchell was convicted for aggravated battery, and the sentence was doubled from two to four years after it was proven he had intentionally selected his victim based on race. Mitchell challenged the constitutionality of the hate crime enhancement statute claiming it violated the First Amendment freedom of expression.

The United States Supreme Court upheld the statute stating bias/ hate crimes were valid for three main reasons:

1. While the government cannot punish an individual's abstract beliefs, it can punish a vast array of depraved motives for crime, including selecting a crime victim based on race, religion, color, disability, sexual orientation, national origin or ancestry.

2. Hate crimes do not punish thoughts, rather they address the greater individual and societal harms caused by bias-related offenses in that they are more likely to provoke retaliatory crimes, inflict distinct emotional harms on their victims and incite community unrest.

3. Hate crime penalty enhancement laws do not punish people because they express their views.

As the above discussion indicates, laws prohibiting certain conduct will be considered constitutionally valid. Nonthreatening bigoted expression is still protected, so long as it does not evolve into bias motivated action. When such beliefs are the basis for hate or bias crimes, professionals in the field should be able to identify them.

Typology of Offenders

Understanding more about those who commit hate crimes allows victim service professionals to help the victim comprehend some of the dynamics involved in this type of crime. Although research is still being developed in this area, Levin and McDevitt have established three categories of offenders: thrill seeking offenders, reactive offenders and mission offenders.[21]

The **thrill-seeking offenders** are generally groups of teenagers that are not otherwise associated with any other formal hate group. They engage in these acts for a variety of reasons including: an attempt to gain a psychological or social thrill or rush, a desire to be accepted by others, and the ability to brag about the act at a later time. Almost any member of a minority group may be a target of these groups. They generally operate outside of their own area or neighborhood and actively look for targets of opportunity. Since these attacks are random and usually fail to follow any pattern, it is often difficult to identify the perpetrators of these types of hate crimes.

The **reactive offenders** have a sense of entitlement concerning their rights or life-style that does not extend to the victim. They usually do not belong to any organized hate group but may associate with one to mitigate a perceived threat to their way of life. When a victim acts in such a manner as to cause these offenders to feel that their life-style is threatened, they may react with violence. They will commit hate crimes to send a message to the victim and/or the victim's community that will cause the victim to stop whatever action is threatening the perpetrator's rights or life-style. These crimes normally occur within the offender's own community, school, or place of work. Examples of these types of hate crimes include burning crosses at a minority's new home in a predominately white neighborhood, beating a minority who takes a job in a traditionally white occupation, and other acts of violence directed at maintaining the status quo.

The **mission-oriented offenders** may suffer from a mental illness including psychosis. They may experience hallucinations, withdrawal, and impaired ability to reason. These offenders may believe they have received instructions from a higher deity to rid the world of this "evil." They typically have a sense of urgency about their objectives and believe that they must act before it is too late. The victim is usually a member of a group that is targeted for elimination. These perpetrators will look for victims in the victim's own neighborhood. An example of this type of offender was Marc Lepine who killed 14 women at the University of Montreal stating that he hated all feminists.

Sapp and his associate developed a typology of hate offenders based upon their ideology.[22] They believed that ideology is used by hate groups to serve as a symbolic set of ideas that provides the group with a perceived social legitimacy. Ideology is a way of thinking used by a group to express its beliefs and social values. Sapp classified hate groups into three basic categories: Christian conservatism, based upon the Identity Movement; white racial supremacy and patriotism and survival.

- Christian conservatism, based upon the Identity Movement, uses passages in the scripture identifying certain groups as superior to others and follows the belief that a nation, rather than being a geographic, political or economic entity, is a culture grouped according to bloodlines and shared history. Racial identity thus becomes the basis for national identity.

These groups may adopt a post-millennium view, which holds that the second coming of Christ cannot happen until Christians purge the Earth of sin and establish the Holy Land.[23] As Gale points out, this is a potential blueprint for genocide in that it allows these groups to cleanse the Holy Land of "sinners." Therefore, mass murders of inferiors and those who oppose these groups and their churches is mandated.[24]

• White racial supremacy groups also include racial purity proponents. **Racial purity** is concerned with the purity of the Aryan race or God's children. Refugees, illegal aliens, legal immigrants, Jews, blacks, Hispanics, Asians, and non-Christians are all considered a threat to white racial purity theorists. The Ku Klux Klan is an example of a white supremacy group. Its founding fathers stated that its purpose was the maintenance of the supremacy of the white race in the republic since that race is superior to all other races.[25]

• Patriotic and survival groups have recently come to the attention of the general public because of the incidents in Idaho and Montana involving various members of militia groups. These groups offer an attractive ideology to some conservative groups in America. They point out the economic troubles, including unemployment, and blame these problems on refugees and other non-white groups. They argue that special interests control the government and decry the moral bankruptcy of our leaders.

These groups blame lax courts for encouraging criminals. They target the media because they believe it glorifies criminals and is responsible for the total breakdown of morals in America. Some of these groups use quotes from the Constitution as a basis for their beliefs and argue that they are no longer subject to the laws of the United States.

Bias and hate crimes do not just happen, they are motivated by a variety of feelings, beliefs and emotions. The result is intimidation of the individual as well as his or her community. Criminal justice professionals must understand these crimes and their impact in order to properly respond to these offenses.

CHILD ABUSE [26]

Theories Regarding Child Abuse

Some scholars would argue that the most effective method of stopping child abuse is to break the cycle of violence. The *Cycle of Violence Theory*[27] is discussed as a distinct and separate aspect of child abuse. Simply separating it from the other theories should not imply that this is a definite answer as to why people commit aggressive acts, rather it is singled out for examination because professionals and lay persons constantly refer to it as a scientifically accepted fact. As with other causes or theories of child abuse, there is no way to prove or disprove the *Cycle of Violence Theory*. However, since there is widespread acceptance of this theory, it is necessary to fully explore both its founding premiset as well as the criticisms directed to it.

The cycle of violence concept has generated continuing controversy among researchers for several decades. Scholars have attempted to determine whether violent tendencies can be inherited from the family of origin as a result of observation or victimization. Other scholars have attempted to explain criminal behavior by reference to this cycle.[28]

The **cycle of violence** is the most commonly used term to describe the process, however, this theory is also known as the *intergenerational transmission of violence theory*. Since many authors, researchers and commentators use the former, that is the term that will be utilized in this text. The Cycle of Violence Theory asserts that violent behavior is learned within the family and bequeathed from one generation to the next. This theory holds that children who are victims of child abuse or who witness violent aggression by one spouse against the other will grow up and react to their children or spouses in the same manner, thus the childhood survivor of a violent family develops a predisposition towards violence in his or her own family. So we have a never ending chain of violence that is passed from one generation to the next.

The sources for most studies of the Cycle of Violence Theory are case studies, clinical interviews, self-reporting and agency records. One of the most widely cited studies in support of the Cycle of Violence Theory is Steele and Polick's research which appeared in Helfer and Kempe's, *The Battered Child Syndrome* in 1968.[29] Their study involved 60 parents who were referred to them as a result of their children being treated for child abuse. Steele and Polick gathered data by testing and interviewing the parents. The parents stated that as children they had experienced intense, pervasive continuous demands from their own parents. Lost within the conclusions of the study was the fact that some parents were physically abused and others were not. The researchers had cautioned against drawing too many inferences from their research, however their study is constantly cited as evidence supporting the Cycle of Violence Theory.

Straus conducted an extensive study by interviewing 1,146 families with children.[30] The results of the study indicated an 18 percent rate of generational transmission of violence. The results of this study may have been low since the researchers limited the definition of abuse to physical acts that occurred during adolescence. Child abuse is more likely to occur at a younger age with a gradual tapering off in incidents as the child reaches the teenage years.

During this same time period, Hunter and Kilstrom interviewed 282 parents of newborn infants.[31] These researchers followed the parents and determined that the intergenerational transmission of violence was 18 percent. However, 82 percent of the parents who were abused as children did not abuse their offspring. Those parents appeared to be able to break the cycle of violence because of social support, healthy children and a more supportive relationship with one of their own parents. Hunter and Kilstrom's study is suspect since it examined only infants who had been admitted to an intensive care nursery. In addition, there was no extended follow up of the families or their children.

In 1984, Egeland and Jacobvitz concluded a major study of 160 single-parent mothers.[32] Each mother had at least one child under the age of five. The sample was divided into three groups: severe physical child abuse including being struck by objects or burned; borderline child abuse including weekly spankings, and finally those children who were being raised by another caretaker. The researchers found a 70 percent intergenerational transmission of violence for those mothers who had suffered severe abuse as a child.

In 1990, Cappell and Heiner analyzed 888 child-rearing families and measured the incidence of aggression in the respondents' families.[33] The presence or absence of aggression was classified into family member relationships: husband to wife aggression; wife to husband aggression, and respondent to child aggression. These researchers found that women who witnessed or experienced violence as children were more likely to aggressively discipline their own children. Perhaps more importantly, these scholars suggested that children who are raised in a violent family learn **inherent vulnerability** (e.g., children who are raised in a violent family learn, without anyone directly teaching them, that they are vulnerable to violence, thus they accept this fact and react accordingly). Cappell and Heiner theorize that this intergenerational transmission of vulnerability causes men and women to provoke violence, accept violence as natural, and select aggressive partners. These scholars rightfully point out that this research is limited because the same group was composed only of intact couples.

As the above discussion illustrates, the Cycle of Violence Theory continues to dominate the literature. This and other theories of family violence will continue to be researched in an attempt to find the cause of family violence, predict its occurrence, and search for a cure.

Rather than attempt to describe all acceptable theories of the cause of child abuse, this section will set forth one model that encompasses several different theories. Cynthia Crosson Tower established a series of categories that grouped several theories into three distinct models: (1) the psychopathological model; (2) the interactional model; and (3) the environmental-sociological-cultural model.[34]

The **Psychopathological Model** stresses the characteristics of the abuser as the primary cause of abuse. The abuser's personality predisposes the abuser to injure the child. This model includes three separate approaches to child abuse: (1) the psychodynamic model; (2) the mental illness model; and (3) the character-trait model.

The **Psychodynamic Model** is based upon the work of C. Henry Kempe and Ray Helfer. This model theorized that a lack of bonding between the parent and child is an important factor in child abuse. This theory assumes that the abuser were part of a cycle of parental inadequacy. These individuals are unable to bond with children and when a crisis occurs, they respond with abusive acts. This model also assumes the abuser will engage in role reversal. In other words, the parents expect the child to nurture them instead of vise-versa.

The Mental Illness Model sets forth the proposition that the parent's mental illness is the primary cause of child abuse. This is an easy theory for lay persons to accept because its easy to believe that anyone who would repeatedly beat or torture a child must be crazy. Justice and Justice suggested this model as a viable category.[35] While some scholars have found abusive parents to be mentally disturbed, many others argue that abusive parents do not fit any existing psychiatric classification. For example, Kempe found that less than five percent were psychotic.

The **Character-trait Model** focus on specific traits of the abuser without regard for how they acquired these traits. Scholars such as Merrill and Delsordo have categorized abusive parents by specific traits that cause child abuse.[36] Merrill's study included such traits as hostility, rigidity, passivity and dependence and competitiveness. Delsordo's categorization of abusive parents' traits included mental illness, frustration and irresponsibility, severe discipline and misplaced abuse.

The **Interactional Model** views child abuse as a result of a dysfunctional system. This category of abuse focuses on the following factors: (1) the role of the child; (2) chance events; and (3) the family-structure.

The role of the child and the perceptions of the parent towards that child are viewed as a cause of child abuse by some scholars. Martin suggests that abuse not only requires a certain type of adult, but that certain acts of the child trigger the abuse. If the parent has certain expectations that the child does not meet, abuse may occur.[37]

Chance events is the somewhat inaccurate name given to events which prevent the parent from bonding with the child. This lack of attachment is viewed as a predisposition towards child abuse. Lynch suggests that difficulties in pregnancy, labor or delivery can have a bearing on the attachment of the mother to the child.[38]

The **Family-structure Model** theorizes that child abuse is a result of a dysfunctional family. The adult members of the family blame the child for their own shortcomings, and this leads to abuse.

The **Environmental-Sociological-Cultural Model** views child abuse as a result of stresses in society that are the primary causes of abuse. This category of abuse includes the following causes of child abuse: (1) the Environmental Stress Model; (2) the Social-learning Model; (3) the Social-psychological Model; and (4) the Psychosocial Systems Model.

The **Environmental Stress Model** accepts the proposition that factors such as lack of education, poverty, unemployment or occupational stress result in child abuse. As these outside forces build, the parent or caretaker is unable to cope and reacts by hitting or injuring the child.

The **Social-learning Model** emphasizes the inadequacy of the parenting skills of abusive parents. These parents never learned appropriate responses to child rearing and, therefore, their lack of skill leads to frustration. This frustration, in turn, causes abusive behavior.

The **Social-psychological Model** assumes stress results from a number of social and psychological factors including marital disputes, unemployment, too many or unwanted children. These factors induce stress which causes the individual to react to the child in an abusive manner.

The **Psychosocial Systems Model** stresses that abuse results from interactions within the family. The family as a system is out of balance and incapable of caring for the child. The child becomes the target for family members' frustration, and abuse is the result.

As the above discussion indicates, there are several theories that attempt to explain who the abusers are and why they abuse children. While no authority can point to one single cause of child abuse, it is clear that it continues to occur. The causes of child physical abuse are multifaceted, therefore it is necessary to review who the victims are (i.e., recipients of this violence) in order to attempt to more fully understand this phenomena.

Are poor children neglected and rich kids well cared for? Unfortunately a substantial number of people in society equate poverty with neglect, but simply being poor does not make a neglectful parent. There are children who live at the edge of poverty or below the poverty level who are loved and nurtured. On the other hand, there are children that live in million dollar homes but are neglected or psychologically abused on a daily basis.

Some scholars have indicated that families who neglect their children live in an environment that is unfriendly and characterized by low morale and hopelessness.[41] Polansky and his colleagues in their classic text, *Damaged Parents: An Anatomy of Child Neglect*, established three major causes of neglect: (1) economic causes, (2) ecological causes, and (3) personalistic causes.[39] The economic theory suggests that neglect is caused by stress as a result of living in poverty. The ecological theory views the family behavior and neglect as a result of social causes. The personalistic theory attributes child neglect to individual personality characteristics of the caretakers.

The more reasoned approach seems to be that of the personalistic theories. In this approach, neglect is viewed as being caused by complex maladaptive interactions and/or lack of essential caretaking behaviors that are influenced by the level of parental skill, knowledge deficits and other stress factors.[42] There are other models that profile personalities of neglectful parents or caretakers, but no one study or theory has gained universal acceptance.

The causes of neglect are varied and wide-ranging. Numerous studies have indicated that poverty is an important factor in the parent's ability to care for their children and the question must be asked if poverty causes neglect, or if poverty is the result of the parents' inability to function. [40]

Numerous studies indicate that those who sexually abuse children do not fit any stereotype. The common lay perception that all these abusers are ugly old men who prey on children is simply not true, but researchers have attempted to find a common thread or factor that connects all child abusers. They have examined the degree of violence, the age of the victim, the age and education of the offender, preoffense social and occupational adjustment, alcohol abuse, physiological responses of offenders and aggression. Conte reviewed the literature in this area and described the following factors which were considered important when evaluating characteristics of child sex abusers:[43]

1. Measurement of sexual arousal is essential to discriminate between various categories of sexual offenders.

2. The role of sexual fantasies with children is important due to its connection to deviant sexuality. Fantasies about children coupled with masturbation during these fantasies serves as a form of rehearsal for contact with the victims.

3. The types of rationalizations used by adult offenders who have sexual relations with children. These rationalizations commonly take the form of statements or thoughts to the effect: "A child who doesn't resist really wants to have sex"; "Having sex with a child is the best way to teach her about sex"; "You become closer to the child when you share sex with him," and so on.

There is no distinct or clear answer as to why adults sexually abuse children. The offender may commit these acts for a variety of reasons. Both psychological forces and social structure enter into this complex mesh of forces to allow individuals to engage in sexual activities with young victims.

We traditionally think of the abuser as a male and the victim as a young female. However, studies indicate that boys may be the victim of sexual abuse at a higher rate than previously thought. One study in San Jose, California indicates a rise in the reported incidents of sexual abuse of boys.[44] Between 1970 and 1975, only 5% of the reported victims of sexual abuse were boys. However, this figure rose to over 22% by 1986.[45]

The high-risk years for child sexual abuse range between the ages of 4 and 9.[46] At the former age, children are naive and sexually curious, and by the time they reach 9 years of age, their loyalty, desire to please and trust of adults are traits manipulated by offenders to accomplish their goal of molestation. Generally, sexual abuse is terminated by the time the child reaches the age of 14. This termination occurs because the victim may threaten the offender with disclosure or engage in activities, such as running away that would lead authorities to suspect abuse.[47]

Contrary to popular belief, the actual physical attractiveness of the female child has little, if anything, to do with whether the child is a victim of molestation. Additionally, the seductiveness of the female child is now discounted as a contributing factor in sexual abuse situations. While we may be able to dispel certain stereotypes about female victims, there needs to be more research on the issue of male victims. Two scholars have isolated at least one factor that may identify why certain male children are molested. Finkelhor and Porter suggest that less assertive boys are more likely to be victims of sexual abuse.[48]

Children are at a higher risk of sexual abuse if they are socially isolated, left alone, and unsupervised. If the mother is absent from the home for long periods, either because of work or other commitments, the child is more likely to be abused. Some authorities theorize that the presence of a stepfather in the home adds to the risk of sexual abuse.[49] All these factors establish situations which make the child vulnerable to the perpetrator.

We are still researching and learning about the characteristics of those who abuse and who or why certain children are chosen for abuse over others. Misconceptions and stereotypes have contributed to the confusion in this very important area. While we do not have all the answers on why and who is involved in child sexual abuse, we are making progress.

Types of Child Abuse

Numerous authorities have defined child abuse. Part of the problem in this area has been the continued struggle to agree on what the term *child abuse* means. Mildred Pagelow, Vincent B. Van Hasselt,

Richard Gelles and other scholars in the field have excellent discussions and definitions of this condition.[50] For purposes of this text and ease of understanding, we have accepted the following definition: **physical child abuse** may be defined as any act which results in a nonaccidental physical injury by a person who has care, custody or control of a child.

There are two key aspects to this definition-- the act is intentional or willful and the act resulted in a physical injury. An accidental injury does not qualify as child abuse. An accidental slip in a bathtub would not qualify as child abuse even if the child received an injury that required several stitches. Child abuse, as discussed in this chapter, is manifested by physical injury which can be proved or documented. Simply yelling at the child is not child abuse within the meaning of this definition. Nor is spanking the child on the hand, the face or the buttocks if those acts did not result in a physical injury that can be documented. While it is true that any form of spanking causes injury in the form of pain and some trauma to the child, unless the force is sufficient to leave marks, most medical and legal authorities will not classify these acts as child abuse. This lack of a clear definition is part of the problem of physical child abuse.

In the past 20 years, there have been numerous texts, articles and studies that deal with the subject of neglect. The literature runs the gamut from examining assessment techniques of neglect,[51] to listing all the different forms of this abuse.[52] Except for rare instances, child neglect does not receive the public attention that child sexual and physical abuse generates. Part of the reason for this lack of emphasis may lie in the definition and nature of child neglect.

Child neglect is the negligent treatment or maltreatment of a child by a parent or caretaker under circumstances indicating harm or threatened harm to the child's health or welfare. While this appears, at first glance, to be a simple and straightforward statement, it covers a wide range of activities or omissions that impact on the physical and emotional well being of a child. At what point does mere inattention or lack of knowledge translate itself into child neglect. The above definition would require an act or omission which results in harm or threatens to cause harm to the child's health or welfare. This act or omission may be physical or psychological. A strict interpretation of this definition would require that parents or caretakers guard their children like prisoners. However, this is unrealistic because children are mobile.

They get into drawers, cabinets, and every corner in the house and yard. Therefore, we are dealing with a continuum that stretches from momentary inattention to gross inaction.

$$\vdash - \dashv$$

Momentary inattention   Gross action or inaction

Somewhere on this line, acceptable parenting ends and child neglect begins. While there is no clear bright line that establishes neglect, it is a common form of child abuse.

Child sexual abuse is sexual exploitation or sexual activities with children under circumstances which indicate that the child's health or welfare is harmed or threatened.[53] This definition includes inappropriate sexual activities between children and adults. The inappropriate behavior may be between family members or between a stranger and the victim. **Intrafamilial sexual abuse** includes incest and refers to any type of exploitative sexual contact occurring between relatives. **Extrafamilial sexual abuse** refers to exploitative sexual contact with perpetrators who may be known to the child (neighbors, baby-sitters, live-in partners) or unknown to the child.[54]

One of the major problems with this definition is the requirement that the child be harmed. From a legal perspective, harm to the victim is not an element of the crime of child sexual abuse. If certain physical acts occur, the crime is complete. In criminal proceedings, it is not necessary to prove that the perpetrator intended to, or actually harmed, the child. However, this definition is useful in exploring the consequences of child sexual abuse and retaining the requirement of an injury to the child will allow for such a discussion.

The following acts are examples of child sexual abuse: exposing one's sexual organs to the child, voyeurism, touching the sex organs of the child, mutual or self-masturbation with the child, oral sex, intercourse and anal sex. In addition, allowing the child to view or participate in pornographic or obscene movies is considered child abuse.

Child sexual abuse may be distinguished from rape in that the perpetrator may use a variety of different "techniques" to achieve the objective of sexual gratification. Rape normally involves sexual acts as the result of force or fear. Child abuse offenders may also use force or fear, however, they also employ other pressures or influences to accomplish their goal. These actions include manipulation of the child (psychologically isolating the child from other loved ones), coercion (using adult authority or power on the child), force (restraining the child), threats or fear (informing the child if they tell, no one will love them).[55]

SPOUSAL ABUSE [56]

Theories Regarding Spousal Abuse

There is a continuing controversy surround the cause and extent of spousal abuse. Authorities in the field cannot agree on a simple definition for this form of violence. For purposes of this section, **spousal abuse is defined as any intentional act or series of acts that cause injury to the spouse.** These acts may be physical, emotional or sexual. Spouse is gender neutral and therefore the abuse may occur to a male or female. The term includes those who are married, cohabiting, or involved in a serious relationship. It also encompasses individuals who are separated and living apart from their former spouse. While there is some disagreement regarding the exact definition of spousal abuse, all scholars and authorities agree it exists.

you don't have to be married

One of the most often asked questions is "Why does the victim stay in an abusive relationship?" The reasons that women stay with abusive partners are complex and multifaceted. There are a number of theories that attempt to explain the dynamics involved in battering. This section will briefly discuss some of the more well-known concepts in this area.

Lenore E. Walker is one of the leading authorities in the area of spousal abuse. She coined the term "cycle theory of violence" as a result of her research in the area of battered women.[57] This concept does not attempt to explain the cause of spousal abuse, rather it examines the dynamics of this form of family violence.

The Cycle of Violence Theory sets forth the dynamics of battering in spousal abuse. Walker's theory has three distinct phases: the tension-building phase, the explosion or acute battering phase and the calm, loving respite phase. These phases can vary in length and intensity depending upon the relationship.

- **The tension-building phase:** As the name of this phase implies, tension increases within the relationship. At which time the husband may engage in minor battering of his spouse. The wife attempts to calm him by agreeing to his demands, becoming more nurturing or simply attempting to stay out of his way during this phase. The victim may rationalize that perhaps she is really at fault and deserves the abuse, accepting the barterers faulty logic as her own. Women, who have been in a battering relationship for any extended period of time, know only too well that the minor battering will increase in time. She may try to withdraw more from the abuser in an attempt to avoid more conflict but the tension in the relationship will continue to increase until the batterer explodes in a fit of rage.

- **The explosion or acute battering phase:** During this phase the abuser loses control and engages in major incidents of assaultive behavior. This intense violent aggression is what distinguishes this phase from the minor or occasional battering that takes place in the first phase. When the first serious attack is over, both parties may feel shock, disbelief and denial. For example, the woman may attempt to minimize her injuries.

- **The calm, loving respite phase:** This phase is characterized by contrite loving acts on the part of the abuser. The batterer may understand that he has gone too far during the previous phase and will beg forgiveness and promise never to let it happen again. The woman will want to accept the abusers promises that he can change, and that his loving behavior is an inducement for her to stay in the relationship.

Walker's theory is generally accepted both in academia and the legal system. Her explanation for the dynamics of battering has been cited in numerous court decisions that deal with battered spouses.

Walker also presented the concept of the ***Battered Person (Woman) Syndrome.***[58] Some authorities prefer the term *battered women's experiences* because they believe that the former (1) implies that there is one syndrome which all battered women develop, (2) it has pathological connotations which suggest that battered women suffer from some sort of sickness, (3) expert testimony on domestic violence refers to more than women's psychological reactions to violence, (4) it focuses attention on the battered woman rather than on the batter's coercive behavior, and (5) it creates an image of battered women as suffering victims rather than active survivors.[59] However, since most court cases and the majority of experts still refer to this experience as the battered woman syndrome, that term will be used in this text.

Walker theorized that victims of spousal abuse gradually become immobilized by fear and believe they have no other options. As a result, these women stay in the abusive relationships coping the best they can. The Battered Woman Syndrome involves one who has been, on at least two occasions, the victim of physical, sexual, or serious psychological abuse by a man with whom she has an intimate relationship. It is a pattern of psychological symptoms that develop after somebody has lived in a battering relationship. This is a gradual process of conditioning in which the victim feels both helpless and hopeless and, according to Walker, is one of the main reasons why spouses stay in these situations longer than people would expect. The abuse tends to follow the three-stage cyclical pattern of "tension-building," "acute explosion," and "loving contrition." The following responses are typical of women suffering from the Battered Woman Syndrome: (1) traumatic effects of victimization induced by violence,(2) learned helplessness deficits and (3) self-destructive coping responses to the violence.[60]

Very similar in dynamics to the Battered Woman Syndrome is a condition referred to as the **Stockholm Syndrome.** This phenomenon occurs when persons who are held as hostages, captives or prisoners of war begin to identify with the captors. These victims are isolated, mistreated and in fear of their lives. They become helpless, confined to the area they are ordered to stay in, and dependent on their captors to supply everything they need to survive. They begin to develop positive feelings for their captors.[61] The syndrome was named after an incident in Stockholm, Sweden where four bank employees were held hostage in the bank's vault for 131 hours by two perpetrators. When the victims were finally freed, they expressed gratitude toward the offenders for sparing their lives.

NiCarthy indicated that the dynamics of spousal abuse is very similar to techniques used to control or brainwash prisoners of war. NiCarthy wrote, "As stated in a report published by Amnesty International, these techniques induce 'dependency, dread and debility.' To the extent that a person is victimized by these techniques, she or he tends to become immobilized by the belief that she or he is trapped, cannot escape."[62] This heightening of fear, helplessness, dependency and dread are all intertwined in the definition and dynamics of spousal abuse.

Dutton and Painter developed the ***Traumatic Bonding Theory*** to explain why battered women stay in abusive relationships.[63] This theory holds that when a woman finally leaves an abusive partner, her immediate fears begin to diminish and her hidden attachment to her abuser begins to manifest itself. Emotionally drained and vulnerable, she becomes susceptible to her partner's loving contrite pressure to return. As her fears lessen and the needs previously provided by her partner increase, she may decide to give him another chance.[64]

Dutton's theory is based on the concepts of power distribution and emotional bonding that focus on the dynamics of the abusive relationship rather than on any personality defect or socioeconomic status of the victim. Dutton states that these two features—the existence of a power imbalance and the intermittent nature of the abuse can explain why an abused woman stays with her abuser or even returns to the relationship. Dutton theorized that when power imbalances exist in a relationship, the person of low power feels more negative in her self-appraisal, more incapable of fending for herself and thus in need of the person with more power. This cycle of dependency and lowered self-esteem repeats itself over and over and eventually creates a strong affective bond to the high-power person.[65]

The second factor in traumatic bonding is the intermittent nature of the abuse. This occurs when the abusive partner periodically abuses the submissive partner by threats or physical acts. The time between these incidents is normally characterized by normal, socially acceptable behavior. Thus, the victim is subjected to negative arousal and the relief or release associated with its removal. This situation of alternating negative and pleasant conditions is known within the learning theory as partial or intermittent reinforcement. Dutton states that this situation is highly effective in producing persistent patterns of behavior that are associated with strong emotional attachment to the abuser that is hard to change or modify.[66]

These four theories or concepts are only a few of the many reasons advanced for why battered women stay in abusive relationships. At this time, controversy continues regarding why victims stay in these relationships.

If we knew the causes of spousal abuse, we could correct it. To date, no one has yet come forward with a definitive answer to this question. However, numerous scholars in different professions have studied this form of family violence and come up with a variety of reasons or causes for this type of abuse. While there are many theories and studies in the area of spousal abuse, space dictates that only a few of the more well known theories be discussed.

Social Stress. The family system in America is a system of contradictions. Americans retreat from the city streets to their homes and install bars on their windows to keep out the violence. Yet, the family structure is one of the most violent settings a person is likely to encounter.

For purposes of this discussion, a **family** is a group of persons who cohabitate. Marriage is not a requirement. Within this living arrangement, forces converge to cause stress. This increased level of stress, in turn, leads to a high rate of violence within the family. Many times this violence is directed at the spouse in the form of physical assaults. It should be pointed out that stress does not cause violence, it is one of the many responses available to persons who suffer from stress.

Family life has a different set of behaviors than other social settings. How the members within a family setting dress, talk and act in their home is different than when they attend social functions. Additionally, violence in the form of physical punishment is accepted by many as a characteristic of the family. Parents can and do slap infants' hands in order to teach them not to touch the hot coffee pot. Thus, this form of physical violence may be used on loved ones for their own benefit. Therefore when stress occurs, there is already a preconditioned response or behavior that has been used, and therefore it is easier to use when one is under pressure.

Power. Power is the ability to impose one's will on another and make life decisions. Couples who share power, or are equals in the decision-making process, have the lowest level of both conflict and violence.[67] When there is a conflict, these families display the greatest resistance to the use of violence.

One of the characteristics of family violence is the use and abuse of power. Additionally, battered women report a feeling of powerlessness as a result of the spousal abuse they have suffered. If the male desires power and control in the relationship, this represents one of the factors that may indicate a potential for violence.

Dependency. Some authorities argue that our society has fostered women's dependency. Women's financial and social success, in many instances, has been dependent upon the man they marry. While this is beginning to change, the "glass ceiling" still remains for the most part an impregnable barrier. A few examples bring home this point; there are only two female United States Supreme Court justices, only six women are United States senators and only a small percentage of women are chief executive officers of major corporations.[68] Statistically, after a divorce a man's standard of living increases, while a woman's declines.[69]

The meaning of marital dependency is subject to debate, but the most common meaning includes economic dependency. The female spouse has little or no earning power and is therefore dependent upon her male partner for the necessities of life. A variation on this theme of economic dependency is the presence of children. While a female may be able to leave an abusive relationship and make ends meet, the addition of children multiplies the difficulties inherent in any separation. A third factor in dependence is society's expectation of women as care givers and the further hidden message that a woman is not whole until she is married.[70]

Thus, **marital dependency** is a multifaced concept that involves economic, emotional and societal forces that result in a women being dependant on her spouse for support. This dependency on a man and marriage for economic, emotional and other support increases a woman's tolerance for physical abuse.

Straus and Gelles and their associates conducted an in-depth study of dependency and violence and reported that women whose dependency on marriage is high tend to suffer more physical violence than women whose dependency is low. Dependent wives have fewer alternatives to marriage and fewer resources within the marriage with which to cope or modify their husbands' behavior.[71] This dependency is a pair of "golden handcuffs" which binds the spouse to the abusive partner.

Alcohol. There is a common perception that males who drink alcohol beat their spouses. Therefore, so the reasoning goes, alcohol causes violence. Movies, books and to some extent our own personal experiences support the concept that alcohol causes problems in relationships. The relationship between alcohol and abuse has been studied extensively, and there are several theories regarding alcohol and its relationship to violence. A few of the more common theories are listed below:

- *Disinhibition Theory*: This theory is based upon the principle that alcohol releases inhibitions and alters judgment. Medical evidence regarding the effects of alcohol on the central nervous system supports this theory. However, recent research into the disinhibition theory reveals that alcohol interacts with individuals based upon varying individual expectancies which is only one aspect of the alcohol-violence equation.[72]

- *Social Learning and Deviance Disavowal Theory*: Coleman and Straus have argued that individuals learn violence by observing others who drink and become violent. This violent behavior is excused, pardoned, or justified because the individual was drunk and therefore not accountable for his or her actions.[73] Other scholars have suggested that individuals use alcohol to increase their sense of power and as an excuse for the exercise of unlawful force against others.[74]

- *Integrated Theoretical Models*: Pernanem's research into alcohol and violence indicates numerous factors that interact in alcohol and violence. These factors may include the inherent conflict present in marriages.[75] A second factor is our society's expectation that drinking is an acceptable and expected form of male behavior.

All of these theories and studies have attempted to determine if alcohol causes spousal abuse. At this stage there is no definitive answer but there appears to be a link between the two. However, there are persons who drink and do not abuse their spouses so it would appear that alcohol by itself cannot be defined as the cause of spousal abuse.

Pregnancy. Pregnancy and spousal abuse is a controversial subject, and studies indicate that there is a relationship between the two.[76] Despite this linkage, there is still the question of whether or not pregnancy causes domestic violence or whether it is just another one of the factors to be considered. Most of the studies are based upon small samples and have internal validity problems however the Straus and Gelles survey of violence, using the National Family Violence Survey, determined that the rates of violence were higher for households where the female partner was pregnant.[77] Subsequently, the authors concluded that previously reported associations between pregnancy and violence was not valid and that age is a more critical factor in determining violence than pregnancy. Young women have higher pregnancy rates and they experience violence more often than older women. Females under the age of 25 appeared to be at the highest level of risk.

Marriage. "The marriage license as a hitting license" was adopted in the early 1970s by Gelles and Straus when they discovered that married couples suffered assault at a much greater rate than strangers.[78] They reasoned that the common law tradition that allowed a husband to discipline his wife was alive and well in this modern age. However, more recent studies indicate that the highest rate of assault is among cohabiting couples. Additionally, violence is most severe in cohabiting couples.[79]

Age may also be a factor, because dating and cohabiting couples tend to be younger than married couples. However, other research indicates that age and marital status have no relationship to violence. Therefore, significant relationships, whether they involve dating, cohabitation or marriage place women at risk. As indicated above, cohabiting couples may be at a higher risk than married couples. In a more recent evaluation of the National Family Violence Surveys, Straus and Gelles set forth the following factors as having more impact on the degree of risk a woman faces in a cohabitating relationship:

- *Isolation*: Couples who are living together may be more isolated than married couples. Part of this isolation may be because of the stigma society attaches to cohabitation over marriage. This isolation allows for spousal abuse because there is little or no supporting network of friends or family available for the abused spouse.

- *Autonomy and Control*: Some persons prefer cohabitation over marriage with the thought that they can retain their own independence. However, any living arrangement brings with it duties, obligations, tensions and the resulting disagreements. Some authorities point out that when the issue of control arises, violence occurs.[80] As the relationship becomes more serious, the issue of control becomes more important and violence is more likely to occur.

- *Investment in the Relationship*: Cohabiting couples may share some characteristics that trigger violence, while lacking others shared by married couples that stop the conflict from escalating into physical violence.[81]

As with other theories of spousal abuse, more study and research needs to occur before we can understand whether or not women who enter into any significant relationship are at risk of spousal abuse. This section has discussed various theories of spousal abuse and it is clear that as of this time, we have not discovered the cause or the cure for this type of abuse.

Types of Spousal Abuse [82]

Physical aggression may take the form of "minor" acts that escalate over time. It may began with an arm being grabbed, a dish thrown, or a slap to the arm or face. This aggression increases in severity until the victim has no way out of the relationship. Only the perpetrators imagination is the limiting factor in the infliction of physical abuse on the spouse. The following is a list of the more common forms of physical abuse suffered by spouses:

- *The abuser may engage in striking acts.* He may strike the face, arms, body or legs of the spouse. The violence may be delivered with an open or closed hand. These acts include punching with his fist.

- *Throwing or destruction of property.* The abuser may throw dishes, small appliances, etc., at the spouse or he may go on a rampage and simply destroy household property.

- *Control or choking acts* are also common. Choking is a common form of abuse. It sends a very clear message that the abuser is stronger and more powerful. Choking allows the batterer to control the spouse and have her beg for mercy.

- *Repeated beating using objects.* Use of belts, sticks or other objects during the assault is not uncommon. Using the same object allows the abuser to completely control the victim simply by laying his hand on the object.

- *Humiliation violence.* Some abusers will require their victims to assume certain positions for the imposition of violence. Having the victim undress before yelling and beating her adds to the feeling of helplessness.

As the above discussion indicates, there are numerous forms of physical violence. The results of these acts will leave certain physical marks or injuries on the women. In the event they require medical treatment, the physician should be alert to the possibility of abuse if an injury is not consistent with the medical history given by the spouse. The second form of spousal abuse discussed below is even harder to detect.

Physical violence is often accompanied by sexual abuse. Sex on demand or after physical assaults is very common. Because the woman does not believe she has any choice or free will, she will submit to the abuser's demands. Additionally, she may fear that a refusal to engage in sexual activity will cause the abuser to react violently.

Sexual acts that humiliate or degrade the wife are not uncommon. The husband may demand oral sex without any regard for his spouses feelings or beliefs. Anal intercourse is a common form of sexual abuse. The abuser may say things to the spouse or require her to say things that are degrading to her. Some abusers may require their spouses to share sex with friends or co-workers.

Violence during the sexual act may occur. The abuser may engage in sexual activities in a violent and forceful manner that is intended to injure or hurt his spouse. This is a form of physical abuse that is accomplished by use of sex.

Sometimes, *sex will occur after a physical altercation.* This may be loving and caring and an attempt by the abuser to "make-up" for the aggression. This offers false hope to the abused spouse and is intended to make her believe that the abuser is really sorry and the physical acts will not occur again.

Sexual abuse may provoke intense emotional and physical reactions in the abused spouse. This intensity and humiliation may become addictive and be looked upon as a form of release. It may, on occasion, take on a narcotic effect for the abused spouse.

At one time in our history, a man had a "right" to sex with his wife. There was no such thing as spousal rape. Today, we have laws that prevent this form of assault. Sexual abuse may not leave physical scars visible to the naked eye but certainly it will leave emotional scars that may be even longer lasting and more devastating.

Emotional abuse is far more than a husband simply calling his wife degrading names. This form of spousal abuse has far-reaching consequences for the victim and leaves scars that require long term treatment. Emotional abuse includes many different acts that all contribute to a feeling of helplessness and inability.

The batterer may engage in **verbal dominance**. At first, the spouse may believe this is simply ego or a strong person speaking. However, in time, she learns her opinions, feelings and thoughts carry no weight and if, in fact, she expresses herself at all, she is subject to verbal and possibly physical abuse.

Isolation is a common form of emotional abuse. The abuser may isolate the victim by limiting her access to money, use of the car or other normal activities. He talks negatively about her family and friends thereby making it uncomfortable for the spouse to maintain outside relations. Isolation forecloses feedback. The only feedback she receives is from the abusing partner who distorts both his and her realities leaving her feeling dumb, lazy and unattractive. After a period of time, the abused spouse comes to accept these statements as true.

Guilt is a common form of emotional abuse. The abuser usually blames the spouse for his assaultive behavior with the rationale that if she had only carried out her duties better, then he would not have had to hit her. After a period of time, the abused spouse begins to accept these pronouncements and blame herself for the battering.

Fear is a common form of emotional abuse. The abuser may threaten to reveal secrets or private information to family and friends or the batterer may threaten the spouse with a beating when he gets home. The spouse then waits hours for the expected assault. The abuser may threaten to harm her or her family if she ever leaves him or does anything else he does not approve of. **Humiliation** is another common form of emotional abuse. The spouse may be "put down" in front of friends, family or children. In extreme cases, the abuser may require her to perform degrading acts in public such as having sex in front of friends or her children, requesting permission before leaving the room or going to the bathroom, etc. This type of emotional abuse destroys the spouses sense of self-worth and ability to resist further acts of control by the abuser.

Using fear, guilt and isolation, the abuser will promote the feeling of helplessness within the spouse. This further ties the victim to the abuser. She believes there is no way to break the cycle and is therefore trapped.

One aspect of emotional abuse that deserves special attention is financial dependence. The abuser may require the spouse to work and turn her check over to him. He will control all finances and insure she never has any funds that he does not approve. The abuser may control the funds in order to isolate the spouse, deny her opportunities to improve herself or to demean her. This financial dependence adds to the spouse's feelings of helplessness and entrapment. Even if she wanted to leave, she would have no money with which to support herself or even rent a room for a night.

Emotional abuse is a serious form of spousal abuse. While it leaves no physical scars, it can bind the abused spouse to the perpetrator far more effectively than chains or ropes. It also can leave psychological scars that may last a lifetime.

Spousal abuse is a special form of violence that more and more authorities are acknowledging is a serious problem. There are a number of dynamics involved in spousal abuse that cause the victim to remain in the relationship. There are also a number of theories that authorities claim cause spousal abuse. More study and research is needed regarding this special crime before we have answers to these issues.

STALKING

Anyone can become a victim of a stalker at anytime or anyplace. However, we are not yet certain exactly who is or may become a stalker. We are still researching this area, and like so many other special crimes, we have yet to agree on a single definition of the term "stalker."

Stalking involves more than simply following another person before committing a crime. If this action were considered stalking, then most street muggings would involve stalking. Stalking also does not have to result in death or injury to another person. Telephone calls, letters, or simply following the victim are acts that can cause a reasonable person to feel threatened and even terrorized. The victim can be a celebrity, related to the stalker by marriage, or a complete stranger.

As indicated above, stalking involves a complex series of acts, that taken by themselves, might be normal everyday occurrences. Stalking has been examined from a psychological perspective, a physical security point of view and from a legal basis. By combining all of these disciplines, we can distill the crime of stalking down to the following definition:

Stalking is a knowing, purposeful course of conduct directed at a specific person that would cause a reasonable person to fear bodily injury or death to himself or herself or a member of his or her immediate family. While the definition may appear simple, it is composed of six distinct elements that must be met before the crime of stalking has occurred:

- **Knowing**: This requires knowledge that the victim will be placed in fear of injury. Acts that occur without knowledge of the victim's fear do not meet this element. However, this knowledge may be inferred from the perpetrator's actions. If a reasonable person would perceive that his acts were placing another in fear, the requirement has been satisfied.

- **Purposeful**: The acts must be done in a conscious course of conduct that a reasonable person would know places another in fear.

- **Course of Conduct**: This element requires more than a single act. Thus, the mugger who follows a victim, then robs her has not engaged in the conduct necessary to be classified as a stalker. However, if an estranged husband followed his former spouse on more than one occasion and if the other elements are satisfied, he may be guilty of stalking.

- **Reasonable Person**: The victim is judged by what a reasonable person would feel, not what the victim may experience. This poses a problem in the area of family violence since battered spouses are very sensitive to the potential injury from their abuser and jurors may not understand the victim's level of fear. However, if this standard is interpreted to mean what a reasonable person would feel having undergone what the victim has experienced, then jurors would be exposed to the feelings of a spouse who has been battered and can then place themselves in her position.

- **Fear of Injury or Death**: The conduct must be more than simply an annoying series of acts. The victim must fear that she will be injured as the end result of the perpetrator's actions.

- **Herself or Immediate Family**: The actions may be directed at the victim or her family. Immediate family is normally considered to be spouses, children or parents.

Legal Issues

Stalking laws are a relatively recent phenomena. As a result of the 1989 stalking murder of actress Rebecca Schaeffer and other reports of stalking of high profile celebrities, California enacted the nation's first stalking legislation in 1990. In retrospect, it is hard to believe that any sane person could oppose legislation that would protect persons from possible danger and harassment. However, proponents of California's stalking law have indicated that there was a great deal of resistance within the legislature to passage of the proposed law.[83] The statute, as finally adopted, was very narrow and required the prosecution to prove a credible threat to kill or commit great bodily injury upon the victim. Fortunately, California, some other states and the federal government have since adopted a more comprehensive series of stalking laws that, in many instances, offer victims of family violence protection where before none existed.

Forty-eight states and the District of Columbia have adopted stalking laws. The remaining two states, Arizona and Maine, utilize their harassment and terrorizing statutes to combat stalking. The federal government also passed an anti-stalking law. States continue to amend their statutes to provide more protection to victims of stalking. Depending on the jurisdiction, various acts are prohibited. For example, a suspect may not be present, approach, pursue or follow, trespass onto property, lay in wait, intimidate, vandalize, conduct surveillance, harass, show a weapon, restrain or commit bodily injury upon the victim. Part of the problem in enacting any legislation that criminalizes certain types of conduct involving expression of thoughts and ideas is the inevitable confrontation with the rights guaranteed under the Constitution.

Any law that attempts to regulate the exercise of speech is subject to scrutiny by the courts. The First Amendment to the U.S. Constitution states, "Congress shall make no law ... abiding the freedom of speech."[84] Some scholars argue that the First Amendment is the most important protection within the Constitution.

Stalking laws, by their very nature, regulate the expression of ideas and thoughts. The stalker may engage in conduct that is intended to express his or her feelings of love or hate toward the victim. This conduct may involve following the victim, sending the victim objects such as flowers and other conduct that, at first glance, is clearly conduct protected by the First Amendment. A stalker may also engage in pure speech activities such as sending letters or phoning the victim proclaiming his/her undying love for the victim. All of these acts raise constitutional issues that must be addressed.

The United States Supreme Court has held that certain conduct which is intended as a form of communication is protected by the First Amendment. Demonstrations protesting government decisions are examples of such speech-related conduct. However, the courts have held that even First Amendment rights can be regulated. The Supreme Court decision in *Madsen v. Women's Health Center, Inc.* illustrates this position.[85] In *Madsen,* the court stated that abortion protestors were exercising their First Amendment rights; however, other considerations such as safety of individuals who worked at the clinics and those who desired to use the services of the clinics were proper factors that the legislature could consider in setting up a zone of protection that the protestors could not enter. Thus, stalking laws may be drafted so as to regulate conduct that otherwise might be argued as protected by the First Amendment.

Another aspect of stalking laws involves punishment for sending letters or making telephone calls. These activities by the stalker are clearly forms of expression. However, the Supreme Court has held that the First Amendment does not prevent the government from regulating speech that contains threats. Threats of violence are outside the protection of the Constitution because they protect victims from a fear of violence and the disruption that such a fear causes.[86] In *Thorne v. Bailey,* the 4th Circuit Court of Appeals upheld the constitutionality of a statute prohibiting telephone harassment that included a provision against using the phone to make threats against persons or property.[87] The appellate court held that harassment was not protected even though it took the form of speech and involved the use of a telephone.[88]

For stalking laws to withstand a constitutional challenge they must prohibit specific activity that is clearly defined. In the legal profession, this requires that the stalking statute not be overbroad or vague. Each of these requirements involve "shades of gray" within the realm of constitutional law.

A statute is overbroad if it prohibits both activities that are not constitutionally protected, as well as activities that are protected. The Supreme Court has stated there are several justifications for voiding overbroad statutes. First, is the fear that if a statute is overbroad, individuals may refrain from carrying out protected activities as well as regulated activity. The second rationale for voiding overbroad statutes is the fear that an overbroad statute will allow law enforcement agencies to selectively enforce it against unpopular groups or activities. This danger is avoided if the statute is narrowly drafted.

A vague statute fails to provide explicit grounds for enforcement. A statute is vague if a person of common intelligence cannot ascertain the limits of lawful behavior.[89] If a statute is vague, it will be struck down or declared void. This *Void for Vagueness Doctrine* is based upon the due process requirements of the Fifth and Fourteenth Amendments.[90] This doctrine requires that all criminal legislation satisfy a two-pronged test. The first requires notice and clarity such that ordinary persons can understand what conduct is prohibited. The second requires all criminal laws to provide explicit standards to prevent arbitrary and discriminatory enforcement.[91] Similar to overbroad statutes, the danger with a vague statute is the fear that individuals will fail to exercise their right to free speech because of a belief that they will be prosecuted under the statute which regulates unprotected activities. However, the Supreme Court does not require that words in a statute reach mathematical or scientific precision to be valid and enforceable.[92]

Understanding stalking requires more than simply setting forth a definition of the act. Stalking is a course of conduct that may occur in a wide variety of situations. This characteristic makes it difficult to establish a clear typology of stalkers.

Typology of Stalkers

Zona, Sharma and Lane have conducted an in-depth review of stalkers in the Los Angeles area.[93] Zona and his associates utilized the files of the Threat Management Unit (TMU) of the Los Angeles Police

Department. This was the first unit of its kind in the United States. During the latter portion of 1989, the Los Angeles Police Department became aware of an increase in unsolicited contacts between mentally ill persons and Hollywood celebrities. After a meeting with various entertainment personal managers, the Threat Management Unit was formed.[94]

Los Angeles Police Department Special Order Number 4 sets forth the background and purpose of this unit as follows:

> Obsessed individuals with abnormal fixations on ce-
> lebrities have recently received a great deal of media atten-
> tion. However, becoming a victim of harassment, threats, or
> being stalked could happen to any member of society. Of-
> ten these situations begin without any specific crime hav-
> ing been committed. If such a case is allowed to escalate, it
> could end in a tragedy to which law enforcement can only
> react after the fact. In response to the rapid increase of threats
> and harassment against a variety of public figures and other
> community members, the Department has developed the
> Threat Management Unit. This Order establishes the threat
> Management Unit within Detective headquarters division.[95]

Zona was able to establish a data base of 74 subjects that had engaged in stalking behavior. Only cases that were officially opened and investigated by the TMU were considered. Unfortunately, none of the cases involved domestic violence situations. However, situations where the couple had physically separated and were living apart were included. All the cases were reviewed by a psychiatrist, and a profile was established. This profile classified stalkers as erotomania, love obsessional and simple obsessional.

- **Erotomania**: This type of stalker has a delusional disorder in which the predominant theme of the delusion is that a person, usually of higher status, is in love with the subject. The victim does not know the stalker and oftentimes will be a public figure or celebrity. The stalker is convinced that the victim, usually of the opposite sex, loves him or her and would return the affection if not for some external influence. The stalker rejects any contrary evidence and will remain delusional for years.

- **Love obsessional**: The love obsessional stalker is similar to the erotomanic in many ways. The subject does not know his or her victim except through the media. This stalker may also suffer from delusions, however, the subject has a primary psychiatric diagnosis. These individuals often believe that if the victim would simply acknowledge their existence then the victim would fall in love with the stalker. These subjects usually engage in a campaign to make their existence known to the victim by writing, telephoning or otherwise attempting to contact the victim.

- **Simple obsessional**: Unlike the two previous categories, there existed a prior relationship between the stalker and his or her intended victim. This relationship may have been a former spouse, employer or neighbor, and in all cases, the stalking begins after the relationship had soured or there was a perception by the subject of mistreatment. The stalking is an attempt to rectify the problem or seek revenge.

- **False victimization:** There were a small percentage of Zona's sample (2 percent) that involved those persons who claimed to be victims of stalkers. By insisting that someone is stalking them, the offender becomes the victim.

The length of time of stalking varied with the type of stalker studied. The duration for erotomanics was 124 months while the love obsessionals was slightly less with an average of 146 months. The simple obsessional stalker maintained contact for 5.1 months. The contact between the stalker and the victim ranged from visits to the subject's home or other location, to mailing letters or making phone calls. In addition, all categories of stalkers made threats to the victim.

Stalking is a serious crime that we are only beginning to study. It covers the continuum of violence from simple threats or the killing of the victim. It may take place over a computer or in a dark alley. Its effect on the victim and society can be devastating.

SUMMARY

- Gangs are a problem for criminal justice agencies. It is difficult, however, to describe what constitutes a gang. Definitions vary from state to state. One solution is to identify gangs based on certain common traits. There is also a controversy as to the number of gangs and the amount of crime committed by gangs. Gangs use graffiti for identification, marking their territory, and communication. Gangs are as varies as any other facet of our society. Communities are responding to the gang problem by mobilizing neighborhoods, increasing social interaction, and more prompt law enforcement responses.

- Hate crimes appear to be increasing over the past years. To assist in measuruing hate crimes, The Hate Crime Act of 1990 was passed. Persons of color have traditionally been targets of hate crimes. Otehr targets include women, gays, and disabled persons. Hate crimes may be defined as "words or actions designed to intimidate an individual because of his or her race, religion, national origin, or sexual preference. Bias crimes are offenses that are motivated by hatred toward a victim based on the victim's membership in one or more of the hate crime classifications. Hate crimes deal with both the expression of beliefs and actions, thus, drafting a criminal statute dealing with hate crimes has been difficult. The U.S. Supreme Court, in looking at this problem, has held that nonthreatening bigoted expression is still protected. When such beliefs, however, are the basis for crimes, they can be punished. There are three types of hate crime offenders—the thrill-seeker, the reactive, and the mission-oriented.

- Some scholars contend that the most effective method of stopping child abuse is to break the cycle of violence. There are several theories regarding the cause of child abuse. Tower established three distinct models—interactional, psychopathological, and psychodynamic. Child abuse includes both physical and psychological abuse.

- Spousal abuse is defined as any intentional act or series of acts that cause injury to the spouse. There is controversy regarding the cause and extent of spousal abuse. It is difficult to understand why a spouse stays in an abusive relationship. Walker uses the Cycle Theory of Violence to explain the dynamics of spousal abuse. She sees three phases—tension-building, explosion, and respite. The Battered Woman Syndrome involves one who has been on ,at least two occasions, the victim of physical, sexual, or serious psychological abuse by a person with whom she has had an intimate relationship. The result is a gradual process of conditioning in which the victim feels both helpless and hopeless.

• Stalking is also a crime in which no single definition has been agreed on. It involves more than simply following another person before committing a crime. It is considered as a knowing, purposeful course of conduct directed at a specific person that would cause a reasonable person to fear bodily injury or death. Almost all states have recently adopted ststutes to combat stalking. For a stalking statute to be constitutional, it must prohibitt specific activity that is clearly identified. Zona has classified stalkers as erotomanic, love obsessional, and simple obsessional.

DISCUSSION QUESTIONS

1. Define the term *gang*. How is it different from the text discussion of gang? Is the definition different for street gangs versus prison gangs? Why? Why not?

2. What is the most serious form of hate crime? Justify your answer.

3. Should hate crimes be punished more severely than other crimes? Which of the following crimes should be considered the most serious: arson of a African American Church, rape of an adult women, battery on a teenage, painting of a Nazi symbol on the home of people of Jewish faith, a drive by shooting?

4. Which theory regarding child abuse do you believe is the most valid? Justify your answer.

5. What type of child abuse is the most serious? Why?

6. Why do people abuse their partners? If you had to list one reason what would it be? Why is this factor more important than the other reasons listed in the text?

ENDNOTES—Chapter 10

1. *Special Report, Victims of Gang Violence: A New Frontier in Victim Services,* (Office for Victims of Crime, US Department of Justice, Washington DC, October 25, 1996), p. 12.

2. James C. Howell, *Gangs, A Fact Sheet,* (Office of Juvenile Justice and Delinquency Prevention, US Department of Justice, Washington DC, April 1994)

3. *Id.*

4. This section has been adapted from *Gangs: A Community Response,* (Office of the Attorney General, Sacramento, California, no date)

5. Much of this information has been adapted from *Addressing Community Gang Problems: A Model for Problem Solving,* (Bureau of Justice Assistance, Department of Justice, Washington DC January 1997) [hereinafter referred to as *Addressing Community Gang Problems]* and Irving Spergel, et. al., *Gang Suppression and Intervention: Problem and Response,* (Office of JuvenileJustice and Delinquency Prevention, Department of Justice, Washington DC, October 1994)[hereinafter referred to as *Gang Suppression and Intervention*]

6. *Gang Suppression and Intervention,* p. 19.

7. This section has been adapted from Harvey Wallace, *Victimology: Legal, Psychological, and Social Perspectives* (Allyn & Bacon, Boston, Mass. 1998) All rights reserved. Used with permission of the author.

8. Peter Finn and Taylor NcNeil, *The Response of the Criminal Justice System to Bias Crimes: An Exploratory Review,* (Abt Associates, Inc. Washington D.C. 1987)

9. Public Law 101-275 (1990)

10. *National Bias Crimes Training For Law Enforcement and Victim Assistance Professionals,* Office for Victims of Crime, U.S. Department of Justice, Washington D.C. January 1995.

11. Marlene A. Young, *Victim Assistance Frontiers and Fundamentals,* (Kendall/Hunt Publishing, Dubuque, Iowa 1993)

12. "1990 Audit of Anti-Semitic Incidents," Anti-Defamation League of B'nai B'rith , New York (1991).

13. For example it was not until January 1995, that the Office for Victims of Crime published a *National Bias Crimes Training Manual for Law Enforcement and Victim Assistance Professionals* (U.S. Department of Justice, Washington D.C. 1995)

14. Harry H.L. Kitano, "Asian-Americans: The Chinese, Japanese, Koreans, Pilipinos and Southeast Asians," 454 *Annals American Academy of Political & Social Science* 125 (1981)

15. Robert J. Kelly, Ed., *Bias Crimes: American Law Enforcement and Legal Responses*, (Office of the International Criminal Justice Administration, Reading, Berkshire, United Kingdom 1993)

16. But see Fred Bayles, "Church Arsons not all Linked to Racism," Associated Press, *Fresno Bee* July 5, 1996, p. A-1 where the reporter points out that after reviewing six years of federal, state and local data, the Associated Press found arsons increasing, but with only random links to racism. Of the 73 African American Church arsons since 1995, fewer than 20 cases had clear links to racism. On the whole, the Associated Press reported that church arsons increased across the nation.

17. *Characteristics of Hate Crime in 1992,* (U.S. Department of Justice, Federal Bureau of Investigation, GPO, Washington D.C. 1993).

18. Kevin Berrill, "Gay and Lesbian Crime victims: What We All Can Do," *NOVA Newsletter*, Vol. 10, No. 12 Washington D.C. p. 3.

19. *R.A.V. v. City of St. Paul*, 112 S.Ct. 2538 (1992).

20. 113 S.Ct. 2194 (1993).

21. Jack Levin and Jack McDevitt, *The Rising Tide of Bigotry and Bloodshed*, (Plenum, New York 1993).

22. Allen D. Sapp, Richard N. Holden & Michael E. Wiggins, "Value and Belief Systems of Right-Wing Extremists," in Robert J. Kelly, Ed., *Bias Crimes: American Law Enforcement and Legal Responses*, (Office of the International Criminal Justice Administration, Reading, Berkshire, United Kingdom 1993).

23. Norman Geiser, *Moody Monthly,* (October 1985) pp. 129-131.

24. William Gale, *Racial and National Identity,* (pamphlet) (Ministry of Christ Church, Glendale, California, undated)

25. William P. Randel, *The Ku Klux Klan: A Century of Infamy*, (NY:Chilton Books, 1965) p.15-16.

26. This section has been adapted from Harvey Wallace, *Victimology: Legal, Psychological, and Social Perspectives* (Boston: Allyn & Bacon, 1998) All rights reserved. Used with permission of the author.

27. Cycle of Violence Theory contends that violence is cyclical. Children learn to be violent from the violence they received from their families and will, in turn, grow up to abuse their children.

28. Larry J. Siegal, *Criminology*, 3rd. (St. Paul: West, 1989) p. 188.

29. B. Steele and V. Pollock, "A Psychiatric study of Parents who Abuse Infants and Small Children," in R. Helfer and C.H. Kempe, Eds., *The Battered Child Syndrome,* (University of Chicago Press, Chicago) 1968. It is interesting to note that later editions of this classic book on child abuse do not contain the article. For example, see the 4th edition published in 1987.

30. M. Straus, "Family Patterns in a Nationally Representative Sample," 3 *International Journal of Child Abuse and Neglect* 23 (1979)

31. R. Hunter and N. Kilstrom, "Breaking the Cycle in Abusive Families," 136 *American Journal of Psychiatry* 1320 (1979)

32. B. Egeland and D. Jacobvitz, "Intergenerational Continuity of Parental Abuse: Causes and Consequences" Paper presented at the Conference on Biosocial Perspectives in Abuse and Neglect, York, Maine (1984)

33. C. Cappell and R.B. Heiner, "The Intergenerational Transmission of Family Aggression," 5(2) *Journal of Family Violence* 135 (1990)

34. Cynthia Crosson Tower, *Understanding Child Abuse and Neglect,* 2nd. (Allyn and Bacon, Mass 1993)

35. B. Justice and R. Justice, *The Abusing Family*, (Human Services Press, New York 1976) p.37

36 . See J.D. Delsordo, "Protective Casework for Abused Children," *Children*, 10 (1963):213-18.

37. H.P. Martin, Ed., *The Abused Child,* (Ballinger, Cambridge, MA 1976)

38. M. Lynch, "Risk Factors in the Child: A Study of Abused Children and Their Siblings," *The Abused Child*, edited by H.P. Martin, pp. 43-56. Cambridge, MA: Ballinger 1976.

39. D.J. Hansen & V.M. MacMilian, "Behavioral Assessment of Child Abuse and Neglectful Families: Recent Development and Current Issues," *Behavior Modification,* 14, (1990) p. 225-278.

40. N. Polansky, M. Chambers, E. Buttenwieser and D. Williams, *Damaged Parents: An Anatomy of Child Neglect,* (Chicago, IL: University of Chicago Press, 1981) p.21.

41. See L. Young, *Wednesday's Children*, (NY: McGraw-Hill, 1964) and S.N. Katz, *When Parents Fail,* (Boston: Beacon Press, 1971).

42. I. Wolock and B. Horowitz, "Child Maltreatment and Maternal Deprivation Among AFDC Families," *Social Service Review*, 53 (1979) p.175-184.

43. See J. Conti, "The Effects of Sexual Abuse on Children: A Critique and Suggestions for Future Research," *Victimology: An International Journal*, 10, 110-130 (1985) and J. Conti, I. Berliner, and J. Schurman, "The Impact of Sexual Abuse on Children: Final Report," Available from the authors at the University of Chicago, 969 E. 60th Street, Chicago, Ill., 60637.

44. E. Porter, *Treating the Young Male Victims of Sexual Assault*, (Syracuse, NY: Safer Society Press, 1986)

45. *Id.*

46. D.J. Gelinas, "The Persisting Negative Effects of Incest," 46 *Psychiatry* 312-322 (1983)

47. C.A. Courtios, "Studying and Counseling Women with Past Incest Experience," 5 *Victimology: An International Journal*, 322-334 (1980).

48. D. Finkelhor, *Child Sexual Abuse* and E. Porter, *Treating the Young Male Victim of Sexual Assault.*

49. D. Finkelhor, *Child Sexual Abuse*, (New York: Free Press, 1984)

50. See for example, Vincent B. Van Hasselt, et. al, Eds, *Handbook of Family Violence*, (New York: Plenum Press, 1988).

51. R.T. Ammerman and M. Hersen, *Assessment of Family Violence*, (NY:Wiley, 1982).

52. J. Myers, *Evidence in Child Abuse and Neglect*, 2d Ed., (New York : John Wiley & Sons, 1992).

53. This is a shortened version of the definition contained in the Child Abuse Prevention and Treatment Act of 1974 which is one of the most widely adopted statutes defining child sexual abuse.

54. D.A. Wolfe, V.V. Wolfe & C. L. Best, "Child Victims of Sexual Assault," V.B. Van Hasselt, R.L. Morrison, A.S. Bellack, M. Hersen, Eds., *Handbook of Family Violence*, (New York: Plenum Press, 1988).

55. J.R. Conte, "Victims of Child Sexual Abuse," in *Treatment of Family Violence*, R.T. Ammerman and M. Hersen, Eds., (New York: John Wiley & Sons, 1990) p. 64-65.

56. This section has been adapted from Harvey Wallace, *Victimology: Legal, Psychological, and Social Perspectives* (Boston: Allyn & Bacon, 1998) All rights reserved. Used with permission of the author.

57. L.E. Walker, *The Battered Woman*, (New York: Harper & Row, 1979).

58. L.E. Walker, *The Battered Woman Syndrome*, (New York: Springer, 1984).

59. See *People vs. Humphrey*, 96 Daily Journal D.A.R. 10609 at 10612 where the California Supreme Court addressed this issue.

60. M.A. Douglas, "The Battered Women Syndrome," D.J. Sonkin, Ed., *Domestic Violence on Trial*, (NY: Springer, 1982)

61. M.D. Pagelow, *Family Violence,* (NY: Praeger, 1984) p. 308.

62. G. NiCarthy, *Getting Free: A Handbook for Women in Abusive Relationships,* (NY: Seal Press, 1986) p. 117-118.

63. D.G. Dutton and S.L. Painter, "Traumatic Bonding: The Development of Emotional Attachments in Battered Women and Other Relationships of Intermittent Abuse, *Victimology*, vol. 6, (1981) p.139.

64. Donald G. Dutton, *The Domestic Assault of Women,* (Vancouver, B.C.: UBC Press, 1995).

65. *Id* at 190.

66. *Id*. at 191.

67. Demie Kurz, "Battering and the Criminal Justice System: A Feminist View," Eve S. Buzawa and Carl g. Buzawa, Eds., *Domestic Violence: The Changing Criminal Justice Response*, (Westport, CT: Auburn House, 1992).

68. For an excellent discussion of these issues, see K. Spiller, "The Feminist Majority Report: Corporate Women and the Mommy Track," A.M. Jaggar and P.S. Rothenberg, Eds., *Feminist Frameworks*, 3rd Ed. (McGraw Hill, New York 1993) p. 316-318.

69. See K. Newman, "Middle-Class Women in Trouble," A.M. Jaggar and P.S. Rothenberg, Eds., *Feminist Frameworks*, 3rd Ed. (NY: McGraw Hill, 1993) p. 319-323.

70. M. Roy, "A Current Study of 150 Cases," M. Roy, Ed., *A Psychological Study of Domestic Violence*, (Van Nostrand Reinhold, New York 1977)

71. D.S. Kalmuss and M.A. Straus, "Wife's Martial Dependency and Wife Abuse," M.A. Straus and R.J. Gelles, *Physical Violence in American Families,* (Transaction Publishers, New Brunswick, N.J. 1990) p. 379-380.

72. K.J. Sher, "Subjective Effects of Alcohol: The Influence of Setting and Individual Differences in Alcohol Expectancies," 46 *Journal of Studies on Alcohol* 137-146 (1985)

73. D.H. Coleman and M.A. Straus, "Alcohol Abuse and Family Violence," *Alcohol, Drug Abuse and Aggression*, E. Gottheil, K.A. Druley, T.E. Skoloda and H.M. Waxman, Eds. (Springfield, IL: Charles C. Thomas, 1983) p. 104-124.

74. D.C. McClelland, W.N. Davis, R. Kalin, and E. Wanner, *The Drinking Man*, (NY: Free Press, 1972).

75. K. Pernanem, "Theoretical Aspects of the Relationship Between Alcohol Use and Crime," *Drinking and Crime: Perspectives on the Relationships Between Alcohol Consumption and Criminal Behavior*, J.J. Collins, Jr., Ed., (NY: Guilford Press, 1981).

76. A. Helton, "Battering During Pregnancy," 86 *American Journal of Nursing* 910-913 (1986)

77. R.J. Gelles, "Violence and Pregnancy: Are Pregnant Women at Greater Risk of Abuse?" M.A. Straus and R.J. Gelles, *Physical Violence in American Families*, (Transaction Publishers, New Brunswick, N.J. 1990) p. 282.

78. M.A. Straus and R.J. Gelles, "How Violent Are American Families? Estimates From the National Family Violence Survey and Other Studies," G.T. Hotaling, D. Finkelhor, John T. Kirkpatrick and M.A. Straus, Eds., *New Directions in Family Violence Research*, (Beverly Hills, CA: Sage, 1988)

79. J.E. Sets and M.A. Straus, "The Marriage License: A Comparison of Assaults in Dating, Cohabitating, and Married Couples," in M.A. Straus and R.J. Gelles, *Physical Violence in American Families*, (Transaction Publishers, New Brunswick, N.J. 1990) p. 227-244 published earlier in 4 *Journal of Family Violence* (1989) p. 161-180.

80. J.E. Stets and M.A. Pirog-Good, "Violence in Dating Relationships," 50 *Social Psychology Quarterly* 237-246 (1987).

81. See J.E. Sets and M.A. Straus, "The Marriage License: A Comparison of Assaults in Dating, Cohabitating, and Married Couples," in M.A. Straus and R.J. Gelles, *Physical Violence in American Families*, (New Brunswick: Transaction Publishers, 1990) p. 227-244.

82. This section has been adapted from Harvey Wallace, *Family Violence, Legal, Medical, and Social Perspectives,* (Boston: Allyn & Bacon, 1996) All rights reserved. Used with the permission of the author.

83. Rhonda Saunders, Los Angeles Deputy District Attorney, "Legal Tools for Case Management," paper presented at the 4th Annual Threat Management Conference, Disneyland Hotel, Anaheim, California, June 29, 1994.

84. U.S. Constitution, Amendment I.

85. 1994 U.S. LEXIS 5087 (June 30, 1994)

86. *R.A.V. v. City of St. Paul, Minnesota,* 112 S.Ct. 2538, 2546 (1992)

87. 846 F. 2d 241 (4th Cir. 1988) , cert. denied, 448 U.S. 984 (1976)

88. *Id.* p. 243

89. *Winters v. New York,* 333 U.S. 507 (1948)

90. Wayne R. LaFave and Austin W. Scott Jr., *Criminal Law*, 2nd Ed. (St. Paul: West, 1986) Section 2.3 pp. 90-91.

91. *Kolender v. Lawson,* 461 U.S. 352 (1983)

92. *Grayned v. City of Rockford,* 408 U.S. 104 (1972)

93. M.A. Zona, K.K. Sharma and J. Lane, "A Comparative Study of Erotomanic and Obsessional Subjects in a Forensic Sample," 38 *Journal of Forensic Sciences* 894 (July 1993)

94. John C. Lane, "Threat Management Fills Void in Police Services," *The Police Chief,* August 1992, p. 27;.

95. Special Order No. 4, Office of the Chief of Police, February 12, 1992.

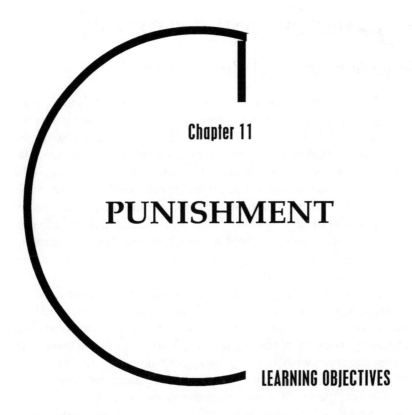

Chapter 11

PUNISHMENT

LEARNING OBJECTIVES

After studying this chapter, you should be able to:

- Explain the beginning of legal punishments and how they developed.

- Examine the concept of punishment in the Middle Ages.

- List the purposes of criminal sanctions.

- Recite the popular justifications for punishment.

- List the guiding principles of punishment.

- Identify the social aspects of punishment.

HISTORY AND PHILOSOPHY

Beginning of Legal Punishments

In primitive societies, the remedy for wrongs done to one's person or property was personal retaliation against the wrong doer. Unlike modern society, in the early primitive societies, personal retaliation was encouraged. From the concept of personal retaliation, developed "blood feuds." A **blood feud** occurred when the victim's family or tribe took revenge on the offender's family or tribe. Often, blood feuds escalated and resulted in continuing vendettas between families or tribes. In many cases, for religious reasons individuals were expected to avenge the death of a kinsman. The duty of retaliation was imposed by universal practice upon the victim or, in case of death, the nearest male relative.

To lessen the costly and damaging vendettas, the custom of accepting money or property in place of blood vengeance developed. At first, the acceptance of payments instead of blood vengeance was not compulsory. The victim's family was still free to choose whatever form of vengeance they wished. Often the relative power of the families or tribes decided whether payments or blood vengeance was used.

The acceptance of money or property as atonement for wrongs became know as **les salica** or **wergeld**. This practice is still used in some Middle Eastern countries. The amount of payment was based on the rank or position of the victim. This tradition of accepting money for property damages was the beginning of the development of a system of criminal law.

One problem with the acceptance of payment as complete satisfaction for the wrong was the concept that punishment of an individual wrongdoer should also include some religious aspects. To many, crime was also a sin against the church and, later, the state. Accordingly, there developed the concept that punishment in the form of wergeld (payment to the victim) should also be supplemented with friedensgeld (payment to the church or later to the crown).

Fines and other forms of punishment replaced personal retaliation as tribal leaders began to exert their authority during the negotiations or proceedings concerning the damages caused by the wrongs committed. The wrongdoers were not required to attend the proceedings. If, however, they failed to follow the recommendations of the tribal leaders, they were banished or exiled and, thus, considered "outlaws."

Since criminal law requires an element of public action against the wrongdoer, the banishment or pronouncement of outlawry was the first criminal punishment imposed by society.[1] Many present day researchers consider the development of this custom as the beginning of criminal law as we know it today. Subsequent legal codes and punishments for different crimes have either stressed or refined the vengeance principle. The concept that a society express its vengeance within a system of rules was present in the ethics of primitive societies.

The two earliest codes involving criminal punishments were the Sumerian and Hammurabic Codes. The punishment phases of these codes contained the concept of personal vengeance. The listed punishments in the codes were harsh and, in many cases, the victim or nearest relative was personally allowed to inflict punishment. Permitted punishments included mutilation, whipping, or forced labor. At first, the punishments were applied almost exclusively to slaves and bond servants and indicated a base or servile mentality towards those being punished. Later they were extended to all offenders.

The use of penal servitude also developed. Penal servitude involved the use of hard labor as punishment. It was generally reserved for the lower classes of citizens. Penal servitude included the loss of citizenship and liberty (i.e., civil death). With civil death, the offender's property was confiscated in the name of the state and his wife was declared a widow. Later, the use of penal servitude by the Romans was encouraged by the need for workers to perform hard labor.

The fact that early punishments were considered synonymous with slavery is indicated by the practice of shaving the heads of those punished as a "mark of slavery." Other marks of slavery used on punished wrongdoers included the branding on the forehead or use of a heavy metal collar that could not be easily removed.

The Greek code, **Code of Draco**, used the same penalties for both citizens and slaves and incorporated many of the concepts used in primitive societies (e.g., vengeance, outlawry, and blood feuds). Apparently, the Greeks were the first society to allow any citizen to prosecute an offender on behalf of the victim. This practice appears to indicate that public interest and protection of society had accepted the concept that crimes affected not only the victim, but society in general.

The Case Against Socrates

Socrates was charged in 399 B.C. with the offense of impiety (corrupting young minds and believing in new Gods). He was tried before a jury of 500 members. The trial lasted only one day. He was found guilty by a margin of thirty jurors. The prosecution proposed the death penalty. Socrates had a right to propose an alternative penalty. He stated:

> Shall I [propose] imprisonment? And why should I spend my days in prison, and be the slave of the magistrates? Or shall the penalty be a fine and imprisonment until the fine is paid? There is the same objection. I should have to lie in prison, for money I have none, and cannot pay. And if I say exile, I must indeed be blinded by the love of life, if I am so irrational as to expect that when you, who are my own citizens, cannot endure my discourses and arguments, and have found them so grievous and odious that you will have no more of them, that others are likely to endure them.

The jury condemned him to death. He committed compulsory suicide by drinking poison, the Athenian method of execution.

Middle Ages

During the Middle Ages, rapid changes were made in the social structure of societies. In addition, the growing influence of the church on everyday life helped create a divided system of justice. The offender in committing a crime, also committed a sin. Accordingly, he or she had two debts to pay—one to the victim and one to the church. **Trials by ordeal** were used by the churches as substitutes for trials. In a trial by ordeal, the accused was subjected to dangerous or painful tests in the belief that God would protect the innocent and the guilty would suffer agonies and die. The brutality of the trial by ordeal ensured that most would die and thus be considered guilty. The practice of trial by ordeal was not abolished until about the year 1215.

It was also during the Middle Ages that the churches expanded the concept of crime to include new prohibited areas. This concept is still present in our modern day codes. Sexual offenses were among the new areas now covered by law. Sex offenses which include either public or "unnatural" acts were punished by horrible punishments. Heresy and witchcraft were also included in the new prohibited areas of conduct. The church inflicted cruel punishments and justified the punishments as necessary to save the unfortunate sinners. For example, the zealous movement to stamp out heresy resulted in the Inquisition. The Inquisition was a tribunal established by the Church with very broad powers to use for the suppression of heresy. The Inquisition searched out offenders rather than waiting for charges to be brought against them.

The Holy Inquisition

The word "inquisition" means an inquiry. In one sense, all modern courts of law are inquisitions. The Holy Inquisition was a court set up by the Church of Rome to inquire into cases of heresy. It was later extended to cover crimes of witchcraft and ecclesiastical offenses committed by members of the Church. The idea of a court of inquiry into religious offenses was of very early origin. For example, Jews found guilty of deserting their faith by an inquisition were sentenced to be stoned to death.[2] The Holy Inquisition flourished in all European countries, but its barbarities were the greatest in Spain and the Spanish dominions. The sentences of the court were generally pronounced on Sunday in a church and consisted of burning, scourging, imprisonment, penances, humiliation, and/or fines.

Whipping was the usual method of punishing persons for minor offenses. Whipping was inflicted on women while kneeling and on men while lying on the ground. Generally the victims were stripped to the waist and the blows inflicted on their backs.[3]

Purpose of Criminal Sanctions

In discussing the purpose of criminal sanctions, various ideologies are presented. For purposes of studying this chapter, **ideology** refers to the belief system adopted by a group and consists of assumptions and values. The **assumptions** are beliefs about the way the world is constituted, organized, and operates. **Values**, however, are beliefs about what is moral and desirable.[4] There are numerous methods to classify ideologies. Three popular classifications based on political theories that influence our corrections system are conservative, liberal, and radical.

The conservative ideology tends to accept the concept that human beings are rational, possess free will, and voluntarily commit criminal misconduct. Accordingly, criminals should be held accountable for the actions. Punishment should be imposed to inflict suffering on the criminal because the suffering is deserved, and it will deter future crime. The punishment imposed should fit the crime. This ideology because of its view on the causes of human behavior, generally does not accept the concept of rehabilitation as an attractive objective of punishment.

The liberal ideology tends to view human behavior as greatly influenced by social circumstances including one's upbringing, material affluence, education, peer relationships, etc. Accordingly, human behavior is more than a simple product of free choice. All of the social influences are important factors in shaping our conduct. Viewing criminal behavior as a product of both social circumstances and individual actions, liberals are more likely to support rehabilitation as the proper purpose of criminal punishment. Most liberals tend to be receptive to a wider range of aims for criminal punishment including deterrence.

The radical ideology rejects both the conservative and liberal ideologies. To them, crime is a natural consequence of our social system. According to the radicals, fundamental changes in the socioeconomic basis of society are required in order to control crime.

The ultimate purpose of criminal sanctions is generally considered to be the maintenance of our social order. Herbert Packer contends that the two major goals of criminal sanctions are to inflict suffering upon the wrongdoers and the prevention of crime.[5]

Robert Dawson sees the major purpose of the criminal justice system as the identification in a legally acceptable manner of those persons who should be subjected to control and treatment in the correctional process.[6] According to Dawson, if corrections does not properly perform its task, the entire criminal justice system suffers. An inefficient or unfair correctional process can nullify the courts, prosecutors and police alike. Conversely, the manner in which the other agencies involved perform their tasks has an important impact upon the success of the process, thus a person who has been unfairly dealt with prior to conviction is a poor subject for rehabilitation.

The four popular goals of criminal sanctions are retribution, deterrence, incapacitation, and rehabilitation. From the 1940s to the 1980s, rehabilitation was considered by most as the primary goal of our system.

Since the 1980s, retribution as received popular support. Each of these four commonly accepted goals are discussed in later in this chapter.

THE JUSTIFICATION OF PUNISHMENT

The problem of punishment causes constant, anguished reassessment, not only because we keep speculating on what the effective consequences of crime should be, but also because there is a confusion of the ends and means. We are still far from the answer to the ultimate questions: What is the right punishment? and On what grounds do we punish others?[7]

Retribution

Retribution generally means "getting even". Retribution is based on the ideology that the criminal is an enemy of society and deserves severe punishment for willfully breaking its rules. Retribution is often mistaken as revenge. There are, however, important differences between the two. Both retribution and revenge are primarily concerned with punishing the offender and neither is overly concerned with the impact of the punishment on the offender's future behavior or behavior of others. Unlike revenge, however, retribution attempts to match the severity of the punishment to the seriousness of the crime. Revenge acts on passion, whereas retribution follows specific rules regarding the types and amounts of punishment that may be inflicted. The Biblical response of an "eye for an eye " is a retributive response to punishment. While the "eye for eye" concept is often cited as an excuse to use harsh punishment, it is less harsh than revenge-based punishment which does not rule out "two eyes for an eye" punishment. Sir James Stephen, an English judge, expressed the retributive view by stating that "the punishment of criminals was simply a desirable expression of the hatred and fear aroused in the community by criminal acts."[8] This line of reasoning conveys the message that punishment is justifiable because it provides an orderly outlet for emotions, that if denied may express themselves in socially less acceptable ways. Another justification under the retribution ideology is that only through suffering punishment can the criminal expiate his sin. In one manner, retribution treats all crimes as if they were financial transactions. You

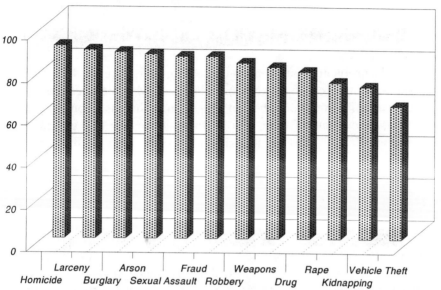

Likelihood of Being Prosecuted
Percentage by type of felony arrest

got something or did something, therefore you must give equivalent value (suffering).

Retribution is also referred to as "just desserts." The just desserts movement reflects the retribution viewpoint and provides a justifiable rationale for support of the death penalty. This viewpoint has its roots in a societal need for retribution. It can be traced back to the individual need for retaliation and vengeance. The transfer of vengeance motive from the individual to the state has been justified based on theories involving theological, aesthetic, and expiatory views. According to the theological view, retaliation fulfills the religious need to punish the sinner. Under the aesthetic view, punishment helps reestablish a sense of harmony through requital and thus solves the social discord created by the crime. The expiatory view is that guilt must be washed away (cleanse) through suffering. There is even an utilitarian view that punishment is the means of achieving beneficial and social consequences through the application of a specific form and degree of punishment deemed most appropriate to the particular offender after careful individualized study of the offender.[9]

Deterrence

Deterrence is a punishment viewpoint that focuses on future outcomes rather than past misconduct. It is also based on the theory that creating a fear of future punishments will deter crime. It is based on the belief that punishments have a deterrent effect. There is substantial debate as to the validity of this concept. Specific deterrence deters specifically the offender, whereas general deterrence works generally on others who might consider similar acts. According to this viewpoint, the fear of future suffering motivates individuals to avoid involvement in criminal misconduct. This concept assumes that the criminal is a rational being who will weight the consequences of his or her criminal actions before deciding to commit them.

One of the problems with deterrence is determining the appropriate magnitude and nature of punishment to be imposed in order to deter future criminal misconduct. For example, an individual who commits a serious crime and then feels badly about the act may need only slight punishment to achieve deterrent effects, whereas, a professional shoplifter may need severe fear-producing punishments to prevent future shoplifting.

Often, increases in crime rates and high rates of recidivism are used to cast doubt that the deterrence approach is effective. Recidivism may cause some doubt on the efficacy of specific deterrence, but it says nothing about the effect of general deterrence. In addition, unless we know what the crime rate or rates of recidivism would be if we did not attempt to deter criminal misconduct, the assertions are unfounded. Are we certain that the rates would not be higher had we not attempted to deter criminals?

Incapacitation

At least while the prisoner is in confinement, he is unlikely to commit crimes on innocent persons outside of prison. To this extent, confinement clearly helps reduce criminal behavior. Under this viewpoint, there is no hope for the individual as far as rehabilitation is concerned, therefore the only solution is to incapacitate the offender. Marvin Wolfgang's famous study of crime in Philadelphia indicated that while chronic offenders constituted only 23 percent of the offenders in the study, they committed over 61 percent of all the violent crimes.[10] Ac-

.cordingly, the supporters of the incapacition viewpoint contend that incapaciting the 23 percent would have prevented 61 percent of the future violent crimes. This approach has often been labeled the "nothing else works" approach to corrections. According to this viewpoint, we should make maximum effective use of the scarce prison cells to protect society from the depredations of such dangerous and repetitive offenders. This approach is present in California's "Three Strikes and You're Out" statute.

There are two variations in the incapacitative viewpoint. **Collective incapacitation** refers to sanctions imposed on offenders without regard to their personal characteristics such as all violent offenders. Selective incapacitation refers to incapacitation of certain groups of individuals who have been identified as high-risk offenders such as robbers with a history of drug use. Under selective incapacitation, offenders with certain characteristics or history would receive longer prison terms than others convicted of the same crime. The purpose of incapacitation is to prevent future crimes and the moral concerns associated with retribution are not as important as the reduction of future victimization.[11] As Herbert Packer states: "Incapacitation is a mode of punishment that uses the fact that a person has committed a crime as a basis for predicting that he will commit future crimes.[12] Packer also states that the logic of the incapacitative position is that until the offender stops being a danger we will continue to restrain him. Accordingly, he contends that pushed to its logical conclusion, offenses that are regarded as relatively trivial may be punished by imprisonment for life.

Rehabilitation

The rehabilitation approach is that punishment should be directed toward correcting the offender. This approach is also considered the "treatment" approach. This approach considers the criminal misconduct as a manifestation of a pathology that can be handled by some form of therapeutic activity. While this viewpoint may consider the offender as "sick," it is not the same as the medical approach. Under the rehabilitation viewpoint, we need to teach offenders to recognize the undesirability of their criminal behavior and make significant efforts to rid themselves of that behavior. The main difference between the rehabilitation approach and the retribution approach is that under the rehabilitation approach the offenders are assigned to programs designed to prepare them for readjustment or reintegration into the community whereas the latter approach is more concerned with the punishment aspects of the sentence. Packer sees two major objections to making rehabilitation the primary justification for punishment. First, we do not know how to rehabilitate offenders. Second, we know little about who is likely to commit crimes and less about what makes them apt to do so. As long as we are ignorant in these matters, Packard contends that punishment in the name of rehabilitation is gratuitous cruelty.[13]

PURPOSES OF PUNISHMENT

English Statement of Purposes

The United States is not the only country that has had problems determining the proper purposes of punishment. It appears that most other countries have the same problem. An examination of the *English Statement of Purposes* indicates that the English have similar problems. The English Prison Service has approximately 43,000 prisoners confined. The Service declares that it "serves the public by keeping in custody those committed by the courts." And that its duty is to "look after them with humanity and help them lead law-abiding and useful lives in custody and after release." The purposes are divided into a series of goals:

√ To keep prisoners in custody

√ To maintain order, control, discipline and a safe environment

√ To provide decent conditions for prisoners and meet their needs, including health care

√ To provide positive regimes which help prisoners address their offending behavior

√ To allow prisoners as full and responsible a life as possible

√ To help prisoners prepare for their return to the community.[14]

Guiding Principles

Certain principles are used in guiding the decision as to the proper disposition of a person convicted of criminal behavior. The principles are simple, yet subject to interpretation according to the philosophy of the individuals involved. The generally accepted principles include:

1. **Parsimony.** The least restrictive sanction necessary to achieve the defined purposes should be imposed. The debate regarding this principle centers on the purpose of criminal sanctions.

2. **Dangerousness.** Whether the likelihood of future criminality should be considered? The controversy on this point is whether we should use predictions of future misconduct as a basis for present criminal sanctions. There are numerous studies which indicate that predictions of dangerousness are unreliable. The studies indicate that we tend to over predict future dangerousness in individuals. There is also the philosophical and due process concerns of punishing a person for conduct not yet committed.

3. **Just Desserts.** Any sanction imposed should not be greater than that which is deserved by the last crime, or series of crimes, for which the defendant is being sentenced.[15]

Social Purposes of Punishment

C. Ray Jeffery, a noted criminologist, contends that the more glaring defect in most analyses of punishments is that the analyses view punishments always in the context of what it means to the individual offender and never in terms of what it means to society. The purpose of punishment, according to Jeffery, should be to establish social disapproval of the act. To him, the use of punishment by society is not as important in terms of whether or not it reforms the individual as in terms of what it does for society. He also contends that punishment serves an important social function in that it creates social solidarity and re-enforces social norms.[16]

SUMMARY

- In primitive societies, the remedy for wrongs done to one's person or property was personal retaliation against the wrong-doer. Unlike modern society, in the early primitive societies, personal retaliation was encouraged. From the concept of personal retaliation, developed "blood feuds."

- Fines and other forms of punishment replaced personal retaliation as tribal leaders began to exert their authority during the proceedings concerning the damages caused by the wrongs committed. The wrongdoers were not required to attend the proceedings. If, however, they failed to follow the recommendations of the tribal leaders, they were banished or exiled, and thus considered "outlaws." Because criminal law requires an element of public action against the wrongdoer, the banishment or pronouncement of outlawry was the first criminal punishment imposed by society.

- The ultimate purpose of criminal sanctions is generally considered to be the maintenance of our social order. Herbert Packer contends that the two major goals of criminal sanctions are to inflict suffering upon the wrongdoers and the prevention of crime. Robert Dawson sees the major purpose of the criminal justice system as the identification, in a legally acceptable manner, of those persons who should be subjected to control and treatment in the correctional process.

- The four popular goals of criminal sanctions are retribution, deterrence, incapacitation, and rehabilitation. From the 1940s to the 1980s, rehabilitation was considered by most as the primary goal of our system. Since the 1980s, retribution has received popular support.

- Retribution generally means "getting even." Retribution is based on the ideology that the criminal is an enemy of society and deserves severe punishment for willfully breaking its rules. Retribution is often mistaken as revenge. Deterrence is a punishment viewpoint that focuses on future outcomes rather than past misconduct. It is also based on the theory that creating a fear of future punishments will deter crime.

- There are two variations in the incapacitative viewpoint. Collective incapacitation refers to sanctions imposed on offenders without regard to their personal characteristics (i.e., all violent offenders). Selective incapacitation refers to incapacitation of certain groups of individuals who have been identified as high-risk offenders (e.g., robbers with a history of drug use). The rehabilitation approach contends that punishment should be directed toward correcting the offender. This approach is also considered the "treatment" approach. This approach considers the criminal misconduct as a manifestation of a pathology that can be handled by some form of therapeutic activity. While this viewpoint may consider the offender as "sick," it is not the same as the medical approach.

DISCUSSION QUESTIONS

1. Explain how the concept of blood feuds developed.
2. Discuss the functions and purpose of the Holy Inquisition.
3. Compare and contrast the three political ideologies regarding punishment.
4. Compare and contrast the rehabilitation and deterrence approaches to punishment.
5. How did the concept of punishment change during the Middle Ages?
6. Explain the various rationales for criminal sanctions.
7. List four popular goals of criminal sanctions.
8. Differentiate between specific and general deterrence.
9. Explain the differences between incapacitation and rehabilitation.

ENDNOTES—Chapter 11

1. Albert Kocourek and John Wigmore, *Evolution of Law*, Vol. II, (Boston: Little, Brown and Co., 1915) p. 15.

2. John Swain, *The Pleasures of the Torture Chamber*, (New York: Dorset Press, 1931) p. 157.

3. *Id.*, p. 27.

4. Alexis M. Durham III, *Crisis and Reform: Current Issues in American Punishment*, (Boston: Little, Brown, 1994) p. 16-18.

5. Herbert L. Packer, *The Limits of Criminal Sanction*, (Stanford, CA.: Stanford University Press, 1968) p. 33.

6. Robert O. Dawson, *Sentencing: The Decision as to Type, Length, and Conditions of Sentence* (Boston: Little, Brown and Company, 1969).

7. Stephen Schafer, *Theories in Criminology*, (New York: Random House, 1969) p. 291.

8. Herbert L. Packer, *The Limits of Criminal Sanction*, (Stanford, CA: Stanford University Press, 1968) p. 37.

9. Elmer H. Johnson, *Crime, Correction, and Society*, (Homewood, IL: Dorsey Press, 1974) p. 173.

10. Marianne W. Zawitz, ed., *Report to the Nation on Crime and Justice* (Washington, D.C.:, Bureau of Justice Statistics, U.S. Government Printing Office, 1983) p. 35.

11. Durham, 1994:26.

12. Packer, 1963:49.

13. Packer, 1963:55-57.

14. As reported in *The Oxford History of the Prison*, eds. Norval Morris and David J. Rothman. (New York: Oxford, 1995), p. xi.

15. Norval Morris, *The Future of Imprisonment*, (Chicago: University of Chicago, 1974, p. xi).

16. C. Ray Jeffery, "The Historical Development of Criminology," in *Pioneers in Criminology*, 2d ed., Hermann Mannheim editor (Montclair, NJ: Patterson Smith, 1973) p. 487.

THE ECONOMICS OF CRIME

SHATTERED LIVES
$170,000,000,000

CRIMINAL JUSTICE SYSTEM
$90,000,000,000

PRIVATE PROTECTION
$65,000,000,000

URBAN DECAY
$50,000,000,000

PROPERTY LOSS
$45,000,000,000

MEDICAL CARE
$5,000,000,000

estimated

425 Billion Dollars
Per Year

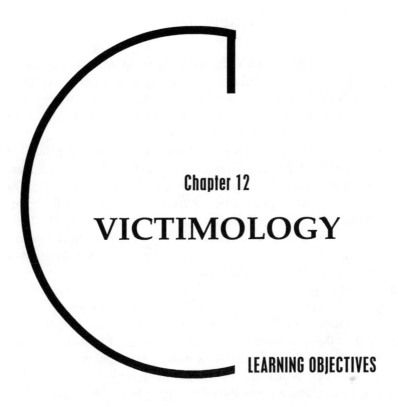

Chapter 12

VICTIMOLOGY

LEARNING OBJECTIVES

After reading this chapter, you should be able to:

- Understand the history and development of victims' rights.

- Differentiate between criminology and victimology.

- Distinguish between restitution and compensation.

- Illustrate the theories that justify victim impact statements.

HISTORY¹

A complete and accurate understanding of the concepts inherent in victimology can only be attained by a review of the development of law, its history, philosophy, and development. Modern criminal law is the result of a long evolution of laws attempting to deal with deviant behavior in society.

Early civilizations accorded victims many more rights than we did until the birth of the victim's rights movement in the United States. Early laws were known as **primitive law** which was a system of rules in preliterate societies. These rules or regulations represent the foundation upon which the modern legal system is built. Primitive laws typically contained three characteristics: (1) Acts that injured others were considered private wrongs, (2) The injured party was entitled to take action against the wrongdoer and (3) This action usually amounted to in-kind retaliation. These types of laws encouraged blood feuds and revenge as the preferred method of making the victim whole.

As society matured, we learned the art of reading and writing. One result of this evolution was the development of written codes of conduct. The Code of Ur-Nammu dates back to the twenty-first century B.C. Many of these codes treated certain wrongs, such as theft or assault, as private wrongs with the injured party being the victim, rather than the state.²

The Code of Hammurabi

The Code of Hammurabi is considered one of the first known attempts to establish a written code of conduct. King Hammurabi ruled Babylon at approximately 2000 B.C. He was the sixth king of the First Dynasty of Babylonia and ruled for about 55 years. Babylon, during that period of time, was a commercial center for most of the known and civilized world. Since its fortune lie in trade and other business ventures, the Code of Hammurabi provided a basis for order and certainty. The code established rules regarding theft, sexual relationships, and interpersonal violence. It was intended to replace blood feuds with a system sanctioned by the state.³

The Code of Hammurabi was divided into five sections:

1. A penal or code of laws.

2. A manual of instruction for judges, police officers, and witnesses.

3. A handbook of rights and duties of husbands, wives, and children.

4. A set of regulations establishing wages and prices.

5. A code of ethics for merchants, doctors, and officials.[4]

The code established certain obligations and objectives for the citizens of Babylon to follow. These included:

1. An assertion of the power of the state. This was the beginning of state administrated punishment. The blood feuds that had previously occurred between private citizens were barred under the code.

2. Protection of the weaker from the stronger. Widows were to be protected from those who might exploit them, elder parents were protected from sons who would disown them, and lesser officials were protected from higher ones.

3. Restoration of equity between the offender and the victim. The victim was to be made as whole as possible and, in turn, he or she forgave vengeance against the offender.

Of noteworthy importance in the code was its concern for the rights of victims.[5] In reality, this code may have been the first "victim rights statute" in history. However, as will be seen, we as a society began to neglect victims in our rush to punish the offender with the result that victims rights would not resurface until the present century.[6]

Other Early Codes and Laws

Another important milestone in the development of American law was early Roman law. Roman law was derived from the Twelve Tables, written about 450 B.C.

These laws existed for centuries as unwritten law. However, they applied only to the ruling patrician class of citizens. A protest by the plebeian class, who were the workers and artisans of Rome, caused commerce to come to a standstill. These workers wanted the law to apply to all citizens of Rome.[7] As a result, the laws were inscribed on 12 wooden tablets and prominently displayed in the forum for all to see and follow. These tables were a collection of basic rules relating to conduct of the family, religion and economic life.

Early Roman legions conquered England in the middle of the first century. Roman law, customs, and language were forced upon the English people during the next three centuries of Roman rule.

Emperor Justinian I codified the Roman laws into a set of writings. The Justinian Code, as these writings became known, distinguished between two major types of laws—public laws and private laws. **Public laws** dealt with the organization and administration of the Republic. **Private laws** addressed issues such as contracts, possession and other property rights, the legal status of various persons such as slaves, husbands, wives, etc. and injuries to citizens. It contained elements of both our civil and criminal law and influenced Western legal theory into the Middle Ages.

Prior to the Norman Conquest of 1066, the legal system in England was very decentralized. There was little written law except for crimes against society. As a society, we had moved away from the teaching of the Code of Hammurabi, and crimes during this period were again viewed as personal wrongs. Compensation was paid to the victim or his family for the offense. If the perpetrator failed to make payments, the victim's family could seek revenge resulting in a blood feud. For the most part, during this period, criminal law was designed to provide equity to what was considered a private dispute.

The Norman Conquest under William the Conqueror established royal administrators who rode circuit to render justice. These royal judges would use local custom and rules of conduct as a guide in rendering their judgment. This system known as *stare decisis* (Latin for the phrase "to stand by the decided law") would have far reaching effects on modern American criminal law.

The next major development in the history of law was the acknowledgment of the existence of common law. Early English common law forms the basis for much of our present day legal system. **Common law** is a traditional body of unwritten legal precedents created by court decisions during the Middle Ages in England. During this period of time when cases were heard, judges would start their deliberations from past decisions that were as closely related as possible to the case under consideration. In the eleventh century, King Edward the Confessor proclaimed that common law was the law of the land. Court decisions were finally recorded and made available to lawyers who could then use them to plead their case. This concept is one of the most important aspects of today's modern American law.

VICTIMIZATION[8]

Introduction

Victimology is a relatively new concept in the United States. It is a study that resides in a number of different academic disciplines across the nation. Some courses that focus on victimology are offered in sociology, social work, criminology and even psychology. At the same time that academic institutions are awakening to the necessity of offering courses in victimology, the victim's movement continues to gain strength and momentum across America. While there is some interaction between these two forces, there is still a great deal that they can learn from each other.

Definitions

In 1947, Edwin H. Sutherland, one of the imminent scholars in America, set forth the following definition of criminology:

> "*Criminology* is the body of knowledge regarding crime as a social phenomenon. It includes within its scope the process of making laws, of breaking laws .... The objective of criminology is the development of a body of general and verified principles and of other types of knowledge regarding this process of law, crime, treatment or prevention."[9]

Other scholars have researched various aspects of criminology and several have put forth definitions of victimology. However, for purposes of clarity, the following definition of victimology is offered:

> *Victimology* is the study of the victim, the offender and society. This definition can encompass both the research

or scientific aspects of the discipline as well as the practical aspects of providing services to victims of crime, This combined definition allows for a wide ranging examination of various issues affecting victims of crime. From its inception in the 1940s to the present day, victimology has been an interdisciplinary approach to violence and its effect on victims.

Mendelsohn's Theory of Victimization

Benjamin Mendelsohn was a practicing attorney. In the course of preparing a case for trial, he would conduct in-depth interviews of victims, witnesses and bystanders.[10] He would use a questionnaire that was couched in simple language and contained more than 300 questions concerning the branches of criminology and associated sciences. The questionnaire was given to the accused and all others who had knowledge of the crime. Based upon these studies, Mendelsohn came to the conclusion that there was usually a strong interpersonal relationship between the offender and the victim. In an effort to further clarify these relationships, he developed a typology of victims and their contribution to the criminal act.[11] This classification ranged from the completely innocent victim to the imaginary victim. Mendelsohn classified victims into six distinct categories:

1. **The Completely Innocent Victim:** This victim may be a child or completely unconscious person.

2. **The Victim with Minor Guilt:** This victim might be a woman who induces a miscarriage and dies as a result.

3. **The Victim who is as Guilty as the Offender:** Those who assist others in committing crimes fall within this classification.

4. **The Victim More Guilty than the Offender:** These are persons who provoke others to commit a crime.

5. **The Most Guilty Victim:** This occurs when the perpetrator (victim) acts aggressively and is killed by another person who is acting in self defense.

6. **The Imaginary Victim:** These are persons suffering from mental disorders such as paranoia who believe they are victims.

Many scholars credit Mendelsohn with coining the term "victimology," and still others consider him the "father of victimology."[12] His typology was one of the first attempts to focus on victims of crimes rather than simply examine the perpetrator. However, Mendelsohn was only one of two early scholars who explored the relationship between victims and offenders. The other noted early researcher in victimology was Hans von Hentig.

Von Hentig's Theory of Victimization

In an early classical text, *The Criminal and His Victim*, von Hentig explored the relationship between the 'doer' or criminal and the 'sufferer' or victim.[13] Von Hentig also established a typology of victims.[14] This classification was based upon psychological, social, and biological factors. Von Hentig established three classes of victims—the general classes of victims, the psychological types of victims, and the activating sufferer victims. His classification identifies victims by examining various risk factors. The typology includes:

✓The General Classes of Victims

- **The Young:** They are weak and the most likely to be a victim of an attack. Youth is the most dangerous period of life.[15]

- **The Female:** The female sex is another form of weakness recognized by the law since numerous rules of law embody the legal fiction of a weaker (female) and stronger (male) sex.[16]

- **The Old:** The elder generation holds most positions of accumulated wealth and wealth-giving power and, at the same time, is physically weak and mentally feeble.[17]

- **The Mentally Defective:** The feebleminded, the insane, the drug addict, and the alcoholic form another large class of victims.[18]

- **Immigrants, Minorities, and Dull Normals:** Immigration means more than a change in country. It causes a temporary feeling of helplessness in vital human relations. The inexperienced, poor, and sometimes dull immigrant, minority or other are easy prey to all kinds of swindlers.[19]

✓The Psychological Types of Victims

- **The Depressed:** These victims may suffer from a disturbance of the instinct of self-preservation. Without such an instinct, the individual may be easily overwhelmed or surprised by dangers or enemies.[20]

- **The Acquisitive:** This type of person makes an excellent victim. The excessive desire for gain eclipses intelligence, business experience, and inner impediments.[21]

- **The Wanton:** Often a sensual or wanton disposition requires other concurrent factors to become activated. Loneliness, alcohol and certain critical phases are "process-accelerators" of this type of victim.[22]

- **The Lonesome and the Heartbroken:** Loneliness causes critical mental facilities to be weakened. These individuals become easy prey for criminals.[23] The heartbroken victims are dazed by their loss and, therefore, become easy targets for a variety of "death rackets" that might, for example, charge a widow an outlandish fee for a picture of her late husband to be included in his biography.[24]

- **The Tormentor:** This victim becomes a perpetrator. This is the psychotic father who may abuse the wife and children for a number of years until one of the children grow up and, under extreme provocation, kill him.[25]

- **The Blocked, Exempted, and Fighting:** The blocked victim is so enmeshed in a losing situation that defensive moves become impossible. This is a self-imposed form of helplessness and an ideal condition for a victim from the point of view of the criminal.[26]

✓The Activating Sufferers

- **The Activating Sufferers:** This occurs when the victim is transformed into a perpetrator. A number of factors operate as activators on the victim such as certain predispositions like age, alcohol, and loss of self-confidence.[27]

Von Hentig theorized that a large percentage of victims, because of their acts or behavior, were responsible for their victimization.[28] This concept has since been repudiated by modern studies which have more closely examined and defined the relationship between the victim and the offender.

COMPENSATION AND RESTITUTION[29]

The growth of victim compensation and restitution statutes within the United States is a relatively recent phenomenon. Much of this slowness to react to the victim's plight was based on our concept of the criminal justice system. As discussed earlier, the victim was viewed as merely one more witness, and the state was the party that was injured when perpetrators committed crimes.

Compensation and restitution are both aimed at making the victim financially whole, however, they are separate and distinct concepts. Victim compensation funds are provided by the state and restitution comes from the perpetrator. Understanding how they operate will assist any professional working in the criminal justice field.

Compensation

Compensation can be defined as state funds that are paid to victims or their families for injuries suffered as a result of another's criminal act. These victim compensation laws allow those that have suffered economic loss to partially recover funds from a state supported fund established for that purpose. Eligible expenses include medical expenses, including the costs of counseling, burial expenses, special services to the victim, and rehabilitation expenses.

In 1965, California became the first state in the union to establish compensation funds for victims of crimes. In 1966, New York followed California's lead by setting up a special board to allocate funds to victims. In 1967, Massachusetts organized a procedure whereby the state attorney general granted compensation to victims. Today, all states have a mechanism in place that allows victims of crimes to be compensated for their loss.

While victim compensation programs vary from state to state, they generally have certain common characteristics.

- All programs grant aid to innocent victims. Perpetrators who were injured during the commission of the crime are not eligible for compensation under these statutes.

- Many states have boards or commissions that investigate victim's claims and eliminate or reduce any award, if the victim contributed to his or her injury participated in or provoked the offender.

- Most of these programs compensate only the more serious offenses. They do not pay for property that was damaged or stolen in burglaries or robberies.

- All the states prevent "double dipping" or recovery from more than one source for the same injury. When the victim receives funds from other state agencies, insurance companies, or the perpetrator in the form of a civil judgment or an order for restitution, that amount is deducted from any award.

- Most states require the victim to report the crime to the police and cooperate with them in any investigation and court proceeding.

From a historical perspective, one of the most troubling aspects of some early victim compensation statutes was the prohibition against awarding any funds to victims if they are related to the offender. Under these programs, battered spouses and abused children were deemed ineligible for compensation. The rationale for this male-oriented rule was that the offender should not be indirectly rewarded by granting money to the family. Other arguments included the fear that families will conspire to defraud the state by claiming injuries where none exist. Fortunately, these antiquated ideas are being thrown out, and all states have now modified this particular prohibition so that victims of family violence can now claim compensation.

While at first glance victim compensation programs appear to provide a long needed solution to the financial problems faced by victims of crime, there are several problems that still exist within most programs.

As indicated above, many of these statutes apply only to victims of violent criminal acts, and, as such, the financial crimes committed against elders would not be covered. Additionally, some of these statutes reimburse the victim only above a certain minimum level and do not provide compensation above a stated limit. State compensation funds are not the only method of making crime victims financially whole.

Rights of Texas Crime Victims

1. The right to protection from threats of harm arising from cooperating with prosecution efforts.

2. The right to have your safety and that of your family taken into consideration when bail is being considered.

3. If you so request, the right to be informed about court proceedings, including whether or not they have been canceled or rescheduled.

4. If you so request, the right to information about procedures in the criminal investigation of your case by law enforcement and about general procedures in the criminal justice system, including plea bargaining, from the prosecutor's office.

5. The right to receive information about the Texas Crime Victim Compensation Fund, which provides financial assistance to victims of violent crimes and, if you so request, to referral to available social service agencies that may provide additional help.

6. The right to provide information to a probation department conducting a presentence investigation about the impact of the crime.

7. If you so request, the right to be notified of parole proceedings by the Board of pardons and Paroles, to participate in the parole process, and to be notified of the defendant's release.

8. The right to be present at all public court proceedings, if the presiding judge permits.

9. The right to be provided with a safe waiting area before and during court proceedings.

10. The right to prompt return of any property no longer required as evidence.

11. If you so request, the right to have the prosecutor notify your employer of the necessity of your testimony that may involve your absence from work.

12. The right to complete a Victim Impact Statement, detailing the emotional, physical, and financial impact that the crime has had on you and your family, and to have that statement considered by the judge at sentencing and by the parole board prior to taking any parole action.

The use of restitution in criminal cases is becoming more and more common.

Restitution

Restitution is part of a criminal sentence that requires the offender to pay for injuries suffered by the victim. The original rationale for restitution was to require the party that injured the victim to pay for his or her injuries. The ability of courts to order restitution has been a part of the common law in the United States. The increased awareness of the victim's plight resulted in the passage of the Victim Witness Protection Act of 1982. This federal statute specifically authorizes the imposition of an order of restitution in addition to, or in lieu of, any other sentence in a criminal proceeding. Every state has restitution statutes which allow courts to order the perpetrator to pay the victim for any injuries suffered as a result of the offender's criminal act or acts.

Restitution statutes, like compensation laws, provide the victims of crime violence with some financial relief. However, many of these restitution statutes have shortcomings (e.g., some statutes prohibit restitution for certain types of injuries such as emotional distress). Other statutes allow the sentencing court to not order restitution if to do so would overly burden the criminal justice system. Still others do not address future costs such as continuing medical expenses.

Restitution and compensation laws provide the victims of crime with some financial assistance. They are not perfect, but are a beginning and an acknowledgment that we must consider the plight of the victim in our criminal justice system. One of the most dramatic examples of including the victim in the criminal process is the use of victim impact evidence at sentencing.

VICTIM-IMPACT STATEMENTS[30]

Introduction

A new series of rights are emerging in our judicial system. These rights confer upon the victims, or the relatives of deceased victims, the opportunity to speak out or be heard during various phases of the criminal justice process. As with many rights when they converge on a single point, there is an actual or potential conflict. How we handle this conflict is a reflection of the morals and ethics of our society. This section will review the history of these various rights and examine the rationale behind the current status of the law as it relates to victim impact statements.

Purpose and Procedure

One of the most controversial "rights" bestowed upon victims is known as the **victim-impact statement**. In essence, this statement presents the victim's point of view to the sentencing authority. Providing the sentencing authority with all relevant information is not a new phenomenon in the criminal justice system. For many years courts have received information regarding the defendant prior to imposition of sentence.

Traditionally, presentence reports have been utilized by judges in determining the proper punishment for criminal defendants. The report, which is normally prepared by a probation officer, details the defendant's background, education and prior criminal record. Many of these reports have included information concerning the victim of the crime.[31]

Victim impact evidence is now admitted in sentencing for a wide variety of criminal acts including those which fall within the realm of family violence. However, the law on admissibility and use of victim impact statements is based upon use of this evidence during death penalty cases. To understand the nature of victim impact statements, it is necessary to review how this evidence is used in the most serious type of criminal case—those involving capital punishment.

The use of victim impact evidence during the sentencing phase of a criminal crime raises serious constitutional issues. The right to confront witnesses comes head to head with the right to have all relevant evidence placed before the sentencing authority. As will be seen, the use of victim impact statements has aroused intense feelings in the Supreme Court when it addressed this issue.

In *Booth v. Maryland*, the Supreme Court initially addressed the issue of the use of victim impact statements in a sentencing jury's determination.[32] In 1983, John Booth and Willie Reed bound and gagged an elderly couple. Believing the couple might be able to identify them, Booth stabbed them numerous times with a kitchen knife. The trial judge in *Booth* allowed the jury to consider a victim impact statement which detailed the family and community's respect and admiration for the victims as well as the impact of the murder on the victim's family.[33]

The Supreme Court, in reversing the death sentence, held that it was impermissible to allow the jury access to such evidence in the sentencing phase of a death penalty proceeding.[34] The Court listed three factors which precluded the prosecution from introducing evidence of the homicide's impact on the victim's family. First, the Court stated that the victim-impact statement (VIS) impermissibly allows the jury to focus on the victim rather than the defendant. Second, the Court held that the sentence of death should not turn on the characteristics of the victim and the victim's family. Specifically, the Court recognized that the imposition of the death penalty should not be determined on the basis of the ability of the victim's family to articulate their anguish and bereavement, whether the victim did or did not leave behind a family, or on the fact that the victim was a stellar member of the community.[35] These factors focus attention on the victim and away from the central inquiry of whether the defendant's characteristics and background are such that the death sentence is warranted.[36] Finally, the Court stated that because a VIS contains the subjective perceptions and feelings of family members, the defendant has limited rebuttal opportunity.[37]

In summing up the Court's holding that introduction of the victim-impact statement violates the Eighth Amendment's prohibition against cruel and unusual punishment, Justice Powell commented:

> One can understand the grief and anger of the family caused by the brutal murders in this case, and there is no doubt that jurors generally are aware of these feelings." The admission of these emotionally-charged opinions as to what conclusions the jury should draw from the evidence clearly is inconsistent with the reasoned decision making we require in capital cases.[38]

As may be apparent at the time of the decision in *Booth v. Maryland*, the relevant considerations at the sentencing phase of a murder trial were those aspects of a defendant's background or character or those circumstances which extenuate or mitigate the defendant's culpability.

South Carolina v. Gathers followed the rationale of *Booth* and held unconstitutional the imposition of a death penalty based upon prosecutorial remarks that were also considered inflammatory.[39] Demetrius Gather and three companions sexually assaulted and killed Richard Haynes, a man they encountered in a park. During the incident, the perpetrators ransacked a bag the victim was carrying. The bag contained several articles pertaining to religion including a religious tract entitled, "Game Guy's Prayer." During the sentencing phase of the trial, the prosecutor's argument included references to Haynes's personal qualities and included a reading of the "Game Guy's Prayer." The Supreme Court reversed the sentence stating that such references to the qualities of the victim were similar to the *Booth* holding prohibiting Victim Impact Statements. The court determined that such evidence was likely to inflame the jury and, thus, violated the defendant's Eight Amendment rights. In a well-reasoned and logical dissent, Justice O'Conner stated, "Nothing in the Eighth Amendment precludes the community from considering its loss in assessing punishment nor requires that the victim remain a faceless stranger at the penalty phase of a capital case." The dissent by Justice O'Conner was a signal that the winds of judicial temperament might be changing.

In *Payne v Tennessee*, the court completely reversed itself and allowed to stand the imposition of a death sentence which was based in part on evidence contained in a victim-impact statement. In 1987, Pervis Tyrone Payne entered the apartment of Charisse Christopher and her two children. Payne stabbed Charisse and the two children numerous times with a butcher knife. Charisse and her daughter died, however, three-year-old Nicholas survived.

Payne was caught and convicted for the murders. During the penalty phase, four witnesses testified regarding the defendant's background, reputation and mental state. All of these witnesses urged the jury not to impose the death penalty. In rebuttal, the prosecution called the maternal grandmother who was caring for Nicholas. She was allowed to testify, over the defendant's objection, that Nicholas continued to cry out calling for his dead mother and sister. The witness was also allowed to testify regarding her personal grief over the loss of her loved ones. During closing argument, the prosecutor hammered on the pain and suffering that Nicholas and his deceased family had endured stating:

"But we do know that Nicholas was alive. And Nicholas was in the same room. Nicholas was still conscious. His eyes were open. He responded to the paramedics. He was able to follow their directions. He was able to hold his intestines in as he was carried to the ambulance. So he knew what happened to his mother and baby sister. . . .

Somewhere down the road Nicholas is going to grow up, hopefully. He's going to want to know what happened. And he is going to know what happened to his baby sister and his mother. He is going to want to know what kind of justice was done. He is going to want to know what happened. With your verdict, you will provide the answer."[40]

The jury sentenced Payne to death, and the case was appealed to the United States Supreme Court. Payne contended that the trial court erred when it allowed the maternal grandmother to testify. Relying on *Booth* and *Gathers*, Payne argued that such evidence was a violation of his Eighth Amendment rights.

After reviewing the principles that have guided criminal sentencing over the ages, the court stated that the consideration of the harm caused by the crime has been an important factor in the existence of the exercise of judicial discretion. The majority opinion went on to state that neither Booth nor Gathers even suggested that a defendant, entitled as he is to individualized consideration, is to receive that consideration wholly apart from the crime which he had committed.

In setting forth the groundwork for overruling *Booth* and *Gathers*, the court stated:

"Under our constitutional system, the primary responsibility for defining crimes against state law, fixing punishments for the commission of those crimes, and establishing procedures for criminal trials rests with the states. The state laws respecting crimes, punishments, and criminal procedures are of course subject to the overriding provisions of the United States Constitution. Where the State imposes the death penalty for a particular crime, we have held that the Eighth Amendment imposes special limitations upon that process. . . .

The states remain free in capital cases, as well as others, to devise new procedures and new remedies to meet felt needs. Victim impact evidence is simply another form or method of informing the sentencing authority about the specific harm caused by the crime in question, evidence of a general type long considered by sentencing authorities. We think the *Booth* court was wrong in stating that this kind of evidence leads to the arbitrary imposition of the death penalty. In the majority of cases, and in this case, victim-impact evidence serves entirely legitimate purposes."[41]

Thus, the Supreme Court overruled *Booth* and *Gathers* to the extent that they prohibited introduction of evidence or argument regarding the impact of the crime on the victim, families and the community. In addition, the Court's decision clearly stated that the decision regarding the admission of such evidence was the prerogative of the individual states. The court ruled it would not intervene unless the evidence introduced was so unduly prejudicial that it renders the trial fundamentally unfair.[42] If this occurred the court reasoned, the Due Process Clause of the Fourteenth Amendment provides a mechanism for relief.

The decision generated controversy in the academic world with a series of articles condemning the court for both allowing victim impact evidence and appearing to repudiate its acceptance of *stare decisis*.[43] While the dissent and certain individuals within academic community may condemn the majority's opinion, it is now clearly the law of the land. In addition, the Supreme Court's decision enhanced the victim's rights movement in the United States. It allows individual states to determine what is relevant evidence in the death penalty phase of a capital crime.

Some would argue that the decision in Payne leaves prosecutors and defense attorneys scrambling to determine what type of evidence is admissible under the guise of victim impact statements. The answer is simply evidence which does not result in rendering a trial fundamentally unfair. This concept of fundamental fairness is not a new untested, or ill-defined doctrine.

There is a long history defining acts which render acts by the state fundamentally unfair. The *Doctrine of Fundamental Fairness* has its roots in two early cases. In *Powell v. Alabama* several black youths were accused of repeatedly raping two young white girls. They were caught, tried, and convicted. Their conviction was overturned on the ground that the failure of the trial court to appoint counsel until the day of the trial was a violation of the defendant's due process.[44] In *Brown v. Mississippi*, a sheriff hung the defendant from a tree and whipped him until he confessed to the murder of a white man. The Supreme court held that such actions are revolting to the sense of justice and the confession was suppressed.[45]

The Ddoctrine of Fundamental Fairness accepts the concept that due process is a generalized command that requires states to provide the defendant with a fair trial. In the instant situation, if the admission of the victim impact evidence "revolts the sense of justice" or "shocks the conscience" of the court, such admission would be error under the due process clause.

Victim-Impact Panels

Victim-impact panels (VIP) differ significantly from victim-impact statements. MADD established victim-impact panels as a method of dealing with the drunk driving problem.[46] MADD does not believe that victim-impact panels should replace traditional criminal sanctions for driving under the influence. They are offered to enhance and supplement such sentencing by placing offenders face-to-face with victims of drunk driving whose lives have been changed by someone who drank and then got behind the wheel of a car.

MADD and other victim groups select a panel of three to four victims to speak briefly about the drunk driving crashes in which they were injured, or a loved one killed, and what the event has meant to them. They do not blame or judge the attendees. A victim-impact panel coordinator moderates the panel, and victims are never allowed to speak at groups in which their own offender is present. The attendees are convicted drunk drivers who are required to attend a panel as an element of their sentences. A probation officer or other agent of the court attends each panel to monitor attendance. Any person who fails to appear for a panel is required to return to court for appropriate action.[47]

SAMPLE LETTER TO VICTIM

Date:
Victim's Name:
Address:

Re: *State v. [Defendant's Name]*

Dear:

Crime has a different impact on each victim. No two victims suffer the same emotional, physical, and financial pains as a result of a crime. You have a right to present a victim-impact satement to be considered by the judge during the sentencing phase of the trial. While you are not required to submit one, only you can provide us with information regarding the impact of this crime on you.

If you would like to submit a victim impact statement for the court's consideration during the sentencing phase of the trial, a form is enclosed. While the enclosed form may seem to be impersonal, when it is completed in your own words, it will help to provide the information to the judge, probation officer, and correctional personnel regarding the impact of the crime on you.

If you are uncomfortable submitting a written statement, you may attend the sentencing hearing and orally present your statement. If you would like to attend the sentencing hearing, and/or present an oral statement, please call my office as soon as possible so that the necessary arrangements may be made.

If you choose to prepare a written victim-impact statement, please complete the attached form and return it to our offices no later than [date]. Once we receive the completed form, the original will be provided to the judge. A copy will be provided to the probation officer so that it may be included in the presentence investigation report. The probation officer may contact you for additional information. The defendant and his attorney will receive a copy of your answers to the questions on the form. The defense attorney may question you in court concerning your answers. The defense will not have access to any personal information such as your telephone number or address.

The victim-impact statement also provides you with the opportunity to present any financial loss that you may have incurred as a result of this crime. The judge may use the information presented in determining the restitution aspects of the sentence. Restitution is the payment the defendant may be required to make to you for your financial losses.

If you have any questions concerning how to complete this form, or how it will be used in the criminal justice system, please contact our offices. Those of us involved with your case believe that it is very important for you to help the court understand how this crime has affected you and those close to you. Thank you for taking the time to provide the court with this important information.
Sincerely,

District Attorney

Victims who have served on these panels find that telling their story lightens their personal pain and assists in the healing process. Victims also report that they have experienced something positive from a previously devastating event, and they believe that by telling their stories, they may be preventing some other family from suffering a similar fate.[48]

The goals of the victim-impact panel are to enhance the emotional healing of victims by offering them an opportunity to speak out about the incident. These panels also enable attendees to understand drunk driving from the victim's perspective. Hopefully these stories will affect the attendees' decisions whether to drink and drive.

Victim-impact panels are different from victim-impact statements. However, they both serve to allow the victim to express his or her feelings regarding the consequences of the crime. The opportunity to express feelings regarding the event can be a valuable healing process. While victim-impact panels are relatively new within the criminal justice system, they offer another sentencing option to judges.

Victim-impact evidence is now an accepted part of the judicial process. The ability of a victim of a crime to inform the court of the impact of the offender's acts on his or her life can only benefit the victim and continue to educate the public regarding the dynamics of family violence.

SUMMARY

- Early civilizations accorded victims more rights than did the United States until the recent victims' rights movement. One of the first attempts to establish a written code of conduct was the Code of Hammurabi in approximately 2000 B.C. One of its stated objectives was the restoration of equity between the offender and the victim. It attempted to make the victim as whole as possible.

- Victimology is a new concept in the United States. It is the study of crime from the victim's viewpoint. Mendelsohn classified victims into six distinct categories—the completely innocent, one with minor guilt, one who is as guilty as the offender, one who is more guilty than the offender, the mostly guilty one, and the imaginary victim. Von Hentig explored the relationship between the criminal and his of her victim. Von Hentig classified victims by examining various risk factors. His general classes of victims were: the young, the female, the old, the mentally defective, and immigrants, minorities, and dull normals. Divided by psychological types of victims, the classes include the depressed , the acquisitive, and the wanton.

- Another aspect of victimology is compensation for injuries suffered as the result of criminal acts. Today, all states have victim compensation programs. Most of the programs grant aid to innocent victims who are seriously injured. Normally, they do not cover property losses. If the victim receives reimbursement from insurance or another fund, they are excluded from "double-dipping."

- Restitution is often a part of the criminal sentence and requires the offender to pay for injuries suffered by the victim. The ability of courts to order restitution was originally a common law power of the courts. Now, there is also statutory authority to require the offender to pay restitution.

- Victim-impact statements allow the victim to present evidence during the sentencing process. There have been constitutional problems in allowing the use of the impact statements because of the right of the defendant to confront the witnesses against him or her. The latest Supreme Court decision allows individual states to determine relevant evidence in capital cases and thus control, to some extent, the use of victim-impact statements. One of the problems with the victim-impact statement, according to many jurists, is that it focuses the sentencing phase on the victim rather than the accused.

DISCUSSION QUESTIONS

1. What historical event had the most impact on victims' rights? Did it involve a change in attitudes? Justify your answer.

2. Can you draft a more complete definition of victimology? Why is it more comprehensive than the one contained in the text?

3. What is the difference between compensation and restitution? If you were the victim of a crime and could only select one of those two options, which one would you choose?

4. Why are victim-impact statements important? Do you believe judges really change their sentencing of offenders based upon evidence presented in victim-impact statements? Justify your answer.

ENDNOTES—Chapter 12

1. This section has been adapted from Harvey Wallace, "History of Law: The Evolution of Victims' Rights," *National Victim Assistance Academy Text* (Washington DC: Office for Victims of Crime, 1997)

2. Sir Henry Summer Maine, *Ancient Law*, 10th ed. (London: John Murray 1905).

3. S. Schafer, *The Victim and His Criminal,* (New York: Random House 1968).

4. Masters and Roberson, *Inside Criminology*, (Englewood Cliffs, N.J.: Prentice-Hall, 1985).

5. Gordon, *Hammurabi's Code: Quaint or Forward Looking*, (New York: Rinehart, 1957).

6. G.O. Mueller & H.H.A. Cooper, "Society and the Victim: Alternative Responses," in I. Drapkin & E. Viano, Eds., *Victimology: A New Focus*, Vol. 2 (Lexington, Mass.:D.C. Heath, 1974) pp. 85-102.

7. O.W. Mueller, "Tort, Crime and the Primitive," 43 *Journal of Criminal Law, Criminology, and Police Science,* 303,1955.

8. This section has been adapted from Harvey Wallace, *Victimology: Legal, Psychological, and Social Perspectives*, (Boston: Allyn & Bacon, 1998) Used with permission. All rights reserved.

9. Edwin H. Sutherland, *Principles of Criminology,* 4th ed.(Philadelphia: Lippincott, 1947).

10. B. Mendelsohn, "The Origin and Doctrine of Victimology," 3 *Excerpta Criminologica* (June 1963) pp. 239-244

11. Steven Scafer, *The Victim and His Criminal,* (New York: Random House, 1968).

12. B. Mendelsohn, "Rape in Criminology", *Giustizia Penale* (1940).

13. Hans von Hentig, *The Criminal and His Victim,* (First published by Schocken Books, New York 1979, republished by Yale University Press 1984).

14. Some scholars have subdivided von Hentig's original typology (probably for ease of understanding). See for example, Doerner and Lab, *Victimology*, (West Publishing, St. Paul, Minn. 1994) where the authors list 13 classifications. They arrive at this number by listing immigrants, minorities and dull normals as separate categories instead of one subdivision as von Hentig did.

15. *The Criminal and His Victim*, p. 404.

16. *Id.* at p.406.

17. *Id.* at p.410.

18. *Id.* at p.411.

19. *Id.* at p.415.

20. *Id* .at p. 420.

21. *Id.* at p.422.

22. *Id.* at p.427.

23. *Id.* at p. 428

24. *Id.* at p.431.

25. *Id.*

26. H. von Hentig, *The Criminal and His Victim*, (New Haven, CT: Yale University Press 1948) p. 433.

27. *Id.* at p. 445.

28. *Id.*

29.

30. This section has been adapted from Harvey Wallace, *Family Violence: Legal, Medical and Social Perspectives*, (Boston: Allyn & Bacon, 1996) Used with permission. All rights reserved.

31. See Phillip A. Talbert, "The Relevance of Victim Impact Statements to the Criminal Sentencing Decision," *36 UCLA L Rev 199*, 202-11 (1988) and Maureen McLeod, "Victim Participation at Sentencing," *22 Crim L. Bull. 501*, 505-11 (1986).

32. *Booth v. Maryland,* 482 U.S. 496 (1987).

33. *Id.* at 500-01.

34. *Id.* at 509. The Court did, however, carefully note that information typically contained in a victim's statement is generally admissible in non-capital cases and may be considered in capital cases if directly related to the circumstances of the crime. Id. at 508 n. 10. For example, the Court noted that the prosecution may produce evidence as to the characteristics of the victim to rebut an argument made by the defendant (e.g., victim's peaceable nature to rebut claim of self-defense.)

35. *Id.* at 505-07.

36. *Id.* at 507-08.

37. *Id.*

38. *Id.*

39. 490 U.S. 805 (1989)

40. 115 L.ED. 728-729

41. 115 L.Ed.734-735

42. 115 L.Ed. 2d 735.

43. See Jimmie O. Clements, Jr. "Casenote:Criminal Law—Victim Impact Evidence," 23 St. Mary's L.J. 517 (1991).

44. *Powell v. Alabama*, 287 U.S. 45, 53 S.C. 55, 77 L.Ed. 158(1932)

45. 297 U.S. 278, 56 S.Ct. 461, 80 L.Ed. 682 (1936)

46. This section has been adapted from Janice H. Lord, *Victim Impact Panels: A Creative Sentencing Opportunity*, (Mothers Against Drunk Driving, Dallas Texas, 1990).

47. *Id.* at p. 6.

48. *Id.* at p. 10.

PART IV

The Criminal Justice System

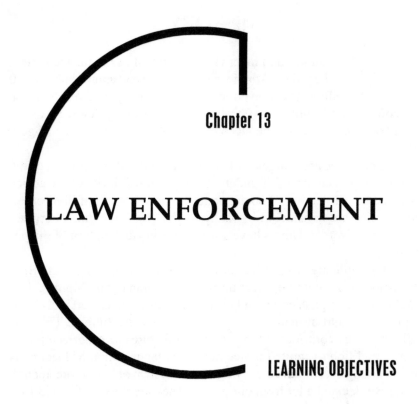

Chapter 13

LAW ENFORCEMENT

After studying this chapter, you should be able to:

- Trace the historical development of law enforcement.

- List the types of police agencies in the United States.

- Name the characteristics of contemporary law enforcement agencies.

- Describe the functions of law enforcement agencies.

- Outline the structure and operation of law enforcement agencies.

HISTORY

The largest and most visible segment of the justice system is the police. American taxpayers spend approximately $30 billion a year on police protection compared to $15 billion on courts and $20 billion on corrections. Accordingly, for every dollar spent on criminal justice, about 45 cents goes to law enforcement agencies.

The police are charged with the prevention and detection of crime and the apprehension of offenders. Other responsibilities of the police include the protection of society and the preservation of civil order. Our police are considered by many as the "thin blue line" between order and disorder. Others have a less flattering description of the police.

Our policing is a product of its English heritage. When the British colonists brought their criminal justice system to the colonies, they included the English common law, the high value placed on individual rights, the court system, and law enforcement institutions. This English heritage contributed three enduring features to American policing: a tradition of limited police authority, the tradition of local control, a highly decentralized and fragmented system of law enforcement.[1]

We demand a lot from our police. They are the only around-the-clock, 365 days a year public service agency with the authority to use coercive force to settle disputes. We expect our police to settle our problems immediately. Demands for police services fall into one of four categories:

(1) Crime fighting

(2) Maintaining order

(3) Providing informational services

(4) Providing emergency services

The modern police department can be traced to the ninth century when Alfred the Great of England structured his kingdom's defenses to prepare for the Danish invasion. To establish internal security, he instituted the system of **mutual pledge**. This system organized the country at the lowest level into groups of ten families. These groups were called **tithings**. Next, ten tithings were grouped together into a hundred families called **constables**. Next, the constables within each geographic area were combined to form the administrative units called **shires** (later called counties). Each shire was governed by a shire-reeve (later called sheriff).

In the thirteenth century the **night watch** was established to protect the streets in urban areas of England during the hours of darkness. The night watch was the first rudimentary form of metropolitan policing. From the thirteenth to the seventeenth centuries, there was little development in the area of policing. During that period of time, in theory, each citizen in England was a policeman because all citizens were charged with the enforcement of the laws of England. In actual practice, however, law enforcement was almost nonexistent.

By the seventeenth century, the chief law enforcement officials were the magistrates and the parish constables. The **magistrates** presided over courts, ordered arrests, called witnesses to investigate criminal behavior and examined prisoners. The **parish constables** were holdovers from the days of Alfred the Great. They had only limited authority to arrest, and their authority was confined to small districts. In addition, in some urban areas there were constable's assistants called **beadles.** The beadles were used primarily to clear the streets of vagrants. Many of the constables, magistrates and beadles were corrupt.

Highway robbery was flourishing in England during the sixteenth and seventeenth centuries. To combat this problem, Parliament, in 1693, passed an act providing a reward of 40 pounds be paid for the capture and conviction of any highwayman or road agent. From this act emerged the **thief-takers**. The thief-takers were private detectives who were paid by the Crown on a piecework basis. They had no official status and only the authority of private citizens. Anyone could be one. They received rewards in return for the apprehension of criminals. The reward was payable upon the conviction of the thief. In addition to the reward, the thief-takers also received any property that belonged to the thief unless someone could prove that the property was stolen. During serious crime waves, the Parliament increased the bounty to 100 British pounds for certain crimes. Later the system was expanded to include burglars, housebreakers, and street robbers. In addition, in some villages the landowners banded together and offered supplemental rewards. Many people have traced the origin of the bounty hunter of the American West to thief-takers.

As the system of thief-takers grew, a class of professional thief-takers developed. While many criminals were apprehended by the thief-takers, probably more crime was created by the system than it suppressed. Many of thief-takers were criminals themselves, because pardons were often used as rewards. In addition, many of them became thief-makers. They would entice people to commit crime and then arrest the unsuspecting people for the rewards. There were also cases where innocent people were framed by the planting of stolen property on them in order to collect rewards.[2]

The period 1750 to 1850 witnessed a marked growth in the development of modern policing. By 1829, there were over 3,000 uniformed constables in the London Metropolitan police force. Henry Fielding, an eighteenth-century novelist who wrote *Tom Jones*, is credited with laying the foundation for the first modern police agency. Fielding was appointed as a magistrate in Westminster near London in 1748. At the time, he lived on Bow Street. It was in his home where he first opened his office and there formed the first modern police department. Fielding's goal was to reduce the burglaries, street and highway robberies, and thefts which were flourishing at the time.

Fielding established a relationship with the local pawnbrokers and requested that they notify him when someone tried to pawn stolen property. He ran advertising in the London and Westminster newspapers inviting anyone who was the victim of a crime by robbers or burglars to immediately send or bring to his Bow street office a description of the property stolen and a description of the criminal. Prior to his actions, there were no formal provisions for the reporting of crimes to authorities. Next, with the help of Saunders Welch who was the Constable of Holborn he formed a small unofficial investigative group of assistants. This group is considered as the first organized police force used in England and were nicknamed the "Bow Street Runners." The Bow Street Runners were not salaried. They earned their money under the standard thief-takers' reward system.

Later, the government supplemented Fielding's efforts by periodically providing financial support for the Bow Street Runners. In 1752, however, Fielding, because of his poor health, was confined to a wheelchair. He persuaded the government to appoint his brother, John Fielding, as his chief assistant. John took control over the operations of the runners. Because John was blind, he was referred to as the "Blind Beak." [*Beak* is an English slang word for judge.]

Henry Fielding died in 1754. In 1763, his brother John was provided with government funds to establish a civilian horse patrol of eight men to patrol the streets of London. After less than a year, however, the horse patrol was disbanded. Later, a permanent foot patrol was established, and in 1804 a new horse patrol was started.

The new horse patrol was outfitted in red vests and blue jackets and trousers. They became England's first uniformed police. One of the promises made to parliament in establishing the new police was that they would wear uniforms to ensure that they were not used as spies and that people who gave information to a constable would know that it was a constable.

In 1789, a Glasgow businessman, Patrick Colquhoun was appointed as a London magistrate. He attempted to get authorization to establish a large, organized police force for greater London. His efforts were unsuccessful because of the English people's love of freedom, their faith in private enterprise, and their distrust of government. He did, however, establish a special river police patterned after the Bow Street model. The majority of his efforts were unsuccessful because of the traditional mistrust of authorities by the English.

As a result of the riots between the Irish immigrants and local English citizens in 1780, the Parliament began debating on how to provide better public safety. Parliament debated this question for almost fifty years until 1829. In that year, Sir Robert Peel, England's Home Secretary influenced Parliament to pass the "Act for Improving the Police In and Near the Metropolis." This act established the first permanent police force in London. It was composed of over 1,000 men. The force was structured along military lines. The police were required to wear distinctive uniforms and were under the leadership of two police commissioners (one a lawyer and one a military officer). At that time, they were known as "the new police." Later they became known as "Bobbies" in reference to Sir Robert Peel's nickname.[3]

The act was referred to by the citizens of England as the "Peelian Reform." The basic tenets of the act are as follows:

√ The police must be stable, efficient, and organized along military lines.

√ The police must be under government control.

√ The best evidence of the efficiency of the police will be an absence of crime.

√ The distribution of crime news is essential.

√ The policeman should have a perfect command of his temper and a quiet and determined manner.

√ Good appearance commands respect.

√ The selection of proper persons and then properly training them is the root of efficiency.

√ Police headquarters should be centrally located and easily accessible to the police.

√ Policemen should be hired on a probationary basis.

√ Police records are essential to the necessary distribution of police strength.[4]

The London Metropolitan Police introduced four new concepts to policing that exist today: 1) new mission, 2) new strategy, 3) new organizational structure, and 4) continual presence of the police. The new mission was one of crime prevention. Until then, the chief role of law enforcement was catching criminals. The new strategy was the concept of preventive patrols. The Bobbies maintained a visible presence in the city by the use of fixed "beats." The organizational structure was the development of a quasi-military style. In addition, the police were professional in that they were full-time paid employees.

EMERGING LAW ENFORCEMENT SYSTEM IN THE UNITED STATES

The first law enforcement agencies in America were created as soon as communities were organized. Whereas the English were reluctant to establish police forces, the colonies did not hesitate in the establishment of local law enforcement agencies. The Puritans, who dominated the intellectual life of colonial America, included in their ideology the belief that government was necessary because man was by nature sinful. Accordingly, it was essential that the government force people to conform to the requirements of the law.

Colonial America

The law enforcement officers in the colonies were the sheriff, the constable, the watch, and the slave patrol. The **sheriff** who was appointed by the colonial governors was the chief law enforcement officer. His responsibilities included the collection of taxes, conducting elections, maintaining bridges and roads, and criminal law enforcement. The sheriff did not patrol his area, but was a reactive agent of social control. The sheriffs received no salaries and were paid through a system of fees. Corruption was common.

The **constable** was initially an elected official in the colonial towns and cities. His duties included criminal law enforcement. Later in some of the larger cities, including Boston, the position became a semiprofessional appointed position. As a general rule in the larger cities, the constable provided law enforcement during the day and the night-watch during hours of darkness.

The **watch** is the closest to our modern-day police force. Members of the watch patrolled the cities to guard against fires, crimes and disorders. At first, the watch was only a nighttime activity. Later in the larger towns and cities, it evolved into a 24-hour activity and became a paid professional force. At first, following the English tradition all adult males were required to serve as a part of the watch. As more males attempted to evade their service in the watch and many hired others to take their place, the volunteers were replaced by paid persons.

In 1801, Boston became the first city to be required by law to maintain a permanent night watch. The hired people were paid fifty cents a night. That same year, Detroit appointed its first civilian full-time police officer.

Frontier Justice

While the cities on the Eastern seaboard were concerned with law and order, there was little law and order on the colonial frontier. Accordingly, two distinct patterns of law enforcement developed—the quest for law and order in the cities on the Eastern seaboard and the lawlessness of the frontier. As a general rule, the only law enforcement officials available on the frontier were the elected county sheriffs and the appointed town marshals. Often crime fighting was a secondary duty to the sheriff. His primary concerns were collecting taxes and judicial assistance duties.

When extra help was needed by a sheriff or marshal for crime sprees or the apprehension of particularly dangerous criminals, they would call upon the male citizens of the local area to form a **posse**. The posse is slang for "posse comitatus," a common law descendant of King Alfred's "hue and cry." By common law, no man could refuse to serve as a member of a legally constituted posse.

Officials in a few frontier states also created their own law enforcement organizations. One of the more famous was the Texas Rangers, which was formed in 1823 by Stephen Austin who hired a dozen bodyguards to protect fellow Texans from the Indians and bandits. Similar organizations included the Arizona Rangers, formed in 1901, and the New Mexico Mounted Patrol, formed in 1905.

The present popular opinion of what a policeman is is based to a great extent on the image created by the Eastern press regarding the western law man. The image created of the ideal policeman was of one who:

- Was large in stature
- Harsh in attitude
- Had a low tolerance
- Extreme courage
- Had ample firepower

Policing in the Nineteenth Century

As occurred in England, the old system of law enforcement could not handle the problems caused by urbanization, industrialization, and immigration.[5] Boston had major riots in 1834, 1835, and 1837. Racial violence grew in the years before the civil war. Angry depositors stormed and destroyed banks. Despite the problems, the cities were slow in creating new police forces. New York City did not create a new police force until 1845, and Philadelphia finally created a consolidated city-wide police force in 1854. Two commonly accepted reasons for the delay in establishing new police forces are: 1) to the Americans, police officers dispersed throughout the community brought to mind the hated British army, and 2) others were afraid that rival politicians would gain control of the police departments and use them for their own partisan advantages.

Four theories are commonly used to explain the development of police agencies during the nineteenth century after the delayed start.

1. **Disorder-control theory**— explains the development in the need to control mob violence that existed in the United States during that time period.

2. **Crime-control theory**— suggests that the increases in criminal activity and the failure of the old systems of law enforcement created a perceived need for a new type of police.

3. **Class-control theory**— blames the creation of police departments on class-based economic exploitation. Advocates of this theory note that the development of new police agencies coincided with the development of urbanization and industrialization. According to those who support this theory, the police are merely tools used by those in power to suppress the lower classes.

4. **Urban dispersion theory**— holds that many of the urban police departments were created just because other cities had them.[6]

Policing in the Early Twentieth Century

At the turn of the century, politics influenced every aspect of the American police agencies. For example, to obtain an appointment to the New York City Police Department, all one needed to do was to pay $300 to the Tammany Hall political machine. Officers were selected entirely on the basis of their political connections. In most cases, the composition of the local police department reflected the ethnic and religious makeup of the cities. Police officers had no job security and could be fired at will. It was not unusual for an entire police force to be fired after a new mayor was elected.

Few departments had any formal training requirements. New officers were handed a badge, a baton, and a copy of department rules (if any). The first police academy was formed in Cincinnati in 1888, but it lasted only a few years. In 1895, New York City started a special training course for new officers, but the course covered only the use of a pistol. It wasn't until 1909 that New York City offered training, other than weapons training, for new officers. As late as 1913, the New York Police Academy gave no tests, and all students were automatically passed.

For the most part, officers patrolled on foot. The foot patrols were, however, inefficient. The officers were thinly spread. For example, the foot patrols in Chicago were often longer than four miles. The lack of a communications system made it difficult for officers to respond to crime and disorder. Supervision was weak, and officers could easily avoid patrolling by spending their time in the local bars and restaurants.

Reform Movement

As police agencies slowly evolved in the latter part of the nineteenth century, the control of the departments by the local politicians impeded effective law enforcement and created an atmosphere of corruption. In the 1850s, to curb police corruption, community leaders in many of the cities created police administrative boards with the power to oversee police agencies. For the most part, the boards failed to curb police corruption because the appointed private citizens lacked the necessary expertise in the intricacies of police work.

In some cities, including New York City, the police departments were taken over by state legislators. These takeovers resulted in police departments that were funded by local budgets but under the control of state legislators. Since most state legislatures at that time were controlled by rural politicians, the control of the police in those cities was also under the control of the rural politicians.

CONTEMPORARY LAW ENFORCEMENT

Presently there are over 15,000 state and local police departments in the United States. Approximately 80 percent of the agencies are local police departments. About 20 percent are sheriff's departments. There are only 49 state police or highway patrol agencies. Federal law enforcement agencies are a very small fraction of the total law enforcement industry. As noted earlier, American policing is highly fragmented. Accordingly, any generalizations about police departments are usually made toward a "typical" department.

Law Enforcement Workforce

percentage distribution by employer

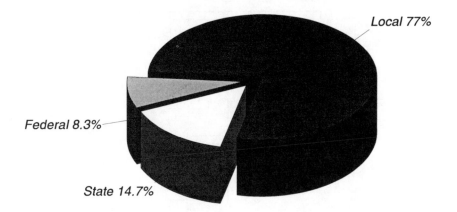

Local 77%

Federal 8.3%

State 14.7%

Police Services

In a typical police department, the law enforcement agency performs the following services to the citizens of the community:

√ Prevent crime

√ Investigate crimes and apprehends criminals

√ Maintain order

√ Provide other miscellaneous services[7]

Metropolitan Police

City police constitute the majority of the sworn police officers in the United States. Police departments range in size from the 33,000 in New York City to one officer departments in smaller cities. More than half of all the police departments have 10 or less sworn officers. Nearly 1,000 departments have only one officer. The FBI estimates that ap-

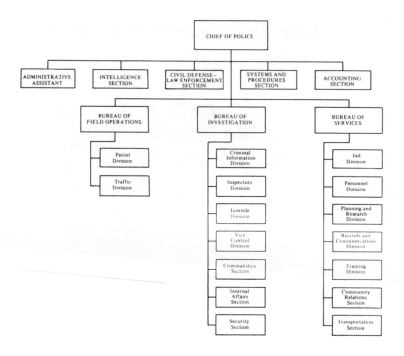

A typical organization chart of a police department serving a city of 500,000.

proximately 390,000 officers and civilians work in city police departments in the United States.

Almost all police departments, from the largest to the smallest,
perform the same standard set of services as noted above. Most maintain jurisdiction over law enforcement matters within their city boundaries. There are a number of auxiliary police agencies that assist them.
The most common auxiliary agencies are park police, airport police,
transit police, and university police. The auxiliary police are created to
handle special problems or special jurisdictional areas like the airports
and parks. The relationships between the city police and the auxiliary
agencies differ in almost every city. In general, the auxiliary agencies
have carved out a small portion of the city police's jurisdiction (normally geographic) over law enforcement. In most cases, in those limited geographic areas like our airports, both the city police and the
auxiliary police have concurrent jurisdiction. Police departments are
headed by a police chief who is appointed by the mayor or city council.

Rural Law Enforcement

While city police have jurisdiction over law enforcement within their respective city, outside of city boundaries the jurisdiction is normally with the sheriff's office. In all states, except Rhode Island and Hawaii, the **sheriff** is an elected official. The county sheriff's office has evolved from that of the early sheriff in England. There are approximately 3,400 rural law enforcement agencies in the United States.

The duties of a sheriff vary according to size and population of the county. The sheriff's role is more complex than the role of the urban police. The county sheriff may serve in three major capacities: (1) law enforcement, (2) service to the courts, and (3) corrections. In many rural counties, the sheriff is also the coroner. In most counties, the sheriff is the process server for court processes such as summons and writs of execution. In general, the sheriff's law enforcement duties are restricted to the unincorporated areas of the county. In counties where the entire county is within an incorporated area (like San Francisco), the sheriff generally has no law enforcement duties. In addition, most sheriffs are charged with the responsibilities of operating the county jails.

Lee Brown classifies the sheriff departments into four models.

1. **The full-service model**—This is the department that performs in all three major capacities—law enforcement, courts, and corrections.

2. **The law enforcement model**—This is where the department has only law enforcement duties.

3. **The civil-judicial model**—This is where the sheriff's duties are limited to court service with no law enforcement or corrections responsibilities.

4. **The correctional-judicial model**—This is where the sheriff has no law enforcement duties but operates the jails and provides service to the courts. The San Francisco Sheriff's Department could be considered a correctional-judicial model, because the San Francisco Police Department has the law enforcement responsibilities. [Note: The entire county is within the city limits of San Francisco.][8]

Sheriff's departments have traditionally been considered the weak link in the law enforcement chain. One reason for this status has been the partisan nature of the sheriff's departments. Sheriffs are elected in all but a few counties. The sheriff must be political in order to be elected. The fact that one is a good campaigner is no guarantee that one will be a good law enforcement administrator. After the sheriff is elected, unlike the chief of police, the sheriff is accountable to no one until the next election. In recent years, great strides have been made to improve the quality of sheriff's departments.

STATE POLICE

Unlike city police, state police are generally created by the legislature to deal with specific problems. Presently, Hawaii is the only state without a state police. Historically, the state police do not have general law enforcement jurisdiction. The trend, however, is to vest the state police with such authority. For example, there are presently 23 state police agencies in the United States with general law enforcement duties. The largest and best known state police agency is the California Highway Patrol (CHP). The CHP specializes in the protection of motorists and directs most of their attention to the enforcement of laws involving traffic safety. The CHP has approximately 6,200 officers and 2,500 civilian employees. The smallest state police unit is probably Wyoming with about 160 officers and 55 civilian employees.

NATIONAL LAW ENFORCEMENT AGENCIES

There is no federal law enforcement agency with unlimited jurisdiction. Unlike Italy or France, there is no national police force. Each federal law enforcement agency has been created to enforce specific laws and cope with particular problems or issues. The more important agencies are discussed below.

The legal arm of the federal government is the U.S. Department of Justice which is headed by the attorney general. The attorney general is appointed by the president and confirmed by the senate. The attorney general, like other cabinet members, serves at the pleasure of the president. The general duties of the Department of Justice are to: (1) enforce federal laws, (2) provide representation in court when the U.S. is a party to a court action, and (3) conduct investigations of possible violations of federal law through one of its agencies.

STYLES OF POLICING

A Harvard University symposium divided American policing into three historical eras. The administrative approach to each era provides us with three different styles of policing. The first period, from 1840 to 1930, was characterized by the interrelationships between the police and politics. The second era was the reform era which lasted from about 1930 to the 1970s. The reform era was characterized by the growth of police professionalism. The present era, from the 1970s to present, is the era of community problem solving. The present era is characterized by a concept of a partnership between the police and the community and the stressing of the service role of police.[9]

James Q. Wilson contends that each era contributed to three styles of policing. His three styles are: the watchman style (from the first period), the legalistic style (from the growth of police professionalism era), and the service style (from the present era).[10]

The **watchman style** of policing has an overriding concern for order maintenance. The police are employed to keep the peace. The average officer sees his or her goal as one of controlling criminal activity and disruptive behavior. Often informal police intervention is used to keep the peace, such as persuasion and threats. In some cases, "roughing up" tactics by the police are used on disruptive persons. Many researchers have condemned this style of policing as being focused on the lower to lower-middle class neighborhoods within a city, especially those neighborhoods where a fair amount of violence or physical abuse is traditionally present.

The **legalistic style** focuses on enforcing the law "to the letter." The legalistic style has also been called the **"laissez-faire" style** because of its "hands-off" approach to behaviors which are not criminal in nature. Often under this style of policing, police do not get involved in community disputes that do not break the law. Uniform, impartial arrests or citations for all violators of the law characterizes the legalistic style. An example of this style of policing would be to issue speeding tickets to motorists who are caught driving 56 m.p.h. in a 55 m.p.h. zone. This style of policing tends to increase the number of criminal complaints filed.

The **service style** of policing is marked by a concern to provide service to the community and to assist the community in solving problems with less emphasis on the enforcement of the law. The police see themselves as helpers rather than enforcers of the law. Often, persons who commit criminal acts are not prosecuted if the individuals agree to seek voluntary treatment through behavior modification courses. Instead of arresting, in many cases, the officers counsel, issue written warnings, or issue oral instructions to offenders. The service style of policing tends to blend into the characteristics of the community. [Note: The service style of policing tends to reduce the number of criminal complaints filed especially in misdemeanor cases.]

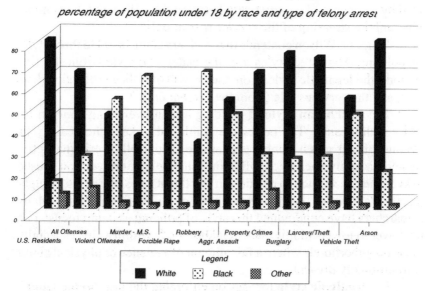

Likelihood of Being Arrested
percentage of population under 18 by race and type of felony arrest

STRUCTURE AND OPERATION

Police departments in the United States are not substantially different from the original British style of policing.[11] There are certain organizational features common to almost all urban departments. The three most important features are bureaucracy, semi-military model, and organizational environment.

The International City Manager's Association's book, *Municipal Police Administration,* offers six general principles of organization for law enforcement agencies:

1. The work should be apportioned among the various individuals and units, according to some logical plan. (Homogeneity)

2. Lines of authority and responsibility should be made as definite and direct as possible. (Delineation of responsibility)

3. There is a limit to the number of subordinates who can be supervised effectively by one officer, and this limit seldom should be exceeded. (Span of control)

4. There should be "unity of command" throughout the organization. (Subordinates under the direct control of only one supervisor)

5. Responsibility cannot be placed without the delegation of commensurate authority, and authority should not be delegated to a person without holding him/her accountable for its use. (Delegation of responsibility)

6. The efforts of the organizational units and of their component members must be coordinated so that all will be directed harmoniously toward the accomplishment of the police purpose. The components, thus coordinated, will enable the organization to function as a well-integrated unit.[12]

Bureaucracy

Bureaucracy is a form of organizational structure that was developed by Max Weber, a German social scientist. Bureaucracy is defined as (1) government by bureaus, administrators, and petty officials, (2) the body of officials and administrators of a government or government departments, or (3) the concentration of power in administrators. Presently, bureaucracy is a term generally cast in an unfavorable light. We blame a lot of our problems and inactions on the "bureaucracy."

Semi-Military Model

Police departments not only tend to be bureaucratic, but are also modeled loosely after the military style of organizations. The characteristics in law enforcement agencies taken from the military style include:

- Centralized command structure with a rigid chain of command
- Clearly marked lines of communications
- Strong discipline
- Differentiation between ranks or positions
- Authoritarian leadership
- Status quo emphasis

The operational units within a police department are also similarly classified to the military units of line, staff, and auxiliary units.

SUMMARY

- The largest and most visible segment of the justice system is the police. The police are charged with the prevention and detection of crime and the apprehension of offenders. Other responsibilities of the police include the protection of society and the preservation of civil order. Our police are considered by many as the "thin blue line" between order and disorder.

- Demands for police services fall into one of four categories: (1) crime fighting, (2) maintaining order, (3) providing informational services, and (4) providing emergency services.

- The modern police department can be traced to the ninth century when Alfred the Great of England structured his kingdom's defenses to prepare for the Danish invasion. By the seventeenth century, the chief law enforcement officials were the magistrates and the parish constables. The magistrates presided over courts, ordered arrests, called witnesses to investigate criminal behavior and examined prisoners.

- Sir Robert Peel, England's Home Secretary, influenced parliament to pass the "Act for Improving the Police In and Near the Metropolis." This act established the first permanent police force in London. The London Metropolitan Police introduced four new concepts to policing that exist today: 1) new mission, 2) new strategy, 3) new organizational structure, and 4) continual presence of the police. The new mission was one of crime prevention. Until then, the chief role of law enforcement was the catching of criminals.

- The law enforcement officers in the colonies were the sheriff, the constable, the watch, and the slave patrol. The sheriff who was appointed by the colonial governors was the chief law enforcement officer. His responsibilities included the collection of taxes, conducting elections, maintaining bridges and roads, and criminal law enforcement.

- In a typical police department, the law enforcement agency performs the following services to the citizens of the community: prevent crimes; investigate crimes; apprehend criminals; maintain order; and provide other miscellaneous services.

DISCUSSION QUESTIONS

1. Explain the present day concepts of policing that we obtained from the English.

2. Why were the cities slow in establishing city police departments?

3. What are Sir Robert Peel's contributions to policing?

4. What was the reason that the English first started requiring their police officers to wear distinct uniforms?

5. What are the functions of our present day law enforcement agencies?

6. How are law enforcement agencies organized?

ENDNOTES—Chapter 13

1. Samuel Walker, *The Police in America,* (New York: McGraw-Hill, 1992).

2. Patrick Pringle, *The Thief-Takers*, (London: Museum Press, 1958).

3. Charles Reith, *A Short History of the British Police*, (London: Oxford University Press, 1948).

4. T.A. Critchley, *A History of Police in England and Whales*, 2d ed. (Montclair, NJ: Patterson Smith, 1972).

5.Samuel Walker, *The Police in America,* 2d ed. (New York: McGraw-Hill, 1992).

6. Roy R. Roberg and Jack Kuykendall, Police and Society, (Belmont, CA: Wadsworth,1992).

7. Samuel Walker, 1992: 37.

8.Randy L. LaGrange, *Policing in America*, (New York: Nelson Hall, 1993).

9. Francis X. Hartmann, "Debating the Evolution of American Policing," *Perspectives on Policing,* No. 5, Washington, D.C.: National Institute of Justice, November, 1988.

10. James Q. Wilson, *Varieties of Police Behavior: The Management of Law and Order in Eight Communities*, (Cambridge: Harvard University, 1986).

11. Randy L. LaGrange, *Policing in America*, (New York: Nelson-Hall, 1993).

12. *Ibid.*

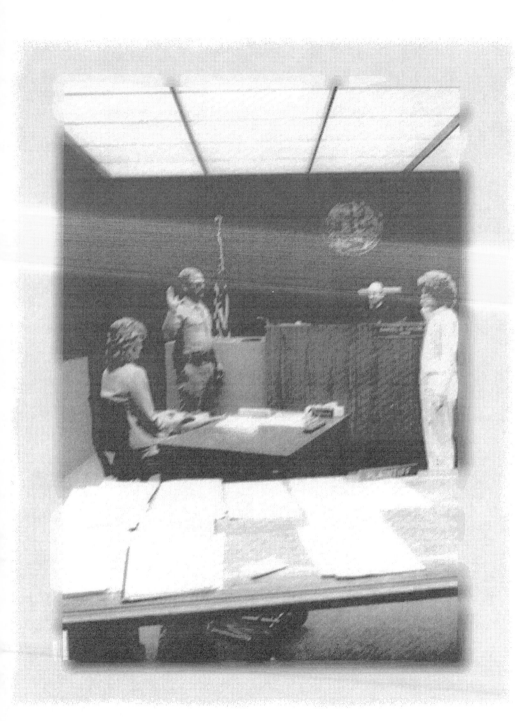

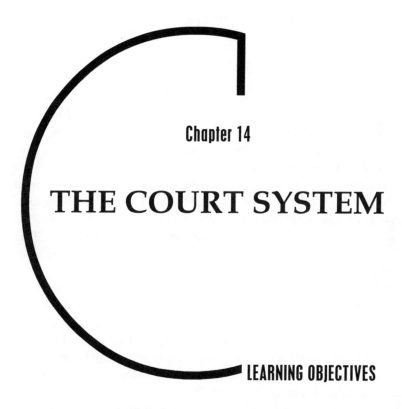

Chapter 14

THE COURT SYSTEM

After reading this chapter, you should be able to:

- Understand the difference between the state and federal court systems.

- Explain the roles and functions of the different parties to a criminal trial.

- List the various types of pretrial procedures.

- Distinguish between the different phases in a criminal trial.

COURT STRUCTURE[1]

Principles and Characteristics

In order to understand the role of federal and state law, it is essential to have a firm grasp of the principles of how the American criminal justice system functions. There is no more confusing, frustrating, and complex environment in the legal system than the criminal court system.

The court system in the United States is based upon the principle of **federalism**. The first Congress established a federal court system, and the individual states were permitted to continue their own judicial structure. There was general agreement among our nation's founding fathers that individual states needed to retain significant autonomy from federal control. Under the concept of federalism, the United States developed as a loose confederation of semi-independent states with the federal court system acting in a very limited manner. In the early history of our nation, most cases were tried in state courts, and it was only later that the federal government and the federal judiciary began to exercise jurisdiction over crimes and civil matters. **Jurisdiction**, in this context, simply means the ability of the court to enforce laws and punish individuals who violate those laws.

As a result of this historical evolution, a **dual system** of state and federal courts exists today. Therefore, federal and state courts may have concurrent jurisdiction over specific crimes. For example, a person who robs a bank may be tried and convicted in state court for robbery and also tried and convicted in federal court for the federal offense of robbery of a federally chartered savings institution.

Another characteristic of the American court system is that it performs its duties with little or no supervision. A supreme court justice does not exercise supervision over lower court judges in the same way that a government supervisor or manager exercises control over his or her employees. The U.S. Supreme Court and the various state supreme courts exercise supervision only in the sense that they hear appellate cases from lower courts and establish certain procedures for these courts.

A third feature of our court system is one of specialization that occurs primarily at the state and local level. In many states, courts of limited jurisdiction hear misdemeanor cases and, in others, state courts of general jurisdiction try felonies. Still other courts may be designated as juvenile courts and hear only matters involving juveniles. This process also occurs in certain civil courts that hear only family law matters, probate matters or civil cases involving damages. At the federal level, there are courts, such as bankruptcy courts, that hear only cases dealing with specific matters.

The fourth characteristic of the American court system is its geographic organization. State and federal courts are organized into geographic areas. In many jurisdictions, these are called **judicial districts** and contain various levels of courts. For example, on the federal level, the 9th Circuit Court of Appeals has district (trial) courts which hear matters within certain specific boundaries and an appellate court that hears all appeals from cases within that area. Several studies have been conducted regarding the difference in sentences for the same type of crime in geographically distinct courts. For example, in Iowa, the average sentence for motor vehicle theft was 47 months while the average sentence for the same offense in New York was 14 months.[2] These variations may reflect different social values and attitudes within specific geographical areas.

The State System

Historically, each of the 13 states had their own unique court structure. This independence continued after the American Revolution and resulted in widespread differences among the various states, some of which still exist today. Because each state adopted its own system of courts, the consequence was a poorly planned and confusing judicial structure. As a result there have been several reform movements whose purpose has been to streamline and modernize this system.

Most state courts can be divided into three levels: trial courts, appellate courts and state supreme courts.

- **Trial Courts:** Trial courts are where criminal cases start and finish. The trial court conducts the entire series of acts that culminate in either the defendant's release or sentencing. State trial courts can be further divided into courts of limited or special jurisdiction and courts of general jurisdiction.

- The nature and type of case determines which court will have jurisdiction. Courts which only hear and decide certain limited legal issues are courts of **limited jurisdiction**. Typically, these courts hear certain types of minor civil or criminal cases. There are approximately 13,000 local courts in the United States. They are county, magistrate, justice or municipal courts. Judges in these courts may be either appointed or elected. In many jurisdictions these are part-time positions, and the incumbent may have another job or position in addition to serving as a judge. However, simply because they handle minor civil and criminal matters does not mean these courts do not perform important duties. Many times the only contact the average citizen will have with the judicial system occurs at this level. Courts of limited jurisdiction hear and decide issues such as traffic tickets or set bail for criminal defendants.

- In addition, courts of limited jurisdiction may hear certain types of specialized matters such as probate of wills and estates, divorces, child custody matters and juvenile hearings. These types of courts may be local courts or, depending on the state, may be courts of general jurisdiction that are designated by statute to hear and decide specific types of cases. For example, in California, a superior court is considered a court of general jurisdiction; however, certain superior courts are designated to hear only juvenile matters thereby becoming a court of limited jurisdiction when sitting as a juvenile court.

Courts of **general jurisdiction** are granted authority to hear and decide all issues that are brought before them. These are the courts which normally hear all major civil or criminal cases. These courts are known by a variety of names, such as superior courts, circuit courts, district courts or courts of common pleas. Since they are courts of general jurisdiction, they have authority to decide issues that occur anywhere within the state. Some larger jurisdictions such as Los Angeles or New York may have hundreds of courts of general jurisdiction within the city limits. Typically, these courts hear civil cases involving the same types of issues that courts of limited jurisdiction hear, although the amount of damages will be higher and may reach millions. These courts also hear the most serious forms of criminal matters including death penalty cases.

Felon Sentencing

by state court in 1992

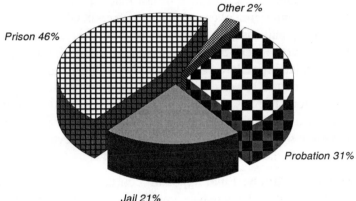

Other 2%

Prison 46%

Probation 31%

Jail 21%

Courts of general jurisdiction traditionally have the power to order individuals to do, or refrain from doing, certain acts. These courts may issue injunctions which prohibit performing certain acts or require individuals to do certain functions or duties. This authority is derived from the equity power that resides in courts of general jurisdiction. **Equity** is the concept that justice is administrated according to fairness as contrasted with the strict rules of law. In early English common law such separate courts of equity were known as **Courts of Chancery**. These early courts were not concerned with technical legal issues, rather they focused on rendering decisions or orders that were fair or equitable. In modern times, the power of these courts has been merged with courts of general jurisdiction allowing them to rule on matters that require fairness as well as the strict application of the law. The power to issue temporary restraining orders in spousal abuse cases comes from this authority.

Appellate jurisdiction is reserved for courts which hear appeals from both limited and general jurisdiction courts. These courts do not hold trials or hear evidence. They decide matters of law and issue formal written decisions or "opinions." There are two classes of appellate courts—intermediate and final.

- **Courts of Appeals:** The intermediate appellate courts are known as courts of appeals. Approximately half the states have designated intermediate appellate courts. These courts may be divided into judicial districts that hear all appeals within their district. They will hear and decide all issues of law that are raised on appeal in both civil and criminal cases. Since these courts deal strictly with legal or equitable issues, there is no jury to decide factual disputes. These courts accept the facts as determined by the trial courts. Intermediate appellate courts have the authority to reverse the decision of the lower courts and to send the matter back with instructions to retry the case in accordance with their opinion. They also may uphold the decision of the lower court. In either situation, the party who loses the appeal at this level may file an appeal with the next higher appellate court.

- **Supreme Courts:** Final appellate courts are the highest state appellate courts. They may be known as supreme courts or courts of last resort. There may be five, seven or nine justices sitting on this court depending on the state. These courts have jurisdiction to hear and decide issues dealing with all matters decided by lower courts including ruling on state constitutional or statutory issues. This decision is binding on all other courts within the state. Once this court has decided an issue, the only appeal left is to file in the federal court system.

The Federal System

While state courts have their origin in historical accident and custom, federal courts were created by the United States Constitution. Section 1 of Article III established the federal court system with the words providing for "one Supreme Court, and . . . such inferior courts as the Congress may from time to time ordain and establish." From this beginning, Congress has engaged in a series of acts that have resulted in today's federal court system. The **Judiciary Act of 1789** created the U.S. Supreme Court and established district and circuit courts of appeals.

Federal district courts are the lowest level of the federal court system. These courts have original jurisdiction over all cases involving a violation of federal statutes. These district courts handle thou-

Cases Handled in Federal District Courts

percentage by type of offense

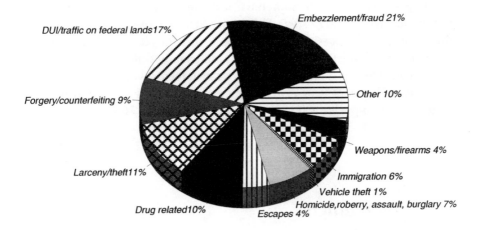

Embezzlement/fraud 21%

DUI/traffic on federal lands17%

Forgery/counterfeiting 9%

Other 10%

Weapons/firearms 4%

Larceny/theft11%

Immigration 6%

Vehicle theft 1%

Drug related10%

Escapes 4%

Homicide,roberry, assault, burglary 7%

sands of criminal cases per year and questions have been raised as to the quality of justice that can be delivered by overworked judges.

Federal circuit courts of appeals are the intermediate appellate level courts within the federal system. These courts are called **circuit courts** because the federal system is divided into 11 circuits. A twelfth circuit court of appeals serves the Washington D.C. area. These courts hear all criminal appeals from the district courts. These appeals are usually heard by panels of three of the appellate court judges rather than by all the judges of each circuit.

The United States Supreme Court is the highest court in the land. It has the capacity for judicial review of all lower court decisions as well as state and federal statutes. By exercising this power, the Supreme Court determines what laws and lower court decisions conform to the mandates set forth in the U.S. Constitution. The concept of **judicial review** was first referred to by Alexander Hamilton in the Federalist Papers where he referred to the Supreme Court as ensuring that the will of the people will be supreme over the will of the legislature.[3] This concept was firmly and finally established in our system when the Supreme Court asserted its power of judicial review in the case of *Marbury v. Madison.*[4]

The Supreme Court has original jurisdiction in the following cases: cases between the United States and a state; cases between states; cases involving foreign ambassadors, ministers and consuls; and cases between a state and a citizen of another state or country. The court hears appeals from lower courts including the various state supreme courts. If four justices of the U.S. Supreme Court vote to hear a case, the court will issue a *writ of certiorari*. This is an order to a lower court to send the records of the case to the Supreme Court for review. The court meets on the first Monday of October and usually remains in session until June. The court may review any case it deems worthy of review, but it actually hears very few of the cases filed with it. Of approximately 5,000 appeals each year, the court hears about 200.

THE PARTIES

Law Enforcement

Law enforcement's role in the court system is critical and was discussed in Chapter 13. Here, it is important to remember that law enforcement's duties do not end with the apprehension of the suspect. They must continue to work the case until it is sent to the jury by the judge. It is common in larger prosecutors' offices to have the lead detective sit with the prosecutor during the trial. That detective may know the case as well as the prosecutor and, many times, will provide critical advice.

The Prosecutor

One of the most important roles in the system is that of the prosecutor, especially the U.S. Attorney. This is the individual who is charged with the responsibility of filing criminal cases. Until the case is filed, it does not become a part of the court system.

We often think that the prosecutor's role is to convict the defendant. This is erroneous. The prosecutor has the duty to ensure justice, not merely to convict. Accordingly, if the prosecutor has a reasonable basis for believing that the defendant is not guilty, the prosecutor should not attempt to obtain a conviction. In such a case, if the prosecutor is the decision maker (e.g., district attorney), then the prosecutor should request that the case be dismissed. If the prosecutor is not the decision maker (e.g., an assistant district attorney), the prosecutor should present the facts to the district attorney and request either that he or she be relieved from the case or that the case be dismissed. It would be unethical for an attorney to attempt to convict an innocent person.

As noted earlier, the prosecutor in federal court is the U.S. Attorney or Assistant U.S. Attorney, probably the latter. In state courts, he or she is the district attorney, state's attorney, commonwealth's attorney, or county attorney. As reflected in the American Bar Canons of Professional Responsibility, the prosecutor's primary duty is not to convict but to seek justice. If the prosecutor believes that the defendant is guilty, and there is sufficient evidence to support the charges, then, and only then, is the prosecutor under a duty to enforce the criminal charge against the defendant.

The prosecutor has absolute and unrestricted discretion to choose who is prosecuted and who is not.

Anonymous

Often, young prosecutors forget this and attempt to obtain as many convictions as possible to build a reputation as a "tough" prosecutor on crime. This conflict can lead to prosecutorial misconduct. Since appellate courts generally uphold convictions in those cases where the misconduct is not serious, some prosecutors, who are overzealous or motivated by personal or political gain, attempt to prosecute using questionable tactics that are marginally acceptable.

Under our adversarial system, only the prosecutor has the authority to refer charges to the courts. A case does not begin until the prosecutor files the charges or grand jury indictment with the court. In most jurisdictions, if the prosecutor refuses to prosecute, the only remedy is to remove the prosecutor for misconduct or elect a new one. The courts will refuse to order a prosecutor to prosecute a case. Prosecutors do not have sufficient assets to prosecute all cases. Accordingly, they select those cases to prosecute. Prosecutors tend to focus on certain types of crimes in deciding which crimes to prosecute. Often the decisions are made based on the personal behavioral norms of the elected district attorney. The prosecutor cannot, however, forget that he or she may soon be up for re-election and may have to answer to the voters for his or her actions.

In the previous paragraphs, the reference to prosecutor has generally been to the elected or appointed prosecutor. In most jurisdictions this individual, as the head of the prosecutor's office, makes policy decisions and rarely tries a case in trial court. Most cases are tried, however, by the assistant district attorneys or assistant state's attorneys. There are approximately 2,300 chief prosecutors in the United States. They employ about 20,000 assistants. About 97 percent of the chief prosecutors are elected to office. The others are usually appointed by the governor.

The general duties of an assistant district attorney or assistant state's attorney include:

√ Helping investigate possible violations of the law

√ Cooperating with police in investigating crimes

√ Interviewing witnesses

√ Subpoenaing witnesses to appear in court

√ Plea bargaining in accordance with policy directions from the elected prosecutor

√ Trying the cases in court

√ Recommending sentences to the court

√ Representing the government in appeals

Assistants need to make many decisions regarding the processing and prosecution of cases. Often there is neither time nor the opportunity to check with the elected prosecutor regarding decisions. The elected prosecutor is, however, held responsible for decisions made by his or her assistants. In most prosecutors' offices, the elected prosecutor provides detailed guidelines or standards for the assistant prosecutors to follow in making decisions. For example, in most offices there are specific guidelines regarding plea bargaining.

Another problem with prosecutors is the high number of part-time prosecutors in small jurisdictions. Many states, like California, have taken steps to consolidate the prosecutors' offices in order to eliminate the need for part-time prosecutors. The part-time prosecutor generally practices law to supplement his or her income. Conflicts often

 ## Duties of the Prosecutor

The American Bar Association's Code of Professional Responsibility, Canon 7-103 provides:

7-103: Performing the Duty of Public Prosecutor or Other Government Counsel

A. A public prosecutor or other government lawyer shall not institute or cause to be instituted criminal charges when he knows or it is obvious that the charges are not supported by probable cause.

B. A public prosecutor or other government lawyer in criminal litigation shall make timely disclosure to counsel for the defendant, or to the defendant if the defendant does not have counsel, of the existence of evidence, known to the prosecutor or other government lawyer, that tends to negate the guilt of the accused, mitigates the degree of the offense, or reduces the punishment.

arise when the prosecutor is also a part-time civil attorney. In addition, most part-time prosecutors receive little or no formal training to handle the complex duties of prosecutor.

The U.S. attorney is the prosecutor or district attorney in the federal system. There is a U.S. attorney for each federal district court. They are appointed by the president and serve at the pleasure of the president. It is customary for every new president to request the resignation of all U.S. attorneys at the start of a new administration.

The U.S. attorneys, therefore, tend to have the same political outlook as the president and probably support the president during the election process. Accordingly, to some extent, the U.S. attorney is a political person. Justice George Sutherland described the role of the U.S. Attorney as follows:

> The United States Attorney is the representative not of an ordinary party to a controversy, but of a sovereignty whose obligation to govern impartially is as compelling as its obligation to govern at all; and whose interest, therefore, in a criminal prosecution is not that it shall win a case, but that justice shall be done. As, such, he is in a peculiar and very definite sense the servant of the law, the twofold aim of which is that the guilty shall not escape or innocence suffer. He may prosecute with earnestness and vigor—indeed, he should do so. But while he may strike foul ones, it is as much his duty to refrain from improper methods calculated to produce wrongful conviction as it is to use ever legitimate means to bring about a just one.[5]

As the chief federal prosecutor for the district court, the U.S. attorney determines which federal crimes will be prosecuted and which will not be. The new federal court sentencing guidelines, however, limit to some extent the plea bargaining that the U.S. attorney may do.

The Defense Attorney

Defending people accused of a crime is the most distasteful function performed by lawyers.

F. Lee Bailey

At a trial in Leningrad, USSR in 1974, the first thing that the accused's attorney did was to apologize to the court for defending "an enemy of the people." This would never happen in our courts. Under our system of justice, the accused has the right to a counsel whose duty is to serve the interests of the accused. While the defense counsel is an officer of the court, he or she is also the representative of the defendant in our adversarial process. The Sixth Amendment provides that in all criminal cases the accused shall have the right to the assistance of counsel. As a member of the courthouse work group, the defense counsel should represent the interests of the accused.

Right to Assistance of Counsel

... in all criminal prosecutions, the accused shall enjoy the right...to have the assistance of counsel for his defense.

Sixth Amendment, U.S. Constitution

The Sixth Amendment of the U.S. Constitution guarantees that the accused shall have the right to the assistance of counsel in all criminal cases. This means that no matter how petty the offense, the accused has the right to assistance of counsel. This issue has never been seriously questioned. The controversial issue is whether when the accused cannot afford an attorney, the government is required to provide the accused with counsel?

As a general rule, the accused is entitled to the appointment of a counsel any time that the accused is subject to punishment which may include jail or prison time and the accused cannot afford to retain an attorney.[6] [Note: If the accused can afford counsel, he or she has the right to counsel in all criminal proceedings.] Typically, the indigent accused has the right to counsel at every significant phase of the trial.

Another problem in our system is that of providing counsel in those cases where the accused cannot afford an attorney. States and the federal government use several different methods. The three methods generally used are: public defender, assigned counsel, and contract counsel.

The first public defender's office was established in Los Angeles County, California in 1914. Thirty states and the federal government use a public defender system to provide legal services to indigent defendants. The **public defender** is an attorney who is employed by the state or federal government to serve as counsel for indigent defendants. In those jurisdictions using a public defender, generally when the trial judge conducts arraignments, a public defender will be available in court to be appointed as counsel for the accused.

In some jurisdictions, the public defenders receive less pay than the prosecutors and their positions are considered less prestigious than those of the prosecutors. Most states have corrected this situation and have attempted to make public defenders' positions as prestigious as that of the assistant prosecutors.

Most public defenders' offices are struggling under a massive caseload, and often the attorneys do not have the luxury to spend sufficient time on particular cases. There are often frequent criticisms regarding the quality of services provided by public defenders. It appears that public defender offices, like other state agencies, vary in the quality of services provided. In each office you are likely to encounter individuals who fail to adequately perform their assigned duties as counsel. But, however, you also find many well-qualified and highly competent counsel. In both the public defender and the assigned counsel systems, attorneys may be found who do not wish to anger judges through the use of extensive motions, arguments, demands for jury trials, etc. It appears that the quality of service provided by public defenders is very similar to that provided by individual attorneys who have been selected and hired by the defendant. In both situations, you find good attorneys and bad ones.

Most jurisdictions which do not have a public defender system normally assign individual attorneys to represent indigent defendants. Judges use several methods to decide which attorney should be appointed. The most common is the use of a list of all attorneys practicing in the local court. From this list, the judge appoints the next available attorney to defend the accused. Assigned counsel generally receives a small fee from the state for the representation of the defendant.

The **assigned counsel system** is the oldest and, until recently, the most widely-used method for providing representation to indigent defendants in criminal cases. There are many problems with this system. The problems include:

√ In many jurisdictions, only new and inexperienced counsel are assigned.

√ In some jurisdictions, "has beens" are assigned as a supplement to their retirement income.

√ In those jurisdictions that use all members of the local bar, frequently counsel will be assigned who do not normally practice criminal law.

√ For those counsel assigned, the pay is substantially lower than the counsel would make on a non-assigned case and most of their out-of-pocket expenses are not paid, accordingly, this discourages attorneys from accepting appointments.

√ Seldom are additional funds available to hire investigators, etc. to assist in the cases.

√ The few attorneys who are financially dependent upon the assignments will be hesitant to vigorously defend the cases for fear of angering the judge.

Despite the above problems, there are some definite advantages of using the assigned counsel system. They include:

√ Counsel may bring a different perspective to the case since counsel is not a part of the courthouse work group.

√ The accused generally feel more comfortable when represented by a private attorney rather than a public defender.

Presently, six states exclusively use the contract system, and several other states use the contract system to supplement the public defender system. It is the newest system, but appears to be growing as more states attempt to obtain more for their limited resources. Under the **contract system**, the jurisdiction publishes "request for proposals" (RFPs). An RFP invites private law firms to bid for the services. The law firms submit proposals on establishing a defender system and the costs involved. The government then selects the firm with the best bid. That firm is responsible for providing indigent defendants with representation in court.

The most popular grounds for appeal in criminal courts is that of ineffective assistance of counsel. The appellate courts generally require not only that the defendant establish that his or her counsel made errors at trial, but also that the errors prejudiced the defendant. The courts are hesitant to engage in second guessing trial counsel (Monday morning quarterbacking). In addition, a defendant who is represented by a retained attorney (one hired by a defendant) has a more difficult time in establishing ineffective assistance of counsel. The rationale for the latter rule is that the accused should not be rewarded for selecting a bad attorney.

No one person has a more demanding and more misunderstood role than that of the defense counsel. Too often we associate the defense counsel with the person he or she represents. Would you defend a person who raped an eight-year-old girl? How could you defend a person who has committed murder?

These questions are commonly asked of attorneys. The people who ask these types of questions fail to realize that under our adversarial system of justice, the accused has the right to have a counsel to appear on his or her behalf and owes a duty to represent the accused within legally permissible bounds. Even if the accused has admitted his or her guilt to the defense attorney, the attorney has the right to force the government to prove the accused's guilt beyond a reasonable doubt. The defense attorney's role is to be the spokesperson and representative for the accused. If the attorney can legally prevent the state from proving the accused's guilt, the attorney must do so.

The defense attorney is an officer of the court and, as such, he or she cannot present false evidence, allow perjury to be committed or break the law in defending the accused. The defense attorney, however, is required to use any legal method to prevent the accused's conviction or in the case of conviction, to obtain the lightest sentence possible for the accused. It is not the attorney's duty to determine what sentence is best for the accused, its his or her duty to obtain the lightest sentence unless requested otherwise by the defendant. An undecided issue in this regard is the defense counsel's duty to fight the death penalty or to attempt to ensure that the death penalty is imposed when the accused is being tried for a capital offense and requests the death penalty.

As noted earlier, the defense counsel cannot violate the law in defending the accused. If for example, the accused tells the counsel that he is going to testify falsely at the trial, the counsel should encourage the accused not to. If the accused insists on testifying and indicates that he will commit perjury, the defense counsel should request that the judge relieve the counsel from the duties to represent the accused before the accused testifies. The problem, in this case, is that the counsel cannot tell the judge why he or she wants to be relieved due to the rules of confidentiality. All the counsel can tell the judge is that there is a conflict between the accused and counsel. This problem could last indefinitely, because when new counsel is appointed, if the accused tells the new counsel that he intends to commit perjury, the new counsel should also be excused. What normally happens, however, is once a counsel has been excused, the accused realizes the problem and doesn't tell all to the new counsel.

A young girl is missing, the girl's parents offer a reward for information regarding the missing girl's whereabouts. You are defending an accused on an unrelated murder charge. He informs you that he killed the young girl and buried her body in the local cemetery. If the police find the body, evidence on the body will lead the police to your client. What do you do?[7]

Information that an attorney receives from his or her client is privileged and cannot be divulged without the client's consent. Accordingly, if an accused tells his attorney that he committed a murder, the attorney cannot divulge this information without the client's consent. This privileged communication is based on the theory that the accused needs to be able to communicate with his or her attorney without fear of the communications being used against him or her. In the above situation, the New York Bar Association ruled that the communication was privileged and the attorney should not have revealed the information regarding the girl's death.

In one Virginia case, the accused told his counsel that the money from a bank robbery was in a locker in a bus station. The counsel advised the accused to hide the money elsewhere. The attorney was convicted of being an accessory after the fact. While the communication as to the location of the money was privileged, the attorney went beyond that when he advised the accused to hide the money in a different location. This conversation was overheard by a nosey telephone operator who reported it to the police. [Note: The privileged communication extends to the attorney, attorney's secretary and paralegal, but not to a third person such as a telephone operator who overhears the conversation.]

The courts have recognized that there is an important relationship between the accused and his or her counsel. Accordingly, an accused has the right to refuse a counsel and in turn, counsel has a right to refuse to represent any accused. An occasional problem in this area is where the accused is assigned a counsel at government expense, and the accused does not like his or her attorney. As a general rule when dealing with "appointed" counsel, the judge will allow the defendant to "fire" one attorney but will require reasons before allowing the defendant to fire the second attorney. Normally a defendant can fire his or her "retained" counsel at any time. The judge, however, may decide not to delay a scheduled trial or other court appearance to allow the defendant time to obtain new retained counsel. [Note: "Appointed counsel" is one provided by the government to indigent defendants. "Retained counsel" is a counsel that has been hired and paid by the defendant.]

The Judge

The judges are the weakest link in our system of justice, and they are also the most protected.

Alan M. Dershowitz

The **trial judge** is an officer of the court. It would be more accurate to describe him or her as the "master of the court." The trial judge's duties are varied and far more extensive than would appear on the surface. During the trial, judges rule on appropriateness of the conduct of all others involved in the court process including spectators. Judges determine what evidence is admissible and, during jury trials, which instructions of law the juries will receive. Any motions, questions of law, objections, and, in most states, the sentence to impose are questions decided only by the judges. The senior judge in any one court or the presiding judge is responsible for the docketing (scheduling) of cases, motions, etc. Judges also have extensive control over probation officers, the court clerks and indirectly, to some extent, the police.

The duties and responsibilities of an appellate judge are very different from those of a trial judge. The responsibilities of an appellate judge include:

1) Examining the record of trial, trial brief, notice of appeal, and other matter submitted with the appeal to determine if the appeal is properly presented and the appropriate issues are properly before the court

2) Presiding over oral arguments

3) Negotiating a decision among the justices considering the appeal

4) Writing an opinion that explains the logic and reasons for the decision

The appellate justice's work is largely confined to reviewing cases tried by trial judges. Instead of the noisy, crowded trial court with numerous distractions, the appellate justice deals mainly with paperwork, (e.g., briefs, records of trial, and research regarding prior court decisions).

There are approximately 26,000 judges in the United States. The vast majority of them are lower court judges. Most states now require that a judge have a law degree and be licensed to practice law in the jurisdiction. Many states like California, Florida, and New Jersey require the judges to be admitted to practice in that jurisdiction and at least "learned in the law." There are still, however, a number of lower court judges who do not have formal legal training.

While judges have the most important role in the judicial process, the current methods used to select judges do not guarantee that the best-fitted and best-trained persons are appointed as judges. Judges are selected by one of three methods: popular election, appointment, or merit plan. Thirty-two states elect their judges. Some elections are partisan (candidates run as members of a political party) and some are nonpartisan (candidates run without a party designation). Some states and the federal system appoint their judges. Other states use a form of merit system or the Missouri Plan.

The **Missouri Plan** was created in the 1940s to overcome the widespread use of political patronage in the appointment of judges. The Missouri plan is where the judges are selected based on their records of achievement in the legal field. After serving an initial term of office, the judge is then on the ballot for confirmation. When the judge's confirmation is presented to the voters, it is normally on a yes or no vote.

California elects its judges, however, in most situations when a vacancy occurs, the governor appoints a new judge. At the next election, the judge stands for election. In 1992, 88 percent of the trial court judges in California were placed on the bench initially by gubernatorial appointments to fill vacancies. In states using nonpartisan elections only 43 percent of the judges were initially elected, the majority were initially appointed by the governor.[9]

Focus — Functions of the Trial Judge

The American Bar Association Standards for Criminal Justice makes the below statement regarding the responsibility of the trial judge.

The trial judge has the responsibility for safeguarding both the rights of the accused and the interests of the public in the administration of criminal justice. The adversarial nature of the proceedings does not relieve the trial judge of the obligations of raising on his own initiative, at all appropriate times and in an appropriate manner, matters which may significantly promote a just determination of the trial. The only purpose of a criminal trial is to determine whether the prosecution has established the guilt of the accused as required by law, and the trial judge should not allow the proceedings to be used for any other purpose.[8]

In most states, like California, it is rare that a sitting judge is defeated by an opponent. An exception to this is Texas. In Texas, the judges are elected in partisan elections and the judicial races are very political in nature. A problem with the partisan election of judges is illustrated in a Texas case. In the 1970s, Texas elected an individual to the state supreme court who was being investigated for criminal homicide in another state and had little prior legal experience. This individual's last name was very similar to that of a popular politician in the state, and it is assumed that many voters thought they were voting for the politician. [Note: This individual resigned from the state supreme court as part of a criminal plea bargain.]

A few states, like New York, use a variety of methods for selecting judges. Appellate court judges are appointed by the governor from a group of candidates selected by a judicial nominating commission and approved by the state senate. Partisan elections are used to select major court trial judges. Municipal judges in New York City are appointed by the mayor of New York City.

As noted earlier, federal judges in constitutional courts hold office "during good behavior" for life. In most states, the judges serve terms of four to seven years. The most common method of removing judges is the failure to re-elect a judge when his or her term expires. In those states, like California, where judges are subject to being removed by a "fail-to-retain" vote, they can be removed by a negative vote. The opportunity to remove by failing to retain or not re-electing the judge occurs only when the judge's term is expiring.

In some states, the judges are subject to recall. The general recall procedures begin with a recall petition with a sufficient percentage of voter signatures is filed with the state election commission. The recall question is then placed on the next general election ballot, and a majority vote at the recall election will remove the judge. This process is time consuming and expensive.

Federal judges and some state judges may be removed by impeachment. The U.S. Constitution provides, in part, that any civil officer of the United States (including judges) may be removed by impeachment for crimes of "treason, bribery, or other high crimes and misdemeanors."[10] In federal cases, the House of Representatives must vote on the articles of impeachment, which is an accusation of criminal wrongdoing. The actual trial occurs before the senate. Two-thirds vote of the Senate is required before the judge is removed from office.

Like recall procedures, impeachment is time consuming and expensive.

The most workable method of judicial removal is by use of the Judicial Conduct Commission. In 1960, California was the first state to establish a judicial conduct commission. Now all states have some form of judicial removal commission. The judicial commission normally consists of judges, nonlawyer citizens, and attorneys. For example, Florida's commission has 13 members—six are judges (two from circuits courts, two from county courts, and two from the district courts of appeal), two attorneys appointed by the state bar, and five nonlawyer citizens appointed by the governor. The members serve staggered six-year terms. The Florida commission is empowered to deal with charges of misconduct, persistent failure to perform judicial duties, and any physical or mental disability that interferes with the performance of duties.

Generally, federal court judges hold their offices for life "during good behavior." The judges are nominated by the president and confirmed by the senate. In most cases, the president nominates judges of the same political party as the president. In fact, of the 107 Supreme Court justices, only 12 were not of the same party as the president. This power to nominate federal judges is an important political power. Especially since the judges appointed by a president generally serve in his or her office years after the president's term has expired. Accordingly, a president's influence will be present for many years after the president has been replaced.

For many years, the president appointed his friends or political supporters to the courts. President Reagan, however, changed this practice. He started the trend, which has been followed by both Bush and Clinton, to appoint judges that seemed most ideologically suited to the president's agenda. In addition, Reagan started the trend of appointing younger judges who would most likely serve longer terms of office.

The practice of selecting judges based on their ideology has had the effect of making the appointments more controversial and more difficult to achieve senate confirmation. Previously, most presidential appointments were quickly approved by the senate. Now, the confirmation hearings are more adversarial in nature and the candidates face an in-depth examination regarding their past career activities and personal conduct.

U.S. Commissioners for many years served the same functions that justices of the peace served for state courts. Commissioners had the authority to issue search and arrest warrants, arraign defendants, hold preliminary hearings, and try cases involving petty offenses. In 1967, the President's Commission on Law Enforcement and Administration of Justice noted that 30 percent of the commissioners were not lawyers and all but 7 of the 700 commissioners had other jobs. The president's commission recommended that the system be either eliminated or reformed. As the result of the recommendations, Congress established the federal magistrate system and provided for a three year phasing out of the commissioners.

Federal magistrates are appointed to assist district courts. There are presently 452 federal magistrates. Magistrates are lawyers appointed by district court judges for eight-year terms. Part-time magistrates are appointed for four-year terms. The Federal Magistrates Act of 1968 empowers them to issue search warrants, hear preliminary stages of felony cases, set bail, and try misdemeanor cases.[11] In 1976, the magistrates were given the authority to review civil rights and *habeas corpus* petitions and make recommendations regarding them to the district court judges.

It is estimated that magistrates perform about 475,000 separate tasks a year for the federal districts. Misdemeanor and petty offense trials account for 20 percent of the magistrates' time. About 30 percent of their time is involved with preliminary proceedings in criminal cases, 40 percent involves the disposition of motions and pretrial conferences, and the remaining 10 percent in miscellaneous duties.[12]

The Jury

Even though most cases are handled with a guilty plea and only a few cases are tried by a jury, the jury is the focal point of the criminal justice system. The Sixth Amendment also guarantees the accused the right to trial by jury. The three major issues regarding the right to a jury trial are (1) whether all offenders, including those being tried on minor offenses, have a right to jury trial; (2) the size of the jury; and (3) whether the jury verdict must be unanimous.

In felony cases, there has never been a question regarding the right to a jury trial. Prior to 1970, the general rule for state criminal trials was that in serious crimes the accused had a right to a jury trial but not in minor offenses. In *Baldwin v. New York*, the court moved away from the serious-minor classification and established the rule that if the accused was facing a possible sentence of six months or more in jail, the accused had a right to a jury trial.[13] If the accused is facing a possible sentence of less than six months, then the accused has no right to a jury trial unless provided by state statute. Many states, like California, provide the right to a jury trial any time the accused faces a possible jail sentence.

The U.S. Supreme Court discussed this issue again in *Blanton v. North Las Vegas*. The issue in this case was whether the accused had a right to a jury trial in cases involving driving under the influence (DUI). The court stated that if the state considered the offense a petty offense, the accused has no right to a jury trial. If the state, however, treats the crime as a serious crime then the accused has a right to a speedy trial. [Note: Nevada had a statute that classified DUI as a petty offense unless aggravating circumstances were present.[14]]

A related issue is whether the accused has a right to a trial by a jury consisting of at least 12 jurors. Historically, trial juries have consisted of 12 jurors. As the result, of *Williams v. Florida*, the U.S. Supreme Court has approved trial by a six person jury. The court stated:

> "We conclude, in short, as we began: the fact that a jury at common law was composed of precisely 12 is a historical accident, unnecessary to effect the purposes of the jury system and wholly without significance...."[15]

After the *Williams* case, many states adopted the six person jury for misdemeanor cases. In some states, like Florida, a six person jury may be used in felony cases. The U.S. Supreme Court has set six as the minimum size for a jury.

A related issue is the requirement for unanimous verdicts in jury cases. The Supreme Court has ruled that in trials with six person juries, the verdict must be unanimous. The court has approved statutes that allow less than unanimous verdicts in cases with 12 person juries. In *Apodica v. Oregon*, the court approved a state statute that allowed conviction based on the vote of 10 jury members in a 12 person jury.[16] The Supreme Court has never approved a less than unanimous verdict in cases with less than 12 jurors.

PRETRIAL AND TRIAL PROCESS

The Decision to Prosecute

The decision to prosecute is a function of the prosecutor and is generally not reviewable. In many states and the federal government, before the prosecutor may file felony charges with a court, he or she must obtain a grand jury indictment. In other states, the prosecutor files an **information** with the lower court.

Generally, after an arrest or on the completion of an investigation, the case is referred to the prosecutor's office. In some jurisdictions, however, the case is not referred until after the accused has made an initial appearance in court. When the case is received in the prosecutor's office, it is reviewed to determine if the case merits prosecution. Because of a lack of resources, prosecutors cannot try all cases referred to their offices.

Additional reasons that prosecution may be declined in a case include:

√ Insufficient evidence

√ Witness problems

√ Interests of justice

√ Defendant pleas in another case

√ Pretrial diversion

√ Referral to another jurisdiction for prosecution

√ Due process problems (e.g., questionable search)

√ Referral to treatment programs (e.g., alcohol rehabilitation programs)

The prosecutor may also reduce the charge to a misdemeanor. Of the above reasons for declining prosecution, insufficient evidence is the most common reason for rejection. For example, approximately one half of all drug cases in which prosecution is declined were based on insufficient evidence. The second most common reason involved witness problems, in that the witnesses were unavailable or unwilling to be involved.[17]

Bail

Traditionally, the bail system required the defendant to guarantee his or her appearance at trial by posting a money bond. This money would be forfeited should the defendant fail to appear in court for trial. The Eighth Amendment of the U.S. Constitution states that excessive bail shall not be required. While the amendment does not grant the right to bail in all cases, all states and the federal government give the defendant the right to bail except in limited situations.

The traditional bail system discriminates against the poor who cannot afford bail. Accordingly, alternatives to the bail system include release on recognizance, conditional release, third-party custody, and citation release.

The U.S. Supreme Court made it clear in 1950 that the purpose of bail was "to assure the defendant's attendance in court when his presence is required."[18] Accordingly, we assume that any bail higher than that necessary to ensure the accused's presence at trial is excessive and, thus, unconstitutional.

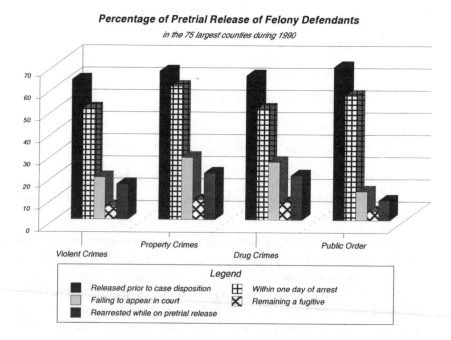

Percentage of Pretrial Release of Felony Defendants

in the 75 largest counties during 1990

Violent Crimes   Property Crimes   Drug Crimes   Public Order

Legend

■ Released prior to case disposition   ⊞ Within one day of arrest
▨ Failing to appear in court   ⊠ Remaining a fugitive
■ Rearrested while on pretrial release

 **Pretrial Releases**

Traditional Bail Bond. In this situation, the defendant, or someone on the defendant's behalf, posts the full amount of the bail.

Privately Secured Bail. A professional bondsperson signs a promissory note to the court for the bail amount and charges the defendant a fee for the service (usually 10 percent of the face amount of the bond). If the defendant fails to appear in court as required, the bondsperson may be required to pay the court the full amount of the bond. Frequently, a bondsperson will require the accused or the accused's family to post collateral in addition to the fee. If the accused fails to appear, the accused owes the bondsperson the amount of money that the bondsperson has to pay the court. This amount is in addition to the 10 percent fee already paid by the accused for bail services.

Deposit Bond. The courts, in many states, allow the defendant to post a deposit, usually 10 percent of the full bail with the court. This is also frequently referred to as the "10 percent Bail" program. If the defendant fails to appear, he or she owes the full amount of the bond to the court. If the defendant appears, most of the deposit is returned. Generally the courts keep one percent of the bond amount for administrative costs.

Unsecured Bail. In this situation, the defendant pays no money to the court, but is liable for the full amount of the bail if the accused fails to appear.

Release on Recognizance (ROR). In this situation, the court releases the defendant on the defendant's *promise* to appear in court as required.

Conditional Release. The court releases the defendant subject to the defendant agreeing to follow certain specified conditions. For example, the judge may release a defendant providing he or she will not leave the city, or bother the witnesses.

Third Party Custody. The defendant is released to the custody of a third person who promises to assure the accused's presence in court. No monetary transactions are involved in this type of release. This type of release is very common with juvenile defendants released into the custody of their guardians.

Citation Release. The defendant is released pending the first court appearance by signing a citation issued by a law enforcement person. Normally the citation release is used only in traffic cases and cases involving minor offenses.

Other key features of the act were its establishment of a "no-bail" presumption for certain types of cases. Many scholars thought that the "no-bail" presumption denied the accused due process since it authorized punishment before trial. The U.S. Supreme Court, in upholding the constitutionality of the Bail Reform Act, stated: "The legislative history clearly shows that Congress formulated the Bail Reform Act to prevent danger to the community— a legitimate regulatory goal— not to punish dangerous individuals.[19]

When the U.S. Supreme Court held this act constitutional, most states enacted similar statutes. Accordingly, now in determining whether to release a defendant from custody prior to the trial, the judge must consider both (1) the likelihood the accused will be present for trial and (2) the safety of the community.

Pretrial Hearings

Felony cases are processed either by indictment or appearance before a preliminary hearing. In those states that require indictments by a grand jury, the case is normally presented to the grand jury by the prosecutor. If the grand jury returns an indictment, the indictment is then filed with the superior or district court.

In states, like California, that do not require an indictment by grand jury, an **information** is presented to a lower court (justice or municipal). The information is a charging document similar to the complaint in a misdemeanor case. The information is presented to the municipal or justice court where a preliminary hearing is held. About half the states use preliminary hearings rather than grand juries. The purpose of the preliminary hearing is to determine if there is probable cause to have the defendant answer to the charge in a felony court. At the preliminary hearing, the judge can dismiss the charges, reduce the charge to a misdemeanor and try the case, or order the defendant to be bound over for trial in felony court.

After the indictment is filed or the accused is bound over by the municipal or justice court on an information, the accused is arraigned before the trial court. In some states, the arraignment may be before the lower court. At the arraignment, the accused is informed of the charge(s) against him or her, advised of the right to counsel, and a plea is entered. In addition, the judge must decide whether the accused should be released on bail or some other form of release while awaiting trial.

At the preliminary hearing, the prosecution presents its evidence, including witnesses, to the judge. The defense counsel may also present evidence favorable to the accused. At this hearing, the judge determines whether probable cause indicates that the accused has committed a felony.

The accused may plead guilty, not guilty, or *nolo contendere* when asked to plead. A plea of *nolo contendere* means that the accused does not contest the charges. It is treated as if the accused entered a plea of guilty. If the accused enters a **guilty plea** he or she admits all of the elements of the offense charged. If the accused enters a **plea of not guilty**, the case is set for trial. Normally both a trial date and a date for pretrial motions are set by the judge after the judge accepts the not guilty plea. On the pretrial motion date, the counsel are afforded an opportunity to present motions. Typical motions include: motion to suppress certain items of evidence, motion for speedy trial, and motion for dismissal of charges.

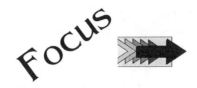

Pleas

Plea of Not Guilty— A plea of not guilty denies guilt and places the burden of proving guilt beyond a reasonable doubt on the prosecution. If the defendant stands mute and refuses to enter any plea, a plea of not guilty will be entered on the defendant's behalf by the judge. [Note: An accused has a constitutional right to be assumed innocent until proven guilty beyond a reasonable doubt.]

Guilty Plea— A guilty plea is not only an admission of guilt but is also a waiver of the right to jury, the right to remain silent, the right to confront the witnesses against you, and the right to require the prosecution to establish guilt beyond a reasonable doubt by admissible evidence. While an accused has a right to plead guilty, the trial judge is not required to accept this plea. If the judge feels that the accused's plea is not providently entered, the judge can enter a plea of not guilty for the accused. In addition, in capital cases the accused cannot enter a plea of guilty if the state is requesting the death penalty. The rationale for this rule is to allow the accused to plea guilty in a death penalty case would be the same as allowing the accused to commit suicide.

Nolo Contendere— This is a plea of "no contest." It is essentially a guilty plea. By entering a nolo plea, the accused waives the above rights, the same as if he or she had plead guilty. Often the *nolo contendere* plea is used in those cases where the accused is also liable in civil court. By pleading nolo, the accused does not admit commission of the act in question. The accused does not have a *right* to plead *nolo contendere*. This form of plea is acceptable in only about one half of the states and the federal government.

Not Guilty by Reason of Insanity— In most states, the accused may plead not guilty by reason of insanity. In states that do not allow the accused to plead insanity, the accused must plead not guilty and raise the issue of insanity as an affirmative (acceptable) defense. The normal plea in insanity cases is "not guilty and not guilty by reason of insanity." This plea requires the government prove that the defendant committed the offense, then the issue of the accused sanity is determined. In all states and the federal government, insanity is an affirmative defense, so the burden of producing evidence as to the sanity or insanity of the accused is first upon the defense. If no evidence is entered at trial regarding the sanity of the accused, it is assumed that the accused is sane.

Statute of Limitations or Double Jeopardy— In most states, before the accused enters a plea as to his or her guilt, the defense of statute of limitations or double jeopardy must be pled. In most cases, if these defenses are not pled before the guilty or not guilty plea, they are relinquished.

THE TRIAL

Jury Selection

The Sixth Amendment guarantees a defendant the right to an impartial jury. In addition, the due process clause of the Fifth and Fourteenth Amendments prohibits juries that exclude members of the defendant's racial, gender, ethnic, religious, or similar groups. To ensure an impartial jury, states and the federal government require that the jury panel (potential members of the jury) be selected from a fair cross-section of the community wherein the court convenes. Most jurisdictions randomly select the jury panel from the local census, tax rolls, city directories, telephone books, drivers' license lists, etc.

After the jury panel is selected, they are directed to appear at a certain time and place. It is from the jury panel that the actual jury is selected. The principle method used by the counsel to ensure that the jury is impartial is the *"voir dire"* of the jury. *Voir dire* is the questioning of the prospective jury members about matters that could influence their ability to serve on a jury. In some jurisdictions, counsel submit their questions to the judge who then asks the questions to the individual jury members. In other jurisdictions, both counsel have the opportunity to question the prospective jurors. Counsel can then challenge the prospective jury members. If the counsel's challenge is sustained by the judge (approved), the prospective jury member is excused.

There are two types of challenges—challenges for cause and peremptory challenges. A **challenge for cause** is based on something that indicates that the person would not be an impartial juror or would not follow the judge's instructions. Both sides have unlimited challenges for cause, but the judge may overrule the challenge (disapprove). An example of a challenge for cause would be where a juror indicates that he was the victim of a robbery and therefore would be prejudiced against the defendant who is charged with robbery.

Peremptory challenges are challenges by the prosecution or defense to excuse potential jurors from the jury panel. No reason is required. Each side is entitled by state or federal statute to a specified number of peremptory challenges.

In capital cases, we often talk about a "death qualified" jury. This refers to the fact that all the members selected for the jury have indicated that in the appropriate circumstances they would vote for the death penalty. The prosecutor asking for the death penalty has the right to challenge for cause any prospective juror who indicates that under no circumstances would the juror vote for the death penalty.

After the *voir dire* is completed and the jury has been selected, they are empaneled (sworn in). The judge then gives preliminary instructions to the jury. The jurors are instructed that they are not to talk to others about the case, to read the papers, or decide on the case until all the evidence has been submitted and the jury has received their instructions from the judge.

Opening Statements

After preliminary matters have been disposed of, the jury is seated in the jury box. The prosecutor has the opportunity to make an opening statement. This statement is not evidence, but may be used to inform the jury of the direction that the prosecutor is attempting to go. The defense counsel may make his or her opening statement immediately after the prosecution finishes or the defense may wait until the defense presents its case.

Case in Chief

The prosecutor, having the burden of proof, begins the trial. Witnesses are called and evidence is presented. After the prosecution rests its case, the defense presents its case. Then, the prosecution may present evidence in rebuttal to counter the defense.

Closing Argument

After both sides have rested, the prosecution presents its closing argument. The defense then presents its closing argument. Finally, the prosecution may present an argument in rebuttal to the defense's closing argument. The reason that the prosecutor goes first and is afforded the last word is based on the concept that the side with the burden of proof has the right to open and close the case. In the arguments presented by counsel, it is unethical for counsel to indicate a personal belief on whether or not the accused is guilty. For example, the prosecutor may argue that the government has proven the guilt of the defendant beyond a reasonable doubt. It is unethical for the prosecutor, however, to state that he or she believes that the defendant is guilty.

After argument has been completed, the judge gives instructions to the jury. This is also called **charging the jury**. The instructions are used to explain the law of the case to the jurors. The subjects covered in the instructions include burden of proof, the elements of the offense, voting procedures to be used by the jury, etc.

The Verdict

Generally in jury trials, the jury makes the findings of guilt or no guilt. After a guilty finding, the judge sets the sentencing. Sentencing will be discussed in Chapter 16. If the jury is unable to reach a verdict, the jury is considered a **hung jury**. In cases involving a hung jury, the jury is excused. The prosecution either retries the case or the charges are dismissed.

Although there are no provisions for it in the statutes, juries have nullification power. The nullification process occurs when the jury brings in a verdict of not guilty despite the fact that the evidence established the guilt of the accused. When jury nullification occurs, the accused cannot be re-tried for that offense. The power of nullification is a common law right that juries have. It is based on the concept that the jury is not required to explain any findings of not guilty.

Before the death penalty may be imposed by a judge, the jury must not only find that the accused is guilty but also that the special circumstances that allow the imposition of the death penalty exist. Death penalty cases are generally bifurcated trials (in two parts). The first part deals with the question of guilt and the second part deals with the question of whether special circumstances are present which would allow the death sentence.

SUMMARY

- Jurisdiction is the ability (power) of a court to enforce laws and punish individuals who violate those laws. We have a dual court system in the United States—state and federal. Each state has their own federal court system.

- Trial courts are where the cases are tried either with a jury or by judge alone. Courts of general jurisdiction have the authority to hear and decide all issues that are brought before them. Courts of limited jurisdiction may hear and decide only limited legal issues. Appellate courts are courts that hear appeals from both limited and general jurisdiction courts. Appellate courts do not hold trials or hear evidence.

- Federal district courts are the major trial courts in the federal system. There are 11 federal circuit courts of appeal. The courts hear appeals from the district courts. The United States Supreme Court is the highest court in the land and makes the final judicial decisions on matters involving federal issues.

- The prosecutor has the duty not to convict, but to ensure justice. Most state prosecutors are locally elected. Federal prosecutors are called assistant U.S. attorneys are appointed. Under our adversarial system, only the prosecutor has the authority to refer charges to a court. If a prosecutor refuses to prosecute, the only remedy is to remove the prosecutor for misconduct and appoint or elect a new one.

- The Sixth Amendment to the U.S. Constitution provides that the accused has a right to the assistance of counsel in criminal cases. The accused must be provided with an attorney if he or she cannot afford one and the accused is subject to confinement. Assigned counsel are appointed either from a public defender's office, contract attorney, or assigned counsel system. The defense counsel has the duty to present the accused's case in the light most favorable to the accused.

- The judge is often referred to as the "master of the court." A trial judge's duties include presiding over jury trials, ruling on admissibility of evidence, instructing the jury, and ruling on motions presented by either the prosecution or defense. In addition, in non-jury trials, the judge also makes findings of fact.

- There is a constitutional right to a jury trial in serious criminal cases. The functions of a jury include making findings of fact. Most criminal juries have 12 members. In non-capital cases (non-death penalty cases), the U.S. Supreme Court has upheld the use of six member juries.

- The decision to prosecute is vested with the prosecutor. The accused has the right, in most cases, to bail. The Eighth Amendment to the U.S. Constitution provides that excessive bail shall not be required. Pretrial releases may be a traditional bail bond, privately secured bail, deposit bail, unsecured bail, release on recognizance, release to third party custody, and citation release. Pretrial hearings are used to rule on the admissibility of evidence and other motions. Generally, an accused is required to enter a plea at arraignment. The types of pleas that an accused may enter include: guilty, not guilty, not guilty by reason of insanity, and nolo contendere.

- The trial is normally started with jury selection. Next, counsel are provided the opportunity to present opening statements, then the prosecution presents its case. After the prosecution has rested, the defense may present its case. Then the prosecution may present a rebuttal case. After all the evidence is presented, the jury is instructed by the judge and listens to arguments by counsel. The jury then makes the decision as to whether the prosecution has established the accused's guilt beyond a reasonable doubt.

DISCUSSION QUESTIONS

1. Explain the differences between the state and federal court system.

2. Name the key players in the court system and compare their roles.

3. Compare and contrast the roles of the defense counsel and the prosecutor.

4. Why doesn't the prosecutor always have a duty to convict?

5. Would you defend an individual accused of murder if you knew that he was guilty?

6. Explain the role and function of the jury.

7. Why does the prosecution have the burden of proof in criminal cases?

8. Explain the process of selecting jurors.

9. Would you qualify for a "death qualified jury"?

ENDNOTES—Chapter 14

1. This section has been adapted from Harvey Wallace, "Role of Federal and State Law," *National Victim Assistance Academy Text*, (Office for Victims of Crime, Washington DC 1997)

2. Pursley, *Introduction to Criminal Justice*, 6th Ed., (MacMillan Publishing Company, New York) 1994.

3. *The Supreme Court of the United States,* (U.S. Government Printing Office, Washington D.C.) no date.

4. 1 Cranch 137 (1803)

5. *Berger v. United States*, 295 U.S. 78 (1935).

6. *Argersinger v. Hamlin*, 407 U.S. 25 (1972).

7. This was an actual case that occurred in the 1970s in Buffalo, NY.

8. American Bar Association, *Standards for Criminal Justice*, approved draft, (1972).

9. N.Gary Holten and Lawson L. Lamar, *The Criminal Courts*, (New York: McGraw-Hill, 1991), p. 96.

10. U.S. Constitution, Article II.

11. 28 U.S.C. 636 (b).

12. Administrative Office of the United States Courts, *The United States Courts*, (Washington D.C.: Government Printing Office, 1989).

13. 399 U.S. 66 (1970).

14. 489 U.S. 538 (1989).

15. 399 U.S. 78, 90 (1970).

16. 406 U.S. 404 (1972).

17. Bureau of Justice Statistics Study, "Felony Arrests," (1987).

18. 342 U.S. 1 (1951).

19. *U.S. v. Salerno*, 55 USLW 4663 (1987).

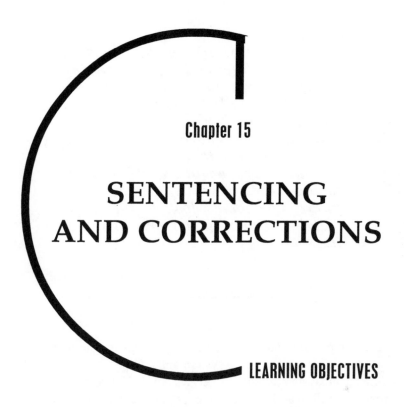

Chapter 15

SENTENCING AND CORRECTIONS

LEARNING OBJECTIVES

After studying this chapter, you should be able to:

- Outline the fragmentation of the corrections system.
- Explain the sentencing process for both misdemeanants and felons.
- Relate the American Bar Association's standards to sentencing alternatives.
- Differentiate between determinate and indeterminate sentencing.
- Describe the sentencing guidelines being used today.
- Explain the use of presumptive sentencing.
- Explain the use of parole guidelines.
- Identify the changes to the "justice" correctional philosophy.
- Define flat time with mandatory supervision.

385

Correctional management is directly influenced by sentencing changes (bigger numbers of offenders, for example) and also by the attendant culture. Whether the "message" of politicians is intended for correctional managers or not, they receive and heed it. I have long thought that if one wants to understand prisons and predict their future, one should look to the larger social environment, for prisons reflect it.

Walter J. Dickey, 1996

It is important to remember that corrections is a subpart of the broader criminal justice system and can be understood only as a subsystem of that larger system. It is also important to remember that before an individual comes under correctional control, he or she has already moved from citizen, suspect, arrestee, defendant and to convict.[1] In other words, the individual has already experienced the other two subsystems of the criminal justice system—law enforcement and the judiciary.

Corrections, like other subsystems (law enforcement and judiciary) in the criminal justice field, is fragmented. This fragmentation makes administrative coordination and linkage to the other criminal justice components difficult. The subsystem fragments into various areas by:

- **Jurisdiction:** federal, state, or local
- **Location:** institutional or community-based
- **Age:** adult or juvenile
- **Other factors:** size of institution, sex of inmates, types of offenses, and special programs

F_{OCUS} ➤ **National Crime Victimization Survey**

The annual BJS Bulletin presents the findings from the National Crime Victimization Survey (NCVS), based on an ongoing survey of households, each year interviewing about 100,000 persons in 50,000 households. In 1994, U.S. residents age 12 or older experienced more than 42 million crimes, about 11 million violent victimizations and 31 million property crimes.

Violent crimes include rape and sexual assault, robbery, both aggravated and simple assault (from the NCVS), and homicide (from crimes reported to the police).

The violent crime rate has essentially been unchanged since 1992, following a slight increase between 1985 and 1991. Property crime continued a 15-year decline. Property crimes include burglaries, motor vehicle thefts, and thefts of other property. Victims reported approximately a third of all property crimes. Motor vehicle theft was the most frequently reported crime (78%), and theft of other property was the least reported crime (27%).

THE SENTENCING PROCESS

Before the correctional process may be involved, the defendant must be convicted of a crime by a court with proper jurisdiction. In this section, we will examine the process by which a citizen becomes a client in the correctional process (i.e., the sentencing process). While there are some variations between the states, generally the processes are very similar. **Sentencing** is the formal process by which the courts deal with defendants convicted of crimes. A **sentence** is an authorized judicial decision that places some degree of penalty on a guilty person.[2] The responsibility for deciding the appropriate sentence is generally delegated to the judges. In a few states, like Texas, the defendant can elect to be sentenced by a jury.

Sentencing involves selecting the appropriate sentence from an array of choices that include incarceration, fine, forfeiture, probation, and alternative corrective programs. Once the sentencing decision is made, the responsibility for administrating the decision is placed with the department of corrections.

California Rules of Court, Rule 410

General objectives of sentencing include:

(a) Protecting society.

(b) Punishing the defendant.

(c) Encouraging the defendant to lead a law abiding life in the future and deterring him from future offenses.

(d) Deterring others from criminal conduct by demonstrating its consequences

(e) Preventing the defendant from committing new crimes by isolating him for the period of incarceration.

(f) Securing restitution for the victims of crime.

(g) Achieving uniformity in sentencing.

Because, in some instances, these objectives may suggest inconsistent dispositions, the sentencing judge shall consider which objectives are of primary importance in that particular case. The sentencing judge should be guided by statutory statements of policy, the criteria in these rules, and the facts and circumstances of the case.

The Chinese Proverb

There is an old Chinese proverb that states: "It is better to hang the wrong fellow than no fellow." This proverb indicates that certainty of punishment is important. When a crime is committed, someone must be punished.

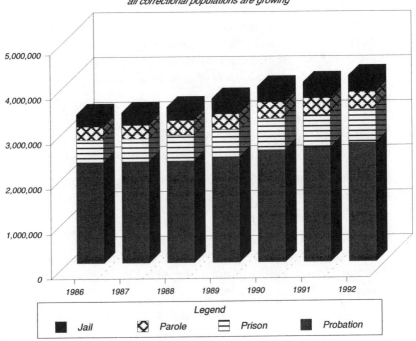

Number of Sentenced Offenders

all correctional populations are growing

Presentence Investigations

In most states, a presentence investigation report is mandatory for felony convictions. The **presentence investigation report** (PSI) is an important document for trial judges in making their sentence determinations. In most cases, the PSI is prepared by the court's probation office. In some states, like California, there are private companies that also prepare alternative PSIs for the judges to consider. The alternative PSIs are commissioned and paid for by the defense. Accordingly, they are generally used only in cases where the defendant or defendant's family can afford their costs.

A PSI generally include the following items:

1. A face sheet showing the defendant's name and other identifying data; case number; the crime for which the defendant was convicted; the date of commission of the crime; the date defendant was convicted; the defendant's present custody status; and the terms of any agreement upon which a plea of guilty was based.

2. The facts and circumstances of the crime and the defendant's arrest, including information concerning any codefendants and the status or disposition of their cases. The source of the information contained in this section should be stated in the report.

3. A summary of the defendant's record of prior criminal conduct, including convictions as an adult and sustained petitions in juvenile delinquency proceedings. Records of an arrest or charge not leading to a conviction generally are not included.

4. Any statement made by the defendant to the probation officer, or a summary thereof, including the defendant's account of the circumstances of the crime.

5. Information concerning the victim of the crime, including the victim's statement or a summary thereof, the amount of the victim's loss, whether or not it is covered by insurance, and any information required by law.

6. Any relevant facts concerning the defendant's social history, including family, education, employment, income, military status, medical/psychological history, record of substance abuse or lack thereof, and any other relevant information.

7. Collateral information, including written statements from: official sources such as police officers, defense counsel, probation and parole officers, and interested persons including family members.

8. An evaluation of factors relating to the sentence, including a reasoned discussion or the defendant's suitability and eligibility for probation. If probation is recommended, a proposed probation plan. If prison is recommended, a reasoned discussion of the aggravating and mitigating factors affecting the sentence length. In addition, a discussion of the defendant's ability to make restitution, pay any fine or penalty which may be imposed, to satisfy any special conditions of probation.

9. The probation officer's recommendation, including the length of any prison term that may be imposed, including the base term. The recommendation shall also include in the case of multiple offenses whether the terms for each offense will be concurrent or consecutive.

10. Detailed information on presentence time spent by the defendant in custody, including the beginning and ending dates of the period(s) of custody; the existence of any other sentences imposed on the defendant; the amount of good behavior, or work, or participation credit to which the defendant is entitled and whether or not a hearing has been requested regarding the denial of good behavior, work, or participation credit.

11. A statement regarding mandatory and recommended restitution, restitution fines, other fines, and costs to be assessed against the defendant.

The source of all information is listed in the report. Any person who furnished information shall be identified by name or official capacity unless a reason is given for not disclosing the person's identity.

American Bar Association's
Standards Relating to Sentencing Alternatives[3]

In all cases, the sentencing court should be provided with a wide range of alternatives, with gradations of supervisory, supportive, and custodial facilities at its disposal so as to permit a sentence appropriate for each individual case.

Until recent years, the determination as to whether a convicted defendant went to prison, and for how long, was left largely to the courts. Judicial decisions were made with few statutory guidelines except for the stated statutory maximum sentence that may be imposed on the conviction of an offense. In the last two decades, however, many restrictions have been placed on the discretion of judges regarding the types of sentences, whether to suspend sentences or grant probation. Concerns regarding disparate sentences and abuses or perceived abuses in sentencing have resulted in six common strategies used by legislatures to maintain control over the sentencing process and reduce the discretion of the judiciary and correctional administrators. The common theme of the six strategies is to "reduce judicial and correctional imperialism." The six strategies are as follows:

1. **Determinate sentencing**. Establishing set sentences whereby parole boards are also restricted from releasing prisoners before their sentences (minus good time) have expired.

2. **Mandatory prison terms**. Statutes which require the courts to impose mandatory prison terms for convictions of certain offenses or for certain defendants.

3. **Sentencing guidelines.** Guidelines designed to structure sentences based on the severity of the offense and the criminal history of the defendant.

4. **Parole guidelines**. Guidelines designed to require parole decisions to be based on measurable offender criteria.

5. **Good-time guidelines**. Guidelines that allow for reducing prison terms based on an inmate's behavior in prison.

6. **Emergency overcrowding provisions.** Regulations that allow early release of prisoners based on systematic provisions to relieve overcrowding.

William Penn

William Penn, the founder of Pennsylvania and leader of the Quakers, brought to America the concept of humanitarian treatment of

The end result of criminal justice in Colonial America often meant punishment by simple yet effective devices (Courtesy of Patterson Smith Publishing Corp.)

offenders. William Penn (1644-1718) was an English Quaker who fought for religious freedom and individual rights. He obtained a charter from King Charles II in 1681 and founded the Quaker settlement that later became Pennsylvania.

At the time, the American colonies were governed under the codes established by the Duke of York, and earlier, the Hampshire code. The Quakers advocated elimination of the harsh principles of criminal law and the more humane treatment of offenders. The Quakers, though very religious, eliminated most of the religious crimes and created a criminal code that was very secular. The Quaker Code which was enacted in 1682 remained in force until repealed in 1718, one day after the death of William Penn. The code was replaced by the English Anglican Code which was even worse than the former codes of the Duke of York. The English Anglican Code restored the death penalty for many crimes and restored mutilation, branding, and other brutal forms of corporal punishments.

Focus — California Penal Code, Section 1170 (a)

(1) The Legislature finds and declares that the purpose of imprisonment for crime is punishment. This purpose is best served by terms proportionate to the seriousness of the offense with provisions for uniformity in the sentences of offenders committing the same offense under similar circumstances....

(2) Paragraph (1) shall not be construed to preclude programs, including educational programs, that are designed to rehabilitate nonviolent, first-time felony offenders. The Legislature encourages the development of policies and programs designed to educate and rehabilitate nonviolent, first-time felony offenders consistent with the purposes of imprisonment.

[Paragraph (2) added in 1995.][Paragraph (3) omitted.]

Suspended Sentences

Suspended sentences are one of two types—suspension of imposition of sentence and suspension of execution of sentence. In cases involving suspension of imposition of sentence, there is a judgment of guilt, but no sentence is pronounced. For example, the defendant is found guilty, but imposition of sentence is suspended for a period of three years. In a case involving the suspension of execution of sentence, there is a judgment and a sentence pronounced, but the execution is suspended. For example, the defendant is found guilty and sentenced to ten years in the correctional institution but the sentence is suspended for a period of five years.

Determinate and Indeterminate Sentencing

A **determinate sentence** is a sentence with a fixed period of confinement imposed by the judge of the sentencing court. The determinate sentence is based on the concept that each crime should have a price tag. You commit the crime, you pay the price. Its underlying ideology is based on retribution, just desserts, and incapacitation. A form of determinate sentencing now being used by the federal government and many states is the "presumptive" sentence. A **presumptive sentence** is a sentence suggested by the legislative body based on certain factors regarding the crime and the criminal. The judge is expected to impose the presumptive sentence. If the presumptive sentence is not given, the judge must justify why it was not imposed. Generally, determinate sentencing is used in adult criminal courts.

The **indeterminate sentence** is based on the concept that the sentence should be tailored to the needs of the defendant. Generally, indeterminate sentences include the a pronouncement by the judge as to the maximum and minimum terms of confinement. For example, the judge may sentence the defendant to serve a period of confinement for not less than two years nor more than ten. The **minimum term** establishes the earliest release date (after adjustments for credits such as good time or time previously confined awaiting trial). The **maximum term** is the maximum length of time that the prisoner will be required to serve. The indeterminate sentence is based on the concept of rehabilitation. The defendant is to be released when he or she is rehabilitated. The decision as to when the defendant is rehabilitated is taken

Minnesota Guideline Grid, Presumptive Sentence Lengths in Months

Severity Levels of Conviction Offense		Criminal History Score						
		0	1	2	3	4	5	6 or more
Sale of a Simulated Controlled Substance	I	12*	12*	12*	13	15	17	18-20
Theft Related Crimes ($2,500 or less)	II	12*	12*	12*	13	15	17	20-22
Theft Crimes ($2,500 or less)	III	12*	13	15	17	18-20	21-23	24-26
Nonresidential Burglary / Theft Crimes (over $2,500)	IV	12*	15	18	21	24-26	30-34	37-45
Residential Burglary / Simple Robbery	V	18	23	27	29-31	36-40	43-49	50-58
Criminal Sexual Conduct 2nd Degree (a) & (b)	VI	21	26	30	33-35	42-46	50-58	60-70
Aggravated Robbery	VII	44-52	54-62	64-72	74-82	84-92	94-102	104-112
Criminal Sexual Conduct, 1st Degree / Assault, 1st Degree	VIII	81-91	93-103	105-115	117-127	129-139	141-151	153-163
Felony Murder, 3rd Degree / Felony Murder, 2nd Degree	IX	144-156	159-171	174-186	189-201	204-216	219-231	234-246
Murder, 2nd Degree (with intent)	X	299-313	319-333	339-353	359-373	379-393	399-413	419-433

☐ Presumptive commitment to state imprisonment.

*One year and one day

from the judge and transferred to an administrative agency. Most juvenile courts operate on the concept of indeterminate sentencing.

Mandatory Prison Terms

Mandatory prison terms are set forth in statutes that required prison terms always be imposed for convictions of certain offenses or offenders. As of 1996, forty-eight states have some form of mandatory prison term statutes. The statutes apply for certain crimes of violence and for habitual criminals. These states have eliminated the judges' discretion regarding the imposition of probation in those cases.

Sentencing Guidelines

In determining the appropriate sentence in most states, the judge must follow required guidelines and statutory restrictions. To assist judges in determining the appropriate sentences, most states require that a presentence investigation report (PSI) be prepared and submitted to the court. The PSI contains a variety of information such as statements describing the seriousness of the crime, the defendant's past criminal history, any history of substance abuse, and aggravating or mitigating circumstances.

Sentencing guidelines are being used by the federal government and many states to guide the judges in making their determinations as to appropriate sentences. The guidelines were developed in an attempt to limit disparity and discretion, and to establish more detail criteria for sentencing. A sentencing commission monitors the use of the guidelines. Written explanations are required when a judge departs from the guideline ranges. Minnesota, for example, provides that while sentencing guidelines are advisory to the judge, departures from the guideline sentences established should be made only when substantial and compelling circumstances exist. In Pennsylvania, failure of the court to explain sentences deviating from the guidelines is grounds for vacating the sentence and resentencing the defendant. In addition, if the appellate court considers that the guidelines were inaccurately or inappropriately applied, the appellate court may vacate the sentence and order a resentencing.

Duty to Provide Corrected Presentence Report

In *State v. Utah*[4], Stephen Thomas Utah pleaded guilty to one count of forgery. At the sentencing hearing, Mr. Utah moved for the presentence report to be thrown out because it contained inaccuracies concerning his prior criminal record.

The district court refused to order a new presentence report. The court stated that it would not consider the disputed items in the report. Mr. Utah appealed. He contended that the district court was required to provide the department of corrections with an accurate presentence report. The state high court disagreed. The appellate court held that the presentence report is used primarily to aid the district court in sentencing. The court stated that any use by the department of corrections is secondary and not grounds for reversal of the sentence.

The **United States Sentencing Reform Act of 1984** advocated the "least restrictive alternative" in sentencing federal prisoners. The U.S. Sentencing Commission has established guidelines that authorize prison terms for all felony convictions. Research indicates that since the adoption of the federal sentencing guidelines, the use of probation and other non-incarcerative sentences have declined.[5]

The federal sentencing guidelines were enacted in 1984 and have governed federal sentencing decisions since 1989. The guidelines which were promulgated by the United States Sentencing Commission created 43 offense levels with each level reflecting increased severity of crime. In addition, offenders were divided into six categories based on their criminal history. The net result is a grid containing 258 cells, each of which has a sentencing range expressed in terms of months. The intent was to have the grids advise as to judicial decision making on sentencing. While the stated objective of the federal sentencing reform was to encourage alternative sanctions to prison, the guidelines are constructed in such a manner to discourage judges from imposing alternative sanctions.

The sentencing court must select a sentence from within the guideline range. If, however, a particular case presents atypical features, the act allows the court to depart from the guidelines and sentence outside the prescribed range. In that case, the court must specify reasons for departure.[6]

In 1984, before the use of the guidelines, approximately 52 percent of felony federal offenders were sentenced to prison. In 1991, the percentage had increased to 71 percent. Since adoption of the guidelines, there has been widespread criticism of the guidelines among the federal district court judges. The judges have called them unduly harsh and mechanical. Other judges consider that the guidelines, in addition to being harsh, are very inflexible. Most agree that the guidelines rely too heavily on imprisonment as a sanction.

United States Sentencing Commission

The United States Sentencing Commission is an independent agency in the judicial branch composed of seven voting and two non-voting, *ex officio* members. Its principle purpose is to establish sentencing policies and practices for the federal criminal justice system that will ensure the ends of justice by promulgating detailed guidelines prescribing the appropriate sentences for offenders convicted of federal crimes. The guidelines and policy statements promulgated by the commission are issued pursuant to Section 994 (a) of Title 28, United States Code.

Presumptive Sentences

One alternative used to limit the discretion of sentencing judges is the use of presumptive sentences. Under this system, the state legislature sets minimum, average, and maximum terms. The judges select the term appropriate for the defendant based on the characteristics of the offender and aggravating circumstances. California has used this system since 1979. For example, in California, if a defendant is convicted of burglary, the punishment range is set forth in Penal Code 461.

That section provides:

Burglary in the first degree: by imprisonment in the state prison for two, four, or six years.

The first decision that the judge would need to make is the "out or in" decision. This decision is whether the defendant should be placed on probation (out) or sentenced (in) to prison. If the judge decides that imprisonment is the correct sentence. The judge would award four years, the average sentence, unless there were mitigating or aggravating circumstances. Under **aggravating circumstances**, the sentence would be six years and under mitigating circumstances, the sentence would be two years. Examples of mitigating circumstances would be that the defendant is a first time offender, the crime was committed under strong peer pressure, etc. Examples of aggravating circumstances include prior criminal record, great harm to victim, etc.

Parole Guidelines

Parole guidelines are procedures designed to limit or structure parole release decisions based on measurable offender criteria. In some states, the parole board has great latitude in making the parole release decisions. In other states, the parole guidelines are closely prescribed and provide only limited discretion to the parole boards.

Good-time Policies

Good-conduct time has traditionally been used by inmates to reduce their time in custody. In most states, by law, good conduct time applies only to an inmate's eligibility for parole or mandatory release. New York, in 1817, was the first state to pass a good-time statute. By 1916, every state had passed some kind of good-time statute. Most states provide for one day of credit for every two days of good time served. Many states have recently modified their good-time statutes. Generally, good-conduct time is awarded based on the law in effect when the crime was committed. Some states now use programming time or earned time in lieu of good time credit. The programming time

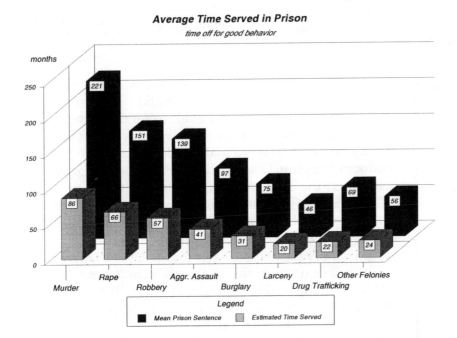

Average Time Served in Prison

time off for good behavior

or earned time allows administrators to consider matters other than time in awarding credit. For example, since January 1983, California eliminated automatic time off for good behavior. Prisoners sentenced after that date must earn all their good-time credit through work or school participation. The California approach has been criticized on the basis that it allows the prison guards and other prison personnel to become sentencers. This is based on the fact that the amount of time that a prisoner may earn in California is discretionary and has therefore enlarged the discretionary power of prison officials to affect the duration of confinement.

In most states, good-time credit is awarded based on an inmate's conduct, obedience to rules, willingness to work, and work/school record. Traditionally, good conduct time is considered as a privilege, not a right. Inmates must follow rules to get good conduct time. Some or all of the good conduct time awarded an inmate may be taken away for breaking rules. In some cases, previously forfeited good conduct time may be restored to the inmate.

Focus — Can Society Afford a Zero Crime Rate?

> Mark A. Cohen, an economic professor at Vanderbilt University states that our society could not afford a zero crime rate, that it would bankrupt us. Cohen estimates that crime costs this country about $500 billion a year and that it is a major industry.
>
> Franklin Zimring, Director of the Earl Warren Legal Institute at the University of California at Berkeley, calls the $500 billion estimate a "phony number." He is worried that by fixing the cost of crime so high, it will make the building of prisons look like a cheap and politically palatable answer to crime. For example in California in 1996, the state will spend more for building and operating prisons than for its public colleges and universities. Prisons are the fastest growing item in almost all state budgets.
>
> John J. DiIulio, professor of public affairs at Princeton University, contends that prisons do pay for themselves. He states that it costs $25,000 a year to keep a prisoner behind bars. He contends, however, that "society saves at least $2.80 in the social costs of crime for every one dollar spent on prisons.

Flat Time With Mandatory Supervision

As noted earlier, a determinate sentence is a "flat time" sentence set by the sentencing judge usually based on legislated guidelines. The defendant is given a definite sentence and once good time or program credit calculations are made, the defendant knows his or her expected release date. Since parole is premised on indeterminate sentencing which allows the correctional administration to set the release date, the move toward determinate sentencing with mandatory supervision on completion of the sentence is seen by many as the way to eliminate the parole system.

Emergency Overcrowding Provisions

The extent of crowding in our nation's prisons is difficult to determine because of the absence of uniform measures for defining capacity. Most jurisdictions are operating above capacity. Prisons generally require reserve capacity to operate efficiently. Dormitories and cells need to be maintained and repaired periodically, special housing is needed for protective custody and disciplinary cases, and space may be needed to cope with emergencies. State prisons are generally operating at between 17 and 29 percent above capacity, while the federal system is operating at 25 percent above capacity.

In some states, there are statutes which provide the governor with the authority to release prisoners prior to their normal release date in order to relieve crowded prison conditions. In some states, the parole boards may consider prison overcrowding conditions in determining the release date of certain classes of offenders, and offenders may be released earlier than normal to relieve crowded prison conditions. For example, in the early 1970s, Florida released thousands of prisoners early to make room for newly sentenced prisoners.

Alternative Sentencing and Diversion

Alternative sentencing involves the use of nontraditional programs, etc. in lieu of fines and custody. One of the most popular alternative sentencing procedures is the use of deferred adjudication. **Deferred adjudication** is a form of probation that is used without a finding of guilt. In deferred adjudication, the defendant pleas guilty and agrees to defer further proceeding. The defendant is then placed on probation or directed to attend counseling, behavior modification courses, etc. After the defendant has successfully completed the requirements, the guilty or *nolo contendere* plea is withdrawn and the case is dismissed. When the charges are dismissed, the defendant does not have a criminal conviction for this misconduct. If the defendant fails to comply with the requirements, then the court sentences the defendant based on his or her original plea.

Pretrial diversion is a form of probation that is granted prior to trial. Under this process, the defendant agrees to waive time and to complete a program or process. Pretrial diversion is used primarily for offenders who need treatment or supervision and for whom criminal

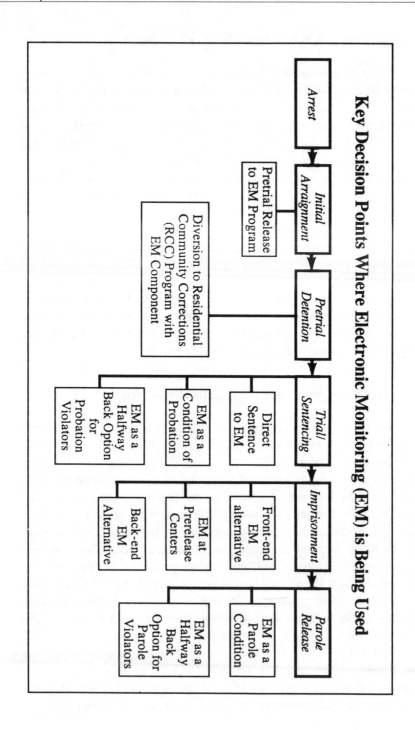

Key Decision Points Where Electronic Monitoring (EM) is Being Used

sanctions would be excessive. Like deferred adjudication, there is no finding of guilt and, thus, no conviction if the program is successfully completed. If the program is not successfully completed, the defendant is then brought to trial on the charges. One of the popular criticisms of pretrial diversion is based on research that indicates that many people are diverted that would not have been prosecuted because of the lack of evidence against them. Accordingly, if this is correct, such action increases the number of persons involved in the criminal justice system.

CORRECTIONS

Judicial Process for Misdemeants

Misdemeanants are individuals convicted of minor crimes (misdemeanors). Their sentences are to jails for periods normally not to exceed one year, fines, community service, and/or attendance at some type of behavior modification course. In studying corrections, we rarely consider the roles of our minor courts and their handling of misdemeanants. More citizens, however, get involved at this level than at the felony level. On any given day, it is estimated that approximately 500,000 individuals are confined in local jails. The lower courts of America are truly involved in an "assembly-line" type justice.

Judicial Process for Felons

In most states, sentences to prison or correctional institutions are decided by judges. Several states, like Texas, allow the defendants to opt for jury sentencing. The incarceration of an individual in a state prison is a dramatic and, all to often, used sanction. The Model Penal Code addresses the problems involved in selecting the appropriate sentence. The code provides that imprisonment should be used as the last resort[7] and only when one of the below conditions exist:

1. There is undue risk that during the period of probation the defendant will commit another crime.

Prison Populations and Rate of Incarceration
In State and Federal Facilities
as of June 30, 1994

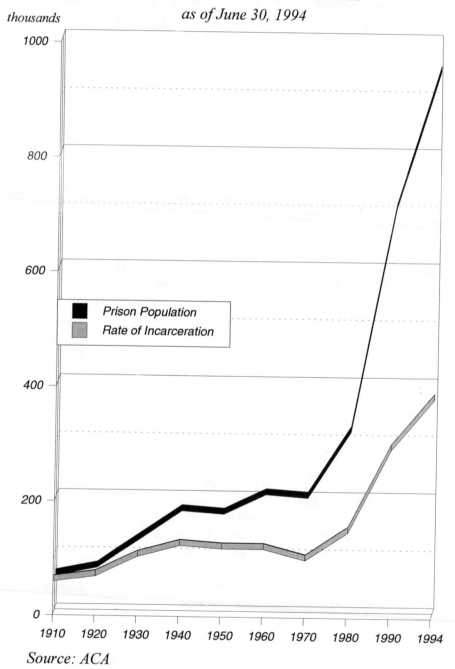

thousands

Prison Population
Rate of Incarceration

Source: ACA

2. The defendant is in need of correctional treatment that can be provided most effectively by commitment to an institution.

3. A lesser sentence will depreciate the seriousness of the defendant's crime.

John Howard (1726-1790)

Until he was appointed sheriff of Bedfordshire, England in 1773, John Howard showed no interest in prisons or prison reform. As sheriff, he was appalled by the conditions of the hulks being used to hold prisoners. **Hulks** were decrepit transport or warships being used to house prisoners in nineteenth century England. He pressed for legislation to alleviate the abuses and to improve sanitary conditions. In addition, he traveled extensively in France and Italy and wrote about the conditions of their prisons.

As the direct result of Howard's actions, the English Parliament passed the Penitentiary Act in 1799. That act provided four principles for reform:

√ Secure and sanitary structures

√ Systematic inspections of the prisons

√ Abolition of fees

√ Reformatory regime

The Penitentiary Act resulted in the first penitentiary in England located at Wyndomhan in Norfolk. Ironically, John Howard died in 1790 of jail fever (typhus) in the Russian Ukraine.

National Conference on Corrections

The National Conference on Corrections held in Williamsburg, Virginia considered the problems and needs of judges in ascertaining appropriate sentences in criminal cases. The conference advocated eight points in regards to more appropriate sentencing:

1. It should be mandatory that trial judges have presentence reports in all felony cases. These reports should be prepared by qualified probation or corrections officers.

2. Diagnostic facilities should be made available to all judges.

3. Jury sentencing should be abolished.

4. Sentencing judges should be required to record the reasons for each sentence.

5. Sentencing judges should educate their communities on the philosophy of sentencing.

6. Defense counsel and the prosecutor should be consulted before imposing the sentence.

7. Probation officers and judges should receive instructions in sentencing and perhaps attend sentencing institutes.

8. Trial judges should be elected or appointed in as nonpolitical a way as possible.

Changes to the "Justice" Correctional Philosophy

The Violent Crime Control and Law Enforcement Act of 1994 was one of the most ambitious crime bills in our history.[8] The act allocated over $22 billion to expand prisons, impose longer sentences, hire more police officers, and to a very limited extent, fund prevention programs. The following year, however, the money allocated to prevention programs was eliminated. The act and similar acts have great political appeal but little support among criminal justice professionals. Most professionals feel that such efforts will do little to reduce crime. This approach has been labeled as the "enforcement model."[9] The popular criticisms of the present "enforcement model approach" are that it is racist, it costs too much, and it fails to prevent young people from entering and continuing lives of crime. The popularity of prison as a response to crime has resulted in changes in the public and professional perceptions of the role of corrections.

The various approaches to correctional philosophy fall into one of three categories: punishment, treatment, or prevention. Often, they

Inmate Profile

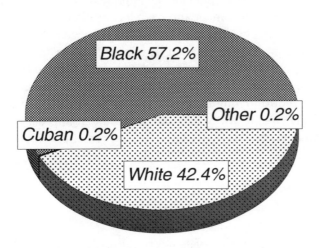

Custody Level

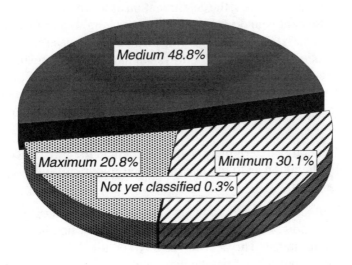

overlap as punishment and treatment can be argued as an approach to prevent crime. The 1960s was a period when treatment was the dominant approach. This changed in the late 1970s. Since that time, society in general has preferred the punishment approach. As was discussed in other chapters, the punishment approach has resulted in overcrowded institutions, budgets stripped of so-called "frills" needed for treatment, and prevention programs curtailed. It appears that in the 1990s the punishment approach may have reached its height, and the future may see the pendulum swing back toward the treatment or prevention emphasis. Note the following excerpt from the California Penal Code, which indicates a shift away from the punishment approach with its 1995 amendment. It is difficult, however, to predict the future of corrections.

SUMMARY

- The criminal justice system is traditionally considered to consist of three subsystems: law enforcement, judicial, and corrections. Before an individual comes under control of correctional agencies, he or she has already moved from citizen, suspect, arrestee, defendant, to convict.

- Until recent years, the determination as to whether a convicted defendant went to prison and for how long was left largely to the courts. Concerns regarding disparate sentences and abuses, or perceived abuses, in the system have resulted in strategies used by the legislatures to maintain some control of the sentencing process. Those strategies include determinate sentencing, sentencing and parole guidelines, and mandatory prison terms.

- Generally, determinate sentences include the pronouncement by the judge as to the maximum and minimum terms of confinement.

- The indeterminate sentence is based on the concept of rehabilitation. The defendant is to be released when he or she is rehabilitated. The decision as to when the defendant is rehabilitated is taken from the judge and transferred to an administrative agency. Most juvenile courts operate on the concept of indeterminate sentencing.

- Sentencing guidelines are being used by the federal government and many states to guide the judges in making their determinations as to appropriate sentences. The guidelines were developed in an attempt to limit disparity and discretion and to establish more detailed criteria for sentencing. A sentencing commission monitors the use of the guidelines. Written explanations are required when a judge departs from the guideline ranges.

- One alternative used to limit the discretion of sentencing judges is the use of presumptive sentences. Under this system, the state legislature sets minimum, average, and maximum terms. The judges select the term appropriate for the defendant based on the characteristics of the offender and aggravating circumstances.

- Good-conduct time has traditionally been used by inmates to reduce their time in custody. In most states, by law, good-conduct time applies only to an inmate's eligibility for parole or mandatory release .

- In most states, a presentence report is mandatory for felony convictions. The presentence report (PSI) is an important document for trial judges in making their sentence determinations. In most cases, the PSI is prepared by the court's probation office.

- Alternative sentencing involves the use of nontraditional programs, etc. in lieu of fines and custody. One of the most popular alternative sentencing procedures is the use of deferred adjudication.

- Deferred adjudication is a form of probation that is used without a finding of guilt. In deferred adjudication, the defendant pleas guilty and agrees to defer further proceedings. The defendant is then placed on probation or directed to attend counseling, behavior modification courses, etc. After the defendant has successfully completed the requirements, the guilty or *nolo contendere* plea is withdrawn and the case is dismissed. When the charges are dismissed, the defendant does not have a criminal conviction for this misconduct. If the defendant fails to comply with the requirements, then the court sentences the defendant based on his or her original plea.

- Pretrial diversion is a form of probation that is granted prior to trial. Under this process, the defendant agrees to waive time and to complete a program or process. Pretrial diversion is used primarily for offenders who need treatment or supervision and for whom criminal sanctions would be excessive.

DISCUSSION QUESTIONS

1. Discuss recent changes to the justice correctional philosophy.

2. Explain the American Bar Associations' Standards Relating to Sentencing Alternatives.

3. Differentiate between determinate and indeterminate sentencing.

4. What is the judicial process for persons convicted of minor crimes?

5. What is contained in a PSI?

6. Explain the overcrowding problems and give possible solutions to correct them.

ENDNOTES—Chapter 15

1. Lawrence F. Travis III, Martin D. Schwartz, and Todd R. Clear, *Corrections: An Issues Approach*, 3rd ed. (Cincinnati: Anderson, 1992) p. 50.

2. Richard W. Snarr, *Corrections*, (Madison, WI: Brown & Benchmark, 1996).

3. *ABA Standards: Standards Relating to Sentencing Alternatives,* (Washington D.C., American Bar Association, 1972).

4. Decided by the Supreme Court of Iowa, No. 348/95-107, Dec. 20, 1995.

5. Elaine Wolf and Marsha Weissman, "Revising Federal Sentencing Policy: Some Consequences of Expanding Eligibility for Alternative Sanctions," *Crime and Delinquency*, Vol. 42, No. 2, April, 1996, p. 192-197.

6. United States Sentencing Commission, *Guidelines Manual*, (Nov. 1995).

7. American Law Institute, *Model Penal Code, Proposed Official Draft*, (Philadelphia, 1962).

8. Joan Petersilia, "A Crime Control Rationale For Reinvesting in Community Corrections," *The Prison Journal*, Vol. 75 No. 4, December, 1995, 479-496.

9. *Id.*, p. 479.

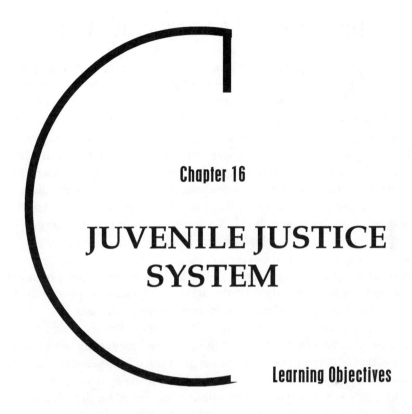

Chapter 16

JUVENILE JUSTICE SYSTEM

Learning Objectives

After studying this chapter, you should be able to:

- Determine whether the juvenile's needs or rights are paramount to society's needs for security.

- Outline the proper scope of authority for juvenile justice.

- Explain what processes should be used to adjudicate and make disposition of juvenile offenders.

- List the reforms that are necessary to improve juvenile justice.

HISTORY OF JUVENILE JUSTICE

A t common law, children over 14 years of age were treated as if they were adults. Children under the age of seven were considered incapable of committing crimes. For children between the ages of seven and 14, it was presumed that they were incapable of committing crimes, however the state could, by establishing the maturity of the child, hold them accountable as an adult. Even when formally treated as adults; however, children were rarely punished as harshly as adults were punished by the criminal courts.

In early English history, the doctrine of *parens patriae* was developed, and, according to this doctrine, the king could intervene in family life to protect the child's estate from dishonest parents or guardians. *Parens patriae* can be roughly be defined as the duty of the state to act as a parent in the interest of the child. This principal expanded and now includes the right of the state to intervene to protect child welfare against parental neglect, incompetency and abuse.[1]

The Reform Movement of the 19th Century also developed a concern for children in general. A "child saving" movement which was directed at children in need or trouble grew out of this general concern. The **child savers** attempted to save children by using houses of refuge and reform schools. These institutions were based on the contemporary idea that children's environment made them bad and that removing the youths from poor homes and unhealthy associations and placing them in special homes or houses of refuge and schools would cause the children to give up their bad and evil habits and would, in fact, reform the children.[2]

ESTABLISHMENT OF THE JUVENILE COURT

The influence of the child savers prompted the development of the first juvenile court in Cook County, Illinois in 1899. The Illinois Juvenile Court Act set up an independent court to handle criminal law violations by children under 16 years of age. The court was also given responsibility for supervising care of neglected, dependent and wayward youths. The Juvenile Court Act also set up a probation depart-

ARREST RATES FOR JUVENILE OFFENDERS
per 100,000 people

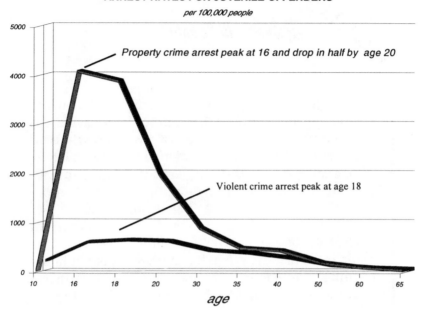

Property crime arrest peak at 16 and drop in half by age 20

Violent crime arrest peak at age 18

age

Source: U. S. Dept. of Justice

ment to monitor youths in the community and it directed juvenile court judges to place serious offenders in secured training schools for boys and industrial schools for girls. The purpose of the Act was to separate juveniles from adult offenders and to provide a legal framework in which juveniles could get proper care and custody.

By 1940, every state in the United States had established a juvenile justice system. The juvenile justice systems were normally created as a division of family court. As the juvenile court movement spread throughout the United States it provided for the use of a quasi legal type of justice. The main concern of the juvenile courts was what was in the best interest of the child. Accordingly, the courts did not adhere strictly to legal doctrine, protect constitutional rights, nor conduct their proceedings according to due process requirements. The general theory was that because these were not criminal courts, the youths did not have the rights as if they were being tried in an adult criminal court.

F_{OCU^S} ➤➤➤ *IN RE GAULT*

FACTS. Jerry Gault, a 15-year-old boy, was taken into custody by the sheriff of Gila County, Arizona. He was arrested based on a complaint of a woman who said that Jerry and another boy had made an obscene telephone call to her. At the time, Jerry was on a six-month probation as a result of having previously been declared a delinquent for stealing a wallet.

Based on the verbal complaint, Jerry was taken from his home. His parents were not informed that he was taken into custody. When his mother appeared in the evening, she was told by the superintendent that a hearing would be held in juvenile court the following day.

The next day, a police officer, who had taken Jerry into custody, filed a petition alleging his delinquency. Jerry, his mother and the police officer appeared at a judicial hearing before a judge in his chambers. Mrs. Cook, the complaining witness, was not at the hearing. Jerry was questioned about the telephone calls and was sent back to the detention home, and was then released a few days later.

On the day of Jerry's release, his mother received a letter indicating that a hearing would be held on his delinquency status a few days later. When the hearing was held, the complainant, Mrs. Cook, was still not present. There was no transcript or a recording of the proceedings. At the hearing, the juvenile officer stated that Jerry had admitted making the lewd telephone calls. Neither the boy nor his parents were advised of any of his rights including the right to be silent, the right to be represented by counsel, or the right to a due process hearing. At the conclusion of the hearing, the juvenile court committed Jerry as a juvenile delinquent to the state's industrial school in Arizona for the period of his minority, i.e., six years.[3]

This, in effect, meant that Jerry got six years for making an obscene phone call. Had he been an adult and convicted of the same crime, the maximum punishment would have been no more than a $50.00 fine and/or 60 days in jail.

Attorneys on behalf of Jerry filed a writ of *habeas corpus* with the Superior Court for the state of Arizona. The request for the writ was denied. The decision was appealed to the Arizona Supreme Court and that was denied. The denial by the Arizona Supreme Court was then appealed to the U.S. Supreme Court.

The U.S. Supreme Court in a far-reaching decision agreed that Jerry's constitutional rights were violated. The Supreme Court indicated that, at a very minimum, notice of charges is an essential right of the due process of law as is the right to confront witnesses and to cross-examine them, the right to counsel, and the privilege against self-incrimination.

Several items not answered by the court in reversing Arizona's determination of delinquency were whether or not Jerry had a right to a transcript and whether or not there was a right to an appellant review.

The significance of the *Gault* case was that it established that a child in a delinquency adjudication proceeding has procedural due process constitutional rights as set forth in the constitution. Note: this case was confined to rulings at the adjudication stage of the judicial process.

For many years, the stated goals of the juvenile justice system were to prevent juvenile crime and to rehabilitate juvenile offenders. In the 1980s, an additional goal was imposed on the juvenile courts— to protect society.

Our early reform schools were generally very punitive in nature and were based on the concept that rehabilitation could only be achieved through hard work. In the 1950s, the influence of therapists, such as Carl Rogers, promoted the introduction of psychological treatment in juvenile corrections. By 1950, group counseling techniques were standard procedure in the vast majority of juvenile institutions.

Just as the due process revolution affected prisoners' rights and defendants' rights, the U.S. Supreme Court also drastically altered the juvenile justice system. In a series of cases, it was established that juvenile delinquents are protected under the due process clause of the Constitution, and therefore, have constitutional rights in juvenile proceedings.

As a result of the influence of constitutional requirements in juvenile proceedings, the distinction between adult and criminal juvenile justice systems are much less now than they were 40 years ago.

PRESENT ROLE OF JUVENILE JUSTICE

Our juvenile justice system is independent but interrelated with the adult criminal justice system. The juvenile court system developed based on the concept of *parens patriae*. Starting in the 1960s, the concept was modified to one of procedural due process and in the 1980s to one of controlling chronically delinquent youths. It appears that the juvenile system will continue to evolve as we hunt for a more efficient system.

What is the present role of our juvenile justice system?

- To provide a social welfare program designed to assist and act as the wise parent.
- To protect the constitutional rights of children.
- To be treatment agency to rehabilitate delinquents.
- To protect society from violent youths.

JUVENILE DIVERSION

The most common screening of juveniles after they have been processed into the court system is through the use of diversion. Diversion is very popular in the juvenile justice system since it was recommended by the President's Commission on Crime in 1967. Several reasons for the growing popularity of diversion are that it helps to reduce the increasing caseload; it provides more flexibility than the juvenile justice treatment programs currently in existence; and it costs less per capita than the use of institutionalization of juveniles.

WAIVER OF JUVENILE COURT JURISDICTION

Prior to the first juvenile court, established in Illinois in 1899, juveniles were tried for violations of law in adult criminal court. Today, most statutes provide that juvenile court shall have primary jurisdiction over children under the age of 17. There are provisions in all state statutes, however, where juvenile court can waive jurisdiction and allow the juvenile to be tried in adult criminal court in cases involving serious crimes. The transfer of juveniles to criminal court is often based on a statutory criteria, and the two major criteria for waivers are the age of the child and the type of the offense alleged in the petition. For example, many jurisdictions require the child to be at least 15 years of age before he/she may be tried as an adult.

The nature and effect of the waiver is significant to the juvenile. Accordingly, the United States Supreme Court has imposed several procedural protections for juveniles in the waiver process. The first major court decision in this area was that of *Kent v. United States*.[4] This case challenged the provisions of the District Court of Columbia which stated that juvenile court could waive jurisdiction after a full investigation. In that case, the Supreme Court held that the waiver proceeding is a critically important stage in the juvenile process, and, therefore, the juveniles must be afforded minimum requirements of due process of law.

Consistent with the minimal requirements, the following conditions are considered necessary before a valid waiver may occur.

1. A hearing must be held on the motion to waiver.

2. The child is entitled to be represented by counsel at the hearing.

3. The attorney representing the juvenile must be given access to all records and reports considered by the court in reaching a waiver decision.

4. The court must provide a written statement of the reasons for the waiver decision.

Prior to 1975, the procedure in most states was that if a juvenile was charged with a serious offense, there would be an adjudication hearing to determine whether or not the juvenile had committed the offense. If the court found that the juvenile committed the offense, then there would be a hearing to determine whether or not a waiver of juvenile court jurisdiction should be entered and the juvenile tried as an adult in adult criminal court. In 1975, however, in the case of *Breed v. Jones,* the Court held that jeopardy attaches when the juvenile court begins to hear evidence as to whether the juvenile committed the offense, therefore, if an adjudication hearing is held prior to the waiver hearing, the juvenile cannot be waived to adult criminal court because that would constitute double jeopardy.[5] After the *Breed v. Jones* case, the courts of all the states were modified to establish a waiver hearing first, and if it was determined that the juvenile should be retained in the juvenile court system, a hearing on the adjudication phase would then take place.

JUVENILE TRIALS

Juvenile courts dispose of about 1.5 million delinquency cases each year. The trial process in juvenile court is referred to as the **adjudicatory hearing**. It is in this hearing that the court determines whether or not the juvenile committed the offense(s) alleged in the petition. During the adjudication process, the juvenile has the constitutional right to a fair notice of the charges, the right to be represented by counsel, the right to be confronted by and cross-examine witnesses, and the privilege against self-incrimination. In addition, the juvenile court, in making a determination in adjudicating the juvenile a delinquent, must use the standard of proof beyond a reasonable doubt.

At the conclusion of the adjudicatory hearing, the court is required to enter a judgment either sustaining the petition (i.e., finding that the accused committed the crimes alleged in the petition) or dismissing the petition. Once the juvenile has been adjudicated a delinquent the court must make a determination as to the disposition of the child.

DISPOSITION

At the separate disposition hearing, the juvenile court should look at the record of the delinquent, the family background, and the needs of the accused and the safety of the public. A juvenile court judge has broad discretion in determining the disposition of the juvenile. Some of the standard dispositions are dismissal of the petition, suspended judgment, probation, placement in a community treatment program, or commitment to a state agency that is responsible for juvenile institutional care. This latter disposition is basically a commitment to a reformatory or other state institution for juveniles. In addition, the court has the power to place the child with parents or relatives under extensive supervision or moderate supervision. It can make dispositional arrangements with private youth-serving agencies, or it can have the child committed to a mental institution.

As in adult criminal court, probation is the most commonly used formal sentence for juvenile offenders. In fact, many states require that before a youth may be sent to an institution, the youth must have failed on probation unless the juvenile has been charged with a serious felony.

Probation may include placing the child under the supervision of the juvenile probation department for the purposes of community treatment. The conditions of the probation are normally spelled out in the state court's order. There are general conditions from which all delinquents are required to obey, such as to obey the law, to stay away from other delinquents, to attend school, etc. Then there are special conditions of probation which require an individual child to participate in certain training, treatment or educational programs.

Disposition of Youths
taken into custody by the police

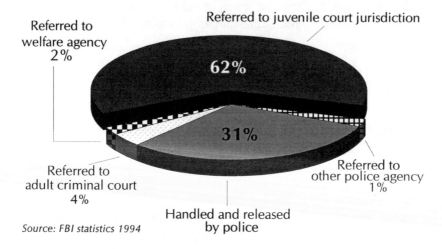

Referred to
welfare agency
2%

Referred to juvenile court jurisdiction

62%

31%

Referred to
adult criminal court
4%

Referred to
other police agency
1%

Handled and released
by police

Source: FBI statistics 1994

INSTITUTIONALIZATION

The most severe disposition that a judge may make at a juvenile court hearing is the institutionalization of the juvenile. In most states, this means that the child can be committed up until the child is 21 years of age. Note that the disposition of commitment to an institution is an indeterminate sentence unlike that of most adult courts.

Many persons involved in delinquency and juvenile law have questioned the practice of committing juveniles to institutions. Deinstitutionalization of juveniles has been attempted by using small residential facilities operated by juvenile care agencies to replace the larger state schools. There has been mixed reaction as to the success of this "deinstitutionalization" of juveniles.

THE RIGHT TO TREATMENT

While not directly stating that juveniles have a right to treatment while incarcerated, it appears that the Supreme Court is leaning in that direction. The Court of Appeals for the 7th Circuit indicates that *Nelson v. Heyne* upheld the constitutional right to treatment for institutionalized juveniles under the Fourteenth Amendment, and recent decisions by the U.S. Supreme Court seem to indicate that juveniles do have a right to receive treatment if committed to a juvenile institution.[6]

TYPES OF CASES HANDLED BY THE JUVENILE COURTS

- **Violent Youths.** Violent youth represent only about 7 percent of juvenile court caseloads. However, they account for 11 percent of the detentions, 12 percent of the out-of-home placements, and 27 percent of the transfers to adult criminal courts.[7]

  The courts are more likely to file petitions in cases involving violent offenses than in any other types of cases.

- **Property Cases.** Property offenses are a major part of the juvenile crime problem. Approximately 30 percent of all juvenile arrests are based on property offenses. Shoplifting was the most common offense for youths under the age of 15. Burglary was the most common property offense for older youths. Female offenders are more likely to be involved in shoplifting, and male youths were more likely to be involved in burglary.[8]

  Approximately 25 percent of the youths arrested for property offenses are detained. Juveniles involved with motor vehicle thefts were the ones most likely to be detained awaiting disposition of the case.

TYPES OF INSTITUTIONS

Currently, juveniles who have been adjudicated as delinquent and committed may be held in one of six types of facilities. The six types include detention centers, shelters, reception/diagnostic centers, training schools, ranches or camps, and halfway houses or group homes.

√ **Detention centers** are short-term, secure facilities that hold juveniles awaiting adjudication, disposition, or placement in an institution.

√ **Shelters** are also short-term facilities that are operated like detention centers, but they are nonsecure facilities with physically unrestricted environment.

√ **Reception/diagnostic centers** are also short-term facilities. They are used to screen youths for assignments to appropriate levels of custody and institutions.

√ **Training schools** are generally long-term secure facilities that are used only for adjudicated delinquents. Ranches, forestry camps, and farms are long-term nonsecure facilities used for adjudicated juveniles.

√ **Halfway houses** or **group homes** are nonsecure facilities that are used to help integrate the youths back into the community. They may be either long- or short-term facilities.

As can be noted from the above, there are two levels of security—secure and nonsecure. **Secure facilities** are characterized by their locks, bars, and fences. Movement is generally restricted in a secure facility. **Nonsecure facilities** are characterized by their lack of bars, locks, and fences. In addition, nonsecure facilities permit greater freedom of movement for the youths.

CONDITIONS OF CONFINEMENT IN JUVENILE FACILITIES

In a recent study of conditions of confinement in U.S. juvenile detention and correctional facilities, conducted by Abt Associates for the Office of Juvenile Justice and Delinquency Prevention (OJJDP), institutional crowding was found to be pervasive.[9] Thousands of juvenile offenders, more than 75 percent of the confined population, were housed in facilities that violated one or more standards related to living space (facility design capacity, sleeping areas, and living unit size). Between 1987 and 1991, the percentage of confined juveniles living in facilities in which the daily population exceeded design capacity increased from 36 percent to 47 percent. Crowding was found to be associated with higher rates of institutional violence, suicidal behavior, and greater reliance on the use of short-term isolation.

The study, required by Congress in its 1988 Amendments to the Juvenile Justice and Delinquency Prevention Act, is the first such nationwide investigation of conditions in secure juvenile detention and correctional facilities. Using nationally recognized correctional standards as a gauge, researchers assessed how juvenile offenders' basic needs were met, how institutional security and resident safety were maintained, what treatment programming was provided, and how juveniles' rights were protected.

The study included surveys mailed in 1991 to all 984 public and private juvenile detention centers, reception and diagnostic facilities, training schools, and ranches. In addition, experienced juvenile correctional practitioners conducted two-day site visits to a representative sample of nearly 100 facilities in the fall of 1991. These facilities held about 65,000 juveniles on the date of the 1991 Children in Custody census, or about 69 percent of the juveniles confined on that date in the United States. During 1990, these facilities received nearly 690,000 admissions, including readmissions and transfers of juveniles from other facilities.

Based on standards conformance and related outcome measures, researchers concluded that serious and widespread problems existed in the areas of living space, health care, institutional security and safety, and control of suicidal behavior. In important areas of treatment, rehabilitation, and education, the evaluation demonstrated the need for more rigorous assessment of how facilities are meeting juveniles' needs in these areas.

The study found three areas in which conditions of confinement appeared to be generally adequate: basic needs, such as food, clothing and hygiene; recreation; and living accommodations. An important overall finding was that generally conformance to existing standards does not guarantee adequate conditions for juveniles in custody. For example, while more than 90 percent of juvenile detention facilities conformed to the fire inspection requirement, more than half of the 30 detention centers visited had at least one unmarked fire exit in a sleeping area. Two-thirds did not have fire escape routes posted, and in some, fire exits were blocked.

In many cases, the standards only require the existence of policies, procedures, or programs, without stipulating performance mea-

The age profile of juvenile arrests in 1995 varied by offense

Offense	Juveniles Age 12 or Younger	Juveniles Ages 13 and 14	Juveniles Age 15 or Older
	Percent of Juvenile Arrests in 1995		
Total	9%	25%	66%
Crime Index total	12	27	60
Violent Crime Index	8	23	70
Murder and nonnegligent manslaughter	3	10	86
Forcible rape	11	26	63
Robbery	6	22	72
Aggravated assault	9	23	68
Property Crime Index	13	28	58
Burglary	12	27	61
Larceny-theft	15	29	56
Motor vehicle theft	4	25	72
Arson	35	33	33
Nonindex			
Simple assault	13	28	59
Forgery and counterfeiting	3	10	87
Fraud	4	22	74
Embezzlement	3	7	90
Stolen property (buying, receiving, possessing)	6	22	72
Vandalism	19	29	53
Weapons (carrying, possessing, etc.)	8	22	70
Prostitution and commercialized vice	5	12	83
Sex offense (except forcible rape and prostitution)	18	33	49
Drug abuse violations	2	15	83
Gambling	3	13	83
Offenses against the family and children	8	22	70
Driving under the influence	2	1	97
Liquor law violations	1	9	90
Drunkenness	2	12	85
Disorderly conduct	9	26	65
Vagrancy	4	17	79
All other offenses (except traffic)	7	21	72
Suspicion	6	21	73
Curfew and loitering	5	24	71
Running away	8	35	56

Note: Percentages may not add to 100% because of rounding.

Source: Authors' analysis of data from the Federal Bureau of Investigation, *Crime in the United States 1995* (Washington, DC: U.S. Government Printing Office, 1996).

Juveniles in Public Facilities, by State: February 15, 1995

	Total Population	Total Delinquent	Total Status Offenders	Total Other
United States	68,910	66,236	1,785	889
Alabama	908	882	22	4
Alaska	223	222	1	0
Arizona	1,083	1,066	11	6
Arkansas	275	274	0	1
California	19,567	19,395	46	126
Colorado	776	771	5	0
Connecticut	371	366	5	0
Delaware	164	164	0	0
District of Columbia	251	211	23	17
Florida	2,674	2,674	0	0
Georgia	2,337	2,240	81	16
Hawaii	101	73	10	18
Idaho	154	154	0	0
Illinois	2,641	2,620	19	2
Indiana	1,704	1,416	233	55
Iowa	461	332	59	70
Kansas	808	787	14	7
Kentucky	593	561	25	7
Louisiana	1,509	1,484	7	18
Maine	369	369	0	0
Maryland	715	713	2	0
Massachusetts	331	307	20	4
Michigan	1,778	1,673	87	18
Minnesota	803	724	62	17
Mississippi	641	590	21	30
Missouri	1,037	901	131	5
Montana	140	125	4	11
Nebraska	419	415	4	0
Nevada	660	633	27	0
New Hampshire	125	125	0	0
New Jersey	1,999	1,900	46	53
New Mexico	662	650	9	3
New York	2,862	2,711	151	0
North Carolina	1,051	1,028	15	8
North Dakota	97	96	1	0
Ohio	3,551	3,245	242	64
Oklahoma	392	371	8	13
Oregon	902	902	0	0
Pennsylvania	1,487	1,407	54	26
Rhode Island	155	155	0	0
South Carolina	1,062	1,031	24	7
South Dakota	261	231	30	0
Tennessee	974	870	44	60
Texas	3,505	3,374	32	99
Utah	465	395	31	39
Vermont	24	24	0	0
Virginia	2,211	2,042	106	63
Washington	1,870	1,850	7	13
West Virginia	148	148	0	0
Wisconsin	1,450	1,385	56	9
Wyoming	164	154	10	0

sures or desired outcomes. Thus, interpretation of standards conformance is problematic. Over the 12 months prior to the mail survey, researchers estimated that:

- Juveniles injured 6,900 staff and 24,200 other juveniles.
- 11,000 juveniles committed 17,600 acts of suicidal behavior, with 10 suicides in 1990.
- More than 18,600 incidents required emergency medical care.
- More than 435,800 juveniles were held in short term isolation (one to 24 hours) and almost 84,000 were isolated for more than 24 hours.
- 9,700 juveniles escaped from custody.

In March 1993, OJJDP officials, Abt researchers, juvenile correctional experts, and youth advocates from across the country assembled in Washington, D.C. to react to the findings. While there was

Between 1960 and 1994, juvenile court delinquency caseloads increased 280%

Estimated delinquency cases

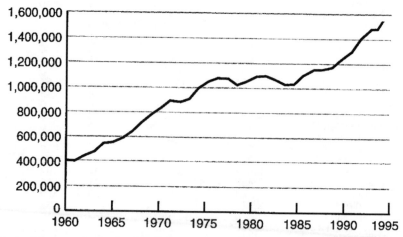

Data Source: *Juvenile Court Statistics* (annual reporting series).
Analysis by Melissa Sickmund, National Center for Juvenile Justice.

general concurrence about the findings, some experts speculated that facility conditions have deteriorated since 1991, citing substantial state and local budget cuts, resulting in staff reductions, staff turnover, and strain on facility program and maintenance budgets.

Compounding these pressures are demographic shifts that already show a steady growth in the juvenile population at risk. Concern was voiced that problems of crowding and related conditions will not only persist, but will increase to the serious detriment of juveniles for whom rehabilitation is still a hope. They were especially concerned about the impact on minority youth. Between 1987 and 1991, the minority populations in detention and correctional facilities grew from 53 percent to 63 percent of the confined population.

In announcing the study's release, Attorney General Janet Reno declared, "This study puts an exclamation point on the obvious conclusion that America must not only take better care of its children before they get into trouble, but also not abandon them once they are in trouble."

PAROLE

Most juveniles, after release from institutions, return to the communities from which they came. Generally, juveniles are released from confinement long before the expiration of their maximum period of commitment. In some states, the juvenile must serve a minimum time before being released. In nine states, the judge who committed the juvenile must agree to the release before the youth may be released early. The problem with this latter practice or requirement is that often the committing judge is too busy with other cases and does not have sufficient time to review the case and make a viable recommendation as to the release decision. In addition, because no new pre-sentencing reports are prepared, the judge may act on dated or incomplete information. For these reasons, judicial involvement in the early release decision has been eliminated in most states.

Most experts assign two goals to parole—protection of society and the proper adjustment of the youth. Presently, it appears that the most important goal is the protection of society. Many see the two goals as conflicting ones involving society versus the youth. A better approach appears to be the concept of protecting society by rehabilitating the youth.

Parole includes the objective of assisting the parolee in integrating into the community. Therefore, the youth must be assisted in coping with the problems faced upon release and to adjust to the status of being a parolee. To be a permanent benefit to society, parole agencies must assist in the development of the youth's ability to make good decisions that are behaviorally acceptable to the community.

The functions of the institution include classifying the youths' readiness for release and the risk factors upon release of the youth. The duty of the parole officer is, among other things, to assist in the rehabilitation and reintegration of the youth into the community and the reduction in the likelihood of the youth committing further criminal acts.

THE RELEASE DECISION

In most states, the parole services in the juvenile justice system are administered by the state agency that is also responsible for the juvenile institutions. There are, however, no clear cut organizational pattern as to who makes the early release decision. In some states, the decision is made by the youth authority, in others by a child welfare agency, adult correctional agency, a lay board, or the correctional institution staff. In addition, in many states, the state officials have delegated the decisional authority to local agencies.

Unlike the process in adult parole, most juveniles' release times are not determined at the post-sentencing hearing. Generally, the juvenile's length of commitment is determined by the youth's progress toward rehabilitation. In some jurisdictions, progress is measured by a token system that awards a specific number of points for various actions. This is very similar to the "task sentences" referred to by Maconochie.

While there is a general agreement that youths should be released as soon as they are ready, there are no valid measures to determine if a juvenile has been successfully rehabilitated or has undergone a real change of attitude. The criteria used to determine if the juvenile has been successfully rehabilitated, and thus should be released, are generally whether or not the juvenile conforms to institutional rules or causes problems. Thus, by appearing to have been reformed, the youth receives the earliest release date. Accordingly, the youth's conduct and behavior in the institution may be based solely on the desire to please his supervisors in order to obtain release.

The question of when to release the youth depends on predictions of the youth's future behavior. The policy considerations that are required to be evaluated before the youth is released include:

√ Has the youth been reformed?

√ Is it likely that the youth will committed another serious offense?

√ Was the youth's behavior acceptable during his confinement?

√ Does the youth have a home or other place, such as a group home, to live?

√ Will suitable employment, training, or treatment be available for the youth on release?

√ What is the youth's own perception of his or her ability to handle reintegration into the community?

√ Are the seriousness of the youth's past offenses and the circumstances in which they were committed sufficiently severe so as to preclude release?

SUMMARY

- Children under 7 years of age were considered incapable of committing crimes at common law. Children between the ages of 7 and 14 were presumed to be incapable of committing crimes, but this presumption could be rebutted. Children over the age of 14 were considered capable of committing crimes.

- The first juvenile court was established in Cook County, Illinois in 1899 as the result of the "child savers" movement. By 1940, every state had a separate juvenile justice system. Until the *Gault* case, the juvenile courts operated infmally with little regard for procedural requirements.

- The role of juvenile justice in our society is continuing to evolve. Present roles include: the protection of society, the protection of the constitutional rights of children, and the rehabilitation of delinquent juveniles.

- The most common result of juvenile court involvement is diversion. Diversion has been popular because it helps reduce the increasing caseloads, is flexible, and costs less than institutionalization.

- The waiver of juvenile court jurisdiction allows the juvenile to be tried in adult criminal court. In most cases, a waiver hearing is required and the juvenile is entitled to certain procedural due process protections. The juvenile trial is referred to as the adjudicatory hearing.

- After the adjudicatory hearing, if the juvenile is found to be a delinquent, the court holds a disposition hearing to determine the disposition of the juvenile. The most severe disposition is that of institutionalization. The most popular disposition after hearing is probation.

- Most of the studies of the conditions of juvenile detention facilities in the United States have determined that the juvenile facilities have violated one or more of the standards related to living space.

- Most juveniles who are released from institutions are returned to the communities from which they came. Most are released on parole or aftercare. Generally, the goals of juvenile parole are the protection of society and the proper adjustment of the juvenile. There is no clear-cut organizational pattern regarding the release decision of juveniles from institutions. The question when to release the juvenile is based on many factors which include a prediction as to whether the juvenile has been reformed and whether the juvenile will be a danger to society.

DISCUSSION QUESTIONS

1. Explain the differences between juvenile corrections and adult corrections.

2. Summarize the history of juvenile justice.

3. What reforms are necessary to improve juvenile justice?

4. When should a juvenile be tried as an adult?

5. How do juvenile trials differ from adult trials?

ENDNOTES—Chapter 16

1. Ralph Weisheit and Diane Alexander, "Juvenile Justice Philosophy and Demise of *Parens Patriae*," *Federal Probation,* December, 1988, p. 56.

2. Anthony Platt, *The Child Savers* (Chicago: University of Chicago Press, 1969).

3. *In re Gault*, 387 U.S. 1, (1967)

4. 383 U.S. 541 (1966)

5. 421 U.S. 519 (1975)

6. 491 F.2d 1430 (7th Cir., 1974)

7. Jeffery Butts and D.J. Connors-Beatty, "Juvenile Court's Response to Violent Offenders," U.S. Department of Justice, Office of Juvenile Justice and Delinquency Prevention, *Special Report*, April, 1993.

8. Ellen H. Nimick, "Juvenile Court Property Cases," U.S. Department of Justice, Office of Juvenile Justice and Delinquency Prevention, *Special Report*, November, 1990.

9. Barbara Allen-Hagen, "Conditions of Confinement in Juvenile Detention and Correctional Facilities," Office of Juvenile Justice and Delinquency Prevention, *Fact Sheet #1*, April, 1993.

GLOSSARY

Actus reus: An illegal act.

Adjudicatory hearing: The juvenile court proceeding that is equivalent to a trial in adult court.

Administrative law: Regulations governing public administrative agencies.

Aftercare: The term used in lieu of parole for juvenile cases.

Age of majority: The legal age at which individuals are no longer considered juveniles.

Aggravated assault: The unlawful attack by one person upon another for the purpose of inflicting severe or aggravated bodily injury.

Aggravating circumstances: Those circumstances that tend to make the crime more serious (i.e., use of a deadly weapon, committing an offense against a law enforcement officer, taking advantage of a position of trust to commit an offense, etc.).

American Society of Criminology: Professional society of the criminological field.

Anomie: A state of normlessness in society which may be caused by decreased homogeneity.

Arraignment: The stage in the criminal trial where the accused is informed of the charges and asked to enter a plea.

Arrest: Taking of a person into the custody of the law, the legal purpose of which is to restrain the accused until he or she can be held accountable for the offense at court proceedings.

Arson: The willful and malicious burning or attempt to burn, with or without intent to defraud, a dwelling house, public building, motor vehicle or aircraft, personal property of another, or forest land.

Assault: See aggravated assault or simple assault.

Atavistic: According to Cesare Lombroso, the primitive physical characteristics which distinguish born criminals from the general population.

Bail: The system of posting bond to assure the defendant's appearance for trial.

Bailiffs: Officers who supervise offenders and maintain order in local and state courtrooms during legal proceedings.

Battered Woman Syndrome: A standard group of psychological, emotional, and physiological reactions suffered by a wife who has been battered by her spouse.

Behavior theory: A theory of crime causation based on the belief that all behavior is learned through consequences that the behavior produced.

Biocriminology: The study of biological variables involved in criminal behavior.

Blood feuds: Blood feuds are actions taken by the victim's family or tribe as revenge on the offender's family or tribe.

Booking: The initial point of entry in the jails, also known as intake, and involves the transfer of responsibility for the arrestee from the law enforcement officer to the jail.

Boot camp programs: Rehabilitative programs based on the military boot-camp routine.

Bribery: The offering or receiving of money, goods, etc. for the purpose of influencing public officials.

Burglary: The breaking and entering of any type of enclosed structure for the purpose of committing a felony or theft.

Capital cases: Those cases in which the government seeks the death penalty.

Career criminals: Those persons who make, or attempt to make, a living committing crime.

Cartographic school: An approach to crime causation that uses population data to ascertain the influence of geographical and sociological factors on criminal behavior.

Child saving movement: A movement which was directed at children in need or trouble which grew out of this general concern and attempted to save children by using houses of refuge and reform schools.

Child abuse: The physical and emotional abuse of children, including sexual abuse and child pornography.

Chronic juvenile offender: According to Marvin Wolfgang, a delinquent offender who is arrested five or more times before he or she is 18 years of age and who stands a good chance of becoming an adult criminal.

Classical theorists: Those who advocate the concept of free will and believe that the punishment should fit the crime.

Classification process: That portion of jail procedure that is concerned with the identification, categorization, and assignment of the inmate to various levels of security, programs, and work.

Classification: A process for determining the needs and requirements of individuals confined and assigning them to housing units and programs in light of individual needs and existing correctional resources.

Code of Hammurabi: Early code of laws established by the Babylonian King Hammurabi around the year 2000 B.C. involving criminal punishments.

Code of Draco: Early Greek code that used the same penalties for both citizens and slaves and incorporated many of the concepts used in primitive societies, e.g., vengeance, outlawry, and blood feuds.

Codes of Ethics: Guidelines for professionals in the field which are not legislative enactments and have no disciplinary actions associated with their violation. The codes provide us with a set of standards that we should strive to meet in our professional lives.

Cognitive development: A psychological theory of crime causation based on the belief that people organize their thoughts into rules and laws and that the way in which those thoughts are organized results in either criminal or noncriminal behavior.

Common law: Unwritten judicial opinion based on customary social practices of Anglo-Saxon society during the Middle Ages.

Community service programs: A sentencing alternative that allows the defendant to stay in the community and uses community services as rehabilitative tools.

Conduct norms: The shared expectations of a group relative to personal conduct.

Conflict approach: An explanation of values and laws based on the assumption that there is no general agreement regarding values and laws. This approach sees values, norms, and laws as creating dissension and conflict.

Consensus approach: An explanation of values and laws based on the assumption that there is a general agreement regarding values and laws.

Constitutional approach: A theory of crime causation that contends that behavior is influenced by body structure.

Containment Theory: A theory of crime causation that focuses on the individual's favorable self-concept (self) and commitment to long-range legitimate goals and the pressures of the external social structure against criminal activity.

Conviction: A judgement of guilt; a verdict by a jury, a plea by a defendant, or a judgement by a court that the accused is guilty as charged.

Corpus delicti: The body of the crime made up of the *actus reus* and *mens rea*.

Crime: Behavior in violation of the criminal laws of the state, federal government, or a local jurisdiction which has the power to make such laws.

Crime rate: The number of offenses per 100,000 population.

Criminal homicide: The UCR category which includes all offenses which cause the death of another human being without justification or cause.

Criminologist: One who is trained in the field of criminology.

Criminology: The scientific study of crime and criminal behavior.

Culture conflict theory: A theory of crime causation based on problems involving the clash of conduct norms.

Date rape: Unlawful forced sexual intercourse with a female against her will which occurs within the context of a dating relationship.

Deferred adjudication: A form of probation that is used without a finding of guilt in which the defendant pleas guilty and agrees to defer further proceeding.

Determinate sentence: A sentence with a fixed period of confinement imposed by the judge of the sentencing court.

Determinism: The concept that one's options, decisions and actions are decided by inherited or environmental causes.

Deterrence: A punishment viewpoint that focuses on future outcomes rather than past misconduct and is based on the theory that creating a fear of future punishments will deter crime.

Differential Association Reinforcement Theory: A crime causation theory that criminal behavior is learned through associations with criminal behavior and attitudes combined with a social learning theory of operant conditioning.

Disposition hearing: The proceeding in juvenile court that is similar to the sentencing phase of an adult criminal trial.

Due process: A fundamental concept of the U.S. Constitution that a person should not be deprived of life, liberty or property without reasonable and lawful procedures. The interpretation of what is required by due process rests with the courts.

Durham Rule: A standard for judging legal insanity which holds that "an accused is not criminally responsible if his unlawful act was the product of mental disease or mental defect."

Ectomorph: A body type described as thin and fragile having long, slender extremities and delicate bones.

Ego: Sigmund Freud's theory of the personality component that is conscious, controls behavior, and is most in touch with external reality.

Embezzlement: Obtaining rightful possession of property with the owner's consent and subsequently wrongfully depriving the owner of that property.

Enlightenment, Age of: Also known as the Age of Reason. A social movement which began in the 18th century and built upon ideas such as empiricism,, rationality, free will, and natural law.

Felony: A serious type of offense, such as murder, armed robbery, or rape, punishable for a year or longer in prison or a more serious penalty.

Felony murder: Special class of criminal homicide whereby an offender may be charged with first-degree murder when his or her criminal activity results in another person's death.

First degree murder: A criminal homicide which was planned or involved premeditation.

Flat time: When an offender serves his or her sentence day for day with no early release.

Folkways: Norms of behavior that are correct because they are the traditional customs, habits, and behaviors.

Free will: A concept that individuals have the ability to make a free choice in their behaviors.

Gang associates: "Wannabee" gang members or individuals who actively support gang activity without being a gang member.

General deterrence: A philosophy of punishment that contends that punishing a person deters others from committing offenses.

Good time credit: Credit resulting in the reduction of prison time; awarded for satisfactory behavior in prison.

Group counseling: A planned activity with three or more offenders present in a counseling session for the purpose of solving personal and social problems.

Guilty but mentally ill: An alternative to the insanity defense. Permits a finding that the defendant was mentally ill, although not insane, at the time the crime was committed.

Juvenile detention centers: Short-term, secure facilities that hold juveniles awaiting adjudication, disposition, or placement in an institution.

Hate crime: Crimes that manifest evidence of prejudice based on religion, sex, race, disability, etc.

Hedonism: The concept that people choose pleasure and avoid pain.

Holy Inquisition: A court set up by the Church of Rome to inquire into cases of heresy.

Id: The aspect of the personality from which urges and desires emanate. Freud's division of the psyche associated with instinctual impulses and demands for immediate satisfaction of needs.

Ideology: The belief system adopted by a group and consists of assumptions and values.

Incapacitation: A punishment philosophy that holds that the confinement of an individual prevents him or her from committing future crimes while confined.

Incest: Sexual relations between members of the immediate family, other than husband and wife, who are too closely related to marry, such as brother and sister, father and daughter.

Indigent: A person with no funds and source of income. In determining indigency for purposes of ability to retain an attorney the general test is "financially unable to obtain adequate representation without substantial hardship to themselves or their families."

Information: The most common formal document used to charge a person with an offense. The prosecutor, acting on evidence from police or citizens, files this document with the court, and it is tested at the preliminary hearing. This procedure does not require grand jury participation.

Insanity defense: A defense that the accused was unable because of mental inability to form the required mental intent to commit the crime charged.

Intent: In the legal sense, the design, determination or purpose with which a person uses a particular means to effect a certain result. It shows the presence of will in the act that consummates a crime.

Jails: Confinement facilities that are used to punish persons convicted of minor offenses and who are sentenced to confinement for a year or less and to detain individuals awaiting trial.

Jurisdiction: The territory of authority within which official authority may be exercised.

Just deserts: The concept that a criminal should be punished because he or she deserves punishment for committing the crime.

Labeling: A theory which sees continued crime as a consequence of limited opportunities for acceptable behavior which result from the negative responses of society to those defined as offenders.

Learning Theory: The belief that crime is an acquired from of behavior.

Manslaughter: The unlawful killing of a human being by a person who lacks malice in the act. Manslaughter may be *involuntary* or negligent, the result of recklessness while committing an unlawful act or *voluntary*, an intentional killing committed in the heat of passion.

Megan's Laws: Sex Offender registration laws.

Mens rea: The required criminal intent for a crime.

Mitigating circumstances: Those circumstances that tend to reduce the severity of the crime (i.e., cooperation with the investigating authority, surrender, good character).

M'Naghten Rule: Also known as the right-wrong test. Maintains that an individual is insane if he or she is unable to tell the difference between right and wrong because of a mental disability.

National Crime Victimization Survey (NCVS): Conducted annually by the Bureau of Justice Statistics which provides data on crime from surveyed households.

Neoclassical school: Those who accept the concept of free will of the classical school with modifications for some who do not have the ability to exercise free will.

NIBRS: The National Incident-Based Reporting System which collects data from 22 crime categories.

Norms: The rules or standards of behavior shared by members of a group or society.

Parens patriae: The concept that the state has the right to be a supervisory parent to minors.

Parole: The discretionary release of an inmate from prison when he or she completes a prescribed portion of his or her sentence and the parole board agrees that the release will not increase the likelihood of harm to the public.

Peremptory challenge: A challenge by prosecution or defense attorneys to excuse a potential juror from the jury panel. No reason is required.

Phrenology: A theory of behavior causation based on studying the bumps on a person's head.

Positive school: Early philosophers and writers who advocated that the study of crime should emphasize the individual, scientific treatment of the criminal, not the postconviction punishment. A belief that punishment should fit the criminal, not the crime.

Premenstrual tension syndrome (PMS): The physiological changes that occur in a woman before menstruation. Examples of symptoms are depression, irritability, and temporary psychosis.

Presumptive sentence: A sentence suggested by the legislative body based on certain factors regarding the crime and the criminal.

Pretrial diversion: A form of probation that is granted prior to trial in which the defendant agrees to waive time and to complete a program or process.

Probation: The conditional release of a defendant based on a promise by the defendant to abide by certain rules.

Probation officers: Officers who supervise probationers and generally work under the supervision of the court system.

Professional criminals: Persons of respectability and high social status who commit crime in the course of their occupations.

Proportionality of punishment: The concept that punishment that the penalty be proportional to the crime.

Rape: Carnal knowledge through the use of force or the threat of force. Includes attempts.

Rehabilitation: The view that punishment should be directed toward correcting the offender.

Restitution: A sanction imposed by an official of the criminal justice system requiring an offender to make a payment of money or service to either the direct or a substitute crime victim.

Restorative justice: A concept of justice whose primary goal is to restore the victim to his or her original position and then take corrective action against the offender.

Retribution: Retribution is based on the ideology that the criminal is an enemy of society and deserves severe punishment for willfully breaking its rules.

Robbery: The unlawful taking or attempted taking of property that is in the immediate possession of another by force or threat of force or violence.

Second-degree murder: Criminal homicide which is unplanned and which is often described as a "crime of passion."

Section 1983 cases: Those cases where officials are sue for violations of individual rights under the provisions of 42 U.S. Code 1983.

Sentence: An authorized judicial decision that places some degree of penalty on a guilty person.

Sentencing guidelines: Guidelines designed to structure sentences based on the offense severity and the criminal history of the defendant.

Simple assault: An attack without a weapon resulting in either minor injury or in undetermined injury requiring less than two days of hospitalization.

Social learning theory: A theory of behavior causation based on the concept that human aggression may be influenced by physiological characteristics and that their activation depends on the learning and is subject to the person's control.

Sociobiology: The application of biological principles to the study of social behavior.

Sociopath: Also referred to as a psychopath. A person who is antisocial, highly impulsive, aggressive, and appears to have little or no concern for society's values.

Somatotyping: The classification of human beings into types according to body build and other physical characteristics.

State jail felony: A relative new crime classification that is more serious than a misdemeanor and less serious than a felony.

Superego: The conscience or moral aspect of personality according to Freud.

Uniform Crime Reports (UCR): The official government source of national crime data.

Utilitarianism: The ethical theory that makes happiness of the individual or society the end and criterion of the morally good and right.

Values: Beliefs about what is moral and desirable.

Victim-impact statement: A written document which describes the losses, suffering and trauma experienced by the crime victim or by the victim's family. In jurisdictions where victim-impact statements are used, judges consider them in arriving at an appropriate sentence for the offender.

Victimology: The study of victims and their contributory role, if any, in crime causation.

Voir dire: To speak the truth; the process of questioning prospective jurors to determine their qualifications and desirability for serving on a jury.

Wergeld: The acceptance of money or property as atonement for wrongs.

White-collar criminals: The traditional name for professional criminals.

Writ of habeas corpus: The writ, traditionally known as the "Great Writ" that is constitutional protected writ designed to require the government to justify why the individual is being held in confinement.

INDEX

INDEX OF NAMES